Systems of General Sales Taxation

Series on International Taxation

VOLUME 33

The titles in this series are listed at the back of this volume.

Kluwer Law International

Systems of General Sales Taxation

Theory, Policy and Practice

Robert F. van Brederode

Wolters Kluwer
Law & Business

AUSTIN BOSTON CHICAGO NEW YORK THE NETHERLANDS

Published by:
Kluwer Law International
PO Box 316
2400 AH Alphen aan den Rijn
The Netherlands
Website: www.kluwerlaw.com

Sold and distributed in North, Central and South America by:
Aspen Publishers, Inc.
7201 McKinney Circle
Frederick, MD 21704
United States of America
Email: customer.service@aspenpublishers.com

Sold and distributed in all other countries by:
Turpin Distribution Services Ltd.
Stratton Business Park
Pegasus Drive, Biggleswade
Bedfordshire SG18 8TQ
United Kingdom
Email: kluwerlaw@turpin-distribution.com

Printed on acid-free paper.

ISBN 978-90-411-2832-4

Printed in Great Britain.

To Heidi

Table of Contents

Chapter 4

Chapter 5

Preface and Acknowledgments

Several chapters have been published earlier in modified form as articles. Section 4.4.2 appeared in the *International VAT Monitor* under the title: "VAT's Regressivity: Empirical Truth or Political Correctness." In the same publication, Chapter 5 appeared under the title: "The Re-emergence of Gross Receipt Taxes in the US." Section 6.2 was published in the *VAT Monitor*, titled: "Introduction to the U.S. State Retail Sales and Use Taxes." Section 6.3 appeared earlier in the *International VAT Monitor*, titled: "Towards a Federal Sales Tax in the US?"

An extended version of section 9.7.2 has been published in *The Tax Lawyer: The State and Local Tax Edition*, but in a different, more philosophical context under the title: "A Normative Evaluation of Consumption Tax Design: The Treatment of the Sales of Goods under VAT in the EU and Sales Tax in the US." Sections 10.2 and 10.3 comprise most of an article, titled: "The Metamorphosis of Corporate Income Tax into a Value Added Tax," which also appeared in the *International VAT Monitor*. Section 10.6.1 appeared in the *International VAT Monitor* under the title: "The American Debate on Taxing Distance Sales and E-commerce." The *International Tax Journal* published: "Third Party Risks and Liabilities in Case of VAT Fraud in the EU," which is found to some extent in Section 10.7. "The Harmonization of U.S. State Sales and Use Taxes" was first published in the *International VAT Monitor* and is reproduced in Section 11.3. Sections 12.1 through 12.3 and 12.4.5 appeared in *Tax Notes* under the title: "Revenue Distribution under Federal/State Consumption Tax." I am grateful to the International Bureau of Fiscal Documentation for their permission to use the articles published earlier in the *International VAT Monitor* for this book.

This book is the result of 25 years of study and practice in the field of sales tax and VAT. But it is far from a complete book. No book can ever be complete on such a complex, multijurisdictional and, indeed, controversial subject. An author has to make choices as to his approach and subject coverage and, even more treacherous, has to decide what to leave out. I can only hope that the reader appreciates the choices I have made in light of the purpose and scope of this book.

Much of what is produced in this book in terms of insights and thoughts has been used during my teaching of courses in the Graduate Tax Program of New York University, School of Law. This gave me the opportunity to amend, change and elaborate where I felt this would improve the text on the basis of the discussions I had with my students. This book is current with literature and case law through 31 January 2009.

I am greatly indebted to all authors whose articles and books I was fortunate enough to consult, and to all colleagues, academics and practitioners, who over the years have contributed to my knowledge of sales taxation and VAT, both in theory and practice.

Foremost, I am sincerely grateful for the forbearance and patience of my wife, Heidi, during long nights and weekends, the writing of this book took precedence over our personal lives. With all my heart, my darling, this book is, therefore, rightfully dedicated to you.

List of Tables and Figures

List of Abbreviations

AEO	Authorized Economic Operator
BAC	Business Advisory Council
CAS	Certified Automated System
CAT	Commercial Activities Tax
CSP	Certified Service Provider
C-TPAT	Customs-Trade Partnership against Terrorism
C-VAT	Compensating VAT
D-VAT	Digital VAT
EC	European Community
ECJ	European Court of Justice
ECSC	European Coal and Steel Community
EDC	European Defense Community
EEC	European Economic Community
ETI	Extraterritorial Income Exclusion Act
EU	European Union
Euratom	European Atomic Energy Community
FCA	Family Consumption Allowance
FTA	Federation of Tax Administrators
GATT	General Agreement on Tariffs and Trade
GDP	Gross Domestic Product
GRTs	Gross Receipt Taxes
GSP	Gross State Product
GST	Goods and Services Tax
IRS	Internal Revenue Service
ITFA	Internet Tax Freedom Act
LCM	Limited Credit Method
MBT	Michigan Business Tax
MGRT	Modified Gross Receipt Tax

MTC	Multistate Tax Commission
MTSA	Mobile Telecommunications Sourcing Act
NCSL	National Conference of State Legislatures
NGA	National Governors Association
NRST	National Retail Sales Tax
NYU	New York University
OECD	Organization for Economic Cooperation and Development
RITC	Reduced Input Tax Credit
RST	Retail Sales Tax
SBT	Single Business Tax
SCAC	Standing Committee on Administrative Cooperation
SCM Code	Code on Subsidies and Countervailing Measures
SLAC	State and Local Advisory Council
SSTIS	Streamlined Sales Tax Implementing States
SSTP	Streamlined Sales Tax Project
SSUTA	Streamlined Sales and Use Tax Agreement
TCA	Tax Collection Accounts
ULITC	Uniform Limited Input Tax Credit
VIVAT	Viable Integrated VAT
WTO	World Trade Organization

List of Cases

Netherlands

United States

Belgium

European Court of Justice

Chapter 1

General Introduction

General sales taxes are not a new phenomenon, but their rise to prominence and extraordinary proliferation occurred in the twentieth century. They vary, however, in coverage, systematic approach and name. These taxes are levied and collected when a sale is made but, depending on the system chosen, this could include all sales or only sales of goods, or only sales to consumers, or only sales at a single or at multiple stages of the production and distribution chain. They are referred to as general taxes to distinguish them from taxes levied on specific products only, such as alcohol, tobacco and gasoline excises. Gross receipt taxes (GRTs) became particularly popular during First World War to pay for the war expenses, and during and after the Great Depression to compensate for reduced revenues from other taxes. Although introduced as temporary measures, they were maintained as a reliable source of income for a much longer time than was initially anticipated. Interestingly, after years of decline in popularity and use, interest in applying GRTs has reemerged, especially in the United States. Retail sales taxes (RSTs) are still in use all over the world, in particular at the subnational level, but in many countries they have been or are in the process of being replaced by value added taxes (VAT). Canada is a good example of how subnational RSTs can coexist with a federal VAT. The United States is the only Organization for Economic Cooperation and Development (OECD) country that does not apply a general sales tax of any design at the federal level. It is not unlikely, however, that the US government will be forced to introduce a federal consumption tax, even as soon as within 10 years, to retain the confidence of the money markets that it is and will remain able to repay the national debt, which is rapidly expanding due to excessive borrowing to finance the economic stimulus plans and bailouts for failing financial institutions and industries.

Because general sales taxes are used all over the world on national and/or subnational levels, it is essential for every tax professional, whether practitioner or academic, and all policy makers involved in budgeting and appropriations to gain knowledge of or improve their understanding of these types of taxes. In terms of revenue they are important as well. In the United States, the retail state taxes yield almost a third of state tax revenue and close to 12% of local tax revenue. On the federal level, some specific taxes on goods and services are levied but there exists no federal general consumption tax. In the United States, 17.4% of total revenue is generated by consumption taxes, of which 8% comes from RSTs. In comparison, in the European Union (EU), 30.3% of revenue comes from consumption taxes, of which the VAT generates 19%.[1] This illustrates the fact that the United States relies much less on consumption taxes than other developed countries.

This book is intended to serve a wide range of people who share an interest in sales taxation, although their interest will likely vary in terms of scope and depth. The idea for this book was developed while preparing for my teaching assignment at New York University (NYU). The search for a single textbook that would deal with all the subjects covered in the course turned problematic. Good books have been written, of course, but these are generally narrow in scope, focusing on a single jurisdiction, or a single type of tax, or approaching the subject from a single academic discipline. There exist excellent legal treatises, for example, on EU-VAT, Canadian GST, or US RSTs. Several books have been published in recent years that focus on consumption tax policy, and proof that the VAT has reached maturity can be found in the emergence of comparative studies. In my assessment, a book was needed that would combine economic theory and legal practice for all general sales taxes to allow for comparative evaluations and tax policy recommendations. The scope of this book is, therefore, wide, covering GRTs, RSTs and different types of VAT. It offers comparisons, identifies similarities and differences, and evaluates advantages and disadvantages of each type of tax.

The book is written for practitioners who would like to deepen their theoretical knowledge, specialists in VAT who seek to obtain a solid understanding of other sales taxes and sales and use tax specialists who want to build or increase their knowledge of VAT, and for academics as well as policy makers and their staff. It is ambitious in that it seeks to provide a solid introduction for novices in the field, while at the same time serving the needs of seasoned practitioners and scholars with an in-depth treatise of each individual subject. Each chapter can be read individually, in order to allow readers to pick and choose depending on their interest and level of knowledge. References to other chapters are made to enable readers to see connections, go back to the basics when needed or explore other territory.

The first chapters lay down the theoretical foundation by categorizing the different types of sales taxes based on their coverage of the production and distribution chain (Chapter 3), and by analyzing certain characteristics of consumption taxes (Chapter 4). The next chapters deal with the most important sales taxes individually. Chapter 5 focuses on GRTs and provides an economic analysis of this type of tax, including advantages and disadvantages, as well as dealing with some specific issues in the United States. In respect of RSTs, the focus is on the situation

1. *Source*: OECD Revenue Statistics 1965–2006; numbers are for the year 2005.

in the United States. The first part of Chapter 6 focuses on RSTs as applied at the subnational level from an economic perspective as well as dealing with cross-border interstate aspects. The second part deals with proposals made for the introduction of a RST at the federal level. Chapter 7 explains the workings of the subtraction VAT. This subtype of VAT is, at the national level, only applied in Japan, but even there many modifications have moved the design closer to the credit invoice method VAT. Interestingly, notwithstanding the dominance of the credit invoice method VAT, all proposals for a federal VAT in the United States are for a subtraction VAT, probably because it offers a closer resemblance of the income tax it is supposed to replace. A large portion of the book is devoted to the credit invoice method VAT, first introduced in the European Economic Community (EEC), and rapidly spreading around the world. Particular attention is paid to problem areas from a design perspective, such as determining rates and rate variation, the treatment of small traders and the agricultural sector, the effect of exemptions in general, the treatment of financial services, immoveable property and the public sector. A separate section deals with the design issues surrounding capital goods, especially how intermediate sales should be treated, including trade-ins and secondhand goods. Chapter 9 takes a closer look at the issues surrounding cross-border transactions, evaluating the World Trade Organization (WTO) rules and the US proposals to mitigate a perceived cross-border disadvantage, explaining the EU tax jurisdiction rules for international transactions, and dealing explicitly with the problems of distance sales and e-commerce. Fraud is an emerging problem with cross-border transactions, and it appears that the solution will not be found in aggressive litigation and in shifting liabilities to bona fide traders but instead in smart design features combined with incentives that invite legitimate traders to join combating fraud.

Harmonization of sales taxes in common or federal markets offers significant economic benefits. Both the EU and the individual states in the United States are pursuing this path. Chapter 10 offers a unique comparison between the approaches taken in these two theaters. The differences may not be as substantial as they appear on first impression. In the United States, the states confirm to a common standard voluntarily, whereas in the EU, confirmation is mandatory but only to the extent that all decisions are made unanimously.

When both the federal or common and subnational levels of government apply general sales taxes, coordination questions arise. How national and subnational sales taxes can coexist is dealt with in Chapter 11. Several models for cooperation are analyzed with particular emphasis on revenue sharing and the taxation of cross-border, interstate transactions, which carry a high risk of fraud.

We conclude in Chapter 12, particularly to evaluate, which type of sales tax is most advantageous from a tax policy perspective.

Chapter 2

Short Overview of the History of General Sales Taxation

Sales taxes have a long history.[1] Taxes on the sale of individual commodities (excises), such as cooking oil, can be traced to 2000 BC, and tomb paintings from around that time depict tax collectors in Egypt. At some point during the eighth or seventh centuries BC, the city-states in Greece developed three types of turnover taxes: on the sale of land, on market sales[2] (probably with rate variations depending on type of product sold) and a general turnover tax. Emperor Augustus introduced a 1% tax on auction sales.[3] Mediaeval Europe mainly followed Roman examples regarding taxes, such as a market tax and fees for the use of weigh stations.

The oldest GRT is the Alcabala as found in mediaeval Spain[4] and later introduced in Spanish colonies in the Americas, where remnants of this tax can still be found today, as well as in the lowlands (roughly present-day Belgium and the Netherlands) of which the Spanish king through inheritance had also become the effective ruler; however, the introduction there failed because of strong resistance. The Alcabala was "modern" in the sense that it was among the first attempts to introduce a permanent system of government financing on a national scale.

---

1. See, for the history of sales and turnover taxes, for example, Rolf Grabower, Detlef Herting & Gottfried Schwarz, *Die Umsatzsteuer, ihre Geschichte und gegenwartige Gestaltung im In- und Ausland* (*Turnover Taxes: Their History and Present Design Here and Abroad*) (Köln, 1962).
2. China and India have market taxes as well, which may have been the inspiration for the Greek cities. It is possible, at least in Athens, that these market taxes were only charged to foreign traders; see Rolf Grabower et al., *supra*, 18, which would constitute one of the earliest examples of tax exporting.
3. Auctions fulfilled an important role in those days and included transactions of present-day agents, commissionaires and brokers.
4. Introduced at 5% in 1342 during the reign of Alphonso XI.

In the early twentieth century, many states in Europe and the United States introduced GRTs, basically as an emergency measure in times of distress, such as economic depression and war, to provide an additional source of income to compensate for declining revenue from income and property taxes. Germany introduced such a tax in 1916 to pay for the war effort; France and Belgium followed in 1920 and 1921, respectively, to finance reconstruction after the First World War; and the Netherlands introduced a manufacturer's sales tax in 1933.[5] In Europe, GRTs were the most widely used form of sales taxation until the 1960s, when they were abolished for reasons of incompatibility with the goals of the EEC, which was established in 1968.

West Virginia was the first state in the United States to introduce a GRT in 1921 under the name of the Business and Occupation Privilege Tax. During the Great Depression, many states followed suit with the introduction of this type of sales tax, generally intended as temporary, emergency revenue measures, and indeed many disappeared before the Second World War. Most of the remaining GRTs were repealed by the end of the twentieth century and were replaced by what were perceived as less harmful revenue sources. New Jersey abandoned its state-level GRT in 1977. Alaska followed in1979;[6] West Virginia and Indiana abandoned their decades-old GRT in 1987 and 2002, respectively. By the end of 2002, Washington remained the only state with a surviving Depression-era GRT. Remarkably, around that time the use of in this type of taxation caught the interest of state policy makers again, when New Jersey introduced its short-lived[7] Alternative Minimum Assessment Tax, which required companies to pay the larger of either regular corporate income tax or a GRT. Kentucky followed in 2005, and Ohio introduced just a few months later the Commercial Activity Tax (CAT), replacing corporate franchise and personal property taxes with a broad-based GRT that is phased in over 5 years. Texas followed per 2007. In addition to broad-based GRTs, many state and local governments over the years have enacted hybrid business taxes that resemble GRTs economically in many ways. Delaware, Hawaii and New Mexico levy GRTs, which incorporate elements of both sales and gross receipts taxes. Michigan levied a "single business tax" (SBT) that incorporated some features of a GRT and some of a European-style value added tax, which has been repealed effective 1 January 2008 and replaced by the Michigan Business Tax (MBT), which is in essence a subtraction type VAT (see Section 7.4). Many states limit the GRT to only certain industries, such as utilities, telecommunications and gambling. More than thirty states and the District of Columbia levy some form of broad-based or industry-specific tax that shares characteristics with a GRT, but are not GRTs altogether. Currently, eight states impose a tax that can, confidently, be classified as a gross receipts tax: Arizona, Delaware, Hawaii, Kentucky,

5. Ben Terra, *Sales Taxation: The Case of Value Added Tax in the European Community,* Series on International Taxation, no. 8 (Deventer-Boston: Kluwer, 1988), 3–4.
6. John F. Due & John L. Mikesell, *Sales Taxation: State and Local Structure and Administration*, 2nd ed. (Washington, DC: Urban Institute Press, 1994), 55.
7. It expired after 4 years in 2006.

New Mexico, Ohio, Texas and Washington. They are levied under different names, such as Transaction Privilege Tax, CAT, GRT, and Business and Occupations Tax. The rates vary from 0.5% and 1% in Texas, from 0.096% to 1.92% in Delaware, and from 5.125% to 7.875% in New Mexico.

The theoretical origins of the VAT are generally attributed to T.S. Adams[8] in the United States and the German industrialist Carl Friedrich von Siemens.[9] It is possible that Adams was aware of the discussions in Germany, as John Due[10] believes to be likely, but this is uncertain. The two concepts are different in approach. Adams' design is in essence a business income type VAT, where Siemens' is a consumption type VAT (see Section 4.3. for an economic analysis of the differences).

It was not until 1953 that the first jurisdiction, the US state of Michigan, adopted a tax based on Adams' theoretical model for the VAT. France was first in adopting a consumption type VAT by gradually modifying its existing turnover (gross receipt) tax. The first step, in 1948, applied the tax only to manufacturers and in 1954 the tax was extended to the production and wholesale stages of the supply chain.[11] In fact, France did not adopt a full VAT until 1968, a year after Denmark had replaced its GRT with a consumption type VAT. The spread of VAT can be credited to the European integration process, which requires the establishment of a common market and mutatis mutandis harmonization of taxes. A destination-based VAT was the logical choice to eliminate the distortion caused by the existing turnover taxes in the Member States and to ensure a level playing field when goods and services were crossing borders within the common market (see further Section 10.2). Nevertheless, it proved quite complicated to achieve political consensus among Member States for the introduction of a VAT because of domestic resistance to a change in tax system. Sectors who believed the current turnover taxes to be beneficial to them did not want to loose their advantage,[12] and sectors who perceived the proposed VAT system to hold a disadvantage had no reason to support it. An alliance arose between Germany and the European Commission tilting the balance to a VAT. Germany needed the European proposals for a VAT as a means to pressure domestic resistance; the European Commission needed German support to convince the European Council, that is, the other

8. Thomas S. Adams, "Fundamental Problems of Federal Income Taxation", *Quarterly Journal of Economics* 35 (1921): 527–556.
9. Carl Friedrich von Siemens, *Veredelte Umsatzsteuer* (*Improved Turnover Tax*), 2nd ed. (Siemensstadt, 1920).
10. John F. Due, *Sales Taxation* (London, 1957), at 138.
11. Maurice Lauré, *La taxe sur la valeur ajoutée* (*The Value Added Tax*) (Paris, 1952).
12. Such as wholesalers enjoying a relatively low tax rate and integrated businesses holding a comparative advantage over nonintegrated traders on the domestic market. Integrated traders were at an advantage as well when exporting because export restitutions of tax were based on averages and, therefore, they would be overcompensated. In addition, the turnover taxes were used as an instrument of social policy to the benefit of the poor (voters). Retailers were opposed to the anticipated increase of compliance costs and consumers feared an increase of the costs of living.

Member States.[13] The new VAT was presented as a modification of the existing turnover taxes, leaving in place the obligation to collect tax on all sales, but introducing the right to recover tax paid on purchases (input tax). This improved the attractiveness of a VAT to businesses already registered for the turnover tax. To support the myth of continuity, officials often called the new VAT laws by the name of the predecessor tax, describing the VAT as the turnover tax.[14]

As a result of its multiple rate structure applying to different outputs and the variable effect of cascading across different industries, the turnover tax regime had markedly dissimilar impacts across commercial sectors. To achieve support for the VAT, governments felt obliged to replicate to some extent the impact of the former turnover taxes by allowing different rates for certain types of supplies and introducing many exemptions. As a result, the VAT legislation of the Member States, at instigation, was quite diverse, but the concept was to harmonize the VAT over time. Because unanimity is required, the policy-making process in the European Communities (ECs) is notoriously slow and driven by a need of compromise to satisfy domestic political opposition and demands. The process can best be described as a step-by-step progress towards further harmonization. Where compromise cannot be reached, controversial issues are pushed into the future and national derogations accepted until the domestic political spectrum has sufficiently changed to reach consensus.[15] After several decades, significant differences still exist and political compromise appears more difficult to reach with the enlargement of the EU. Crucial to the attractiveness of a VAT is its promise of economic neutrality in terms of business organization and processes, investments and consumption choices and that explains the gradual proliferation of the European model VAT notwithstanding the imperfections in the actual design applied in the EU. In 1986 both Japan and New Zealand introduced VATs that significantly improved the European model. Japan applies a single rate to a comprehensive base of taxable supplies and a limited number of exemptions. The administration and structure, however, seem to be designed uniquely for the Japanese situation and are difficult to apply elsewhere.

The New Zealand VAT offers similar improvements but remains in line with the European model regarding its administrative structure. The New Zealand VAT is highly regarded among technical experts and considered to be the world's most efficient system. Although some call it the "Modern VAT," it is not a completely new design but rather a modification of the European model. It became the new standard for other countries – such as Canada, South Africa, Singapore and Australia – who modeled their VAT on New Zealand's VAT.

---

13. Donald J. Puchala, *Fiscal Harmonization in the European Communities: National Politics and International Cooperation* (London and Dover, NH: Francis Pinter Publishers, 1984), at 44.
14. To this day, many official EU documents and European Court Judgments continue to refer to the VAT as the turnover tax as does the VAT legislation itself in several EU countries, for example, *Umsatzsteuergesetz* in Germany and *Wet op de omzetbelasting* in the Netherlands.
15. Puchala, *supra*, at 125.

The credit invoice method VAT is the fiscal success story of the twentieth century. Currently, approximately 150 countries, and essentially every developed country except the United States, levy a VAT. VATs are generally imposed at the national level, but some countries – notably Brazil, Canada and India – have VATs at the subnational level or combine national and subnational VATs or a national VAT with subnational RSTs.[16] Fewer than thirty countries have no form of consumption tax, but Hong Kong is contemplating introducing one, Swaziland has announced its intention to do so and the United Arab Emirates on the initiative of Bahrain are on the verge of implementing a VAT in 2009 or 2010.

---

16. For an overview of counties applying VATs and sales taxes, see Fabiola Annacondia & Walter van der Corput, "Overview of General Turnover Taxes and Tax Rates," *International VAT Monitor* 19 (2) (2008): 2–11.

Chapter 3

Systems of Sales Taxation: General Overview

One of the first determinations policy makers have to make is whether to levy a tax on all stages of the production and distribution chain, or on a single stage or on several stages. As a consequence, they will have to determine whether such a tax would be designed as a business tax or a consumption tax. A simplified model of the manufacturing and distribution chain is shown in Figure 1.

Figure 1. Manufacturing and Distribution Chain

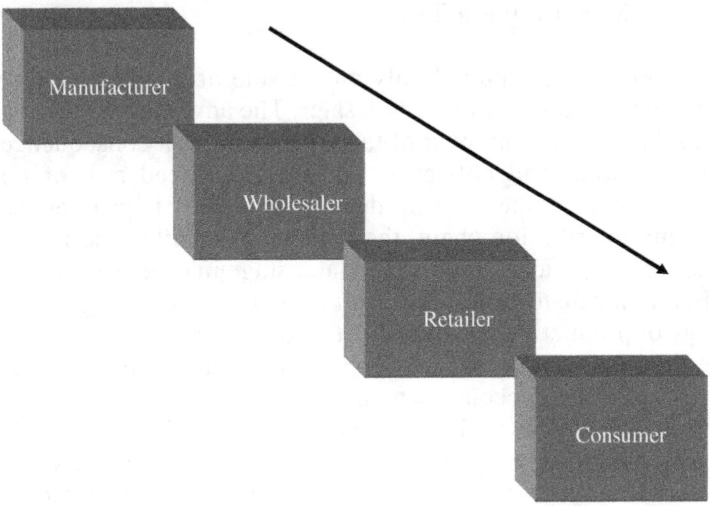

Generally, a distinction is made between single stage, multiple stage and all stage taxes.

3.1. SINGLE STAGE TAXES

As the name indicates, a single stage tax is levied on only one of the stages of the manufacturing and distribution chain (see Figure 2). Generally, they are classified according to the stage of the production and distribution chain at which the tax is applied.[1] As a consequence, such a tax will be a manufacturer tax, a wholesaler tax or a retailer tax.

Figure 2. Single Stage Tax

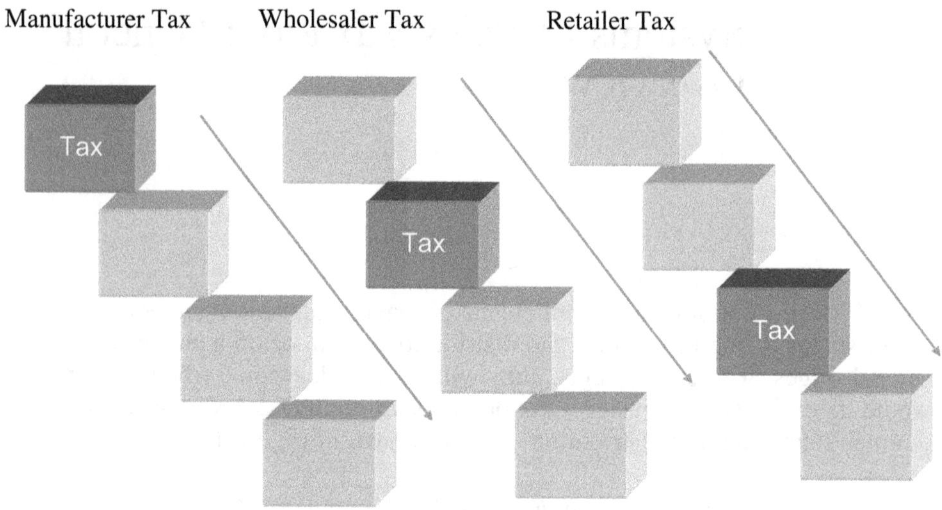

3.1.1. MANUFACTURER TAX

A manufacturer's tax is applied only on the sale of goods by a manufacturer, normally but not necessarily to a wholesaler. The advantage of such a tax is that there are a relatively low number of taxpayers and, as a consequence, there are lower administration and collection costs and reduced risk of tax evasion. Because the market value of a product increases as it progresses along the production and distribution chain, the tax base is smaller and rates need to be higher than the rate of a tax applied at a later stage in order to generate the same revenue. Economic distortions may occur depending on the degree of integration and the stage of production at which the item becomes subject to the tax. Since in reality the production process of a certain good may include several manufacturers, tax accumulation occurs, which in itself creates an incentive to vertical integration and cost forwarding beyond the point of impact of the tax. For example, a manufacturer may decide to allocate certain functions, such as transportation or warranty, at the wholesaler's stage to avoid taxation on their value. This may lead to economic inefficiencies because these decisions are made for

1. For a comprehensive study, see John F. Due, *Sales Taxation* (London, 1957).

the purpose of creating tax advantages only and are not driven by sound operational needs.

In the production and distribution chain models that we use, it is always assumed for simplicity reasons that there is only a single manufacturer, a single wholesaler and a single retailer. In reality it is far more complex. Not only can several businesses fulfill a similar function in the chain but also a single business may fulfill multiple functions. Frequently, a manufacturer also sells directly to consumers, in which case he functions both as manufacturer and as retailer in relation to a particular good. To warrant neutrality, that is, to ensure that identical goods are exposed to the same tax burden, it will be required to estimate the wholesale and retail margins, which will need to be subtracted from the price charged by the manufacturer to the consumer to arrive at an equitable tax base. A simple example may clarify this. Assume a manufacturer as such sells for 100 to the wholesale stage, which in turn sells for 125 to the retailer who in turn sells for 175 to the consumer. Only 100 will be subject to the tax. It may be expected that the manufacturer would sell directly to consumers at the same price or a price close to the retailer price. In case of a direct sale to a consumer, the manufacturer would have to remit tax on the basis of 175 instead of on 100, unless margin corrections are made. Table 1 shows the difference between a chain of sales transactions from manufacturer through wholesaler and retailer to a consumer, and direct sales from manufacturer to consumer with and without margin corrections. It is assumed in all situations that the tax is shifted forward to the final consumer. The wholesaler margin is 25 and the retail margin is 50. The tax rate is 10%.

Table 1. Margin Corrections under a Manufacturer's Tax

Tax Rate 10% (t)	Standard Chain Transaction	Direct Sale	Direct Sale with Margin Corrections
Manufacturer	100 + 10 = 110	175 + 17.50 = 192.50	175 + [175 – (25 + 50) × *t*] =
Wholesaler	110 + 25 = 135		
Retailer	135 + 50 = 185		
Consumer	185	192.50	185

As we can see, the tax burden and the final consumer price are the same in the case of a direct sale from manufacturer to consumer when margin corrections are applied, compared to a series of sales that includes the wholesale and retail stages. Determining these margins, however, is not a straightforward process. For obvious reasons, businesses do not advertise their margins. The margins, therefore, need to be estimated on the basis of a statistical survey, which may produce reasonably accurate average margins. However, an average margin is always too low for one manufacturer and too high for another. Distortion of competition under a manufacturer's tax as a result of direct consumer sales can be reduced but never fully mitigated. The size and impact of such distortions will depend not only on the accuracy of the estimated margins but also on the height of the statutory rate. The distortion impact relates directly to the rate in the sense that a tax rate increase would likely enhance the impact of the distortion.

Countermeasures could be and have been designed to combat avoidance behavior such as integration and function forwarding, but these lead to a significant increase in the complexity of the tax and subsequently of the cost of compliance and administration.

Domestic products may find themselves at a competitive disadvantage when a similar good is imported at a more advanced stage than that at which the domestic product is taxed. The importation itself may be taxed, but the value declared at importation may be lower than the price of identical domestically produced goods, because they likely escape advertising and other costs that a domestic producer cannot avoid. To create a more level playing field the sales tax rate on importation could be set higher than the domestic rate, but it is rather complex to make accurate determinations in this respect.

3.1.2. Wholesaler Tax

The wholesaler tax is levied on the transaction prior to that at which the good reaches the consumer. For convenience reasons this is generally referred to as wholesale tax, but one should realize that not all sales by wholesalers are made to the retail stage. At times, wholesalers may sell to other wholesalers, or directly to consumers.

The number of taxpayers is greater than under a manufacturer's tax, which allows for relatively lower rates to generate the same revenue. However, an increase in the number of taxpayers also leads to higher administrative costs for the taxing authorities.

The problems posed by the imposition of a wholesale tax are very similar to the ones discussed previously for a manufacturer's tax. The degree of integration of a certain business will influence the effective tax rate borne by the final consumer, which may lead to distortions of competition. The effect of this type of distortion can only be prevented or reduced by taking legislative countermeasures, such as levies on internal sales, which we will take a closer look at in Section 5.3.5 in the context of GRTs. Clearly, these countermeasures complicate the tax and lead to an increase in compliance costs for businesses, and administrative and collection costs for the taxing authority.

Since wholesalers may be involved in direct sales to consumers as well, to ensure neutrality, a correction of the sales price with the retail margin would be required. As discussed in the previous section, this can only be achieved through statistical estimations. Margins differ depending on the type of product and the intended market segment. Luxury goods, generally, allow for higher margins than necessities. Using a single retail margin would lead to a relatively lower tax on luxury goods than on these necessities, which could be solved through rate differentiation.[2] Moreover, the same product may be offered at different prices, that is, with different margins, in dissimilar demographic areas as a result of price maximization.[3] Another practical problem arises when luxury items are mixed with necessities, for example food items in a luxury gift box.

A drawback of a wholesale tax is the complexities that arise when the tax base is extended to services. Services should be exempt at the wholesale stage unless they are rendered to consumers, but it is difficult for a services supplier to determine in what capacity a buyer is buying a service. For that reason, services are generally not included in or exempt from a wholesale tax. However, that makes this type of tax less desirable when the objective is to levy a general consumption tax.

3.1.3. Retail Tax

A retail tax is applied to all sales to final consumers, including those made by manufacturers and wholesalers. This requires the latter categories to make an administrative distinction between taxable consumer ("business-to-consumer" or B2C) sales and exempt business ("business-to-business" or B2B) sales. Generally, this is done by the tax authority issuing certificates to businesses as proof of their status. Problems may still arise when a business certificate is used for personal purchases, and regular auditing of businesses on the basis of a risk analysis selection would be needed to counter this type of evasion, adding to the costs of administering the tax. When certificates are limited in scope, that is, when they do not cover all business procurements, the tax would become part of the cost base of a business and, depending on a trader's ability to shift the tax burden forward, it would become (partly) a business tax. Tax cascading would also occur, the size of which will depend on the stage at which the tax would be incurred and the length of the remainder of the chain (see further Section 6.2.5).

A RST would require that there be a much larger number of taxpayers who are accountable for its collection, increasing the administrative costs for the tax authorities. A large number of taxpayers does allow for a relative lower tax rate than required under a wholesale or manufacturer's tax to generate the same revenue.

Another problem with taxing the retail stage is that it is so difficult to apply for the many small businesses engaged at this level. For this reason, policy makers may be reluctant to introduce a RST or to include the retail level in, for example, a VAT. However, it appears more rational to design special provisions for small businesses than to exclude a complete stage from a VAT or to refrain from the introduction of a RST (see Section 8.2.3).

A broad-based, general consumption tax should include services. In practice, this has posed complex problems in a retail tax system. Only services to consumers

2. See Ben Terra, *Sales Taxation: The Case of Value Added Tax in the European Community*, Series on International Taxation, no. 8 (Deventer-Boston: Kluwer, 1988), 23.
3. Gas and grocery prices, for example, tend to differ between towns of diverse prosperity.

should be subject to the tax, which would require the seller to make the distinction between consumers and businesses. Many services can be used for private purposes and for business purposes without the provider having any means of establishing with any certainty what the purpose is. Transportation services are an excellent example in this respect. A certificate system would become extraordinarily burdensome if every employee taking a taxi needed to carry a certificate for business travel. Even if this were doable, a taxi driver has no means of verifying whether its use is justified. For this reason, most states exclude services from the tax base, but this opens the door to tax avoidance opportunities. If the service is ancillary to the supply of goods, and its value, therefore, is included in the overall taxable price, tax could be avoided by dividing activities in a nontaxable service and a taxable supply of goods, reducing the overall tax costs.[4]

3.2. ALL STAGE TAXES

A multiple stage tax levies the tax on two or more stages of the manufacturing and distribution chain, and an all stage tax is levied on each and every stage of the chain (see Figure 3).

Figure 3. All Stage Tax

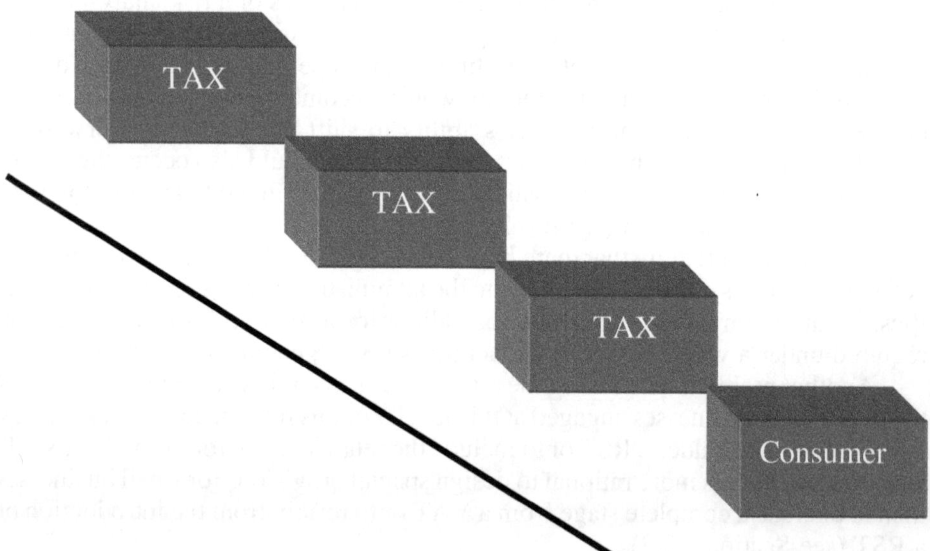

4. Terra, *Sales Taxation*, 25, makes a reference in this respect to the experiences in Norway and Denmark when they applied a retail sales tax. In response to tax avoidance, lists of taxable services were made, but they made the system extraordinary complex, which encouraged Denmark to switch to a VAT.

The tax is due on the total sale price charged to the customer. The tax can be imposed at a single rate for all stages, or different rates may apply for each stage or for some stages. Generally, a distinction is made between cumulative and non-cumulative all stage taxes.

Tax cascading occurs when taxes, as part of the cost price for goods and services supplied to a business, are absorbed in the business' selling prices and, thus, are shifted to its customer. It has the effect that an amount of tax paid at a previous stage is again subject to the tax at a later stage and, as a result, the same amount of tax may be taxed multiple times in the processes of production and distribution, creating a "tax-on-tax" effect, the magnitude of which is determined by the length of the chain of transactions.

It is difficult to measure to what extent cascading occurs in practice because it depends on factors, such as the price elasticity of the goods or services in question[5] and the supplier's market position. Moreover, the cascading effect is likely to vary from state to state and from industry to industry and it also depends on the category of goods. Whether tax shifting occurs and to what extent is subject to debate (see further Sections 4.4.1, 5.3.4 and 6.2.5.2). The Austrian school of economic thought reasons that all taxes are ultimately borne by businesses because price maximization leaves no room for shifting taxes forward. All prices are determined by the interaction of supply and the demand schedule for that good. If a sales tax is introduced, a business cannot raise its prices to cover the additional tax cost because prices, at all times, tend to be set at the maximum net revenue point for each seller. In other words, prices are already at their highest net income levels for each firm when the tax is levied. Any increase in cost, therefore, will have to be absorbed by the firm and cannot be passed forward along the supply chain to the consumers. Tax, therefore, is not shifted forward but backward to either or both the capital and labor factors.[6]

In any event, it is important to note that consumption taxes are designed on the assumption that the tax is, indeed, fully shifted forward along the manufacturing and distribution chain to the final consumer. Consumption taxes in their legal design can, therefore, only be properly understood while keeping this underlying assumption in mind.

Tax accumulation leads to distortion of competition. The tax burden will increase with the length of the distribution chain. The longer the chain, the higher the tax; conversely, the shorter the chain the lower is the tax. Tax cascading,

5. Percentage decrease in demand for goods (or services) resulting from a percentage increase of their price.
6. See, Murray N. Rothbard, *Power and Market: Government and the Economy*, 2nd ed. (Kansas City, 1977), 88–93; Harry Gunnison Brown, "The Incidence of a General Sales Tax," in *Readings in the Economics of Taxation*, eds. Richard A. Musgrave & Carl S. Shoup (Homewood, IL, 1959), 330–339; Murray N. Rothbard, "The Consumption Tax: A Critique," *Review of Austrian Economics* 7 (1994): 75–90.

therefore, favors integrated businesses over nonintegrated businesses or insourcing over outsourcing. Moreover, the tax discriminates against capital-intensive businesses over labor-intensive businesses. In practice, countermeasures have been designed to combat the disadvantages of cumulative taxes. Integration charges have been introduced to discourage vertical integration. Lower rates for the wholesale sector are applied in view of their small margins, and exemptions have been created for sales between manufacturers to reduce the overall tax burden. They remain bandages to stop the bleeding, but they do not cure the underlying disease. We deal with these countermeasures, notably the integration charges, in more detail in Section 5.3.5. A major problem with a cascading system is that border tax adjustments can never be accurate. The tax burden will vary with the length of the production and distribution chain, which will be different even for similar products. Under a tax system that applies the destination principle (see Section 9.1.2), an export product should leave the country of production free of tax, and an equalization tax should be levied in the country of destination to create a level playing field with domestically produced goods. Under a cumulative tax system export rebates and import levies can only be based on estimates, which bear the risk of economic distortion when these estimates are deliberately or accidentally set to high. Higher rebates result in export subsidies and provide a price advantage for exported goods. Higher import charges provide market protection for domestic products competing with the imports.

On the basis of past experience, economists contend that cumulative tax systems can only be effectively, that is, without significant distortion, applied at relatively low rates.

Noncumulative taxes, however, apply a methodology of determining the tax liability of a business that provides a discount for tax paid in previous stages of the production and distribution chain. This can be done in different ways as we will discuss further in Section 3.2.2. Noncumulative taxes avoid the disadvantages of tax cascading or tax pyramiding and, in particular, allow for exact border tax adjustments, which explains why they are preferred by economists and policy makers.

3.2.1. Gross Receipt Taxes

The cumulative tax system most frequently applied both in the past and in the present is that of a GRT. As a consequence, it is also associated with all the disadvantages of cumulative taxes outlined above. Typically, a GRT is levied on total outputs, that is, total sales or turnover of a business without any credit or deduction for tax incurred on procurement. To the extent that tax is shifted forward, accumulation will occur, which is demonstrated for a single product in Chapter 5, Table 10. If we take a car manufacturer as an example, it is easy to see how tax can pyramid when many functions are outsourced.

Figure 4. Tax Accumulation in an Extended Supply Chain

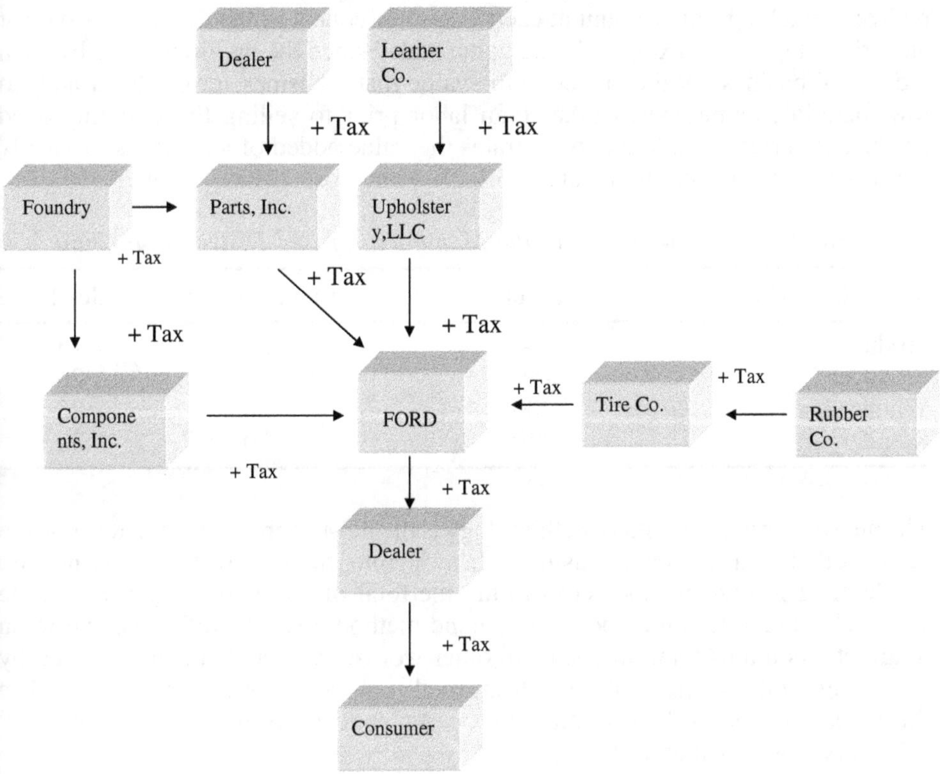

A car manufacturer uses many parts and components produced by other manufacturers who, in turn, buy from other specialized producers. In addition, all incur costs of advertising, accounting and so on. If all these sales are subject to a GRT, which is shifted forward, a potentially large sum of tax will accumulate at the car manufacturers level to be subsequently shifted forward to the dealer and then to the consumer. The more functions are outsourced, the more tax eventually will accumulate in the end price of the product. The car manufacturer could reduce the total tax burden by including all or several of the outsourced functions within the company (insourcing). This process is generally referred to as vertical integration and is the cause of serious economic disadvantages (see Section 5.3.9).

3.2.2. Value Added Taxes

Tax accumulation or tax pyramiding is perceived as a detrimental economic effect that disturbs economic neutrality between businesses. For this reason, many countries favor sales tax systems that are imposed at all stages of the production and distribution chain without the tax accumulation effect. This can be realized by taking into account at each stage subsequent to the first the tax paid at an earlier stage, and taxing only the value added since the previous stage by each individual business. Value added is the value that a business or producer adds to raw materials or purchases other than labor prior to selling the thus-improved product or service. Table 2 demonstrates the value added of a business, basically the difference between gross turnover (sales) and costs of procurement.

Table 2. The Value Added in the Manufacturer and Distribution Chain

VAT rate 10%	Input	Value Added	Sales Price
Producer 1	—	150	150
Producer 2	150	50	200
Wholesaler	200	30	230
Retailer	230	70	300

The question arising is which methodology is the most appropriate to determine the value added of a particular business. In principle, three distinct approaches are available. The first method seeks to tax the total of all elements that constitute value added (addition method). The second method taxes the difference between total outputs minus total inputs, or in other words, value added is determined by deducting total procurement costs from total turnover (subtraction method). The third method deducts the tax paid on procurement costs from the tax due on total sales (tax from tax method).

3.2.2.1. Addition Method

Under the addition method, all elements of the turnover of a business are taxed insofar as they have not been taxed at previous stages of the distribution chain. In essence, the value added of a business is determined by adding up its profit; wages (including employer's social insurance tax); and income in the form of government subsidies, royalties and interest, and multiplying the sum with the statutory tax rate. On a national scale, the addition method VAT has not been adopted anywhere, but Israel applies it to the financial sector.[7] The state of Michigan applied a SBT from 1976 through 2007, which was, in essence, a modified addition VAT. It deviated from the standard form in that it provided for an apportioned formula, allocating one-third of the tax base to the place of production and two-thirds to the place of sale, mixing origin and destination principles. As a result, imports received a competitive advantage since they were taxed significantly lower than domestically

7. See Alan Schenk & Oliver Oldman, *Value Added Tax: A Comparative Approach* (New York: Cambridge University Press, 2007), 328.

produced goods.[8] The New Hampshire Business Enterprise Tax (BET) is also an addition VAT levied on businesses with turnovers beyond a certain threshold. The tax base is apportioned to New Hampshire on the basis of a three-factor formula. The BET-liability can be credited against a business' liability under the state's business profits tax.[9]

The addition method cannot accommodate multiple rates because company accounts do not distinguish different product categories within their sales that coincide with different sales tax rates, nor do they divide inputs by differential tax liabilities.[10]

3.2.2.2. Subtraction Method

Like the addition method, the subtraction method is an accounts-based method that relies on aggregative data over a fixed period of time (generally a year) to compute the value added. The subtraction method VAT is imposed on gross receipts of a business but allows certain deductions. Total purchases in a certain tax period are deducted from total sales in that same period to arrive at the value added generated by the business, and the tax liability is calculated by multiplying the value added with the statutory tax rate, or t (output – input). Generally, business gross receipts neither include interest or similar income nor proceeds from the sale of notes, bonds, and similar assets. Inputs are immediately deductible, that is, expensed, and capital goods, therefore, are not subject to depreciation rules. Typically, however, wages and interest payments are nondeductible.

This method cannot accommodate multiple rates and because of its close resemblance of an income tax there exist serious doubt whether border tax adjustments of a subtraction VAT are permissible under WTO rules (see Sections 9.2 and 9.3).

3.2.2.3. Tax Credit Method

The tax credit method calculates the tax on a transaction-by-transaction basis and has, therefore, the advantage of accommodating a multiple rates consumption tax. In principle, each transaction is subject to the tax. A business will charge tax on its sales and incur tax on its purchases. Over a statutory reporting period (generally a calendar month, quarter or calendar year, depending on the level of total gross turnover or the estimated total tax due) a business will compute its tax liability by deducting the total amount of tax paid on procurement in the period from the total amount of tax charged on its sales in the period.

8. *Supra*, at 400.
9. *Supra*, at 403.
10. Alan A. Tait, *Value Added Tax: International Practice and Problems* (Washington, DC: IMF, 1988), at 5.

Table 3. Tax from Tax Method VAT

VAT Rate 10%	Sales	Tax on Sales	To Treasury
Producer 1	1,000	100	100
Producer 2	2,000	200	200–100 = 100
Producer 3	3,000	300	300–200 = 100
Wholesaler	4,000	400	400–300 = 100
Retailer	5,000	500	500–400 = 100
Total			500

In this simplified model, we assume that each stage of the production and distribution chain creates an additional value of 1,000 to a single product. Producer 1 made a product from scratch and has, therefore, no inputs. When producer 1 sells this product for 1,000, he has to charge an additional 100 in tax (rate 10%) for a total sales price of 1,100. On his periodical tax return, producer 1 has to account for the 100 in tax and remit this amount to the taxing authority. Producer 2 adds 1,000 in value and sells the product for 2,000 plus 200 in tax, thus for a total of 2,200. On his tax return producer 2, will account for the tax on the sale but also will receive a credit for the tax paid on his procurement. Producer 2 deducts the 100 in tax paid to producer 1 from the tax due on his sale to producer 3 and remits the difference (200–100) of 100 to the taxing authority. Each business will be required to operate two bookkeeping ledgers in record of the tax. One ledger to register the tax payable on sales (output-tax), and another to register the tax credit on procurements (input-tax). The total amount of tax credits over the statutory period is then deducted from the total amount of tax payable, and the difference is the tax due.

Because a discount is provided at each stage of the production and distribution chain for tax paid to the previous stage, in the end, the final consumer pays exactly 10%, the statutory rate, in tax over the retail price, and no tax accumulation occurs.

As this example demonstrates in simplified form, each stage of the production and distribution chain pays, in effect, tax over its value added, measured as the difference between tax on sales and tax on procurement. Tax is charged on each sale, and a tax credit arises regarding each purchase. In this sense, this system qualifies as a transaction tax. However, the value added over the statutory tax period is not calculated on a transaction basis. Tax payable is computed as the total tax charged on all transactions, and the tax credit is the total tax incurred on all purchases in a given tax period. In practice, a business may very well buy products that are not sold in the same tax period. Products bought remain tax free in stock until they are resold or used in the production of another good or service that is resold. In addition, most tax from tax systems allow for the immediate deduction of tax paid in relation to capital goods, although they are used over a longer period of time. In other words, the value added of a particular business is estimated on an aggregate level over an arbitrary time period. In this sense, the name VAT is not completely accurate. The value added is assessed indirectly by applying the tax rate "to a component of value added (outputs and inputs) and the resultant tax liabilities are subtracted to get the final net tax payable."[11]

3.3. SUMMARY AND EVALUATION

There are, in essence, two methods and four subsystems to tax value added. Value added is approached either from a composite perspective and it is determined by adding those elements that constitute the value added, or from a subtractive perspective, deducting costs from turnover. In other words, value added can be defined in terms of additive elements or subtractive elements:

$$\text{Value added} = \text{Wages} + \text{Profits}$$
or
$$\text{Value added} = \text{Output} - \text{Input}$$

The four basic forms lead to the same result and can be classified as either direct or indirect.

The direct additive or accounts method	$= t(w + p)$
The indirect additive method	$= t(w) + t(p)$
The direct subtractive method	$= t(\text{output} - \text{input})$
The indirect subtraction method	$= t(\text{output}) - t(\text{input})$

Where t = tax, w = wages and p = profit

The direct methods resemble in approach most taxes in the sense that they first determine the tax base, such as income or wealth, and then apply the tax rate to that value. Interestingly, it is the indirect subtraction or credit invoice method that has enjoyed unsurpassed proliferation. According to Tait,[12] there are four principle reasons for this. Most importantly, under a credit invoice VAT, the tax liability is attached to the transaction, which makes it superior from a legal and technical perspective. The second advantage is the audit trail created by the mandatory invoicing on a transaction basis. Thirdly, direct methods cannot accommodate a multiple rate VAT, whereas indirect methods can. The fourth reason is that the credit invoice method VAT is the most practical one because the tax liability can be calculated on a weekly, monthly, quarterly or annual basis.

In the next sections, we will first look at some determining characteristics of consumption taxes in general. Then we will concentrate on four of the most commonly applied sales taxes, namely GRT, RST, the subtraction VAT and the credit invoice VAT. Our focus is on how they actually work in current practice but references are made to past experience where appropriate.

---

11. Tait, at 5.
12. *Supra*, 5 and 6.

Chapter 4

Characterization of Consumption Taxes

4.1. DIRECT VERSUS INDIRECT TAX

One way to categorize different types of taxes is by distinguishing between taxes that are imposed directly on the person who is legally supposed to bear the tax and is assessed directly on a measurement of income or expenditure, and taxes that are imposed indirectly, that is through an intermediary collecting the tax on behalf of the government through an add-on to his prices.

Figure 5. Direct versus Indirect Tax

Direct Tax:

Statutory Incidence = Economic Incidence

Indirect Tax:

Statutory Incidence ≠ Economic Incidence
(Former to shift tax to latter)

In other words, under a direct tax, the tax is levied on the person identified or destined in the law to actually bear the tax. Put another way, the place of statutory incidence is the same as the place of economic incidence. Under an indirect tax, the tax is levied on a third person who is supposed to shift the tax forward by increasing his prices with the statutory tax rate to the person intended to bear the tax. In this case, the place of statutory incidence is different from the place of economic incidence. The assumption of forward shifting of tax along the production and distribution chain to the ultimate consumer is an essential element of the design of consumption taxes with which we will deal more extensively in Section 4.4.1.

Examples of direct taxes are personal income tax, levied on wages, dividends, interests and lottery winnings; corporate income tax, levied on net profits; and property taxes, levied on the owners of real property, such as land, homes and commercial buildings as well as on certain machinery, equipment and motor vehicles.

Examples of indirect taxes are the general RST and the VAT, levied on all consumption expenditure, and excises, imposed on the expenditure for specific goods.

Although most consumption taxes are indirect, a direct consumption tax is feasible and has been proposed by Nicolas Kaldor in 1955.[1] Income can only be used in two ways. It is either consumed or it is saved. Therefore, the tax base is defined as annual income minus net additions to savings during the year. A direct consumption tax would be paid through the filing of annual forms by individuals or households, declaring their net expenditure. The tax would be directly remitted to the government instead of to sellers of goods and services in their capacity as third-party tax collectors. This structure allows the tax burden to be more easily geared to individual circumstances than other means of taxing consumption because the tax would be collected from individuals rather than vendors. This characteristic makes the direct consumption tax a more effective structure for achieving desired degrees of horizontal and vertical equity.[2] Equity goals in relationship to people's incomes can only be approximated under indirect consumption taxes, such as a VAT or RST. Direct consumption taxes, also called consumption-based or consumable income taxes are seldom used, although they have been proposed frequently.[3] However, the subtraction from taxable income of contributions to 401K and

1. Nicholas Kaldor, *An Expenditure Tax* (London: George Allen & Unwin Ltd., 1955). The idea of taxing individuals through their expenditure rather than on their income goes back to Thomas Hobbes in *Leviathan* and has been supported, inter alia, by John Stuart Mill, and Irving Fisher.
2. Horizontal equity refers to comparisons of the tax burden for people with a similar capacity to pay tax, and vertical equity refers to comparisons of the tax burden for people with different capacities to pay tax. *Progressive*, *proportional*, and *regressive* taxation are terms applied to vertical equity.
3. For example, David Bradford, *Blueprints for Basic Tax Reform* (Washington, DC: US Department of the Treasury, 1977; 2nd ed. 1984); US Tax Act of 1995, proposed by Senators Samuel A. Nunn & Pete V. Domenici, S. 722, 104th Cong., 1st sess., 141 Cong. Rec. S. 5664 (24 April 1995); Simplified US Tax Act of 2003, proposed by Congressman Phillip English, H.R. 269, 108 Cong., 1st sess. (8 January 2003).

IRA[4] retirement savings programs incorporates an element of a direct consumption tax into the US income tax, transforming it, to a modest extent, to a hybrid of a general income tax and a consumable income tax.

Within value added type consumption taxes, the direct versus indirect distinction is made in relation to how the value added is calculated. As we have seen in Sections 3.2.2 and 3.3, the addition method VAT and subtraction method VAT allow for the value added to be determined either directly [$t(w + p)$ and t(output – input)] or indirectly [$t(w) + t(p)$ and t(output) – t(input)].

4.2. GENERAL COVERAGE

Consumption taxes can be product specific, i.e., imposed on particular products, such as alcoholic beverages, tobacco, gasoline and other petrochemical fuels, motor vehicles and so forth. These taxes are generally called excises and are effective insofar as they are levied on products with a high degree of demand inelasticity. RSTs and VATs are general taxes on consumption. In other words, they seek to tax all private consumptive expenditure. As a consequence, the scope of a consumption tax should include both goods and services. Taxing both goods and services also offers the advantage of preventing substitution. If services were not taxed, one could easily substitute a like service for a taxed good. For example, instead of buying a washing machine, a consumer could decide to employ a third-party laundry service. Incomplete coverage will have an undue influence on consumers' expenditure decisions because it discriminates against taxed supplies in favor of nontaxable supplies. In addition, it would reduce the tax base significantly, demanding a higher tax rate on taxed items to realize the revenue needed.

4.3. CLASSIFICATION ON THE BASIS OF THE SCOPE OF THE TAX

A distinction between VATs is made on the basis of the treatment given to depreciation of investments.

4.3.1. Consumption Type

Under the consumption type VAT, all tax paid on purchases for use in the production process is immediately and fully recoverable. In other words, business procurement is eliminated from the tax base or, formulated differently, it can be

4. Individual Retirement Account, enacted by the Pension Reform Act of 1974, P.L. 93–406, s. 2002 (a).

expensed. As a result, capital investment is not penalized through an additional tax burden, and the tax does not favor any method of production over another since substituting labor for capital or vice versa does not influence the total tax burden incurred by a firm.

If we ignore economic relations with foreign countries and exemptions, gross national income (Y) is the sum of total consumption (C) and total investments (I), or $Y = C + I$. When we deduct the value of investments, we find the value of consumption, or $Y - I = C$. For this reason, the tax is referred to as consumption type VAT because the tax base equals total private consumption expenditure.

Ideally, the VAT should include both private and public consumption. However, in the public realm it proves difficult to realize an adequate identification of, and to arrive at a precise distinction between, investments and consumption. Moreover, public services are financed through taxation, and are, generally, supplied free of charge. In the end, public consumption is only included in the tax base to the extent of nonrecoverable input tax, incurrent on government procurement.

4.3.2. Income Type

If expensing of capital investment is replaced by a system of depreciation pro rata temporis (D), the character of the VAT changes accordingly from a consumption type into an income type. The VAT basically mimics the approach under corporate income taxes where capital goods are to be written off over their life cycle as the value of these goods depreciates, by allowing only part of the purchase to be treated as a deductible input in computing value added. Again, ignoring foreign economic relations, the net national product or income is the sum of all domestic income, or $Y - D = C + I - D = Y_{net} \cdot Y_{net}$.

The tax base equals total personal income and is identical to the base of the personal income tax without exemptions. Under the income type of VAT, calculation of depreciation will be required, and an incentive arises to classify purchases as current expenditures.

4.3.3. Product Type

A third category is the product type VAT, under which no depreciation is allowed for investments, or, in VAT terminology, no input VAT incurred on the purchase of capital goods can be recovered or deducted. In effect, this leads to the taxation of gross national income, or $Y = C + I$. Capital investments will be taxed at the time they are purchased and again when the products they help to produce are sold to consumers. The choice for a product type VAT creates an incentive for insourcing (i.e., the self-production of capital goods) and for classifying the purchase of capital goods as current expenditures. Such a tax is not neutral (see Section 4.5 for definitions of neutrality) because it favors labor-intensive methods over capital-intensive methods of production. Currently, only China applies an origin-based, product type VAT, but it is changing gradually to a consumption type VAT.[5]

4.4. TAX INCIDENCE

4.4.1. WHO BEARS THE BURDEN OF A CONSUMPTION TAX?

Tax incidence and tax shifting are not new notions: in the late nineteenth century, economists were quite aware of the essential question of who bears the burden of taxation.[6] The true tax burden is not determined by where and on whom it is imposed initially because taxes affect taxpayers' behaviors, which in turn generate economic changes, regularly shifting part or the entire tax burden to others. Taxes reduce and distort the choice and decision of what and how much people are willing to produce in their respective roles as workers, savers and investors. Taxes increase the prices of their services or products. Changes in the prices and quantities of economic output, consequently, affect consumers in their decisions on how to spend their incomes. The real costs of taxation exceed the amount of revenue collected because lost economic output and compliance costs are additional burdens for taxpayers; this is called the excess burden of a tax.[7]

There exists no certainty that the burden of a given tax rests on the person statutory elected to bear it. Policy makers, generally, rely on assumptions and simplifications regarding tax incidence when they assign various taxes to consumers, capital or labor. Assumptions, however, are not realities, and a considerable mismatch between the former and the latter may, and in many instances do, derail policy objectives incorporated in many tax laws.

The VAT is imposed with the implicit assumption that producers of goods and services will increase their prices with the tax and, thus, shift the burden fully forward to the final consumer. If, before the imposition of a 20% VAT, a certain product sells for USD 100, it is assumed it will sell for USD 120 after its introduction. In that case, the tax burden would, indeed, be shifted to the consumer. However, a seller may choose to reduce its selling price to enhance or secure its relative competitiveness. In our example, the seller may have concluded that it is necessary for him to maintain the same consumer price level. To accomplish this, he will reduce the net price to USD 83.34 and add the 20% VAT, or USD 16.66, to arrive at the preferred consumer price of USD 100. In the latter case, the tax is shifted backward and borne by both or either the labor and capital factors. In another scenario, the seller and consumer could both bear the tax, that is, the seller

5. See Richard M. Bird & Pierre-Pascal Gendron, *The VAT in Developing and Transitional Countries* (Cambridge, 2007), at 216.
6. Alfred Marshall, *Principles of Economics*, 8th ed. (1890), Philadelphia, 1920 (reprinted 1982), Ch. IX, 343–345.
7. See, regarding tax incidence and excess burden, for example, Stephen J. Entin, *Tax Incidence, Tax Burden, and Tax Shifting: Who Really Pays the Tax?* (The Heritage Foundation, Center for Data Analysis, Report 04–12, 5 November 2004), <www.heritage.org/research/taxes/cda04-12.cfm>.

reduces his price only with a fraction of the imposed tax. In our example, the seller could set his net price at USD 95 and yield a final selling price (including tax) of USD 114. These examples also show that the reality of tax incidence can have a direct influence on the amount of revenue generated by the tax. In case of fully or partial back shifting, the amount of tax collected is lower than anticipated and budgeted under the assumption of fully forward shifting of that tax.

The extent and direction of tax shifting depend on the relative price elasticities of supply and demand. In the end, the tax burden will fall on those consumers or producers who have the least shifting capabilities.

Elasticity is the percentage change in the quantity of a product, or the factor of production, such as labor, capital, land and so on, supplied or demanded divided by the percentage change in its price. It measures the sensitivity to price change of a given product or factor. The supply or demand for a product or factor can be either elastic or inelastic but to a degree that can vary. In the case of a perfectly elastic supply, the net-of-tax price is fixed at marginal cost, and demand will be matched as long as the market price is paid. If demand is not willing to pay the price, supply will simply drop to zero. In this situation all tax is borne by the consumer. If demand is price sensitive, output (quantity) will fall.

The reverse situation appears when demand is perfectly elastic. Any rise in the price would cause a collapse in consumption. The market price is fixed, and tax imposed will reduce the net-of-tax price for the producer, who, as a result, will bear the whole tax. If supply is price sensitive, output will fall.

Supply could also be perfectly inelastic. In that case, the same quantity of product must be offered regardless of the price (e.g., perishable products). The market price fully depends on what consumers are willing to pay (fixed by demand), and taxes will reduce the net-of-tax price of the producer, who ultimately incurs the tax burden. Output will not change, but it may be reduced at the next production cycle.

If demand is perfectly inelastic, price changes will not affect the level of demand. Output will remain unchanged in case of a price increase. All taxes would be borne by the consumers.

These examples provide extreme positions, of course, and in reality elasticities of demand and supply are never perfect, but they help explain the concept and implications of elasticity. Figure 6 shows, in simplified form, the implications of the introduction of a tax for a single product.

Before the introduction of the tax (*t*), supply would equal demand at the equilibrium point *E*o, with a unit price of *P*o and a quantity of *Q*o units. The introduction of the tax per unit of product creates a difference between the price paid by the consumer (*P*c) and the price received by the producer (*P*p) at the amount of (*P*c – *P*p). The increase of the gross consumer price will lead to a reduced demand, which triggers a lower price for the producer, who in turn will reduce the quantity of units produced. The quantity of output falls from its original value (*Q*o) to its new value (*Q*1). Market equilibrium shifts from *E*o to *E*1.

Figure 6. Implications of the Introduction of a Single Product Tax

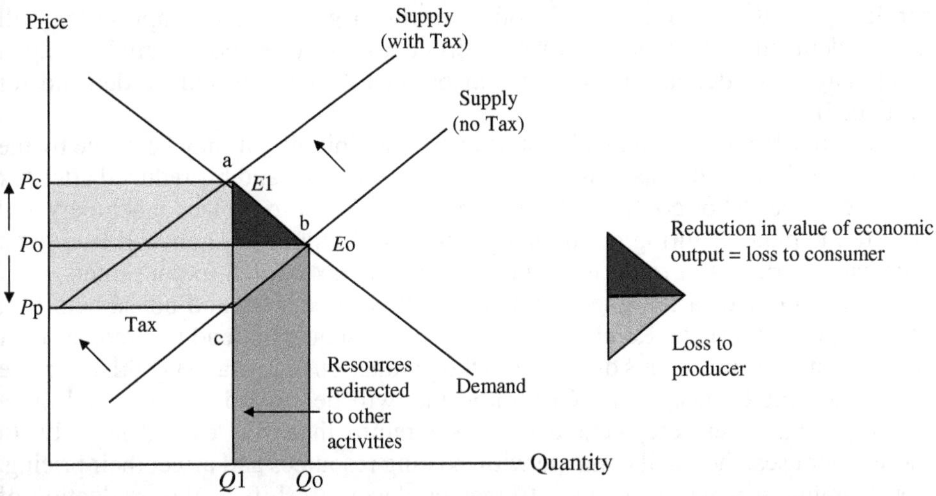

The tax received is not related to the quantity of the original production (*Q*o) but equals the statutory tax times the reduced quantity (*t* x *Q*1). Generally, the upper portion of the revenue rectangle, (*P*c – *P*o) x *Q*1, is considered to be the share of the tax that falls on the consumer because she/he now pays a higher tax-inclusive price. The bottom portion of the rectangle, (*P*o – *P*p) x *Q*1, is considered to be the share of the tax incurred by the producer in the form of a lower net-of-tax price received for the product.

The triangle between the supply and demand curves (a-b-c) is the excess burden or deadweight loss of the tax, representing the excess value of the lost product over its resource cost, divided between the consumer and the producer. The smaller the deadweight loss, the less effect on choices made, for a given level of revenue, and the more economically efficient the tax.

A tax can be described as being paid by the producer or by the consumer, but the outcome is the same: The rise in the price to the buyer to *P*c, the drop in the price to the seller to *P*p and the drop in production to *Q*1 are identical whichever view is taken, and they depend entirely on the rate of the tax and the slopes (elasticities) of the supply and demand curves.

When a tax is levied on a single product, for example, an excise tax, consumers may substitute another comparable product for the newly taxed one. For example, a tax on wine may shift consumer preference to beer. It is argued that a general consumption tax, such as a VAT or RST, do not pose that risk because they do not impact the relative prices of goods and services. The price of all products and services are similarly affected by the tax. However, this reasoning does not provide us with a complete picture of economic reality because price elasticities are not homogeneous but will be different for each product and service offered on the market. In other words, a general consumption tax still affects demand and supply of a single product or service. For example, a 20% VAT may leave demand unchanged for product A but may reduce demand for product B.

The burden of a tax may also shift over time. Initially, it may be borne by the producer as long as his machinery earns more being used and his reduced after-tax revenues cover labor costs, but later he may decide not to replace machinery and shift to the manufacturing of another product. The reduced output will lead to an increase of prices and room is created to shift the tax burden to consumers.

The impact of a tax goes beyond the direct producers and consumers of a certain good or service. Reduced demand will consequently lead to a reduction of production. Resources thus driven from the production of the taxed good or service must find employ elsewhere. Generally, this will be second-best use and these resources will, therefore, generate a lower return than was earned initially. In these other uses, they will compete with existing resources and affect their pricing. For example, a wine excise may trigger producers to shift to the production of tomatoes. If the additional supply is not met with a corresponding increase of demand, prices will be lower. Insofar as the field laborers have transferable skills, they will be able to maintain the level of their earnings, but workers with specialized winemaking skills may find no alternative use for them and will incur a wage loss.

In conclusion, the assumption, generally postulated in legal literature on consumption taxation, that the tax is always and fully shifted forward to the final consumer is obviously an inaccurate simplification. For the tax burden to be fully borne by private consumers and to be correctly characterized as a mere wash through for traders would require supply to be perfectly elastic and demand to be perfectly inelastic. In reality, the tax burden will fall on those who are the least able to shift the burden to someone else. In this sense, the tax burden is on the shoulders of consumers, labor factor and capital factor to the extent of their respective elasticities.

Under the consumption type VAT, the tax is an add-on to the price of each individual producer in the manufacturer and distribution chain. Businesses are relieved from tax by allowing them a credit for VAT paid on procurement that they can exercise against the tax collected on their sales. The credit invoice method VAT has, therewith, created a mechanism to enable tax shifting. In many countries, certain goods and services are exempt from VAT for a variety of reasons (see Section 8.2.4.2.). No VAT is charged on the sale of an exempt item, but on the flipside the trader is not eligible for a credit for the VAT paid on his purchases related to the exempt sale. This would create a tax burden for the business sector engaged in exempt sales, unless and insofar as they are able to shift the tax forward to the final consumers. Shifting of the noncreditable input VAT will, in reality, not be possible for all sectors of the economy or for each and every individual business, or cannot be realized in full for the reasons explained afore.

The extent to which the VAT is borne by the business sector will vary among countries. For Germany, research indicates that the VAT is in effect borne for about 37% by the business sector.[8]

4.4.2. REGRESSIVITY OF CONSUMPTION TAXES

4.4.2.1. Introduction

The assumption that VAT, or any other indirect consumption tax, is a regressive tax has had an immediate effect on the design of the tax in many countries and dominates policy debate when its introduction is under discussion. Our starting point is the requirement that taxes must be fair, and we will investigate the evolution of that concept from its birth in natural law to today's application. Since moral values change over time, the concept of fairness is not carved in stone. The statement that a progressive income tax is fair and just is merely a statement of political correctness; it is not a statement of fact. In this same sense is the rejection of, for instance, a VAT on the grounds of its presumed regressive nature, a statement of political correctness. However, whether VAT, or any other consumption tax, is indeed regressive can be empirically tested. For practical reasons we will refer in this section to VAT only, but our findings have bearing for all consumption taxes. This section examines the arguments pro and con VAT's regressivity and, from a combination of perspectives, concludes that it is in fact a proportional tax.

4.4.2.2. Terminology

4.4.2.2.1. Progressive Taxes

Generally, a tax is called progressive when, as a percentage of income, the tax rises as income rises. For income taxes this means that the tax rate increases as the amount to which that rate is applied increases and, as a result, people with higher disposable income pay a higher percentage of that income in tax than those with lower income.

Consumption taxes, such as VAT or sales tax, do not apply the rate directly to income, but tax consumptive expenditure. By my knowledge, there exists no VAT system in the world designed to be progressive. The only way to make an indirect consumption tax progressive is by rate variation. Theoretically, a VAT or other indirect consumption tax would be progressive if the tax rate on a certain good or service varied with income. In other words, higher-income groups would pay a higher tax rate than lower-income groups on the purchase of the same good or service.

---

8. Peter Gottfried & Wolfgang Wiegard, "Exemption versus Zero Rating: A Hidden Problem of VAT," *Journal of Public Economics* 46 (1991): 308. For the year 1988, 21% of the tax was effectively borne by intermediate products and 16% by capital goods.

Clearly, from a practical perspective the implementation of such a system would be extremely difficult, if not, in fact, impossible. Progression can be built into the design of a VAT through rate variation more effectively (see, however, the remarks in Section 4.4.2.6.3) by applying reduced rates on goods and services predominantly procured by lower-income groups and by applying increased rates on goods and services presumably favored by the better off.

Progressive taxes reduce the tax incidence of people with lower incomes, as they shift the incidence disproportionately to those with higher incomes.

4.4.2.2.2. Proportional Taxes

A tax is called proportional when, as a percentage of income, the tax rate is constant at all income levels. However, even under those circumstances, there is still progression in the sense that persons who earn twice as much as others pay twice as much in taxes.

Proportional or flat taxes were commonly levied during the nineteenth century and are recently making a strong comeback. Flat taxes have been adopted in Estonia, Lithuania, Latvia, Russia, Serbia, the Ukraine, Slovakia, Georgia and Romania. In the United States, although the federal income tax is progressive, five states (Illinois, Indiana, Massachusetts, Michigan and Pennsylvania) apply a single rate tax to household incomes.

4.4.2.2.3. Regressive Taxes

A tax is called regressive when, as a percentage of income, the tax falls as income rises. For income taxes this means that the tax rate decreases as the amount to which that rate is applied increases. In relation to consumption taxes, regression means that the ratio of consumption to income falls when moving up the income scale, as does the ratio of tax burden to income. The tax incidence rests disproportionately on those with lower incomes.

4.4.2.3. Philosophical Perspective

As to the justification of taxation, there exists general consensus that every member of society must somehow contribute to its common costs. There exists also general consensus that taxation should be fair. The definition of "fair" is less clear, and the interpretation of that concept probably varies from person to person and from time to time. Nevertheless, it seems correct to state that fairness must be interpreted relative to the extent a person derives benefits from society, relative to her or his wealth and relative to what others contribute. By writing this down, I am already making a moral statement, and it is important to realize that moral statements are not absolute but, indeed, relative, and that morality and concepts of justice and equality are conceived of differently in various cultures and across time.

When absolute power of the ruler was the norm in Europe, the idea that taxation should be based on fairness was considered absurd. In those days, the ruler, at his discretion, would tax whenever, whatever and whomever he pleased. Only in the eighteenth century, during the age of enlightenment, were ideas of fairness in taxation postulated. In England, Adam Smith laid down his concept of fairness in four canons, the first of which stated that taxes are fair when the tax burden is universal and applies equally to all in society.[9] Smith's ideas on fairness, including the notion that the equal must be treated equally and, as a consequence, the unequal must be treated unequally in proportion to their individual inequality, became an ethic guideline for the next century.[10] Based on the idea of a contract between the individuals and the State,[11] all subjects ought to contribute in proportion to the revenue they respectively enjoyed under the protection of the State. In France, Montesquieu and, later, Rousseau came to similar conclusions, but they were opposed to proportional taxation, arguing that income should be exempt from taxation insofar as it is needed to cover the minimum cost of living, and that excess income should be taxed higher.[12]

John Stuart Mill and later Edwin Seligman argued strongly that the quid pro quo approach of Smith is indefensible because it is impossible to accurately measure the benefits individual members of society derive from the activities of the government.[13]

In the nineteenth century, taxation was no longer perceived as payment for state protection but rather as a personal sacrifice for the totality of benefits the state generated for society as a whole and, therefore, was unrelated to, by whatever measure, the personal advantages individuals derived from the same governmental activity. Where, under the social contract theory, a proportional tax seemed adequate, this more abstract view ultimately leads to taxation based on the ability to pay. Since the latter depends on many factors, such as income, savings, family size, cost for health care and so on, it is basically impossible to exactly measure the ability to pay in individual cases. Another problem involves determining a fair rate of taxation. A progressive tax rate seemed acceptable on the basis of the economic theory of diminishing marginal utility.[14] This means that, in relation to income,

---

9. Adam Smith, *Inquiry into the Nature and Causes of the Wealth of Nations* (first published 1776; New York: The Modern Library, 1937), 777.
10. Although Smith based his conclusions on an economic approach to taxation and never spoke of "Equity" or "Justice."
11. A legal theory supported by the leading philosophers of the seventeenth and eighteenth centuries, including Thomas Hobbes (1588–1679), Hugo Grotius (1553–1645), John Locke (1632–1704) and Jean Jacques Rousseau (1712–1778).
12. Charles de Montesquieu, *De l'Esprit des Lois* (The Spirit of Laws), (1748) and Jean Jacques Rousseau, *Discours sur l'Economie Politique* (Treatise on Political Economics), (1755).
13. John Stuart Mill, *Principles of Political Economy* (1848), 485, and Edwin R.A. Seligman, *Progressive Taxation in Theory and Practice* (1908), 717.
14. Hermann Heinrich Gossen, *Die Entwicklung der Gesetze des menschlichen Verkehrs und der daraus fließenden Regeln für menschliches Handeln* (The Development of the Laws of Human Intercourse and the Consequent Rules of Human Action) (1854), was the first to elaborate on this theory. His work was originally largely ignored but was rediscovered in 1870 by William Stanley Jevons, who, together with Leon Walras and Carl Menger, reintroduced and built on this theory.

additional monetary units offer the receiver reduced utility. In simple words, the more money you earn the lesser value it has. An extra USD 50,000 means a lot when you earn USD 100,000 a year (person A), but where you earn USD 5 million (person B), an additional USD 50,000 does not really make much difference. From that perspective, a tax dollar paid has a different impact on persons whose incomes are significantly different. Under the diminishing marginal utility approach, a fair distribution of the common cost of society means that individuals should make a financial sacrifice that is comparatively the same at different income levels. In terms of utility, every subject contributes the same to the common cost, which principle will then have to be translated into monetary units at the individual level. Since for person B, a dollar has less utility than for person A, B should pay in accordance with a rate of progression that corresponds to the diminishing utility of his earnings. The concept of the ability to pay, in this sense, also serves the objective of ensuring economic neutrality in taxation.

However, economics is not an exact science, and where the ability to pay cannot be measured at the individual level, the same is true for the concept of utility. Everybody's situation is different and, therefore, individual utility curves[15] will be divergent as well. Even where two individuals have the same income and their circumstances are otherwise identical, that is under ceteris paribus conditions, their utility curves may be different because utility is not only an economic phenomenon but also a psychological one. For example, someone who employs his wealth for charitable purposes may gain the psychological satisfaction of doing good, which, clearly, cannot be measured either in terms of utility or in monetary units.

Although the concepts of ability to pay and marginal utility, in abstracto, seem to have sound theoretical foundations, as indicated previously, they do not have much practical value.[16] Therefore, these concepts are, in essence, useless to us. That gives rise to the question of why we still have progressive income taxes in the Western world, and why they have such a strong support.

At the end of the nineteenth century, Adolph Wagner was the founding father of an approach, which is still applied today, that includes the use of taxation for social policy, including the redistribution of income and wealth.[17] With John Keynes, a strong and influential interest emerges in using taxation as an instrument of economic cyclical policy,[18] which means that tax revenue and tax rates must depend on economic conditions. Today's income tax structure is based on a combination of the aforementioned approaches; in effect, taxation serves a myriad of conflicting and contradicting functions. Redistribution of income conflicts directly and essentially with the tax neutrality of the utilitarian model. Under the (post-)

15. A graph expressing the relationship between income and utility of the last-earned monetary unit.
16. Also: John F Due, *Government Finance* (1977), 372: "the concept of ability has no clearly defined universally accepted meaning or measure."
17. Adolph D. Wagner, *Finanzwißenschaft* (Public Finance), vol. 2 (Leipzig/Neurenberg, 1880), at 288.
18. John Maynard Keynes, *The General Theory of Employment, Interest and Money* (London, 1936).

Keynesian theory, taxation is primarily an instrument for realizing economic policy goals; however, the principles of fair tax distribution approach taxation from the perspective of the individual contributor.

Nevertheless, in public opinion and political debate, the argument is still made that a progressive income tax is fair because it is based on the ability-to-pay principle. In my view, that argument is partly based on the apparent misconception that a progressive tax, whose objective it is to realize redistribution of income, is in fact a tax based on the ability to pay; for another part, I am afraid, the argument must be attributed to the short-term benefit of simplistic rhetoric. The misconception has proved to be persistent. In 1999, the Dutch Labor Party held a conference on a new tax system for the twenty-first century based on the premises of ability to pay[19] and redistribution of income, unaware that those two objectives are in essence irreconcilable. The notion that a progressive income tax is fair because it is presumably based on the ability-to-pay principle has become part of the public domain. Everybody seems to accept this as an unalienable truth to the extent that it has become an almost religious dogma not open to discussion or challenge. Whereas a progressive tax is considered fair, a regressive tax is consequently perceived as unfair. This has become a generally accepted idea, as demonstrated by an episode of the television drama series *The West Wing*, in which the character of deputy chief of staff makes the angry remark that a VAT is wrong because it is regressive, which means that poor people pay more than rich people.

Simplicity creates powerful rhetoric but should not be confused with empirical truth. However, perceived truth is what really matters. A certain degree of social acceptance of a tax is essential for its successful implementation. With fairness being a requirement for acceptable taxation, an element of morality has been introduced into the political and public debate. Whereas progressive taxes are perceived as morally correct, regressive taxes are seen as unacceptable, even as immoral. Naturally, politicians are sensitive to the sentiments of their constituents. Obviously, from a political perspective, it is difficult to propose the introduction of a tax that in the public mindset is morally inferior. This provides all the more reason to offer nuances and new perspectives, and to test empirically what is perceived as truth, in order to develop an environment in which tax reforms can be discussed properly, that is, on the basis of facts, not emotions and political correctness.

4.4.2.4. Regressivity in the Political Debate

It is essential to establish whether, and if so, to what extent, a VAT is regressive because it determines the validity of the arguments pro and con in policy debates on the introduction of that tax. The presumed regressivity of a VAT is used as a supporting argument by those who are opposed to its introduction, for example, in the United States. Because of its regressivity, a VAT is perceived to be unfair and its introduction is even seen as a roadblock on the way to social justice. In fact,

19. "De sterkste schouders moeten de zwaarste lasten dragen" (The heaviest loads should rest on the strongest shoulders).

VAT's regressivity has become an axiom elevated beyond proper discussion, at least in policy circles, and probably also in the public's mind.

In countries that already apply a VAT, reduced rates applicable to essential goods and/or increased rates on luxury items have been introduced as measures to reduce or neutralize the regressive effect of the tax. Several authors and politicians even suggest that the introduction of a VAT should be accompanied by an increase of the progressivity in personal income tax in order to offset the regressive effects of the VAT.[20] In the preceding section, I have discussed the element of political correctness in qualifying taxes as "progressive" or "regressive," and the effect of such qualifications on the public's acceptance of a tax as fair or its rejection as unfair. A serious debate on the introduction of a VAT, however, should be based on facts, not myths, and for that reason it is important to establish whether, and if so, to what extent, the VAT is regressive. It neither makes any sense to reject a VAT for the wrong reasons nor wise to make a VAT unnecessarily complicated and more costly in terms of administrative and compliance costs on the basis of an incorrect premise.

4.4.2.5. The Argument for VAT Being Regressive

In economic studies the impact of a tax, or the tax burden, is, generally, measured relative to income. Low-income groups spend a relatively larger part of their incomes on consumption than higher-income groups; consequently, the low-income groups pay more consumption tax (VAT) relative to their incomes.

When a tax is levied on specific goods or services, the regressivity of the tax would depend on the taxpayer's propensity to engage in the taxed activity or transactions relative to their incomes. In other words, where goods and services subject to the tax are predominantly purchased by the poor and to a lesser extent by the rich, the tax would be labeled as "regressive."

A VAT on food and other essentials can be regressive. Because the income-elasticity of food is usually less than 1[21], expenditure on food tends to take up a higher percentage of the budgets of persons or families with a lower incomes as compared to persons or families with higher incomes.

To determine whether a consumption tax is regressive, the income-elasticity of the goods and services[22] being taxed, as well as possible income-substitution[23] effects, must be considered.

The regressive nature of VAT can be illustrated by means of the following highly simplified example. Person A earns an income of 10,000 and person B's income is 5,000. Both A and B pay a tax of 1,000 on their purchases. Consequently, the effective tax rate is 20% for B and 10% for A. Thus, a tax that is fixed to the

20. Not only by applying higher top rates but also by applying higher rates to low-income brackets.
21. An income-elasticity of less than 1 means that, where income increases by 10%, expenditure on the goods or services in question increases by less than 10%.
22. The percentage change of demand for specific goods or services (δC) relative to a percentage change of income (δY), that is, the income-elasticity of the goods and services is $\delta C/\delta Y$.
23. The extent to which demand for specific goods and services is substituted by demand for other goods and services as income changes.

value of the good or service (disregarding exemptions or rebates) would likely result in a higher rate of taxation on people with less purchasing power. Hence, a VAT is, in effect, regressive. In this simple model, regressivity is measured on an annual basis and, as a result, an economic unit is supposed to be captured within a certain income category; the level of consumption is assumed to be stable regardless of income, and savings are not subject to the tax.

4.4.2.6. Preliminary Remarks

Before taking a closer look at, and analyzing the validity of, the argument just presented in what I will refer to as the regressive model, the following should be borne in mind before VAT is rejected as being a regressive and unfair tax.

4.4.2.6.1. The Effect of Regressivity Is Relative

A regressive tax system does not mean that low-income earners pay more taxes than the wealthy, and that probably will not be the case. It only means that the effective tax rate relative to income constitutes a heavier tax burden on low-income earners as compared to high-income earners. For VAT, regressivity means that low-income groups pay a larger percentage of their income in VAT. In absolute terms, they may pay less tax. For example, a low-income family earns 30,000 (after income tax) per annum and spends 8,000 on the home mortgage, leaving the family a disposable income of 22,000. With two children, a cat and a dog, they spend it all on consumptive expenditure. At a tax rate of 6%, the family pays 1,320 in tax. A middle-income family of a similar size earning 60,000, paying 20,000 on the mortgage and saving 5,000 pays a total of 2,100 in tax, which is 5.25% of its disposable income. Finally, a third family earning 150,000, paying 40,000 on its mortgage and saving 30,000 pays 4,800 in taxes, which is 4.36% of its disposable income.

Although the two families with the higher income pay less as a percentage of their respective disposable incomes, in absolute terms they pay a higher amount of tax than the low-income family.

4.4.2.6.2. VAT Is Only One Tax in a Tax System

Even if VAT were a regressive tax, that would not necessarily lead to the conclusion that the tax is unfair. It would only be unfair if it were the only tax levied in a country. In reality, however, every country levies multiple taxes, some of which are progressive, others proportional and still others might fall into a third category being possibly regressive, and those characteristics may even vary regarding individual taxes. For the purpose of assessing the fairness of a tax, its effects should not be considered in isolation. Instead, the total effect of the entire tax system should determine whether the tax burden is distributed equally among all members of society. To make the matter more complicated, grants and subsidies, child support and other payments individuals receive from the state and which, in effect, offset part of the tax burden, should be taken into account.

4.4.2.6.3. *Countermeasures*

Proponents of VAT often point out that the regressive effect of VAT can be mitigated by applying exemptions and reduced rates to goods and services primarily procured by low-income families and by applying increased rates to luxury items supposedly favored by high-income consumers. Theoretically, this proposition is correct. However, in practice, the situation is more complex.

Multiple rates lead to classification problems regarding goods and services on the dividing line of the definition; they violate the principle of economic neutrality in that final consumers may substitute standard-rated goods and services for those subject to a reduced rate, and they may result in a significant increase in the compliance costs for businesses and administrative costs for the government. Moreover, it is not so simple to determine which goods and services are predominantly acquired by the relative poor and which by the better off. Consumption patterns of high- and low-income categories tend to converge and, as a result, the impact of rate variations is much less than expected. Apart from that, it should be borne in mind that reduced rates aimed at benefiting low-income groups also benefit high-income groups, and sometimes even more so. In many countries, public transportation is exempt from tax or subject to a reduced tax rate under the apparent assumption that low-income households make regular use of it. However, commuters from the suburbs taking the train or subway to the city center or to Wallstreet derive the same benefit from a reduced transportation rate. In addition, research shows that expenditures on certain reduced-rated goods and services, as a percentage of total expenditure, increases as family income increases.[24] Irish research shows that, in absolute terms, the rich spend twice as much on food as compared to the poor because they purchase more expensive varieties, go to restaurants more frequently and more often throw away food.[25] As a result, exempting food from VAT[26] in Ireland provides the better off with twice as much tax relief as compared to low-income groups.

In conclusion, VAT's regression can theoretically be reduced or mitigated by exemptions and rate variances, but, in practice, it is impossible to apply those measures efficiently due to many factors that are unknown or cannot be sufficiently quantified, qualified or defined; moreover, the countermeasures themselves add to the complexity of the VAT system and reduce its transparency.

4.4.2.7. Empirical Verification of VAT's Regressivity

Let us take a closer look at the methodology and findings of the regressive model.

24. Irish Commission on Taxation, *Third Report of the Irish Commission on Taxation: Indirect Taxation* (Dublin, June 1984): 71, regarding footwear and children's clothing.
25. *Supra*, Appendix 9.
26. Through the application of the zero percent rate.

4.4.2.7.1. *Level of Expenditure Is Constant*

In its most basic model, the proregressive argument distinguishes between, on the one hand, a low-income category, whose representatives spend their entire income (Y) on consumption (C), that is $Y = C$ and, on the other hand, middle-income and high-income categories spending the same amount of money on consumptive expenditure and saving the remainder ($Y = C + S$; C being constant). If we take the families used in the example in Section 4.4.2.6.1 and assume that they all spend the same absolute amount on consumption, their tax burden, as a percentage of their income, is as outlined in Table 4.

Table 4. Regressivity for Different Income Groups at the Same Consumption Levels

Tax = 6% C = constant

Income Group	Disposable Income	Consumption	Saving	Taxes	Tax Burden
Low	22,000	22,000	0	1,320	6%
Middle	40,000	22,000	18,000	1,320	3.3%
High	110,000	22,000	88,000	1,320	1.2%

The tax burden as a percentage of disposable income is by far the highest for the low-income group, and regression is rather steep: as income increases, the tax burden diminishes from 6% to 1.2%.

However, the assumption of the regressive model that consumption is a constant can be falsified by simple observation. The fact is that people who earn higher incomes spend more money but not necessarily all of it. Consumption is not a constant but a variable determined by long-term income perspectives. This is relevant because with increased consumption comes increased taxation.

If we assume that the families in the middle- and high-income groups spend an increasing amount on consumption, the regression becomes rather moderate.

Table 5. Regressivity for Different Income Groups at Variable Consumption Levels

Tax = 6% C = variable

Income Group	Disposable Income	Consumption	Saving	Taxes	Tax Burden (%)
Low	22,000	22,000	0	1,320	6
Middle	40,000	35,000	5,000	2,100	5.25
High	110,000	80,000	30,000	4,800	4.36

On the basis of a more realistic assumption that consumptive expenditure varies with income, in the sense that expenditure will increase when income increases, albeit not at the same rate, a VAT remains regressive in nature, but a more nuanced picture appears showing that VAT has a moderate regression rate.

Under an income tax, the savings in these examples would have been taxed as earned income. Under a VAT, savings remain untaxed because they are not used for consumptive expenditure. The exclusion of saving in the model has a direct influence on the degree of VAT's regressivity. A VAT is regressive to the extent that the saving ratio increases with income.

Where *T* is the tax rate, this is demonstrated by the following equation:[27]

$$\frac{{}_{T}C}{Y} = {}_{T}\left(1 - \frac{S}{Y}\right)$$

Therefore, the aspect of saving needs further attention in order to assess the validity of the assumption that savings remain untaxed and are correctly excluded when determining the VAT's regressivity.

4.4.2.7.2. *Savings Remain Untaxed*

Under the regressive model, it is assumed that savings are not taxed in the present (which is true) and also remain untaxed in the future, which would imply that savings serve no purpose at all. They are deposited in a bank account and remain there merely generating interest. Clearly, that is generally not the case. People generally save money for two reasons. First, they make reservations for foreseeable costs of repair or replacement of durable goods in the near or semidistant future (automobiles, washing machines, lawnmowers, refrigerators and so on must to replaced every so many years; homes must regularly be maintained, repaired or renovated). Second, savings serve the purpose of a retirement fund aimed at covering the cost of living during the retirement period. In both cases, the savings are postponed expenditures and, consequently, will be subject to the tax in the future. With the exception of top-income earners, households generally consume all their savings over lifetime.[28] That conclusion has a direct impact on the regressivity of VAT as demonstrated in Table 6 in the following section.

---

27. Since income (Y) is consumed (C) or saved (S), $Y = C + S$ or $C = Y - S$. The total amount of consumption tax is ${}_{T}C$, which means that ${}_{T}C = T(Y - S)$. The amount of consumption tax relative to income is ${}_{T}C/Y$. Consequently, ${}_{T}C/Y = {}_{T}(Y/Y - S/Y) = {}_{T}(1 - S/Y)$. This formulation is derived from the Haig-Simons theorem that income equals consumption plus savings, see: Robert M. Haig, "The Concept of Income – Economic and Legal Aspects," in *Readings in* the *Economics of Taxation*, ed. Richard A. Musgrave & Carl S. Shoup (1959), 54 et seq.; and Henry C. Simons, *Personal Income Taxation: The Definition of Income as a Problem of Fiscal Policy* (reprint, University of Chicago Press, 1965) (1938).
28. Franco Modigliani, "The Role of Intergenerational Transfer and Life Cycle Saving in the Accumulation of Wealth," *Journal of Economic Perspectives* 2 (2) (1998): 15–23.

4.4.2.7.3. *Individual Income Levels Are Constant*

In the regressive model, a comparison is made between income categories, regardless of the fact that their constituents may change. The basic assumption is not necessarily that the composition of income categories is static and rigid, as if – by divine predestination – people are imprisoned for life in a certain income category, but that social mobility is simply ignored. By doing so, the model presents a distorted picture of reality because people generally do not remain in the same financial position all their lives and, for that reason, it seems more appropriate to assess the fairness of an individual's tax burden over his whole life span and not over an isolated period of time. Generally, people earn their highest income during middle age and a lower income in their youth and old age. In a cross-sectional annual analysis, low-income categories will include young and elderly people. The latter people's incomes may be low but they may not have had low incomes during their active periods and they may even be wealthy. On the other hand, people in high-income categories include persons who are at the peak of their income; their incidental high income may not be an appropriate criterion for determining their propensity to consume.

In Table 6, the development of a family's income is followed over its lifetime; it assumes that the household's income begins when the breadwinner is 20 and ends when he reaches the age of 80, that the retirement period begins at the age of 60 and that the flow of income is not interrupted due to unemployment. In the first 10 years, the family's annual disposable income is 22,000, which is entirely spent on consumptive expenditure; from age 30 to 39, annual disposable income is 40,000, of which 5,000 per year is saved; from age 40 to 49, annual disposable income is 70,000 and savings are 6,000; and from age 50 to 59, annual disposable income is 110,000 and savings are 30,000 per year. At retirement, the household receives an annual income 60,000, which they supplement by withdrawing 20,000 per year from their savings. The tax rate remains at 6% over the years.

Table 6. Life Cycle Income and Tax Burden Variation

Tax = 6%

Age	Income	Consumption	Saving		Taxes	Tax Burden
20–29	220,000	220,000	0	0	13,200	6%
30–39	400,000	350,000	50,000	0	21,000	5.25%
40–49	700,000	640,000	60,000	0	38,400	5.49%
50–59	1,100,000	800,000	300,000	0	48,000	4.36%
60–80	1,200,000	1,600,000	0	–400,000	96,000	8.00%
Total	**3,620,000**	**3,610,000**	**410,000**	**–400,000**	**216,600**	**5.98%**

Measured over 10-year periods, as income increases, the family's tax burden decreases, except for the third decennium in which savings are comparatively low.

However, during retirement, the tax burden, as a percentage of disposable income, shows a sharp increase due to the appropriation of savings for consumptive purposes. However, measured over lifetime, the tax is unmistakably proportional, if (almost) all savings are used for consumptive purposes. This should not come as a surprise since we concluded in Section 4.4.2.7.1 that on an annual basis a VAT's regressivity correlates with the saving ratio. Where all savings are eventually consumed, lifetime income (Y_t) will equal the value of lifetime consumption (C_t), as in the equation $Y_t = C_t$. At a single and fixed tax rate, the lifetime tax payments, TC_t, would equal TY_t, and the average tax rate would be the same as the statutory rate T, which means that the VAT in this model is proportional. Studies in the United States confirm that, measured over a lifetime, indirect taxes are only slightly regressive or even proportional.[29]

In Table 6, the very high-income groups have purposely been ignored. People in this category will have no or very little need to withdraw funds from their savings and will bequeath most of their funds to their heirs.

4.4.2.8. The Very Poor and the Very Rich

In the examples, people close to the subsistence level as well as the extremely rich have been ignored because the fairness of a tax should not be measured by its effects on groups whose income is peripheral.

The very poor are unlikely to be able to improve their positions, and their social mobility is negligible. As a group, they pose to society a challenging question of justice. However, it is indeed their lack of social mobility, not the tax system, that causes the problem. That problem could be addressed through the provision of direct income support, additional education and so on. As shown in Section 4.4.2.6.3, application of reduced rates, zero rates or exemptions in VAT are not effective remedies.

The regressivity of VAT for the very poor could be mitigated by allowing them a tax credit for income tax purposes. The credit would be applied against their tax liability, if any, and where the credit exceeds the liability, the excess could be refunded ("negative" income tax). The credit could take the form of a fixed amount or, more effectively in reducing regressivity, a credit that decreases as income increases. Alternatively, low-income families could be granted a stand-alone credit, which would avoid the need of filing income tax returns. Eligible

29. For example, James M. Poterba, "Lifetime Incidence and the Distributional Burden of Excise Taxes," *American Economic Review* 79 (2) (1989): 325–330; James M. Poterba, "Is the Gasoline Tax Regressive?," *Tax Policy and the Economy* 5 (1991): 145–164; Donald Fullerton & Diane L. Rogers, "Lifetime versus Annual Perspectives on Tax Incidence," *National Tax Journal* 44 (1991): 277–287; Donald Fullerton & Diane L. Rogers, *Who Bears the Income Tax Burden?* (Washington, DC: The Brookings Institute, 1993); and Erik Caspersen & Gilbert Metcalf, "Is a Value Added Tax Regressive? Annual versus Lifetime Incidence Measures," *National Tax Journal* 47 (4) (1994): 731–746.

households would only need to file a simple refund application form.[30] In its preferred form, this rebate would be equal to the tax rate times the poverty threshold for a given family size in a particular country.

The very rich should remain outside the assessment of the fairness of VAT for the same reason, that is, extremes distort the overall picture. Households in the top-income category do not need their savings to help finance their retirement period. A study by Menchik and David suggests that ignoring bequests only has the effect that the regressivity of a VAT is underestimated for the very top of the income pyramid.[31] As I concluded earlier, under those circumstances, VAT will be regressive to the extent of the saving ratio. This discussion does not aim to examine the fairness of taxation in general; the analysis is limited to an assessment of the fairness of consumption taxes, such as VAT, and other taxes only play a role in providing a framework (see Section 4.4.2.7.1) in which VAT's fairness is analyzed. As a category, the very rich constitute less than 1% of all income earners; therefore, their atypical situation and consumption pattern are of marginal importance for an overall assessment of the regressivity or fairness of VAT.

4.4.2.9. Conclusions

The regressive model, which analyzes the burden of VAT for different income groups on an annual basis, presents a simplification of reality. It disregards saving and social mobility. A life cycle approach is more appropriate to test the VAT's presumed regressivity, and that approach produces the result that VAT is proportional for low- and middle-income groups and mildly regressive where the top-income groups are included. In my opinion, the very poor and very rich should not be included in an assessment of the fairness of a consumption tax because of their extreme positions in the income pyramid. In my opinion, a society may afford the rich to be rich but not the poor to remain poor. Poverty is a problem not caused by taxation. It should be solved by means of social measures, which may include financial support granted through the tax system.

4.5. NEUTRALITY

One of the advantages attributed to the credit invoice method VAT is its neutrality in relation to decisions made by economic factors, such as capital and labor, and by consumers. In other words, these decisions should be made based on their economic merits and not for tax reasons. Tax neutrality is a widely accepted concept in principle. In some cases, however, neutrality cannot be realized and policy makers have to accept a certain level of distortion as inevitable. Also, policy makers may give preference to other specific goals over neutrality. In practice, it proves

30. James M. Bickley, *Value-Added Tax: A New U.S. Revenue Source?* (CRS Report, 22 August 2006), 11–12.
31. Paul Menchik & Martin David, "The Incidence of a Lifetime Consumption Tax," *National Tax Journal* 35 (1982): 189–203.

difficult to find an adequate balance between neutrality and other goals. Nevertheless, the concept itself may assist in guiding the tax policy debate towards the most economically efficient design.

For VAT and other general consumption taxes, a distinction is made between internal and external neutrality. Internal neutrality relates to the domestic impact of consumption taxes on economic decisions by traders, consumers, workers and capital providers. External neutrality relates to relations with other countries. In turn, internal neutrality is sometimes divided into legal and economic neutrality.[32] Basically, this division offers a view of the same phenomenon but from different angles.

Legal neutrality in the context of a tax on individual consumptive expenditure tax refers to equal treatment in the sense that each consumer should pay tax in accordance with his level of consumption. In other words, there should be a direct relation between the quantity of consumption and the tax incurred by an individual consumer. To accomplish this, the tax has to be measured as a percentage of the retail price. In addition, the tax rate should be the same for identical goods and services. Legal neutrality is an approach from the consumer's perspective.

GRTs cannot realize legal neutrality because the total tax burden will depend on the length of the production and distribution chain. Vertical and horizontal integration would reduce the length of the chain, and, as a result, the effective tax rate at the retail level would be lower for integrated businesses (see Sections 3.2.1 and 5.3.7). As a result, identical and similar products or services may be subject to different effective tax rates.

Economic neutrality is realized when the tax does not unduly influence the optimal allocation of means of production. To achieve this, the tax base should be as broad as possible. Broadening the base helps make the tax code more neutral between different activities by including more types of consumption in the definition of consumption and allowing fewer deductions and exemptions for specified activities. In addition, rate variation should be avoided because this would distort the relative prices of goods and services and may artificially steer consumers to lower-taxed and less desirable outputs. Neutrality also requires that the tax on a product or service will not vary according to the level of integration of a firm, which is realized under the credit invoice method VAT through the input tax credit system. Because the intention of general consumption taxes is to be borne by private consumers, but is collected by businesses who are supposed to forward the tax to the consumer as an add-on to their sales prices, it is imperative that such a shifting is accommodated in the design of the tax. If the tax burden would vary due to the extent of business integration, businesses that incur a higher tax on their products than their competition will not be able to (fully) shift the tax forward, and, to the extent that forward shifting fails, it would become a business tax in violation of the tax's inherent objective.

In some cases, policy makers deliberately depart from the principle of neutrality to achieve specific policy goals, such as combating the presumed

32. Ben Terra, *Sales Taxation: The Case of Value Added Tax in the European Community*, Series on International Taxation, no. 8 (Deventer-Boston: Kluwer, 1988), 15–19.

regressivity of general consumption taxes (see Section 4.4.2), encouraging the use of some products by imposing lower tax rates and discouraging the use of others, such as alcohol and tobacco products. In these cases, the tax should be set to capture the external costs of the activity, that is, the costs that users of these products impose on other people.[33] General consumption taxes are not the best tool to accomplish such policy goals. Instead of higher VAT or RST rates, it seems more practical to increase the consumer prices of these demerit goods through excises, and direct income supplements to low-income groups are more efficient in neutralizing regressivity than reduced rating or exemptions.

In addition to distorting choices, non-neutralities in the tax system also result in socially wasteful efforts by firms to change the form or substance of their activities to reduce their tax payments, for example by hiring lawyers and accountants to structure their transactions in a manner that minimizes tax liability.

In the context of consumption taxation based on the destination principle, external neutrality relates to the border tax adjustments required to create fair competition between domestically produced goods and imports. The tax levied on importation has to be equivalent to the tax imposed on similar domestic products, otherwise it would become a protective measure; and the relief provided to exports may not exceed the domestic tax, otherwise it would in fact be an export subsidy (see Sections 9.1.2 and 9.4).

4.6. ECONOMIC EFFICIENCY

Economic efficiency refers to the revenue performance of a tax, that is, the ability to raise revenue with the least distortion to incentives and, therefore, the least loss of real incomes.

Commonly, two measures of VAT collection efficiency are used. The first is the ratio of tax to gross domestic product (GDP), divided by the standard tax rate. A low rate is seen as evidence of erosion caused by exemptions and reduced rates and/or by imperfect enforcement. It has been noted that GDP may be subject to greater measurement error than consumption. Total consumption seems to offer a more appropriate benchmark for a VAT.[34] This C-efficiency ratio can be defined as the ratio of the VAT revenue to aggregate consumption, divided by the standard VAT rate. Essentially, the GDP efficiency ratio is targeted towards an income type VAT and the C-efficiency ratio towards a consumption type VAT.

The benchmark is a uniform tax on all consumption, which would give a C-efficiency ratio of 100. Higher or lower values indicate deviation from the single

33. In the form of, for example, the cost of health care and a police force. The costs that users impose on themselves, such as lost output on account of early death or lower productivity reflected in reduced wages, should be left out of consideration.
34. Liam Ebrill, Michael Keen, Jean-Paul Bodin & Victoria Summers, *The Modern VAT* (Washington, DC: IMF, 2001), 41.

rate tax on all consumption. Reduced or zero rates would drive the ratio below 100%. Tax cascading or incomplete functioning of the input-tax credit system would result in a ratio greater than 100%. Table 7 provides an overview of rates, total consumption, revenue raised through VAT and the consumption efficiency ratio for a total of twenty-nine countries as compiled by an OECD study of 2006.

Table 7. C-efficiency Ratio for VAT, 2003

Country	Standard Rate	Consumption*	VAT-Revenues*	C-efficiency Ratio
Australia	10.0	643,615	34,121	53.0
Austria	20.0	169,610	17,944	52.9
Belgium	21.0	210,017	18,938	42.9
Canada	7.0	906,450	42,181	66.5
Czech Republic	22.0	1,919,439	164,250	38.9
Denmark	25.0	1,046,742	135,092	51.6
Finland	22.0	107,091	12,455	52.9
France	19.6	1,267,458	112,440	45.3
Germany	16.0	1,703,090	137,568	50.5
Greece	18.0	128,880	11,951	51.5
Hungary	25.0	14,905,069	1,539,868	41.3
Iceland	24.5	671,892	80,940	49.2
Ireland	21.0	84,241	9,814	55.5
Italy	20.0	1,040,063	79,486	38.2
Japan	5.0	370,658,900	12,107,000	65.3
Korea	10.0	485,380,400	33,447,000	68.9
Luxembourg	15.0	14,409	1,474	68.2
Mexico	15.0	5,586,952	254,433	30.4
Netherlands	19.0	352,566	34,754	51.9
New Zealand	12.5	106,035	12,775	96.4
Norway	24.0	1,074,245	135,296	52.5
Poland	22.0	681,313	60,315	40.2
Portugal	19.0	108,607	11,072	53.7
Slovak Republic	20.0	917,663	81,876	44.6
Spain	16.0	583,760	46,767	50.1
Sweden	25.0	1,894,364	224,134	47.3
Switzerland	7.6	314,959	17,156	71.7
Turkey	18.0	288,590	29,367	56.5
United Kingdom	17.5	956,789	77,630	46.4

Table 7. (contd)

Country	Standard Rate	Consumption*	VAT-Revenues*	C-efficiency Ratio
Unweighed Average:				
OECD Total (ua)	17.8			52.9
OECD European Union (15) (ua)	20.21			50.6

* Data in national currency, at current prices, in millions. 2003 is the most recent year for which complete data are available.
Source: OECD, Consumption Tax Trends, 2006.

The revenue raised by a VAT depends on several broad factors, that is, the tax base, the rate structure, the size of the economy and the degree of compliance. The broader the tax base, the more activities are included and thus subject to the tax, and the higher the revenue. Exemptions will, on the one hand, reduce the amount of tax collected because the value added of the exempt business or activity will remain untaxed, but, on the other hand, the nondeductible input-tax may be shifted forward depending on price elasticities and lead to tax accumulation, increasing revenue. Reduced rates and zero rates (except when applied to exports) will naturally reduce the amount of revenue raised.

It is important to note in this context that all these elements interact with each other. Tax base and revenue goals have a direct influence on the rate structure, in this sense that the latter will be determined in light of the former. The complexity of the tax structure may not determine, but is evidently crucial for, the degree of voluntary compliance. Multiple rates and exemptions, for example, may lead to misclassifications of goods ands services. The rate structure may also affect the degree of tax evasion where high tax rates provide an incentive to shift activities and procurement to the shadow economy (see also Section 8.2.1.3).

Research into the key determinants of VAT yield is hardly available or substantial. Apart from the factors mentioned previously, other elements play an important role. Strong revenue performance is enhanced by a relatively high ratio of trade to GDP because of the ease of collecting VAT at importation; by high literacy rates, which increase the potential of administrative compliance of taxpayers as well as the administrative capacity of tax collectors; and by the passage of time, in the sense that over time the revenue raised increases, perhaps due to improved compliance and administrative experience.[35] In addition, political stability, penalties and audit probability determine collection efficiency as well.

35. *Supra*, 46.

Collection is also impacted by structural factors affecting the ease of tax evasion, such as the urbanization level, the share of agriculture and trade openness. One study evaluated the evidence on VAT collection efficiency in a panel of 44 countries during 1970–1999. The results showed that a one standard deviation increase in durability of political regime, and in the ease and fluidity of political participation, increased the VAT collection efficiency by 3.1% and 3.6%, respectively. A one standard deviation increase in urbanization, trade openness and the share of agriculture changed the VAT collection efficiency by 12.7%, 3.9% and 4.8%, respectively. In addition, a one standard deviation increase in GDP per capita increased the tax efficiency by 8.1%.[36]

Overall, the efficiency of VAT systems as demonstrated in Table 7 is not impressive. New Zealand is the only country close to the 100% benchmark with an efficiency ratio of 96.4%. Of the remaining twenty-eight countries, only five (Canada, Japan, Korea, Luxembourg and Switzerland) have ratios higher than 60%. Governments are generally aware of the degree of inefficiency of their VAT systems. The Irish government, for example, acknowledges the existence of valid arguments that maintaining zero rates is economically inefficient but recognizes in the same breath that it is difficult to gain public support for their removal because it would be impossible to compensate all those affected by such a measure.[37] As this notion indicates, once facilities are created within a tax system, it is politically difficult to remove them in order to create efficiency gains. In other words, policy makers have to be extremely prudent in allowing facilities to appease political opposition and special interest groups when designing tax law because the assumption that these facilities can be reversed in the future will, in all probability, prove illusionary.

---

36. Joshua Aizenman & Yothin Jinjarak, "The Collection Efficiency of the Value Added Tax: Theory and International Evidence," paper 605 presented at the Department of Economics, University of California, Santa Cruz (1 August 2005), <http://repositories.cdlib.org/ucscecon/605>.
37. Tax Strategy Group (2001), Vat Issues (01/08) [Online]. *Department of Finance*, <www.finance.gov.ie/publications/tsg01/0108.doc>.

Chapter 5
Gross Receipt Taxes

5.1. INTRODUCTION

GRTs can be traced back to the Middle Ages in Europe. Unfortunately, they are not distinguished only because of their age and heritage. In contemporary settings, they have been introduced in times of financial crises but have been gradually abandoned during subsequent decades. Interestingly, in recent years, GRTs have become popular again with state policy makers in the United States. The historical background of GRTs was discussed in Chapter 2. An overview of current GRTs in the United States is provided in Section 5.2. Both positive and negative economic characteristics are attributed to GRTs (Section 5.3). However, in evaluation, the positive effects of these taxes remain questionable, whereas the economic distortions that they generate seem to have a destructive impact on a state's overall economy.

GRTs are facing similar legal questions as sales and use taxes have encountered. This is especially true regarding the nexus standard developed by the US Supreme Court on the basis of the commerce clause of the US Constitution (see Section 5.4.1), and the need for functional apportionment rules to establish tax jurisdiction and decide revenue allocation across states in relation to cross-border sales of goods and in particular services (Section 5.4.2).

5.2. OVERVIEW OF CURRENT GRTs IN THE UNITED STATES

GRTs trace their roots to the fourteenth century, but they became popular in the early twentieth century when many European countries and many states in the United States introduced them to provide additional sources of income to compensate for declining revenues from income and property taxes. In Europe, GRTs were the most widely used form of sales taxation until their replacement with the VAT in about 1970 as a consequence of the establishment of the EEC.

In the United States, GRTs were introduced mostly during the Great Depression as temporary, emergency revenue measures, and many disappeared before the Second World War. Most of the remaining GRTs were repealed by the end of the twentieth century and replaced by what were perceived as less harmful revenue sources. By the end of 2002, Washington remained the only state with a surviving Depression-era GRT. Since then, the tax has become popular again among policy makers. Currently, eight states impose a tax that can, confidently, be classified as a GRT: Arizona, Delaware, Hawaii, Kentucky, New Mexico, Ohio, Texas and Washington. They are levied under different names, such as the Transaction Privilege Tax (TPT), the Commercial Activities tax (CAT), GRT, and Business and Occupations Tax. The rates vary from 0.5% to 1% in Texas, from 0.096% to 1.92% in Delaware and from 5.125% to 7.875% in New Mexico. See Table 8 for an overview of these US GRTs.

Table 8. Overview of US Gross Receipts-Type Taxes

State	Taxable Items	Deductions and Exemptions
Arizona	Transaction Privilege Tax. Imposed under 16 separate business classifications. Rates vary from 0% to 5.6%. All sales subject to TPT are also subject to applicable county excised taxes.	More than 100 exemptions, ranging from food and medical supplies, most services, rodeo animals, hotel soaps, to health club memberships and a variety of other exemptions.
Delaware	All nonexempt goods or services. Rates depend on type of business activity or industry.	Tobacco, fuel taxes and transactions between entities owned by the same five or fewer persons or by one family.
Hawaii	4% (4.5% on Oahu) on retail sale of goods, sale of services, contracting, commissions, rent, interest and other activities. Lower tax rates apply on resold services and subleases. 0.5% on wholesaling, selected intermediary services, manufacturing, production, real property subleasing, canning; and blind, deaf or totally disabled persons; 0.15% on insurance solicitors.	Contracting and other services exported out of the state.

Table 8. (contd)

State	Taxable Items	Deductions and Exemptions
Kentucky	Alternative minimum calculation for business taxes of 0.095% of gross receipt or 0.750% of gross profits. School district may levy a 3% GRT on utilities.	Dividend income, 50% of income from coal disposal and income from safe harbor leases. Exempt from alternative calculation are investment companies, sole proprietors, partnerships and some limited liability companies (LLCs).
New Mexico	General GRT. Widely considered to resemble a RST. Rate is 5%. Counties may add 2.1875%. Railroad car companies are taxed at 1.5%.	Prescription drugs, certain food and medical expenses, interest and dividends, salaries/wages, commissions, homeowner dues, and earnings from farms and Internet businesses.
Ohio	When fully phased-in, rate is 0.260% of gross receipts. Imposed on all activity, legal or illegal, that is conducted for or results in gain, profit or income. Utilities are taxed separately at 4.75%, except oil pipelines, which are taxed at 6.75%.	Nonprofit organizations, entities with less than USD 150K in receipts and utilities paying utility taxes. Allows deductibility of either compensation or cost of goods sold.
Texas	Hybrid GRT. Rate is 1%, calculated on the minimum of either (a) total revenue minus total cost of goods or (b) total revenue minus total compensation and benefits. Wholesalers and retailers are taxed at 0.5%.	Sole proprietors and general partnerships, and businesses with less than USD 300,000 in gross receipts.
Washington	The nation's oldest general GRT. Rates vary widely based on industry.	Entities with gross income less than USD 28,000. Features dozens of specific deductions and exemptions, including investments, dues, interest on agricultural loans, health care providers, beef processing, research and development, insurance premiums, real estate sales, nonprofit organizations, janitorial services, and fruit and vegetable processing.

This reemergence of GRTs is particularly surprising because they were repealed after serious criticism from economists and persistent lobbying by the business community. The question arises as to why GRTs are gaining in popularity with policy makers again. Basically, the answer can be found in the perceived complexity of corporate income taxes. The tax base for income tax is sales minus production costs. Although sales are relatively simple to measure, assigning business costs to arrive at taxable income is full of complexities, which makes corporate income tax difficult to administer. With an increasing number of companies operating in multiple states, problems have emerged in determining tax jurisdiction and income allocation.[1] For these reasons, lawmakers have developed a keen interest in taxes that are simpler in design and administration. Indeed, a GRT is conceptually straightforward. Companies simply have to apply the statutory rate to the total of in-state revenue and pay the tax, which explains the attractiveness of GRTs.[2] In light of the reemergence of GRTs, it seems worthwhile to examine their economic consequences, presumed advantages as well as distortions, in detail.

5.3. ECONOMIC EVALUATION

GRTs are mainly criticized for the following inherent disadvantages: tax cascading, providing artificial incentives for vertical integration, creating disparities in effective tax rates (unfairness), violating external neutrality between domestic production and imports and lacking transparency. Proponents hail the tax for the broad base it allows under a low rate and for being a stable source of revenue.

5.3.1. Broad Base

A GRT easily can be designed, and often is, to have a broad base. In most cases, the tax will apply to each business transaction, including intermediate transactions leading up to the final product. In other words, the tax is levied at every stage of the production and distribution chain and, as a result, the base will be broader than gross product of the state. This can be illustrated by the following examples. The value of printers sold by Hewlett Packard is part of the gross product of the state of California, but the GRT also covers the value of supplies made to Hewlett Packard, such as microchips, metal and plastic parts, and utility services. The value of automobiles sold by General Motors in Detroit will be measured as part of the

1. Arthur P. Hall, *The Compliance Costs and Regulatory Burden Imposed by the Federal Tax Laws* (Washington, DC: Tax Foundation, Special Brief, January 1995), and Chris Atkins, *A Twentieth Century Tax in the Twenty-First Century: Understanding State Corporate Tax Systems*, Background Paper, no. 49 (Washington, DC: Tax Foundation, September 2005).
2. Andrew Chamberlain & Patrick Fleenor, *Tax Pyramiding: The Economic Consequences of Gross Receipt Taxes*, Special Report, no.147 (Washington, DC: Tax Foundation, December 2006).

gross product of the state of Michigan, but the GRT applies as well to the supplies, such as tires, sheet metal, body parts, and electronics made to General Motors. Clearly, the GRT base must exceed the gross product of a state. Mikesell questions whether it is rational to have an annual tax on a flow whose base is larger than the sum of economic production in the state.[3] The tax base for the state of Washington, for example, is 177% of the total economic product of the state. Indiana's tax base is 137% of its gross product.

A tax is not a good choice for raising revenues simply because it has a broad base. "Coverage of an economically sensible base should be as broad as possible, without exemptions or special provisions that create inequities and distortions. Broad coverage of a reasonable base, not broad coverage alone, is the accepted standard."[4]

5.3.2. LOW RATE

Low rates are not an inherent attribute of GRTs. Other taxes could be levied at low rates as well. Rates are determined by how much a certain tax is required to contribute to a state's revenue portfolio. There exists consensus among economists that low rates are to be preferred over high rates because distortions and taxpayer inequities are magnified by and to the extent of higher rates. In any event, the purpose of a tax is to raise meaningful revenue, which is hardly the case with GRTs in the United States. For the fiscal year 2005, the GRT yields 6.1% of total revenue for Delaware[5] and 16.4% for Washington.[6] The 2007 forecast in Ohio is USD 600 million in GRT on total revenue of USD 19.4 billion, or roughly 3%.[7] The Netherlands turnover tax in its final years yielded about 20% of total tax revenue.[8]

When GRTs were still applied in Europe, there existed consensus that this type of tax can only be applied at relatively low rates because tax cascading has a multiplier effect on the tax burden borne by the end consumer which becomes more manifest at higher rates. This aspect will be further discussed in Section 5.3.4.

---

3. John L. Mikesell, *Gross Receipt Taxes in State Government Finances: A Review of Their History and Performance,* Background Paper, no. 53 (Washington, DC: Tax Foundation, January 2007), 7.
4. *Supra*, at 8.
5. Delaware Department of Finance, Fiscal Notebook, <www.state.de.us/finance/publications/fiscal_notebook_05/Section02/Section2.pdf>
6. Washington Department of Revenue, Summary of Washington State Tax Collections, Fiscal Years 2004 and 2005. <http://dor.wa.gov/Docs/Reports/2005/Tax_Statistics_2005/Table1.xls>
7. State of Ohio, Executive Budget, Fiscal Years 2006 and 2007. Columbus, OH: Office of Management and Budget, 2005.
8. A.E. de Moor, *De belasting over de toegevoegde waarde en haar betekenis voor de ondernemer* (Value Added Tax and Its Meaning for Traders). (Alphen aan den Rijn/Brussel: Samson, 1967), 9.

5.3.3. Stable Source of Revenue

Stability of a tax means that the revenue it generates is less subject to fluctuations than other state tax bases. John Mikesell, in a recent study,[9] compared the Washington State Business and Occupation (B&O) Tax, the same state's RST, and the Oregon individual and corporate income taxes for the period 1995–2005. He found that the average change in the GRT base was 5.28% over the period of analysis, which was slightly below the average change for the RST base at 5.89% and somewhat above that for the individual and corporate income taxes at 5.09% and 4.96%, respectively. In other words, there was not much difference between the bases of the four in terms of annual rates of change. The study also established whether the annual percentage change varied considerably or was more or less the same. The standard deviations found were 0.0461 for the B&O tax, 0.0387 for the sales tax, 0.0537 for the personal income tax and 0.2655 for the corporate income tax. The GRT proved to be slightly less stable than the retail tax and slightly more stable than the personal income tax but much more stable than the corporate income tax. In conclusion, a GRT offers, indeed, revenue stability but at about the same degree as a RST.

5.3.4. Tax Cascading

A GRT is a broad-based, low-rate tax imposed on all income received by a business without any deductions for the costs of doing business, such as a deduction for wages. GRTs are not based on a company's profit or loss for a given tax year; rather, they are owed on all income, regardless of whether the business is profitable and regardless of its source. The tax is levied each and every time a commercial exchange takes place. As a result, tax paid becomes part of the cost price of goods and services supplied to a business, and when it is absorbed in the selling price, tax paid at a previous stage is again subject to tax at a later stage. The same amount of tax may be taxed multiple times in the processes of production and distribution, creating a "tax-on-tax" effect, the magnitude of which is determined by the length of the chain of transactions. To demonstrate the effect of tax cascading, we compare a taxation flow in a styled distribution chain under a VAT (Table 9) with the taxation flow that would occur under a GRT (Table 10). For simplicity reasons, we assume that the value added at each stage of the chain is exactly 1,000. The tax rate applied in both examples is 10%.

9. Mikesell, *Gross Receipt Taxes in State Government Finances*, 8–9.

Table 9. Tax Effect of Distribution Chain under a VAT

	Price	Tax on Sales	Credit	To Revenue
Producer 1	1,000	100	—	100
Producer 2	2,000	200	100	100
Producer 3	3,000	300	200	100
Wholesaler	4,000	400	300	100
Retailer	5,000	500	400	100
Total				500

A taxable business must collect VAT on every sale (output – VAT) and receives a credit for VAT paid on its purchases (input – VAT). The difference is remitted to the government and resembles the tax on the value added of each stage. No accumulation occurs, because the total tax remitted to the revenue equals the statutory rate applied to the final consumer price (10% × 5,000 = 500).

Table 10. Tax Effect of Distribution Chain under a GRT

	Input	Sales Price	Tax	Total
Producer 1	—	1,000	100	1,100
Producer 2	1,100	2,100	210	2,310
Producer 3	2,310	3,310	331	3,641
Wholesaler	3,641	4,641	464	5,105
Retailer	5,105	6,105	610	6,715
Total			1,715	

Since under a GRT no credit is given for tax paid on purchases, the tax becomes part of the cost price of the next stage of the distribution chain. Assuming that it is economically possible to shift the tax forward to the next stage, producer 2 would not sell for 2,000 as under a VAT (see Table 9) but for 2,100. At a statutory rate of 10%, the tax due would be 210 instead of 200 under a VAT, the 10 representing the tax rate applied to the tax incurred in the previous stage. The total tax burden in this example is 1,715 instead of 500 under a VAT. In other words, the effective tax rate (measured on the original retail price exclusive of tax) has increased from 10% under a VAT to 34.3% under a GRT in our example.

The effect of tax cascading on the final tax burden of the end consumer depends ultimately on the length of the distribution chain and the statutory rate applied.

If in Table 10 the number of stages were reduced from 5 to 3, the total tax paid would be 641 on a consumer price (excluding tax) at that stage of 3,000. The effective tax rate would be 21.36%. However, if we added two stages with 1,000 value added each, the effective tax rate would also be higher.

Table 11. Extended Distribution Chain

	Input	Sales Price	Tax	Total
Producer 1	—	1,000	100	1,100
Producer 2	1,100	2,100	210	2,310
Producer 3	2,310	3.310	331	3,641
Producer 4	3,641	4,641	464	5,105
Producer 5	5,105	6,105	610	6,715
Wholesaler	6,715	7,715	771	8,486
Retailer	8,486	9,486	949	10,435
Total			3,435	

The total tax burden is 3,435 relative to an exclusive tax base of 7,000. The effective tax rate is 49.07%.

Cascading is subject to a multiplier effect. In other words, as a percentage of the statutory rate, the effective tax rate grows faster at higher statutory rates than when lower statutory rates are applied. This is the reason that in Europe it was believed that GRTs could only be introduced at relative low rates.[10] This is demonstrated by comparing Table 10, where the statutory rate is 10%, with a GRT of 2% in Table 12, and an increased rate GRT of 25% in Table 13.

Table 12. Low-Rate GRT (2%)

	Input	Sales Price	Tax	Total
Producer 1	—	1,000	20	1,020
Producer 2	1,020	2,020	40	2,060
Producer 3	2,060	3,060	61	3,121
Wholesaler	3,121	4,121	82	4,203
Retailer	4,203	5,203	104	5,307
Total			307	

The total tax paid is now 307 relative to an exclusive tax base of 5,000. The effective tax rate is 6.14%.

10. However, the definition of a low rate is subjective to a certain extent of course. The rates for the Netherlands turnover tax of 1954 varied from 0.9% for wholesalers; 4.8% for services with the exception of transportation services, which were taxed at 3.6%; and a standard rate of 6%. In addition, manufacturers were either taxed at the standard rate or at elevated rates of 18% and 25%. See, J.C. Hanhart, *De BTW in schema's en tabellen* (VAT in Figures and Tables) (Alphen aan den Rijn/Brussel: Samson, 1968), 97 et seq.

Table 13. High-Rate GRT (25%)

	Input	Sales Price	Tax	Total
Producer 1	—	1,000	250	1,250
Producer 2	1,250	2,250	562	2,812
Producer 3	2,812	3,812	953	4,765
Wholesaler	4,765	5,765	1,441	7,206
Retailer	7,206	8,206	2,051	10,257
Total			5,257	

The total tax paid is 5,257 relative to a tax exclusive consumer price of 5,000. The effective tax rate is 105.14%.

If we compare the mere growth of the effective tax rate under the three scenarios, we have the following results. Where the statutory rate is 2%, the effective rate becomes 6.14%, or 3.07 times the statutory rate. At a statutory rate of 10%, the effective tax rate is 34.3%, or 3.43 times the statutory rate. At a statutory rate of 25%, the effective tax rate turns out to be 105.14%, or 4.20 times the statutory rate. This demonstrates the acceleration of the effective tax rate at higher statutory rates.

Although it is not impossible to apply a GRT at a single low rate, in practice, most states have applied or apply multiple rates. A single rate would naturally be set at the maximum level that the enterprise with the least tax paying capability can bear. Vertical rate differentiation would enable revenue maximization at each stage of the distribution chain. By applying the optimum rate for each stage and by varying rates depending on type of product or service, overtaxing and undertaxing would become manageable for the purpose of maximum revenue generation. In Europe, it was recognized that applying a relatively high standard rate for every segment of the distribution chain was impossible due to low profit margins of some stages. In the Netherlands, a reduced rate of 0.9% was applied to the wholesale stage because the standard rate of 6% was found to be too high where profit margins varied between 10% and 20%.[11] Although rate variation may be able to ease the economic disadvantages of tax cascading, it has proven to be impossible to accomplish full neutrality under GRTs. For example, Washington State's B&O Tax was enacted in 1935 with a uniform rate of 0.25% for all industries. Over time, with tax rates rising to meet revenue demands, concerns about the inequity and inefficiency of the tax prompted lawmakers to enact separate rates for various industries, along with a range of targeted tax incentives. By 2005, lawmakers had enacted six separate tax rates ranging from 0.138% to 1.6% based on industry, as well as eight distinct tax incentive programs for the B&O tax alone.[12] All attempts to reduce tax cascading have basically failed. Studies routinely find

11. Hanhart, *supra*, at 97.
12. Washington State Department of Revenue, Descriptive Statistics for Tax Incentive Programs: 2006 Report Covering Activity during Calendar Year 2005, September 2006.

substantial tax cascading under GRTs, despite the best efforts of lawmakers.[13] Instead, the main effect of lawmakers' attempts to mitigate tax cascading through differential rates and tax credits has been to sharply increase tax complexity and, henceforth, to effectively abandon the purported simplicity of GRTs.

In 2002, a tax reform commission appointed by Washington State's legislature concluded that the B&O tax results in substantial cascading and is highly non-neutral across products and industries, violating basic principles of good tax design. The commission found that the B&O tax causes cascading of up to 6.7 times on some manufacturing industries, whereas some services are taxed only 1.4 times. On average the tax accumulates 2.5 times, but this rate varied considerably across industries, leading to potentially large economic distortions in the state's economy.[14]

5.3.5. Vertical Integration

The total taxes accumulated at previous stages of the production and distribution chain constitute a production cost for a firm, the amount of which will depend on how many exchanges have previously occurred. This creates an artificial incentive for vertical integration, that is, an integration driven by fiscal motives instead of by business efficiency motives. This is an undesirable result where it is accepted wisdom that any tax should raise revenue with the least interference of the functioning of the market. As demonstrated in Table 14, by merging with its suppliers or by insourcing, a firm can reduce the number of exchanges in the chain, thereby reducing its tax burden.

Table 14. Effect of Vertical Integration

	Input	Sales Price	Tax	Total
Producer 1	—	1,000	100	1,100
Producer 2	1,100	2,100	210	2,310
Producer 3	2,310	3.310	331	3,641
Producer 4	**3,641**	**6,641**	**664**	**7,305**
Producer 5				
Wholesaler				
Retailer	7,305	8,305	830	9,135
Total			2,135	

Producers 4 and 5 integrate with the wholesaler, effectively eliminating two stages of taxation. Their total value added remains 3,000, but no tax is levied on their internal supplies. Compared to Table 11, the wholesaler's price (including tax) has been reduced from 8,486 to 7,305. The retail price (including tax) has been

13. For example, studies of Washington State's gross receipts find substantial tax pyramiding, despite the state's differential tax rates and incentives. See Washington State Tax Structure Study Committee, *Tax Alternatives for Washington State: A Report to the Legislature,* vols 1 & 2 (November 2002).
14. Washington State Tax Structure Study Committee, *Tax Alternatives.*

reduced from 10,435 to 9,135. Total tax is now 2,135 instead of 3,435 and the effective tax rate has come down from 49.07% to 30.5%.

To combat the tendency to vertical integration or insourcing, that is, to self-produce goods and services instead of procuring them from third parties, under GRTs such self-production is taxed. Similar problems arise and similar solutions are being applied under VAT (see Section 8.2.4.3.3.1 and RST (see Section 6.2.12). For GRTs, we take a somewhat closer look at the specific rules of self-supply as applied in the Netherlands from 1941 until 1969 when VAT was introduced.[15] The Netherlands Turnover Tax Act contained three specific and complementing rules to equalize the positions of a business procuring parts, semi-products or ingredients from a wholesaler or manufacturer and one that produces these parts or products itself.[16] The first rule is designed to prevent economic distortions in the construction sector.[17] It creates a tax on self-produced goods that are used in the construction of real property. Without this specific provision, self-produced goods would escape a cycle of taxation. Examples of self-supplied goods covered by this provision include custom made windows and window frames,[18] custom made roof frames,[19] self-manufactured parts of heating boilers to be installed in an immoveable property,[20] modified drainage pipes for a sprinkler installation in a warehouse,[21] and sand distracted from public waterways and used to support and construct levies and dikes.[22]

However, an exception was created for goods not generally available for sale at the wholesale of manufacturer stage.[23] This kind of good remained, therefore, out of scope of the tax, which appears to satisfy the *ratio legis* of the provision since no competitive distortions would occur.

A parallel provision created a taxable supply for the use of self-manufactured goods in the course of one's own business.[24] For example, if a business buys tools or a machine from a manufacturer, the business would incur a 5% turnover tax. Without this provision the business would be able to avoid the tax by self-producing these items. Internal instructions provided for the Revenue Service to abstain

---

15. The Netherlands applied a single stage manufacturer's tax from 1934 until 1941 when an all stage GRT was introduced, modeled after the German GRT, by the Besluit op de Omzetbelasting 1940 (Turnover Tax Decree 1940). This tax was replaced by a multiple stage GRT with the Turnover Tax Act 1954, which excluded the retail stage from the tax. For practical reasons, the legal provisions of only the 1954 act are being used here, but reference is made to case law from 1941 on.
16. My information is based on the following sources: C.P. Tuk, *Inleiding tot de Omzetbelasing* (Introduction to the Turnover Tax) (Gorinchem: J. Noorduijn en Zoon, 1956), 77–81; J. Reugebrink, *Omzetbelasting* (Turnover Tax) (Amsterdam: Fiscale Studieserie no. 6, FED, 1962), 52–57; L.F. Ploeger (ed.), *Fiscale Encyclopedie "De Vakstudie", Deel XIX, Wet op de Omzetbelasting 1954*, (loose-leaf) (Deventer: Kluwer, suppl. 62, April 1968), 282–292.
17. Article 3(1) (g) of the Wet op de Omzetbelasting 1954 (Turnover Tax Act 1954).
18. Tariefcommissie, 20 January 1964, no. 9363 O, BNB 1964/131.
19. Tariefcommissie, 2 July 1963, no. 9052 O, BNB 1963/289.
20. Tariefcommissie, 12 April 1954, no. 7031 O, BNB 1954/257.
21. Tariefcommissie, 19 September 1961, no. 9233 O, BNB 1962/5.
22. Tariefcommissie, 11 December 1962, no. 9210 O, BNB 1963/76.
23. Section 11 of the Leidraad Omzetbelasting (Turnover Tax Instructions for Revenue Service).
24. Article 3(1) (h) of the Wet op de Omzetbelasting 1954 (Turnover Tax Act 1954).

from taxation in a limited number of situations in which distortion of competition was unlikely or negligible.[25] Examples of self-manufactured goods covered by this provision include packaging, such as tin containers made by the producer of preservatives,[26] wooden boxes,[27] boxes for cigarette paper[28] and polyethylene bags for peanuts;[29] printed materials, such as auction catalogs made by auctioneers for their customers;[30] electricity used to power the turbines of an electric power plant;[31] jackets and aprons made by a linen rental company;[32] and detergent created by a kettle cleaning company by mixing a number of components according to its own formula.[33]

The mere display of goods in a shop's window or showcases, or the demonstration of goods to potential customers, does not constitute a use for the purpose of this provision. The main exclusion from this provision is the use of self-produced ingredients and raw materials. This has led, unsurprisingly, to disputes over the exact definition, but in general terms an ingredient or raw material is a material that becomes integrated with the end product during the production process. Ingredients and raw materials, therefore, lose their individual identity. By not taxing ingredients and raw materials, inequality arises between producers who buy these ingredients and raw materials, and those who manufacture these themselves. With the introduction of the VAT Act of 1954 this inequality was partly removed by taxing the use of specifically identified, self-manufactured ingredients and raw materials.[34] The objective was to address only situations of severe distortion of competition.

The use of self-manufactured goods is always taxed unless they are excluded from taxation. The reverse is true for the use of self-manufactured ingredients and raw materials, which are not taxed, but by exception.

5.3.6. Disparities in Effective Tax Rates

It is generally accepted that a tax should raise the revenue needed in ways that do not disturb, or interfere only to a minimal degree with, the competitive market and business decisions regarding resource allocation. Because, under GRTs, the effective tax rate will depend on the length of the manufacturing and distribution

25. Sections 12(2) and (3) of the Leidraad Omzetbelasting (Turnover Tax Instructions for Revenue Service).
26. Tariefcommissie, 18 December 1950, no. 5381 O, V-N 1951, no. 7 (20).
27. Tariefcommissie, 27 April 1953, no. 7135 O, V-N 1953, no. 20 (23).
28. Tariefcommissie, 22 February 1955, no. 7815 O, BNB 1955/202.
29. Tariefcommissie, 17 February 1964, no. 9665 O, BNB 1964/182.
30. Tariefcommissie, 12 May 1953, no. 7063 O, V-N 1953, no. 17 (14).
31. Tariefcommissie, 26 November 1945, no. 3103 O, B. no. 8099.
32. Tariefcommissie, 7 December 1954, no. 7748 O, BNB 1955/120.
33. Tariefcommissie, 15 May 1962, no. 9117 O, BNB 1962/281.
34. Article 3(1) (i) jo. Tabel I of the Wet op de Omzetbelasting 1954 (Turnover Tax Act 1954).

chain of a product or service, the rates will generally differ considerably, even for similar products. This is cause for distortion of the economic neutrality of the tax, the impact of which may be enlarged by the decision of firms to vertically integrate their activities.

Vertical integration effectively leads to discrimination against nonintegrated production and distribution systems. Especially smaller firms, unable to realize any or a sufficient level of integration, would become victims. Nonintegrated, smaller firms will encounter a price disadvantage compared to integrated firms, completely caused by a higher level of taxation, and they will be unable to shift their tax burden forward. The higher the applicable tax rate, the larger the negative effect of vertical integration will be. However, larger, integrated firms also suffer a disadvantage in that they lose the advantages of economies of scale and specialization. Because of the cascading effect of GRTs, insourcing is encouraged and outsourcing discouraged, except for outsourcing to companies in another state.

5.3.7. External Neutrality

Tax accumulation also distorts the competitiveness of domestic producers relative to out-of-state producers. Imports have a relative price advantage over similar domestically manufactured products. Even if a state imposes the GRT on imports as well (see the nexus discussion in Section 5.4.1) in an effort to counterbalance the non-neutrality, the imported product would still be relieved from the tax accrued at previous stages of the chain. For the same reason, exports find themselves at a disadvantage, even if the actual export sale is exempt. In foreign markets, products and services generated in states that apply a GRT are at an apparent competitive disadvantage relative to products produced in states that do not impose these types of taxes. GRTs are, essentially, not tailored to efficiently tax cross-border trade within a common or federal market. Efficient in this context means without causing economic distortions while realizing a fair allocation of total revenue to each state. For this reason, when creating the European Common Market, the existing GRTs were abolished and replaced by a destination based VAT.

Taxation is also the reason that outsourcing to companies in another state is encouraged. The sale by the outsourcee to the domestic firm may be taxed in the destination state, but tax would be avoided on the inputs of the outsourcee firm.

5.3.8. Lack of Transparency

From the previous discussions, it is clear that the effective tax rate differs from business to business and product to product. Similar products or services can easily be found taxed at different levels depending on the integration efficiency of the particular production and distribution system. In a modern democracy, it is a maxim that citizens are fully aware of the costs of government. Transparency in taxation is necessary for the proper functioning of a participating democracy, allowing citizens to make reasonable assessments regarding government services and to ensure accountability of the public sector.[35] The GRT fails the standard of transparency in two respects. First, it is impossible to identify who or what – consumers, capital factor or labor factor – actually carries the burden of the tax and to what degree. Second, it is impossible to establish to what extent the tax has increased the price as a result of tax cascading, except that the total burden as a percentage of the retail price will be higher than the statutory rate.

Clearly, transparency is not served by a tax that is complex in its design and execution. GRTs can be simple but, in practice, they seem almost always to be extremely complex. This is caused by several factors, such as multiple tax rates that depend on the type of business or type of product and which may lead to difficult classification problems; exemptions introduced for social policy purposes; measures introduced to neutralize integration, that is, self-supply charges on products manufactured by a business to be used in the course and furtherance of its enterprise; and other measures to improve the economic neutrality of a GRT, such as fictitious manufacturer or fictitious trader status found in the Netherlands turnover tax of 1954.[36]

5.3.9. Economic Assessment

In the discussions of the preceding paragraphs, several economic disadvantages of a GRT have become manifest. The tax distorts economic decisions by both businesses and consumers because, as a result of tax cascading, competing products and services may be available at quite different price levels. The tax leads to discrimination of integrated firms over nonintegrated firms, and benefits large firms over smaller ones. Insourcing is strongly encouraged, even where this makes less business sense. Imports are favored over domestic products, and exports are put at a competitive disadvantage in foreign markets, such at the detriment of domestic production and employment. Moreover, the tax discriminates against capital-intensive industries as opposed to labor-intensive industries. Insourcing as a strategy to avoid taxation of capital goods seems much less feasible. As a result, substitution of labor for capital in the production process is encouraged. Because the tax has no relation to profits, high volume – low margin businesses are at a clear disadvantage compared to low volume – high margin businesses. Start-up companies may find this tax an obstacle to growth and profitability. Mikesell

35. Richard M. Bird, "A New Look at Local Business Taxes," *Tax Notes International* 30 (2000): 695.
36. See, for example, de Moor, *De belasting over de toegevoegde waarde en haar betekenis voor de ondernemer*, 9–14.

concludes from data for the state of Washington that the GRT has likely contributed to the above national average of business closures in that state.[37]

5.4. US LEGAL ISSUES

GRTs pose similar constitutional questions as do sales and use taxes. The scope of the tax leads to nexus issues, and apportionment issues arise regarding interstate service supplies.

5.4.1. NEXUS ISSUES

In 1967, the US Supreme Court established physical presence as the standard for imposing a state tax[38] and has upheld this standard in subsequent cases,[39] which all dealt with sales and use taxes. In the absence of substantial physical presence, a state cannot require a seller to collect use tax because this would cause an undue burden on interstate trade, which is prohibited by the commerce clause of the US Constitution.[40] The Supreme Court's lack of explicit clarity regarding application of that standard to taxes other than sales taxes has given several states reason to assert that the physical presence requirement and, therefore, the restraints of the commerce clause only apply to sales and use taxes. South Carolina introduced economic nexus as a requirement to impose its corporate income tax, which was accepted by the state supreme court in the 1993 *Geoffrey* case.[41] Until this case, taxpayers generally assumed that physical presence was required for a state to impose corporate income tax. In *Geoffrey*, however, the South Carolina Tax Commission asserted, and South Carolina's Supreme Court affirmed, income tax nexus through a company's use of, and income from, intangible licenses in the state. South Carolina's Supreme Court explicitly states that in its opinion the physical presence requirement as reformulated by the US Supreme Court in *Quill* only applies to sales and use taxes but that such physical presence in a state is not required for income to be taxable.[42] This decision may have far-reaching

37. Mikesell, *Gross Receipt Taxes in State Government Finances*, 11. Total business death rates are 8.9% and small business death rates 14.1% over the national average.
38. *National Bellas Hess v. Dept. of Revenue for the State of Illinois*, 386 US 753 (1967).
39. Most notably in *Quill Corporation v. North Dakota*, 504 US 298 (1992).
40. Article 1(8), clause 3 of the US Constitution; see, for more detail, Robert F. van Brederode, "The American Debate on Taxing Distance Sales and E-commerce," *International VAT Monitor* 18 (5) (2007): 352–361.
41. *Geoffrey, Inc. v. South Carolina Tax Commission*, 313 SC 15: 437 S.E. 2d 13 (6 July 1993).
42. In rejecting the commerce clause argument, the Court stated that a tax would survive challenge under the commerce clause if the tax (a) was applied to an activity with a substantial connection to the taxing state, (b) was fairly apportioned, (c) did not discriminate against interstate commerce and (d) was fairly related to the services provided by the state.

    The Court found that the presence of intangible property alone was sufficient to establish a substantial connection. In addition, a state may tax the part of a nonresident's income that was

consequences. Geoffrey, Inc., received royalties from Toys-R-Us on the basis of a franchise agreement[43] and, in principle, every state could apply the criteria developed in this case to tax franchisors for royalties received from franchisees operating in the state, which could have a significant impact on the franchise chains operating on a national scale. Franchisors may find themselves taxable for income tax in virtually every state.

Many states[44] have adopted rules mirroring the *Geoffrey* case, and similar jurisprudence has surfaced. In *Lanco*,[45] New Jersey's Supreme Court upheld the state's corporate business tax on income from licensing intangibles by a company with no physical presence in the state. In support of its position, the court dismissed earlier US Supreme Court cases as applicable only to sales and use taxes. In *MBNA*,[46] the West Virginia Supreme Court of Appeals held that the state could impose income and franchise tax on a bank that distributed credit cards to West Virginia residents, although it had no physical presence or personnel in the state. As in *Lanco*, the court ruled as well that earlier US Supreme Court cases are limited to sales and use taxes. The court also went further and indicated that physical presence standards can no longer be accepted as the correct measure of nexus due to the growth of electronic commerce. In the court's opinion, significant economic presence is a better indicator of substantial nexus than a physical presence test.

Until now, the US Supreme Court has refrained from involvement in this matter. On appeal by Geoffrey, Inc., the Supreme Court denied certiorari,[47] that is, refused to hear the case, which gave many states and commentators reason to believe that the *Quill* criteria, indeed, apply to sales and use tax only. The state of Ohio, for example, imposed its CAT in 2005 under the explicit assumption that the commerce clause restraints would not apply because the CAT is not a sales or use tax but a GRT. The nexus standard applied in GRTs is generally much broader than

---

reasonably attributable to property located in the state or to events or transactions which, occurring there, are within the benefits that the state confers. *Geoffrey* had raised no argument that the challenged tax was not fairly apportioned or discriminated against interstate commerce.

43. In 1984, Geoffrey, Inc., a wholly owned subsidiary of Toys-R-Us, became the owner of several valuable trademarks and trade names (including "Toys-R-Us"). Geoffrey executed a license agreement with Toys-R-Us that allows Toys-R-Us to use the "Toys-R-Us" trade names as well as other trademarks and trade names in most states. As consideration for the licenses granted, Geoffrey receives a royalty of 1% of the net sales by Toys-R-Us and its subsidiaries. Although Toys-R-Us deducted the royalty payments from its state income tax as a cost, Geoffrey did not report the royalties as income in any state because of lack of physical presence, creating a double nontaxation benefit on the royalties. The so-called Trademark Holding Company strategy is widely applied, generally with the holding company residing in Delaware, which does not tax the income of a corporation whose only activity in the state is the ownership, maintenance, and management of intangible assets.
44. Florida, Illinois, Massachusetts, New Jersey, New Mexico and Washington.
45. *Lanco, Inc. v. Director, Division of Taxation,* 908 A 2d 176 (N.J. 2006).
46. *MBNA America Bank v. Tax Commissioner, State of West Virginia,* 640 S.E. 2d 226 (W.VA 2006).
47. Cert. den, 510 US 992, 114 S.Ct. 550 (29 November 1993).

the one contained in *Quill*. The Ohio standards extend jurisdiction for GRT purposes to anyone who has:

- property in the state valued at USD 50,000 or more at any time during the calendar year;
- payroll of USD 50,000 or more during the calendar year;
- gross receipts of USD 500,000 or more during the calendar year;
- at least 25% of total property, payroll or sales in Ohio at any time during the calendar year; and
- legal or commercial domicile in Ohio.

With these broad standards, foreign residents with no physical presence in Ohio at all could easily end up with a tax liability without even realizing it. An incidental sale of, for example, a small yacht between an out-of-state private seller and an Ohio resident private buyer, if the sales price exceeds half a million dollars, would make the seller subject to the CAT, and the buyer would be subjected to the use tax over the purchase price. Under such broad standards, every business and private citizen could become an Ohio tax evader, and it is important to obtain clarity as to whether these standards violate the commerce clause, and especially the practical effect test, as formulated in *Quill*.

If the US Supreme Court agrees to hear one of the pending cases, it will have the opportunity to consider whether the physical presence standard applies to state income and franchise taxes as well as to GRTs. It is urgent for the US Supreme Court to do so because the jurisprudence of the states' highest courts is in many instances conflicting. The Tennessee Supreme Court found that the state cannot impose franchise taxes on a bank with no physical presence, but solely on borrowers, in the state.[48] Interestingly, although the ruling in this case contradicts *Geoffrey*, the US Supreme Court refused to hear the case, leaving the uncertainty in place.

West Virginia's Supreme Court's reasoning in *MBNA*, that the physical presence standards are unfit for today's electronic reality, could be reversed. The purpose of the commerce clause is to avoid tensions between individual states, thereby promoting the national economy by providing protection of interstate business against taxation by states from which they receive no benefits. The level of economic integration among states is markedly greater than that in the past,[49] which enhances the possibility for states to reach beyond their borders for funding, a practice the commerce clause explicitly was designed to prevent. It is remarkable in this respect that exporting the tax base is one of the guiding principles of Ohio tax reform.[50] From another perspective, the enhanced economic interrelationships among the states also suggest a far greater elasticity of response

---

48. *J.C. Penney National Bank v. Johnson*, 19 S.W.3d 831 (Tenn. Ct. App. 1999), cert.denied, 531 U.S. 927 (2000).
49. Daniel Shaviro, An Economic and Political Look at Federalism in Taxation, 90 *Michigan Law Review* 90 (1992): 895, 902.
50. Ohio is not alone. Exporting the tax burden, that is, shifting taxation to nonresidents, is a popular practice in times of budgetary restraints of both states and local jurisdictions. See Herbert

to locational tax disparities.[51] Where new technologies enable even the smallest enterprises to do business across state borders, their exposure to tax compliance and liability risks in states where they have no physical presence but only customers may reduce their willingness to expansion, which in turn will hurt the nation's economic growth potential. If vague economic presence standards would replace physical presence standards on a national scale, businesses would be required to register in and collect taxes for potentially every state, which would increase compliance costs significantly, especially for small businesses. In all probability, this would have a negative impact on the free movement of goods, services and capital within the United States of America.[52] Legal uncertainty and rising compliance costs will be important factors when an enterprise has to decide whether to do business in a certain state. If and when the US Supreme Court decides to intervene in any of the pending cases, it will not only determine whether and, if so, to what extent, an economic presence standard is acceptable but it will also set boundaries for the scope and reach of taxes such as GRTs.

5.4.2. Apportionment Issues

As to the sale of tangible property, it is an established principle in the United States that such sales can only be taxed by the destination state. The application of GRTs on interstate services is more complicated. In the past, states relied on some basic rules to determine tax jurisdiction and allocate revenue.[53] In essence, these rules centered on the location where the income-producing activity was performed. The vast majority of service providers operated exclusively within the boundaries of their home states. Special rules were developed for industries that did reach beyond their local jurisdictions, such as trucking companies, financial institutions, and radio and television broadcasting, tax allocation for which was determined on the basis of mileage, loan asset location and audience share. Particularly with the emergence of the Internet, tax jurisdiction has become a precarious problem in light of the budgetary needs of the states in combination with the increasing volume of Internet sales and the risks of double taxation and nontaxation. This is

---

Kaylor, "The Experience of Several Cities in Implementing a Commuter Tax," *State Tax Today* (2004): 133. It can be realized by using several mechanisms, such as increasing car rental taxes and hotel taxes, introducing GRTs and introducing economic nexus standards.

51. R. Todd Ervin, "State Taxation of Financial Institutions: Will Physical Presence or Economic Presence Win the Day?," *Virginia Tax Review* 19 (2000): 521.
52. During a moratorium on state taxation of national banks that ended in 1976, Congress authorized several studies on the impact that state taxation of out-of-state financial institution would have on the economy, banking and money; see, for example, *Report of the Board of Governors of the Federal Reserve Board on State and Local Taxation of Banks* (1972), and Senate Committee on Banking, Housing and Urban Affairs, 94th Congress, *Report of the Advisory Commission on Intergovernmental Relations on State and Local "Doing Business" Taxes on Out-of-State Financial Depositories* 23 (1975). Both reports predicted serious economic consequences, including a reduction in the mobility of capital and increased compliance costs.
53. See paras 17 and 18 of the Uniform Division of Income for Tax Purposes Act (1957) and Art. IV of the Multistate Tax Compact (1967).

not a problem limited to GRTs alone but applies as well to sales and use taxes.[54] Fair apportionment as a requisite for acceptable taxation by a state under the provisions of the commerce clause of the US Constitution has been developed by the US Supreme Court in *Complete Auto Transit v. Brady*,[55] the central purpose of which is to ensure that each state taxes only its fair share of an interstate transaction. Basically, a tax must pass both the internal and external consistency tests. Internal consistency demands that a tax is fairly apportioned to activities carried out in the state. Under this requirement, the consequences have to be examined for every state that has adopted the same tax and it must be determined whether multiple taxation would occur. The external consistency requirement is aimed at preventing discrimination against interstate commerce.

In several cases, the US Supreme Court has shown a preference for treating a sale of services as a local state event. In *Western Live Stock*,[56] a New Mexico GRT on advertising revenues for a magazine distributed within and without the state was upheld because the magazine was wholly prepared, edited and published within the state, and the taxpayer's office and place of business were located in New Mexico and payments for the services were made to these offices. In *Jefferson Lines*[57] the US Supreme Court agreed with the state of Oklahoma in requiring the bus company to collect sales tax on interstate transportation purchased and originating in that state. In an earlier case, *Greyhound Lines*,[58] the Supreme Court invalidated an unapportioned New York GRT on the gross receipts of a bus company that sold tickets exclusively for interstate travel. The US Supreme Court held that the statute violated the commerce clause because of a lack of apportionment by New York based on the mileage traveled within New York and other states. The US Supreme Court based its decision on the difference between a sales tax and a GRT. According to the Court, although the services subject to taxation in both cases are similar, the identity of the taxpayers and the opportunities for multiple taxation of the same taxpayer diverge. The GRT on the bus company in *Greyhound Lines* could have been imposed by the other states in which the buses traveled. Without apportionment, the bus company would have been paying the same tax to more than one state. In the case of the sales tax at issue in *Jefferson Lines*, however, the tax fell on the buyer, who would not be subject to taxation by another state. The sale occurred in Oklahoma because the combined events of agreement, payment and partial delivery could be located in that state. The sales tax in *Jefferson Lines* was sustained, without overruling *Greyhound Lines*, because the risk of multiple taxation was absent in the former case but present in the latter case.

The majority opinion in *Jefferson Lines* was centered on the location where the sale took place and the identity of the taxpayer. If the tax at issue in this case had been imposed on the seller, or if the sale had not been consummated in Oklahoma,

54. See, for example, van Brederode, "The American Debate on Taxing Distance Sales and E-commerce."
55. *Complete Auto Transit v. Brady*, 430 US 274 (1977).
56. *Western Live Stock v. Bureau of Tax Revenue*, 303 US 250 (1938).
57. *Oklahoma Tax Commission v. Jefferson Lines, Inc.*, 514 US 175 (1995).
58. *Central Greyhound Lines Inc. v. Mealey*, 334 US 653 (1948).

then a tax on the seller for the entire gross receipts, without apportionment to the mileage traveled in the taxing state, would not have cleared the fair apportionment hurdle.[59] In relation to a trip from Oklahoma City to Dallas, the US Supreme Court noted that Texas could not tax the bus company on the full value of the bus service when the ticket was sold in Oklahoma because that tax would, in that situation, fail the internal consistency requirement. Texas, however, could impose a GRT on the bus company if it apportioned the tax based on the mileage traveled in Texas and also taxed all in-state bus service similarly.

5.4.3. Path to Collision

As noted previously, different standards can lead to double taxation, thereby opening the door for a successful commerce clause challenge. The broad standards applied by Ohio could easily attract tax liability for a company taxed for the same services in another state. For example, assume that an Internet company based in the state of Washington performs marketing services for another company based in Ohio, generating total annual gross revenue of USD 625,000. The revenue would be subject to Washington's Business and Occupation Tax because all costs of performance are incurred in that state, and would also be taxable under the Ohio CAT because the services are billed to that state, with total revenue exceeding the threshold, and enjoyed by an Ohio resident.

5.5. CONCLUSIONS

Although the introduction of a GRT in times of economic distress may be excusable, there exists no justification for their imposition in present-day economic circumstances. The tax leads to a wide range of economic distortions. For example, it violates both internal and external neutrality, leads to tax cascading and artificial vertical integration, favors labor-intensive industries over capital-intensive industries and imports over exports. As a result, GRTs have a negative impact on domestic production and employment.

GRTs as they are levied in the United States at the subnational level also are not without legal challenges. States, generally, apply rather broad nexus standards to ensure that out-of-state companies exporting to their state are liable for the tax, which leads to questions about the constitutionality of those standards, which is still awaiting US Supreme Court decision. With the emergence of the Internet, determining tax jurisdiction and revenue allocation among states has become increasingly difficult. Where states apply conflicting apportionment rules, risks of double taxation and nontaxation are apparent.

59. *Supra*, at 1342.

Chapter 6
Retail Sales Taxes

6.1. GENERAL

A RST is a general sales tax with the objective of taxing private consumptive expenditure. It is a close cousin of VAT but differs in some of its defining features. It is a single stage tax, levied at the retail level, but its scope is generally limited to goods and does not include services. RSTs have the advantage of simplicity but do not provide full neutrality. Especially, they fail to provide full relief for business purchases. RSTs are applied in several countries, either at the national or subnational level. Although their application is retreating because of the growing popularity of VATs, they remain persistent, especially in the United States. For that reason we will focus in this chapter on RSTs as applied in the United States from general characteristics to specific features, such as scope, distributional effects, cross-border sales, merits and demerits, fairness; we then consider proposals for the introduction of a national (federal) sales tax.

6.2. RST IN THE UNITED STATES AT THE SUBNATIONAL LEVEL

6.2.1. INTRODUCTION

Under the principle that governments are responsible for the financing of the public services[1] they provide, tax policy and administration in the United States are to a very large extent decentralized. The states have an almost unlimited discretion as to

1. Public services in this context have to be understood in the broadest sense. They include national security, justice, road maintenance, health care, social security, education, general legislation and so forth.

the taxes they levy and, henceforth, are responsible themselves for their administration, collection and enforcement. As a result, in the absence of a centralized federal administration of state and local taxes,[2] the administrative structures of tax collection vary considerably from state to state. Local governments operate within the rules and guidelines determined by their states. In some states, the local governments administer their own taxes, whereas, in other states, they rely on the state tax administration.

Traditionally, the federal government relies heavily on income tax; the states, on income tax, sales tax and excises (on gasoline, tobacco and alcoholic beverages); and local governments (towns and municipalities), on property taxes (on real estate, motor vehicles and business machinery and equipment) and, to a lesser extent, on sales tax.

In their present form, sales taxes were introduced in the 1930s to compensate for the profound effects of the Great Depression on state finances. Facing drastic declines in revenue from established sources, especially real property taxes and income taxes, the states urgently needed to develop alternative sources of income, and, with only a minimal level of technology required for its collection, the sales tax was expected to be capable of generating sufficient revenue to allow the continuation of the states' public services. Although the tax was introduced in some states as a temporary measure, it has turned out to be enduring in nature.

Currently, 45 states and the District of Columbia have a sales tax,[3] which contributes about 25% to 30% to their total tax revenue. Moreover, 33 states permit local governments (counties and towns) to levy the tax, and additional sales taxes are now levied by about 7,500 local jurisdictions, generating an average of 12% of their total revenue. Indeed, the local sales tax is the second-largest source of tax revenue to local government – a distant second to property taxes. There is no federal general sales tax. Gross revenue generated by the sales and use taxes for the year 2006 ranged from USD 209 million in Alaska to USD 40 billion in California, totaling nationwide revenue of USD 330 billion.[4]

In their design and scope, the state sales taxes follow a common pattern, but details, rates and coverage vary considerably. This discussion focuses on the common elements of these taxes and, as a result, provides generalizations that, by nature, do not apply in all and every state.

2. From 1976 to 1992, the Internal Revenue Service (IRS) was, on a federal level, permitted to administer the state income taxes, but all states declined to take advantage of this offer because they perceived central administration as an infringement on their tax autonomy. However, cooperation between the federal and state tax authorities does exist in joint training of tax officials and exchange of information.
3. Alaska, Delaware, Montana, New Hampshire and Oregon do not have a state sales tax. Together, those states comprise about 3% of the US population. However, in Alaska, sales tax is levied at the local level.
4. Source: US Bureau of Census, Governmental Finances, 2006.

6.2.2. General Description and Characterization

Ideally, a sales tax is aimed at taxing final consumption of goods and services.[5] The tax should be imposed on taxable sales made to households and other final consumers, not to businesses. In its economic effect, a RST is therefore similar to a VAT.

Under a VAT, business purchases are relieved of the tax burden through the mechanism of input VAT deduction; whereas, under a sales tax, business purchases should remain entirely outside the scope of the tax. In practice, however, the typical state sales tax in the United States is also imposed on a significant portion of the business-to-business sales.

When the tax was introduced, the legislators realized very well that business-to-business transactions should somehow be exempt.[6] In order to accomplish this, two methods are generally used. All states exempt items bought for resale;[7] in addition, materials and component parts to be physically incorporated into other goods destined to be sold (known as the "physical ingredient" rule). For example, leather sold to a shoe manufacturer is exempt under the latter rule. However, a wide range of business assets remain that are subject to the tax, regardless of the fact that they are used to produce final products that are themselves subject to the sales tax (see Section 6.2.3).

As a result, the sales tax is a hybrid tax. Insofar as it taxes sales to final consumers at the retail level, it is a consumption tax, and insofar as, in effect and by intent, it is levied on business purchases, it is a business tax.

Contrary to the situation in Europe where VAT is included in the listed retail sales price, the US sales tax is an addition to the price. There is a dual rationale for separating price and tax. In the first place, by stating the tax separately, customers are made aware of what they are paying for public services. Second, it makes it easier for suppliers to shift the tax forward to their customers and it reduces or prevents loss in sales volume when prices increase on introduction of the tax or when existing rates are increased[8] because the listed price is never affected by the tax.

The tax point is the sale of goods, or sometimes services, and the taxable amount is the price actually paid, not including freight or delivery charges, and

5. For a general treatise of the US state retail sales taxes, see *State and Local Sales Taxes*, Research Publication no. 23 (New York: Tax Foundation, 1970); and John F. Due & John L. Mikesell, *Sales Taxation: State and Local Structure and Administration*, 2nd ed. (Washington, DC: The Urban Institute, 1994).
6. The terms *exempt* and *exemption* in this section are used to indicate that a supply of goods or services is not taxed, regardless of the methodology applied to achieve this, and should not be confused with the more specific meaning of these terms in the context of VAT.
7. The definition of *resale* may vary from state to state. Some states apply the resale exemption under the restriction that the goods must be resold in the same physical form as they were purchased, which narrows the scope of the exemption considerably. See Perry D. Quick & Michael J. McKee, "Sales Tax on Services: Revenue or Reform?," *National Tax Journal* 41 (1998): 398.
8. Tax Foundation, 1970, *supra*, 15.

financing, provided that those charges are separated. Generally, the states have allowances for transactions in traded-in goods.

The sales tax applies only to domestic supplies. In the case of cross-border transactions, the sales tax in the country of origin cannot apply because the good (or service) is exported. Sales tax in the state of destination does not apply because the transaction originated in another state and is, therefore, not domestic. To fill this void, use taxes have been introduced. The use tax relates to the sales tax as the flip side of the same coin. The use tax kicks in when the sales tax fails to apply. When a good is sold to a customer in another state and is subsequently shipped to that other state, or a service is rendered to a customer located in another state, the sale will be subject to a use tax in the destination state. For the European reader, the use tax resembles a combination of the acquisition tax, levied on cross-border transactions of goods within in the European Union, and the reverse charge levied on the acquisition of (some) cross-border services. There are differences as well. Contrary to the EU, in the United States there exist no place-of-supply rules determining the tax jurisdiction of supplies of cross-border goods or services. Basically, all exports of goods and services are taxed in the state of destination through the application of use tax, provided of course that they are taxed at all. Moreover, final consumers are liable for reporting and paying the tax as well.

The sales tax is collected from the customer by the seller, who has to remit the total amount of tax collected to the authorities at the end of the monthly or quarterly tax period, when he must file a sales tax return. However, in some states, large retailers must make an advance payment in the course of the year on the basis of their sales volume in the preceding year. In the case of use tax, the tax must be remitted to the authorities by the customer, which can be either a private consumer or a business (see Section 6.2.7),[9] unless the supplier has sufficient nexus in the state of destination, in which case the supplier has to collect and remit the use tax.

6.2.3. Scope of the Tax

Sales tax is primarily levied on sales of goods to final consumers and, to a considerable extent, to businesses. With some minor exceptions, although their share in the total consumption has risen considerably over the years, services remain outside the scope of sales tax (see Section 6.2.6). In an effort to reduce the assumed regressivity[10] of the sales tax, many goods, such as food and other

9. Most states also tax casual (i.e. consumer-to-consumer) sales of (used) motor vehicles, campers, other vehicles, boats and so on by requiring payment of the tax from the purchaser on registration. Because the seller paid the tax on the full dealer price when he bought the vehicle originally, imposition of the tax on its residual value at the private resale constitutes double taxation.
10. A tax is regressive when the tax burden as a percentage of income increases where income decreases. In other words, lower-income households pay a higher percentage of their income in sales tax than higher-income households. This conclusion seems correct when measured on an annual basis. Because most people do not stay within the same income group during their lives, it seems more adequate to measure tax incidence on a life cycle basis, in essence including

groceries, medical supplies, educational materials and other goods and services are exempt. In the end, only about 38% of the total consumption in the United States is actually subject to sales tax.[11]

The rules on exemptions vary widely. Food for off-premises consumption[12] is generally exempt, whereas restaurant meals are not. About half the states exempt prescription drugs, sometimes also nonprescription drugs and orthopedic appliances. Clothing is exempt in a few states and subject to a reduced rate in others. A large number of states exempt products subject to excise taxes, such as gasoline. Utilities supplies, such as gas, electricity, telephone and water; local transportation; repair services; laundry and dry cleaning; hairstyling, barbershop and beauty parlor services; and general admissions (e.g., to zoos, museums or theaters) may all share in exempt treatment in a considerable number of states. Professional services, such as financial, accounting, legal and medical services, are generally exempt. In addition to these objective exemptions, also subjective exemptions apply: purchases made by entities of the federal, state and local government and by philanthropic, religious and educational organizations are also generally exempt.

Equipment sales are in principle subject to sales tax in all states, but exemptions or reduced rates apply to equipment used in agriculture and manufacturing, and for the purposes of public utilities. Sometimes this is a categorical exemption applicable to specific categories of machines regardless of their actual use; other states exempt machinery through a "direct-use" rule, under which only items directly used in the production of tangible goods remain outside the scope of the tax. For example, lumber for the manufacturing of furniture will be exempt under the "ingredient-rule," the machines to make the furniture will be exempt under the "direct-use rule," but the forklift used to store the items in a warehouse remains subject to taxation. Vessels, aircraft, trucks and busses used in interstate commerce may be exempt as well. All other physical business assets, such as computers, office furniture, office supplies and so on remain fully taxed.

Land and buildings are exempt, but sales tax can still affect the acquisition cost of buildings insofar as the components and materials used for their construction were subject to the tax.

---

savings as postponed expenditure. As with VAT, life cycle incidence measurements indicate that sales taxes are in fact proportional. See, for example, Robert F. van Brederode, "VAT's Regressivity: Empirical Truth or Political Correctness," *International VAT Monitor* 18 (2) (2007): 86–92.

11. Donald Bruce & William F. Fox, "E-commerce in the Context of Declining State Sales Tax Bases," *National Tax Journal* 53 (4) (2000): 1373–1388; Robert Cline, John Mikesell, Tom Neubig & Andrew Phillips, *Sales Taxation on Business Inputs* (Council on State Taxation, 25 January 2005), 1 (further: COST report 2005).
12. Legal presumptions can lead to complicated and rather impractical rules. For example, in Connecticut, bakery products are exempt, unless they are consumed on the premise or taken out for immediate consumption, which is assumed for individual items, unless six or more items are bought, or, for cookies, more than a pound. Bread and whole cakes are exempt under all circumstances.

6.2.4. Rates

The RST rates at the state level vary from 2.9% in Colorado to 7% in Mississippi, New Jersey, Rhode Island and Tennessee. In many states, local jurisdictions are allowed to levy an additional sales tax up to a certain maximum determined by the state, so the actual rates can be much higher and vary within a state as well. For example, in Baton Rouge, the capital of Louisiana, the total rate is 9%, which consists of 4% state and 5% local tax, and in Nevada, the state tax is 6.5%, but in the Las Vegas area, total tax amounts to 7.75%.

The differences in rates frequently result in border tax effects, in that consumers may adapt their shopping behaviors and make their purchases in another state or area with a lower tax and, consequently, lower prices.

6.2.5. Distributional Effects

6.2.5.1. Tax Revenue

Final consumers contribute approximately 60% of the states' sales tax revenues, and the remaining 40% comes from businesses.[13] As a national average, the business share of all general sales taxes measured for 2006 is 44.9%.[14]

Total sales tax revenue derived from sales to businesses was USD 124.7 billion in 2006. To put this in perspective, the state corporate income tax collections for that year were about USD 51.8 billion.

Personal consumption expenditures in 2003 totaled USD 6.6 trillion. Because of exemptions for most services and a large number of goods, about USD 4 trillion of household purchases were in fact exempt from sales tax. Total sales tax revenue from household expenditures was USD 133 billion for the year 2003.[15]

6.2.5.2. Cascading Effect

In a 1989 study[16] on behalf of the Office of Tax Analysis of the US Treasury Department, the average state sales tax rate on business equipment was estimated at 4.2%, whereas structures bore 1.6% and land and inventories 0%. These figures, however, did not include the effect of tax cascading. Tax cascading occurs

13. Raymond J. Ring, "Consumer's Share and Producer's Share of the General Sales Tax," *National Tax Journal* 52 (1) (1999: 79–90.
14. Robert Cline, Tom Neubig, & Andrew Phillips, *Total State and Local Business Taxes: Fifty-State Estimates for Fiscal Year 2006* (study prepared by Ernst & Young LLP in conjunction with the Council on State Taxation, February 2007).
15. Council on State Taxation, *Total State and Local Business Taxes: A Fifty-State Study of the Taxes Paid by Business in FY 2003* (study prepared by Ernst & Young LLP for the Council on State Taxation, January 2004).
16. David Joulfaian & James Mackie, "Sales Taxes, Investment, and the Tax Reform Act of 1986," *National Tax Journal* 45 (1992): 89–105. The figures are for the year 1987.

when taxes, as part of the cost price for goods and services supplied to a business, are absorbed in the selling prices of the business and, thus, shifted to its customers. It has the effect that an amount of tax paid at a previous stage is again subject to the tax at a later stage and, as a result, the same amount of tax may be taxed multiple times in the processes of production and distribution, creating a "tax-on-tax" effect, the magnitude of which is determined by the length of the chain of transactions.

It is difficult to measure to what extent cascading occurs in practice because it depends on factors, such as the price elasticity of the goods or services in question[17] and the supplier's market position. Moreover, the cascading effect is likely to vary from state to state and from industry to industry, and it also depends on the category of goods. It should be noted, that investments made by suppliers of exempt goods and services are taxed as well, which means that the prices for exempt goods and services contain an element of hidden sales tax.

In so far as the market conditions enable suppliers to shift the tax to their customers, the sales tax retains its character as a consumption tax. However, in so far as the suppliers assume the tax themselves by accepting a lower margin, the tax becomes a business tax. Studies suggest that the cascading rate is at least 1.72 on a national basis.[18] A study group for Washington State estimated that the tax cascades an average of 2.5 times, which means that 1 dollar of initial tax generates additional tax revenue of USD 1.50.[19]

6.2.5.3. Regressivity

Just like VAT, general sales taxes are stigmatized by the belief that they are regressive, which means that lower-income groups bear a higher burden of the tax relative to their income. In an effort to mitigate the regressive nature of the tax, exemptions for food and other essential products have been introduced in all or most states. However, those concessions increase the administrative and compliance costs for governments and businesses respectively and, since they are not based on the purchasing power of the individual customer, apply to purchases by higher-income groups in the same manner. Moreover, they are costly in terms of loss of revenue for the government. Most economists, however, believe that the burden of the tax is almost proportional to the consumers' income.[20]

When taxable goods and services are exported to another state or a country outside the United States, or are bought by nonresident travelers, it is likely that, at least to a certain extent, the tax will be borne by the nonresident customers, which implies that the burden of the tax is exported.

---

17. Percentage decrease in demand for goods (or services) resulting from a percentage increase of their price.
18. COST Report, 2005, Table 3.
19. Washington State Tax Structure Study Commission, *Tax Alternatives for Washington State: A Report to the Legislature*, vols 1 & 2 (November 2002), 110–112.
20. See n. 10.

6.2.6. Tax on Services

With some exceptions, services are not subject to US state sales tax. Private consumption of services in the United States in the year 2003 totaled USD 3.5 trillion, and business purchases of services totaled USD 3.1 trillion. Only an estimated 11% of the value of those services was subject to sales tax.[21]

There is an understandable reluctance on the part of states to apply a tax to services. Basically, there are three reasons for excluding services from the scope of sales tax. In the first place, taxing services requires criteria to determine where the services are effectively used in order to tax them in the state of destination; in the absence of clear criteria to determine the place of their actual use, taxation of services may lead to double taxation. Second, as with taxing goods, taxation of services would lead to economic distortions and inefficiencies due to tax cascading. And third, taxing services rendered to businesses may have a negative effect on the state's economy.[22]

6.2.7. Interstate Services

It is important to note that there are no federal rules or any other form of coordination between the states[23] to resolve cross-border tax issues between them. In other words, the United States have no rules (comparable to the place-of-supply rules under the EU VAT legislation) to determine the tax jurisdiction regarding cross-border, interstate services. In addition, there is no uniformity in the definition of what constitutes a service. As a result, it is apparent that rules applicable in one state may conflict with those applicable in other states and, therefore, may lead to situations of double or nontaxation.

The approach taken by the State of South Dakota regarding legal services may be illustrative of the problems that can be encountered. South Dakota law requires out-of-state attorneys to collect sales tax on their total legal fees, if the following apply:

- their client resides or has nexus in South Dakota;
- the legal issue concerns property located in South Dakota or events or transactions that took place there; and
- the attorney enters into South Dakota or makes an appearance in court there.

21. COST Report, 2005, 2 and 3.
22. If businesses shift additional tax to their customers, they will face reduced competitiveness relative to companies in other states that do not tax services. If, for this reason, a business absorbs the tax, it faces reduced profit margins and, therefore, reduced ability to further invest. Possibly businesses may relocate to states with a more beneficial tax regime.
23. The states have, however, initiated the Streamlined Sales Tax Project (SSTP) in an effort to cope with these problems. A working group is charged with developing common definitions, rules and procedures to be implemented at some time in the future by all states.

If all three conditions are not met, the attorney's tax liability is determined on the basis of actual work done or time spent in South Dakota.

If, for whatever reason, the attorney does not collect the sales tax, use tax is due by the recipient of the legal service. In addition, South Dakota applies comprehensive and detailed rules to determine under what conditions services are exempt as a purchase for resale.

In principle, a service can be contracted in one state, performed in another, delivered in a third, and redistributed by the client to subsidiaries in several other states. Florida had a short experience[24] with sales tax on general services purchased by multistate businesses based on income (profit) apportionment. If, for example, 10% of the total profits could be allocated to Florida, 10% of the total services purchased were assumed to have taken place in Florida for sales tax purposes.[25]

Although we can appreciate the efforts by the states of South Dakota and Florida to define their tax jurisdiction, the results are, in essence, arbitrary and, in the absence of tax coordination between the states, it will be impossible to tax interstate services equitably without the risk of double or nontaxation.

6.2.8. Interstate Trade in Goods

The United States is a single market to a large extent similar to the EU. There exist no physical borders between the fifty states. Goods exported to another state cannot be taxed in the state of origin,[26] which means that such exports are tax exempt. The sales tax is levied as a "domestic" tax and applies only to sales made within the boundaries of a single state. States have no authority over out-of-state suppliers because interstate commerce is the exclusive domain of the federal government. Henceforth, buying in another state would offer an immediate price advantage. In the case where goods are purchased by a business or final consumer and shipped to another state, no tax would be charged; when a consumer or any other entity that cannot provide proof of being a business purchases a good and transports it personally to his or her home state, the supplier would charge local (domestic) sales tax, which could still be advantageous in cases where the tax in the state of purchase is lower than that in the destination state. In order to close this gap, all states that apply sales tax also impose use tax to resident businesses and final consumers that make their purchase in another state,[27] generally with a tax credit for sales tax paid in the state of purchase.

Use taxes apply to the same categories of goods and sometimes services as sales taxes and at the same rate. They serve the dual purpose of filling in the

---

24. For 6 months in 1987.
25. See James Francis, "The Florida Sales Tax on Services: What Really Went Wrong?," in *The Unfinished Agenda for State Tax Reform*, ed. Steven D. Gold. Denver: National Conference of State Legislatures, (1988), 136.
26. Article 1(9) (5) of the US Constitution.
27. As accepted by the Supreme Court in *Henneford v. Silas Mason*, 300 US 577 (1937).

interstate gap in sales tax coverage and of preventing a competitive disadvantage for "domestic" as compared to out-of-state sellers. From an outsider's perspective, it makes sense to assume that vendors would be obliged to withhold use tax for "export" sales to other states. However, under the current judicial interpretation[28] of the constitutional prohibition for states to impose an undue burden on interstate commerce, only vendors with adequate physical presence (nexus) in a state are required to register as use tax collectors. Without nexus, remote sellers, such as Internet vendors and mail-order retailers, are not required to charge (destination state) use tax on out-of-state sales. This is, of course, a problem that has existed for decades, but, from the perspectives of loss of revenue and competitive fairness, it is becoming increasingly pressing with the advancement of technologies that make remote selling and buying easier and cheaper. A solution can only be found at the level of federal legislation eliminating or substantially altering the physical-presence rule.

However, in the current legal environment, the states have no option but to collect the tax on out-of-state purchases directly from the customers. In their aim to protect revenue for the state of consumption, there is a strong resemblance between the collection of use tax in the United States and that of VAT on intracommunity acquisitions in the EU. However, in the United States, the state use tax applies to both business and private purchases.[29] If the purchaser is a business, it will have to account for use tax in a separate box on its periodical sales tax return. A private consumer has to file a separate use tax return or can account for it on her or his state income tax return at the end of the year.

In sum, use taxes are due on out-of-state purchases (imports) of goods and sometimes services. The tax is collected by either the supplier if he is registered for use tax, either voluntarily or because of nexus, in the destination state, or by the customer. Where these customers are businesses already registered for sales tax purposes in the state of destination, that state avails itself of means of auditing, checking and controlling the customers, albeit that those means are not abundant and certainly not efficient.[30] Private persons are obviously not registered for sales tax purposes and remittance of use tax by the latter group is extremely difficult if not impossible to enforce (see section 6.2.9).

---

28. US Supreme Court, *National Bellas Hess v. Dept. of Revenue for the State of Illinois*, 386 US 753 (1967), and *Quill Corporation v. North Dakota*, 504 US 298 (1992).
29. In the EU, private purchases of goods are in principle taxed in the country of origin, but distance sales (mail-order supplies) are taxed in the country of arrival when the seller exceeds certain annual monetary thresholds, see Arts 32, 33 and 34 of Directive 2006/112. In that case, however, the supplier must register in the customer's Member State and remit the tax to the authorities. With the exception of new means of transport, the tax is not collected from the private consumers.
30. Generally, states lack sufficient manpower to audit all businesses and with sufficient frequency. In addition, extraterritorial limitations of their jurisdiction prevent states from auditing out-of-state vendors and, therefore, cross-checking of administrations is not possible.

6.2.9. Compliance

The general assumption is that sales taxes have a high rate of compliance, exceeding that of state income taxes, but that use taxes have a low compliance rate. Only a few states give priority to measuring the compliance rates, but the information available confirms the assumptions. Minnesota estimates noncompliance at 8.2% of the total tax liability but does not distinguish between sales and use tax.[31] Washington State's estimates are 1.3% for sales tax and 27.9% for use tax.[32]

As to use tax, compliance is ensured from out-of-state vendors who voluntarily register in a state to remit use tax and also in relation to purchases of goods that require registration, such as motor homes, cars, boats and airplanes.[33] Due to the high cost of compliance, out-of-state vendors are very reluctant to register voluntarily. Private consumers have a low awareness of the use tax.

About fifteen states and the District of Columbia link the collection of use tax from consumers to the collection of individual income tax, either by enclosing a separate form with, or by including a separate box on, the income tax return. Nonetheless, compliance seems to be very low. Kentucky reports that about 1% of the income tax filers report something with an average tax liability of USD 37. Maine, with the highest compliance rate, reports that 10% of the income tax filers report use tax due for a total amount of USD 1.6 million on total use tax revenue of USD 78.6 million. It estimates a USD 30 million to USD 100 million loss due to underreporting.[34]

In relation to remote sales, the US General Accounting Office estimates the revenue erosion at between USD 2.6 billion and USD 20.4 billion.[35] The midpoint of that range, USD 11.5 billion, is about 4% of total revenue the states expect to receive from sales and use taxes. Estimates made by private institutions[36] range from USD 15.4 billion to USD 16.1 billion for 2003 and project a revenue loss ranging from USD 21.5 billion to USD 33.6 billion for 2008.

31. Minnesota Dept. of Revenue, 2001. This figure is misleading. Because the sales volume subject to use tax is much narrower than that for sales tax (about 8% of the combined tax base) and under the likely assumption that most of the gap will be caused by noncompliance in relation to use tax, the actual figure for use tax relative to total liability of use and sales tax combined would be significantly higher.
32. Washington Dept. of Revenue, 2003.
33. If sales taxes are not collected by the dealer, or in the case of out-of-state purchases or purchases from private persons (C2C), use tax will be collected on registration with the Department of Motor Vehicles in a state.
34. Maine Dept. of Revenue, 2006.
35. General Accounting Office, *Sales Taxes: Electronic Commerce Growth Presents Challenge; Revenue Losses Are Uncertain*, GAO Report OCE-00-165 (Washington, DC: General Accounting Office, 30 June 2000), 21.
36. Donald Bruce & William F. Fox, *State and Local Sales Tax Revenue Loss from E-commerce: Estimates as of July 2004* (University of Tennessee, July 2004), 5.

6.2.10. Coordination of State and Local Sales Taxes

Nationwide, about 7,500 local governments levy a RST as a supplement to the state tax. Although some local governments administer their own sales tax, the local sales tax is commonly administered by the state[37] and collected in tandem with the state sales tax. In that case, transparency is certainly served and the tax rules and specifics (taxable items, exemptions, due dates, returns) are all fully harmonized. Clearly, a single return to be filed with a central administration is simpler from a compliance perspective. However, multibranch businesses are still required to segregate their sales and tax collections according to tax jurisdiction to allow proper distribution of revenue.

Where the local government collects its own sales tax, the taxable base frequently differs from that of the state tax. The different tax rules, in combination with the requirement of duplicate accounting and the obligation to report the tax to two different administrations, highly complicates vendor compliance.

6.2.11. Merits and Demerits

There are several, mostly economic, merits and demerits contributed to the sales tax as to revenue productivity and stability, tax efficiency and economic distortions, operational cost, resource allocation, fairness, and reduced taxpayer awareness.

6.2.11.1. Revenue Productivity

Potentially, the tax scores high for revenue productivity, even at relatively low rates. The sales tax yields 34% of the total state tax revenue and 11% of local government revenue. For both local and state government combined, the yield is 23% of total tax revenue.[38] Both in absolute terms and in relation to total revenue, the sales tax yield could be increased significantly by reducing the number of exemptions and by increasing the number of services included in the tax base.

6.2.11.2. Revenue Stability

Governments generally prefer a tax base that is relatively stable because it leads to smaller variations in revenue over time and allows for more efficient budget management. Most economists believe that aggregate consumption is more stable over time than aggregate income. When their incomes decline, consumers are presumed to borrow money or use their savings in order to maintain their level of expenditure. When their incomes rise, the increment is expected to be used to pay off debts or to

37. Generally at no cost, but some states charge the local governments for the service of collecting and administering the sales tax.
38. See Due & Mikesell, *Sales Taxation*.

increase savings. Statistical research in the United States for the period 1959–1995 confirms that consumption varied less and was, therefore, a more stable basis for taxation, as compared to income.

6.2.11.3. Tax Efficiency

A sales tax is an efficient tax if it is a truly "general" tax, that is, has a broad base with a minimum number of exemptions and exclusions. However, the sales taxes in the United States are full of exemptions, which may generate substitution effects and, henceforth, create economic inefficiencies due to the fact that consumers are induced to purchase more exempt and less taxed goods and services. The size of those inefficiencies also depends on the price elasticity of the goods and services concerned. Evidence in economic literature of the existence and size of these inefficiencies has always been scarce. However, recent studies[39] confirm their existence, and Hawkins[40] estimates the excess burden – the reduction in economic welfare beyond the increase of revenue – to range between 17% and 39%.

The cascading of the tax also has a number of negative economic effects. It encourages vertical integration of businesses in order to avoid taxable transactions between them, imposes an unjustified burden on the outsourcing of activities (purchased goods or services lead to higher effective taxes as compared to self-produced goods and services), distorts consumer choices where similar products have different effective tax rates as a result of cascading, and may lead to a competitive disadvantage for businesses exporting to other states where the same product is subject to a lower effective rate.

6.2.11.4. Operational Cost

The administrative cost for the government and the compliance cost for businesses are relatively low, estimated at ranging between 1% and 3% of the revenue collected.[41] However, the compliance costs are probably significantly higher for businesses operating in multiple states because the tax rules and legal definitions are not harmonized between the states and/or are operating in states where the tax is levied by multiple tax jurisdictions.

6.2.11.5. Resource Allocation

The effects of a sales tax on resource allocation are manageable because, in theory, the tax is designed to minimize disruption of the market patterns. In principle, this

39. Donald N. Baum, "Economic Effects of Eliminating the Sales Tax Exemption for Food: An Applied General Equilibrium Analysis," *Journal of Economics* 24 (1) (1998): 125–148; Aled Ab Iorwerth & John Whalley, "Efficiency Considerations and the Exemption of Food from Sales and Value Added Taxes," *Canadian Journal of Economics* 35 (1) (2002): 166–182.
40. Richard R. Hawkins, "Popular Substitution Effects: Excess Burden Estimates for General Sales Taxes," *National Tax Journal* 55 (4) (2002): 755–769.
41. Tax Foundation, 1970, 40–50.

argument may be true; however, the sales taxes in the United States distinguish themselves from the ideal model by a large number of exemptions and by application of reduced rates that, by their very nature, have a potentially disruptive impact on allocation patterns.

6.2.11.6. Fairness of the Tax

There exists no gold standard for tax fairness. The concept of fairness of taxation is highly subjective and varies over time. As a proportional tax, the sales tax is fair from the perspective of the ability to pay. Those who believe that the tax is regressive also claim that it is unfair, precisely for that reason.

With their narrow base, the sales taxes in the United States discriminate the goods and few services that are subject to them in favor of the large sectors of the economy that remain untaxed, which constitutes a violation of the principle of equal treatment.

6.2.11.7. Reduced Taxpayer Awareness

Finally, it has been argued that a sales tax offers a psychological advantage over other taxes because the taxpayers are hardly conscious of the total amount they actually pay during the course of a year because payment occurs in small installments, and any pain felt over paying tax on the occasion of a purchase may be mitigated by the consumer's felicity of the acquisition. The fact that the sales tax is an inconspicuous tax makes it also easier for lawmakers to increase its rate.[42] Whether this psychological advantage should be classified as a merit seems, to a large extent, to depend on personal views.

6.2.12. Self-Supply Rules

Where the RST, to a large extent, is in effect a business tax due to the limited scope of the exemptions, a preference for insourcing over outsourcing may arise, disturbing economic neutrality. Strong similarities exist with vertical integration under a GRT (see Section 5.3.5) and the tendency to insourcing among exempt businesses under VAT (see Section 8.2.4.3.3). The solutions to combat insourcing under VAT, GRT and RST are similar as well: taxing self-produced goods to create a level competitive playing field. The rules among the states in the United States vary in this respect, but as a general rule a use tax is levied on self-manufactured products.

The main difference between the states is in how they determine the tax base for self-produced goods. For example, in Connecticut the tax is levied on the sales price of the materials;[43] in Florida the use tax is measured on the total cost of

---

42. Tax Foundation, 1970, 15.
43. CT Regs. Ch. 219, s. 12-411(1). <www.cga.ct.gov/2005/pub/Chap219.htm#Sec12-411.htm>

producing the good, including cost of materials, labor and transportation;[44] and in Georgia the tax is based on the fair market value, that is, the deemed sales price of the article.[45]

6.2.13. Conclusions

The sales taxes in the United States are effective and stable taxes that generate a significant portion of revenue for the states. Extending the scope of sales taxes to all services and the goods that are currently exempt could substantially increase its yield. The US sales taxes are hybrid in character, being in effect both consumption and business taxes. Because of its actual structure, the tax has many economic deficiencies. The US state sales taxes are not harmonized, which increases the compliance costs for businesses active in multiple states. In addition, cross-border (interstate) transactions remain to a large extent effectively untaxed because of the low compliance rate of use taxes. In essence, the state sales and use taxes are not prepared for the twenty-first century and are in need of a total overhaul.

6.3. FEDERAL SALES TAX IN THE UNITED STATES

6.3.1. Introduction

Discussions about tax reform occur in the Unites States on a regular basis both in academic circles and at the political level. In the past decade, three proposals have gained more-than-average attention: the flat tax[46] that would eliminate all tax deductions and lower the annual tax rate to 17%; the USA tax,[47] which combines a consumed-income tax[48] and a business transfer tax, in essence a subtraction method VAT;[49] and the national retail sales tax (NRST).[50] This discussion

44. FL Rule 12A-1.043(1)(a). <www.flrules.org/gateway/ruleNo.asp?ID=12A-1.043>
45. GA Rule 560-12-1-.14(5). <http://rules.sos.state.ga.us/docs/560/12/1/14.pdf>
46. HR 1040 (The Freedom and Fairness Restoration Act of 1997), introduced by Representative Dick Armey (R-TX) on 12 March 1997; the flat tax is in essence an origin-based, subtraction method consumption tax.
47. S 722 (USA Tax Act of 1995), introduced by Senators Sam Nunn (D-GA) and Pete Dominici (R-NM) on 25 April 1995. The USA tax is also a subtraction method consumption tax.
48. Tax on income less savings and plus dissavings.
49. Tax is paid on sales less purchases, where purchases include capital purchases but not wages.
50. For a short treatise on the flat tax and USA tax, as well as other and predating tax reform proposals, including VATs, see Alan Schenk, "Recent Activity in the United States Involving Value Added Tax," *VAT Monitor* (August/September 1992): 2 et seq.; Alan Schenk, "VAT Debate Stimulated by Tax Reform Hearings in the United States," *VAT Monitor* 4 (July/August 1995): 204–210; Oliver Oldman & Alan Schenk, "The Business Activities Tax: Have Senators Danforth and Boren Created a Better Value Added Tax?," *Tax Notes International* (2 January 1995), 55–74; William H. Morris, "Proposed Business Activities Tax Signals Renewed Interest in U.S. VAT," *The Journal of International Taxation* (October 1994),

deals exclusively with the latter, which was proposed for the first time in 1996[51] and again, under the Fair Tax Act, in 1999 and later years. It was introduced for the last time in 2007 to the 110th Congress.[52] Interestingly, the purpose of the proposals is not to generate additional revenue for the federal government but to replace existing taxes. The discussion is ongoing and contains many elements of interest to a wider audience outside the United States. In light of the budget deficits during most of the Bush administration's tenure, the size of the national debt, urgent financing needed for infrastructure, Social Security and lapses in health care coverage, the practice of deficit financing of the military expeditions in Iraq and Afghanistan, the magnitude of the economic depression, and the election of President Barack Obama, it is likely that tax reform, including a national consumption tax, will take the political stage again.

First, I will present an overview of the background, purpose and main features of the NRST based on the Fair Tax Act proposal. Introducing a new tax as a replacement for others has significant economic effects that are examined in Section 6.3.3. Introducing a sales tax at the federal level, while the individual states maintain their sales and use tax systems, gives rise to important questions in relation to tax coordination and federalism that are considered in Section 6.3.4. In the next section an attempt is made to determine the tax rate for such a national sales tax. Before we come to our conclusions, attention is paid to the likelihood and size of tax evasion and fraud under a federal sales tax.

6.3.2. Outline of the Proposed National Retail Sales Tax

6.3.2.1. General

To a large extent, the proposals for a national consumption tax are fueled by dissatisfaction with the current corporate and personal income taxes. The income tax is considered excessively complicated,[53] wasteful, counterproductive regarding economic growth, inequitable due to the influence of special interests and costly with compliance costs estimated at USD 225 billion annually. The initiative for the fair tax was in the hands of a private, nonprofit advocacy group, Americans For Fair Taxation, who assembled a team of economists to design a tax that would make federal tax simpler, fairer and more progressive, and that would "unleash the potential" of the US economy. The concept is ambitious where it seeks to simplify the current tax code, expand home ownership, untax the poor, improve global

---

466–470; and James M. Bickley, *Flat Tax Proposals and Fundamental Tax Reform: An Overview*, Congressional Research Service Brief for Congress (30 September 2004).

51. H.R. 3039 (National Retail Sales Tax Act of 1996), sponsored by Representatives Dan Schaefer (R-CO) and Billy Tauzin (R-LA).
52. H.R. 25/S 1025 (Fair Tax Act of 2007), introduced by respectively Representative John Linder (R-GA) with sixty-eight cosponsors in the House on 1 April 2007 and by Senator Saxby Chambliss (R-GA) with four cosponsors in the Senate on 29 March 2007.
53. The Internal Revenue Code comprises currently more than 54,000 pages.

competitiveness, promote higher education and charitable giving, and create more jobs. The underlying assumption is that consumption provides a more stable and fairer base for taxation than income. The Fair Tax Plan is a comprehensive proposal that replaces all federal income and payroll-based taxes with an integrated approach, including a progressive NRST and a prebate to ensure no US citizen pays federal taxes on spending up to the poverty level. The fair tax would be a broad-based, destination type consumption tax with statutory tax liability on final consumers and tax collection in the hands of sellers of goods and services to these consumers. The tax base would include all supplies of goods and services, which would mean a substantive enlargement compared to the tax base of the current state sales and use taxes. Neutrality is served and tax cascading prevented by taxing all final consumption of goods and services, and by exempting business inputs. To ensure a level playing field, all imports of consumable goods and services would be subject to use tax. To the extent possible, tax will be collected in tandem with import duties, which should work reasonably well for tangible goods but will likely encounter problems regarding services and intangible products, such as electronic downloads of music, books and so on. Input purchasers would find tax relief through a system of exemption certificates, providing much broader relief than the parallel state sales tax by applying more generally to tangible and intangible inputs.[54] It is likely, however, that the federal government would engage the same definition problems as the states have encountered in deciding what constitutes an exempt input. The states use sale-for-resale, ingredient and component part exemptions; the federal exemption format is not completely clear. Exports, used goods and property (including the pre-existing housing stock),[55] education tuition, intangibles (e.g., copyrights, trademarks, patents), and intercompany sales would also receive exempt status. Nonprofit organizations would pay tax on their input purchases at the same time that charitable donations lose their tax-exempt status under the income tax, unless and in so far as they engage in taxable sales of goods and services. Government goods and services that represent final consumption, so-called government enterprise sales, would be taxed with input purchases subject to exemption. General government activities are not taxed, but tax will be due on all input purchases related to these government activities.

Nonresident alien individual and corporate income, sourced to the United States, would be subject to 23% tax, conditional on international tax treaties.

6.3.2.2. Abolition of the IRS

It will come as no surprise that the Internal Revenue Service (IRS) is no candidate to win any popularity contest. From that perspective, proposing the abolishment of

54. It is estimated that 40% of revenue generated by state sales and use taxes is actually paid by businesses; see Ring, "Consumers' Share and Producers' Share of the General Sales Tax"; Cline, Neubig & Phillips, *Total State and Local Business Taxes*.
55. Credits will be available for business acquisition of property held by final consumers for which sales tax has been paid.

the IRS seems to be a smart populist political move. Under the Fair Tax Act, the IRS should be disbanded as quickly as possible after the establishment of the NRST. Some transition period is, of course, required so that the IRS can administer the income tax for the years prior to its abolition. Out-year appropriations for the IRS should decline and then be suspended as part of the enacting legislation. All IRS tax records should be destroyed within 5 years of the new law's enactment. A new excise tax bureau would be established within the Department of the Treasury to collect remaining excise taxes. The Social Security Administration would collect Social Security and Medicare payroll taxes. The NRST will be collected by the revenue services of the individual states.

On a Shakespearean note, one may wonder how material the abolishment of the IRS really is, where the Fair Tax Act creates new federal bureaucracy in the form of a sales tax bureau that will operate within the Department of the Treasury and will be charged with administering the sales tax in those states that do not have a sales tax at the state level, and other federal duties and powers relating to the national sales tax, including an office of revenue allocation and a problem resolution office. It seems unlikely that the change of name will remove the sweet smell of unpopularity. It is true that the new offices would be much smaller in size and have less responsibility, but that is only an optical change since the remaining bureaucratic authority will be delegated from the federal to the subnational level of government. Whether that would make a big difference to individual taxpayers remains questionable.

6.3.2.3. Collection Costs Reimbursement

Under the income tax, compliance costs are borne by the taxpayers and employers. The NRST envisions compensating businesses for compliance and collection costs by allowing them to withhold a 0.25% of tax collected and remitted to the State revenue service. In turn, the states would administer the NRST in exchange for an administrative fee of 1% of revenue collected and remitted to the federal government.

6.3.2.4. Low Income Prebate

Partly to offset the presumed regressivity of the national sales tax and partly to compensate for *de minimis* thresholds under the federal income tax, the Fair Tax Act provides tax relief for low-income households up to the poverty level, called the Family Consumption Allowance (FCA). A household making an income equal to the poverty level pays 0% tax, a household making less than the poverty level receives an actual rebate equal to the tax rate times the difference between the poverty level and earned income. Above the poverty level, households pay a flat tax rate. The effective tax rates are demonstrated in Figure 7.[56]

56. Source: Fair Tax Organization.

Figure 7. Effective Fair Tax Rate

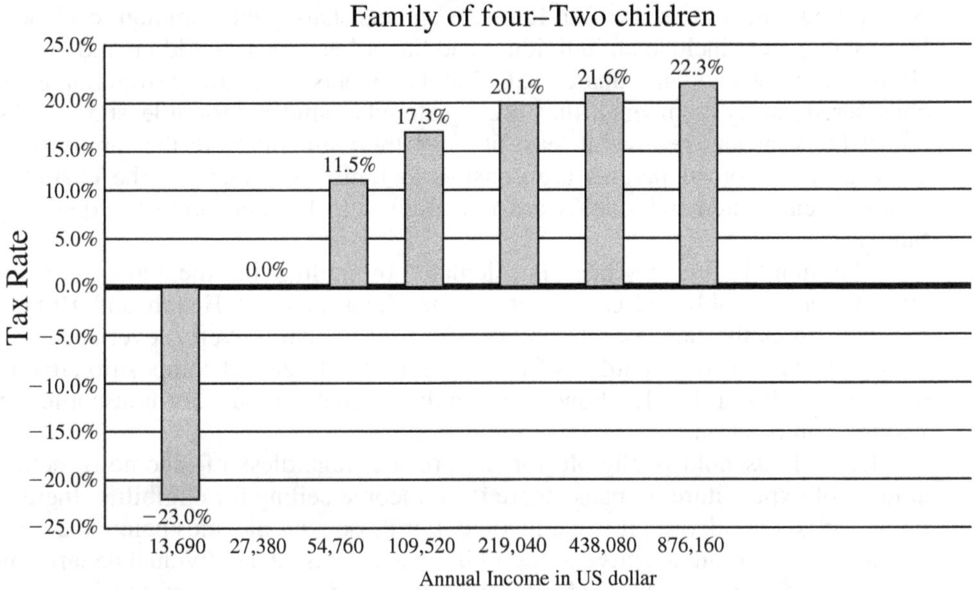

Proponents of the tax call it progressive, but the example in Figure 7 demonstrates that the progression is only marginal at higher expenditure levels. At lower expenditure levels, the tax is slightly more progressive. Moreover, the progression rate edges off as income rises. Whereas the income of the households in this example doubles compared to the previous one, the effective tax rate increases from 0% to, respectively, 11.5%, 5.8%, 2.8%, 1.5% and finally 0.7%.

Of course, under a RST, only consumptive expenditure is taxed and saving is not. *Progressive* and *regressive*[57] are terms related to income and not to consumption. The Figure 7 is, in essence, misleading where it presents expenditure as income and uses it as a base to make conclusions on progressivity. The picture changes significantly, if we assume that people with higher incomes are able to save a portion of their income. The effective tax rate would be lower to the extent of the relative weight of the fair tax on income saved. If the household making USD 219,040 spent only USD 200,000 and saved the remainder, the effective tax rate would be 19.85% instead of 20.1%. In my opinion, it is more accurate to characterize the fair tax as a proportional tax with a redistributive income subsidy for households up to the poverty level (see my additional comments to Table 15).

57. Regressivity in this context means that lower-income groups bear a higher burden of the tax relative to their income than higher-income groups. Progressivity by contrast means that the tax burden rises, as a percentage of income, as income rises. See van Brederode, "VAT's Regressivity."

All qualified families are entitled to receive the monthly prebate. The term *qualified family* means one or more family members sharing a common residence. A qualified family consists of all family members sharing the common residence. Family members include an individual and his or her spouse, children and grandchildren, parents, and grandparents. Children/students living away from home are considered family members if they are registered as students for at least 5 months out of the year and receive at least 50% of their support from the family unit. Children of divorced parents are considered family members of the custodial parent. Incarcerated individuals are not eligible to be members of a qualified family.

The monthly prebate check is calculated by multiplying the annual poverty level spending published each year by the Department of Health and Human Services times the fair tax rate and dividing by twelve. Poverty level spending represents what it costs families of varying household size and composition to buy their necessities. Table 15 shows the monthly prebate amount for households of varying composition.

Every household is eligible for the prebate, regardless of income or actual amount of expenditure. Because there is no income ceiling for eligibility, there is no incentive to underreport wage income. For those with incomes below the poverty level, there is an incentive to report income because the individual benefits by the amount of the sales tax rate for every dollar of wage income reported. The risks of fraud, however, seem to be relatively small. The act provides for procedures to prevent fraud and audits applications in advance, and levies both civil[58] and criminal[59] penalties.

The amount of refund does not depend on the actual level of expenditure or on the amount of tax actually paid. A household of four, consisting of two adults and two children will receive an annual rebate of USD 6,297 even if they paid less in fair tax in the year. In that sense, the prebate contains an element of income redistribution. The rebate is a transfer payment that operates entirely independently of the NRST and is only linked to it through the tax rate. It is a different way of providing relief than applied by most states under their sales tax. Under the state sales tax, relief is provided for in the format of exemptions of food and clothing, in essence, therefore, by exempting part of the tax base.[60] Relief can only be realized under that system to the extent those particular goods are indeed purchased, whereas the FCA prebate is basically unconditional in terms of expenditure.

58. Repayment of rebates not due and monetary penalty of the greater of USD 500 or 50% of the amount overpaid.
59. Up to 1 year imprisonment.
60. Instead of sales tax exemptions, five states, Hawaii, Idaho, Kansas, South Dakota and West Virginia, provide relief through credits against the income tax.

Table 15. 2007 Fair Tax Prebate Schedule

	One-Adult Household			Two-Adult Household			
Family Size	Annual Consumption Allowance (USD)	Annual Pre-bate (USD)	Monthly Prebate (USD)	Family Size	Annual Consumption Allowance (USD)	Annual Prebate (USD)	Monthly Prebate (USD)
1 person	10,210	2,348	196	N/A	N/A	N/A	N/A
and 1 child	13,690	3,149	262	Couple	20,420	4,697	391
and 2 children	17,170	3,949	329	and 1 child	23,900	5,497	458
and 3 children	20,650	4,750	396	and 2 children	27,380	6,297	525
and 4 children	24,130	5,550	462	and 3 children	30,860	7,098	591
and 5 children	27,610	6,350	529	and 4 children	34,340	7,898	658
and 6 children	31,090	7,151	596	and 5 children	37,820	8,699	725
and 7 children	34,570	7,951	663	and 6 children	41,300	9,499	792

Source: The 2007 Dept. of Health and Human Services Poverty Guidelines, 24 January 2007. The annual consumption allowance is the amount of spending that is "untaxed" under the Fair Tax.

6.3.3. Economic Effects of NRST

A single rate federal consumption tax, replacing the current income taxes, is assumed to generate significant economic benefits, mainly due to increased capital investment. As a result of the introduction of a national consumption tax, increases in GDP have been predicted in the past, ranging from 7% to 14%.[61] More robust growth than these predictions is feasible, because these models do not account for productivity gains from reduced compliance costs and from increased technological innovation, or increased capital inflows from abroad likely to result from the introduction of a NRST.

An immediate consequence of a NRST is that interest rates would fall. To what extent interest rates would fall is uncertain because demand for credit would rise as well, given the increased after-tax rate of return on capital investment under an NST approach. Clearly, this would be beneficial to industries and individuals that are sensitive to interest rates.

The complete removal of all taxation of nonconsumed income would enhance the attractiveness of the United States for foreign investors, and expatriated U.S. investment dollars can also be expected to return home, leading to increased net capital inflows.[62] Given the proposed tax treatment and the political stability of the United States, the nation could become the ultimate global tax haven to the advantage of US industry, workers and consumers.

Another economic advantage of eliminating the income tax would be found in strongly reduced administrative and compliance costs, and the utilization of these savings for productive expenditure.[63] With a NRST, compliance costs could be reduced by more than 90%.[64] This is especially relevant to small businesses and start-ups, which disproportionally bear the compliance costs burden, even in excess of tax collected.[65] Private individuals would no longer have to file income tax returns, and businesses would file administratively much simpler

---

61. Dale W. Jorgenson, "The Economic Impact of Fundamental Taxing Consumption," Testimony before the House Ways and Means Committee, 27 March 1996. See also Dale W. Jorgenson, "The Economic Impact of Fundamental Tax Reform," Testimony before the House Ways and Means Committee, 6 June 1995; and, Laurence J. Kotlikoff, *The Economic Impact of Replacing Federal Income Taxes with a Sales Tax*, Policy Analysis no. 193 (Washington, DC: Cato Institute, 15 April 1993).
62. In the 1980s, when top federal tax rates were reduced from 70% to 28%, the United States attracted a net inflow of roughly USD 500 billion; see Stephen Moore & John Silvia, *The ABCs of the Capital Gains Tax*, Policy Analysis no. 242 (Washington, DC: Cato Institute, 4 October 1995).
63. These cost savings, however, would not improve the overall standard of living because compliance cost expenditure is income for accountants, lawyers, revenue service employees and so on, and as such included in the gross national product.
64. See Arthur Hall, *The High Cost of Tax Compliance for U.S. Business*, Special Report (Washington, DC: Tax Foundation, November 1993); and James L. Payne, *Costly Returns: The Burdens of the U.S. Tax System* (San Francisco: Institute for Contemporary Studies Press, 1993).
65. Up to 3.8 times tax collected according to the so-called Kemp Commission Rapport, National Commission on Economic Growth and Tax Reform, *Unleashing America's Potential* (January 1996), 9.

NRST returns instead of corporate income tax returns. Since B2B sales would be exempt under a NRST, vendors need only to keep copies of their purchasers' exemption certificates and report only sales to final consumers, requirements very similar to those under their state retail tax systems. If the individual states were to harmonize their state sales tax systems with the federal sales tax (see Section 6.3.5), and taking into account the cost compensation envisaged under the Fair Tax Act, the NRST would hardly lead to additional compliance costs.

When introducing a national sales tax, it is essential to ensure that the prices of government services remain the same as under the previous income tax relative to similar services provided by the private sector. The NRST creates neutral taxation of public and private production because the tax is the same on private and public production (i.e., consumers must pay the tax on any private goods they purchase and on any production by the state and local governments), whereas taxes are generally paid only on private consumption and production today.

Under the Fair Tax Act, a progressive income tax is being replaced by a flat-rate sales tax. In principle, a sales tax affects decisions to work (the labor/leisure choice) much like the income tax because the tax is imposed on items purchased with earnings but is not levied on leisure. However, as a result of the replacement of an income tax by a sales tax, the marginal tax rate is increased for low-income taxpayers and reduced for high-income groups. In so far as these groups have different work elasticities with respect to after-tax wages, this could affect work effort. Moreover, work will increase if future consumption is complementary with leisure, which seems reasonable if future consumption is thought of as occurring during retirement. However, though these two price effects might encourage more work, the income effect of being able to save more easily for retirement should reduce work effort. Once combined, these offsetting influences probably have a modest effect, if any, on total work effort.

Relative prices of goods and services would remain unchanged by the introduction of the NRST because the tax is imposed on all consumption.

6.3.4. Effects on Federal/State Relationship

Implementation of a NRST would have a variety of consequences for state and local governments.[66] Currently, the state income taxes are harmonized with their federal counterparts in the sense that they apply similar definitions and interpretations in structuring and administering their systems. This common basis would disappear with the elimination of the federal income tax, which would lead to

66. U.S. Joint Committee on Taxation, *Impact on State and Local Governments and Tax-Exempt Organizations of Replacing the Federal Income Tax* (Washington, DC: U.S. Government Printing Office, 1996); Robert P. Strauss, "Federal Consumption Taxes: Implications for the State and Local Sector," *Tax Notes* (22 February 1999): 1173–1190; William F. Fox & Matthew N. Murray, "A National Retail Sales Tax: Consequences for the States," paper presented at the Symposium on Federal Tax Reform and the States (Washington, DC: National Press Club, 13 May 2005).

increasing disparities and variation among state systems and, as a result, higher compliance costs for businesses. Elimination of the IRS would also make it extraordinarily difficult for the states to enforce their income taxes because they rely on cooperation and information-sharing agreements with the IRS, which is essential regarding taxpayers with a multistate presence. New compacts must be formed between the states as is done for sales tax, at least to a considerable extent, through the Multistate Tax Commission (MTC). States could also eliminate their income taxes and conform their sales taxes to the NRST, in which case the combined tax rate would be much higher than under the current proposal (see the next section).

State policymakers perceive a federal retail tax as an intrusion into a traditional state tax source and they fear pressure to conform their state and local tax systems. In other words, the introduction of the NRST may strain the relationships in the federal system. However, the NRST would also establish a new model of cooperation between the federal and state governments because the state would administer the national retail tax on the federal government's behalf.

State and local government costs would rise due to the payment of NRST to the federal government on inputs, the largest increase of tax burden being encountered by states with the largest public sectors. The costs in monetary terms would depend on the statutory exclusive tax rate, but at the rate suggested by the sponsors of the bill, state and local governments would pay just over USD 300 billion to the federal government. In comparison, the total nationwide revenue generated by state sales and use taxes for the year 2006 was USD 330 billion.[67] Capital costs would rise as well because state and local debt would automatically lose its tax-exempt status with the elimination of the federal income tax.

6.3.5. Rate for the NRST

Several studies have been conducted to arrive at a budget neutral NRST rate by taking the quotient of current tax revenues (of the taxes to be replaced) and an estimate of the NRST base. One critical consideration is the tax rate that would be required to maintain government programs at current levels. If government purchases of goods and services are themselves subject to taxation, then the nominal revenues required to fund these purchases will also increase. In other words, a sales tax that merely replaces current nominal tax revenues will be insufficient to fund existing government programs at a level that is unchanged in real terms. Tax rate calculations also depend on whether the monetary authority will hold the consumer price level constant or will allow it to increase by the amount of the NRST. Under a constant consumer price scenario, the producer price level will fall, following the tax reform, shrinking the tax base.

67. Source: US Bureau of Census, Governmental Finances, 2006.

Government transfer-payment programs will also be affected by the introduction of a NRST, requiring a higher amount of funding in order to hold the real purchasing power of the transfers constant.[68]

To avoid confusion, it is also important to determine whether the rate quoted is on a tax-inclusive or tax-exclusive basis. Tax-inclusive rates equal the percentage by which the net-of-price is below the gross-of-tax price. However, tax-exclusive rates measure the percentage by which the gross-of-tax price exceeds the net-of-tax price. Current income taxes and the proposed flat tax are imposed on a tax-inclusive basis, whereas the state sales taxes and the VATs in most countries are imposed on a tax-exclusive basis. If someone pays USD 20 in tax on an income of USD 100, the tax-inclusive tax rate would be 20% (20/100 × 100), but the tax-exclusive tax rate would be 25% (20/80 × 100). To be consistent, sales tax rates in this section will be quoted on a tax-exclusive basis.

In calculating the NRST rate that would replace the revenues generated by the current federal income tax and payroll tax systems, it is not legitimate to simply divide current tax revenues by current consumption expenditures. Taking into account the aforementioned factors as well as a reasonable assumption of base erosion,[69] calculations in academic research for the appropriate tax rate range between 35% and 40%, and some scholars believe that the rate may reach the 60% level if all payroll taxes are to be replaced as well.[70] This is much more than quoted by the supporters of the fair tax proposals, who quote a 23% tax inclusive tax rate, which is 30% on a tax-exclusive basis. The lack of professional consensus regarding the appropriate posttax reform rate makes the policy debate confusing, fuzzy and uncertain.

If the states were to decide to conform their sales taxes to the new NRST, the combined rate would be higher. The existing weighted-average state and local tax rate is about 7%. Conforming to the NRST would double the state and local tax base from about 40% currently to about 80% (corrected for a 20% base erosion) and in effect reduce the average tax rate. However, the states and local governments need to raise additional income to finance the federal NRST incurred by

68. Only in the case where the prereform, tax-exclusive income tax rate would exactly match the postreform sales tax rate will it be possible to hold the real purchasing power of transfers constant by holding nominal transfer-payment spending constant.
69. It is virtually impossible to achieve tax to be collected on 100% of the tax base due to political concessions and avoidance and evasion. Most scholars assume a base erosion of 20%. By comparison, only about 40% of consumption is taxed under the current state sales and use tax systems, an erosion of nearly or just over 60%.
70. Alan J. Auerbach, Laurence J. Kotlikoff, Kent Smetters & Jan Walliser, *Fundamental Tax Reform and Macroeconomic Performance*, in Joint Committee on Taxation Tax Modeling Project and 1997 Tax Symposium Papers (Washington, DC: US Government Printing Office, 1997); William G. Gale, "The Required Tax Rate in a National Sales Tax," *National Tax Journal* 52 (3) (1999): 443–458; and Evan F. Koenig, "Achieving 'Program Neutrality' under a National Retail Sales Tax," *National Tax Journal* 52 (4) (1999): 683–698.

them on their inputs, which would lead to an increase of the average tax rate.[71] These offsetting effects seem to balance out at a federal NRST rate of about 33%. Taken together, a combined state and federal NRST would require an exclusive tax rate ranging between 37% and roughly 50%, depending on which calculation method one prefers to accept. Of course, rates would vary considerably among states, depending on the arithmetic sum of the state's current reliance on sales taxes and the payments that the state must make for the federal NRST,[72] divided by the nonstate and local government NRST base in the state.

6.3.6. Tax Avoidance and Evasion Effects

Under general perception, there exists a correlation between tax avoidance and evasion on the one hand, and the rate of taxation on the other hand. Low tax rates trigger none or only limited avoidance behavior among taxpayers and high tax rates make avoidance and evasion particularly attractive. Both taxpayers and tax policymakers are caught in a cost-benefit analysis. At low rates, the potential costs of interest and penalties may prevent taxpayers from engaging in tax evasion schemes. At high rates, the potential benefits may outweigh the adverse risks of interest and penalty payments. Policymakers find themselves at the flipside of cost-benefit reasoning. High rates, naturally, tend to realize higher revenue but also trigger increased avoidance and evasion behavior. For policymakers, the art is to locate that perfect balance point between maximum rates and revenue on the one hand, and minimum tax avoidance and evasion on the other. If the NRST is to replace the federal corporate and personal income taxes as well as the payroll taxes, the required rate may be too excessive to sustain the threat of substantial tax evasion. A revenue-neutral fair tax would most probably exceed 30%, and combined with the state sales taxes, rates on consumption expenditure will be close to, and may even exceed, 40%. Incentives to underreport gross sales and taxes withheld would increase with the rate of the NRST, and successful evaders would have a potentially enormous competitive advantage over legitimate vendors. Basically, there are two risks: underreporting of gross sales and overstating exempt business inputs (including intercompany sales and exports). Under the state sales and use taxes, noncompliance, avoidance and evasion are found predominantly among small firms, and almost half of income tax shortfall is attributed to nonfarm sole proprietorships.[73] Clearly, a high rate NRST would encourage the growth

71. If states conform to the NRST base, the necessary state and local tax rate is assumed to equal the amount required to replace existing state and local sales tax revenues plus the amount required to finance the NRST imposed by the federal government on state and local government consumption and investment divided by the NRST base.
72. Which is a function of the relative size of each state and local government. Differences in the amount paid to the federal government are an important source of the cross-state variation in the required tax rate.
73. US Department of Labor, *The Underground Economy in the United States* (Washington, DC: US Department of Labor, 1992).

of the underground economy, especially in relation to direct sales of goods and services to private consumers, especially services with a high labor component, such as hairdressing and house painting. There is little empirical research on the volume of tax avoidance and evasion regarding sales and use taxes in the United States.

The only way to prevent and discourage tax evasion or to reduce its volume is a combination of strict enforcement through frequent and thorough audits and severe penalties. Although cross-reference audits with income tax statements will not be possible because the income taxes will be abolished, it is possible to identify high-risk categories of entrepreneurs and industries based on experiences with the state sales and use taxes and experiences with similar patterns of VAT evasion in the EU. In response, enforcement efforts and audits could be tailored to the specific circumstances of these risk categories.

The single rate NRST would prevent economic distortions caused by consumers substituting lower-taxed goods for similar higher-taxed goods, which can be viewed as a form of tax avoidance, an effect encouraged under the current multirate state sales and use tax systems. Nor would it be possible for consumers to relocate to a low-tax jurisdiction within the United States to reduce the tax burden on their consumption because the tax would be levied uniformly in the United States as a whole. Emigration to a low-tax country is possible. However, to the extent that individuals face roughly comparable burdens under the existing income tax versus a NRST, there is little motivation to change country of residence. This consideration suggests that any incentives to emigrate may be highest for the elderly. The reason is that the assets and savings of the elderly have already been taxed under the system of income taxation, and the introduction of a national sales tax would substantially increase their lifetime tax burden. But even the elderly would have little motivation to emigrate because they would likely be subjected to some form of indirect tax (albeit at a lower rate) in the new country of residence, and emigration also entails considerable costs.

Some international cross-border shopping, especially with Canada and Mexico, may likely occur. Foreign purchases would be subject to use tax in the United States under the NRST, but voluntary compliance levels will probably be low, given the current experience with use tax compliance under the state sales and use tax systems.

The NRST would most likely face problems with the collection of use tax due on distance sales, that is, on purchases of goods and services by consumers from mail-order and Internet sellers, similar to the collection problems of the individual states, estimated by some authors to range between roughly USD 20 billion and USD 30 billion for 2008.[74] Of course, since the NRST would be a federal tax,

74. Bruce & Fox, *State and Local Sales Tax Revenue Loss from E-commerce*, 5; for a general treatise on sales and use tax regarding distance sales, see van Brederode, "The American Debate on Taxing Distance Sales and E-commerce," 352–361.

tightening the nexus rules to include all sales of goods and services by foreign suppliers to US private consumers would not raise concerns under the commerce clause. For NRST purposes, the tax jurisdiction rules for distance sales to private consumers could be made similar to the ones currently applied in the EU for VAT purposes, in which case distance sellers would be required to register in the United States and remit the tax, beyond *de minimis* thresholds, to the tax authority.

6.3.7. Conclusions

The NRST is a destination type, broad-based consumption tax that would tax all final consumption. Because it would replace the federal income tax on a revenue-neutral basis, the NRST would have no impact on the purchase power of consumers. In a simplified model with no saving, there is no economic difference between a single rate income tax and a single rate consumption tax. The tax is either taken out before income is taken home (income tax) or is paid in higher prices after all income is taken home (sales tax). As long as the actual tax burden is the same, they will generate similar effects on behavior, and substituting the one tax for the other at the federal level would not lead to base narrowing and a reduction of revenue.

The NRST offers many desirable macroeconomic consequences. A level playing field would be established between public sector expenditures and private sector expenditures. Exports would gain a competitive edge because indirect tax can be rebated under WTO rules, whereas income tax cannot and would be part of the cost price of a product or service.

Introduction of the NRST would also lead to negative effects on state and local finances because they would be subject to the tax on their purchases, which would constitute a considerable cost, and the enforcement of state income taxes would become less viable with the elimination of the IRS.

States could decide to follow in the federal footsteps and replace their income and/or sales taxes with a NRST base tax. The combined tax rate would make the new consumption extremely vulnerable to tax avoidance and evasion. In the end, it will come down to an assessment of the overall benefits and disadvantages of the change to a national consumption tax, in combination with the overarching question of the political feasibility.

Chapter 7
Subtraction VAT

7.1. GENERAL

In Section 3.2.2.2, a direct subtraction VAT was characterized as a tax that determines value added on an aggregate level and over a certain time period by taxing the difference between total turnover/sales and total purchases from other businesses. It is accounts based rather than transaction based, such as the tax-from-tax, credit invoice method VAT. The tax base should be the same as that when the credit invoice method is used. The subtraction VAT does not create a paper trail by requiring invoicing, which is a disadvantage from an enforcement perspective. Moreover, a subtraction VAT can only be implemented at a single rate because the information necessary for determining the tax base is acquired at an aggregate level. A single rate limits the room to maneuver for policymakers, reducing their ability to appease constituents with reduced rates. This may explain the relative unpopularity of the subtraction VAT, which is currently applied only in Japan, compared to the credit invoice method VAT, which is used in about 150 countries. However, once a subtraction VAT is introduced, its inflexibility in terms of rate variation provides a certain degree of protection against changes in the law for the benefit of special interest groups. Table 16 demonstrates the calculation of value added under a subtraction VAT for a business generating USD 1,000 in turnover; purchasing for USD 450 from other businesses; and paying USD 20 in dividends to shareholders, USD 50 in interest to the bank and USD 250 in salaries to its workers.

The difference between gross business sales and deductible purchases is then multiplied by the tax rate.

Although there are differences between a credit invoice method VAT and a subtraction VAT in administration, and the calculation of value added, the revenue generated under both methodologies should be identical because the tax value of subtracting purchased inputs from the tax base is arithmetically identical to a credit for all previous VAT paid at the same tax rate on those inputs.

Table 16. Value-added under a Subtraction VAT

Gross turnover		1,000
Nondeductible costs:		
– Wages	250	
– Dividend payments	20	
– Interest payments	50	
Total	320	
Deductible purchases		450
Taxable turnover (value added)		550

7.2. THE JAPANESE CONSUMPTION TAX

Since Japan is the only country that applies a form of subtraction VAT, their system is of particular interest. The Japanese consumption tax[1] took effect in April 1989 and, although the tax base has narrowed since its adoption through the expansion of the exemptions, is a broad-based VAT levied at a single rate. The Japanese consumption tax is judged favorably by international experts for its functionality but is rather unpopular at home.[2] Earlier attempts to introduce indirect taxes failed,[3] and it required political maneuvering, an effective promotion campaign[4] and expedited enactment to pass the consumption tax law. To promote its acceptability, the tax was cautiously crafted with a low rate, simplified reporting and calculation methods, and an exemption for small businesses.

The Japanese VAT resembles a prototypical subtraction method VAT in the sense that Japanese VAT taxpayers are allowed to derive the amount of credit for VAT paid based on total purchases from domestic entities instead of adding up

1. Shohizei-ho (Consumption Tax), Law no. 108 of 1988, pt. IV. English translation in *Japan: National Consumption Tax Law*, CCH International, 1989. For a general description, see Alan Schenk, "Japanese Consumption Tax after Six Years: A Unique VAT Matures," *Tax Notes International* 11 (21) (1995): 1379–1393; Vicki Beyer, "Japan's Consumption Tax: Settled in to Stay", *Revenue Law Journal* 10 (1) (2000): 98–106; and Alan Schenk & Oliver Oldman, *Value Added Tax: A Comparative Approach* (New York: Cambridge University Press, 2007), at 41.
2. The government that enacted the consumption tax law lost the next election in July of the same year.
3. Japan had adopted a VAT in 1950 as part of its postwar tax reform but was forced by public opinion to repeal it before it came into effect. The memory of the defeat of this unpopular tax contributed to the failure of several successive governments between 1979 and 1987 to introduce any form of broad-based indirect tax. See Hiromitsu Ishi, *The Japanese Tax System,* 2nd ed. (Clarendon Press, 1993), at 316.
4. The government convinced the public that the consumption tax would help secure stable revenues in a time when the tax-paying population was rapidly ageing; see Vicki Beyer & Koji Ishimura, "The Progress of the Japanese National Consumption Tax," *Revenue Law Journal* vol. 3 (2) (1993): 117.

amounts shown on credit method invoices.[5] Furthermore, the Japanese VAT uses an annual accounting period: the calendar year for sole proprietors and unincorporated businesses, and the fiscal year for corporations. Annual returns are due, but depending on the size of the business, interim returns on a monthly, a quarterly or 6-month basis are required.

Domestic sales of goods and services as well as the importation of goods into Japan are subject to the tax, the rate of which is currently 5% (consisting of a national rate of 4% and a local tax rate of 1%). A further distinction is made between goods and services that are exempt with credit, mainly exports, and those that are exempt without credit, such as medical services, certain real estate transactions, insurance, certain financial and banking services, specified social welfare services, postage and revenue stamps, and burial and cremation services.

Small traders are exempt from tax if their annual sales remain below a certain threshold. As such, they are ineligible to recover consumption tax incurred on their purchases. They are allowed, however, to elect treatment as a taxable business in order to be able to recover tax paid on their inputs. For new businesses, except for medium or large businesses, voluntary registration is for a minimum period of the first 2 years, after which a business may continue the registration or elect to return to its exempt status.

Tax liability is calculated using a simplified subtraction method. A taxable business must account separately for its total sales and the amount of tax due. Then the amount of tax charged on its taxable purchases is deducted. In this sense, where input tax is deducted from output tax, the Japanese consumption tax applies the credit method. A business is required to maintain records to substantiate claims made, but tax need not be shown on invoices. As a consequence of this subtraction system, a business can also claim an input-tax credit for purchases from exempt traders who did not actually charge a consumption tax.[6] However, no input-tax credit can be exercised for purchases of exempt goods and services. For this reason, a business needs to make an administrative distinction between taxable and exempt purchases.

Businesses making both taxable and exempt (without credit) supplies can only deduct part of the tax paid on their purchases. They have a choice in determining input-tax credit eligibility on a per item basis or on a pro rata basis. The Japanese VAT also includes simplified rules for small and mid-sized businesses that allow them to calculate the annual consumption tax payable by deducting a formula credit from total output tax. The formula or fixed credit rate depends on business type: manufacturing 70%, wholesalers 90%, retail 80%, services 50% and others 60%. Special rules apply for businesses of mixed character.

5. The issuance of VAT invoices is not required at all.
6. There is some rationale for this because the exempt business may have included its own irrecoverable input tax in its sales price, which would thus be recovered at the next stage of the supply chain, but it would still leave an unjustified advantage in terms of a tax credit over the profit margin of the exempt trader.

7.3. SUBTRACTION VAT PROPOSALS IN THE UNITED STATES

The only OECD country without a federal level VAT is the United States. That does not mean its possible introduction has not been subject to discussion. During the past 30 years, many proposals have been made by politicians and academics to either replace or supplement the federal income tax,[7] several of which are in fact modified subtraction VATs, also often referred to as two-tiered consumption taxes. These generally combine a business-level subtraction VAT with either a yield-exemption (prepaid)[8] or a consumed-income (postpaid) tax[9] at the individual level.[10] The first two-tiered tax was the Flat Tax designed by Hall and Rabushka[11] and later amended by David Bradford's proposal for X-Tax.[12] Under a traditional

---

7. Concrete legislative proposals have been advanced for a national sales tax; see National Retail Sales Tax, H.R. 3039, 104th Cong. (1996) (proposed by Congressman Dan Schaefer, CO); H.R. 2001, 105th Cong. (1998) (proposed by Congressman Dan Schaefer, CO); H.R. 1467, 106th Cong. (1999) (proposed by Congressman W.J. Tauzin, LA); the Fair Tax Act, H.R. 25, 108th Cong. (2003) (proposed by Congressman John Linder, GA); S. 1493, 108th Cong. (2003) (proposed by Senator Saxby Chambliss, GA); and a European style VAT, see the Tax Restructuring Act of 1979 and 1980, H.R. 5665, 96th Congress (1979) and H.R. 7015, 96th Cong. (1980) (proposed by Congressman Al Ullman); The Revenue Restructuring Act of 1996, H.R. 4050, 104th Cong. (1996) (proposed by Congressman Sam Gibbons, FL); the National Health Insurance Act, H.R. 16, 106th Cong. (1993) and S. 237, 104th Congress (1993) (proposed by Congressman John D. Dingle, MI, and Senator Ernest F. Hollings, SC, to finance this health plan); and the War Financing Act of 2003, S. 112, 108th Cong. (2003) (proposed by Senator Ernest F. Hollings, SC, to finance the Iraq war).
8. Under a yield-exemption tax, income is taxed when earned, but the yield on capital is not taxed until it is used for consumption.
9. Under a consumed-income tax, income and interest earned on that income is not taxed unless it is consumed. These types of taxes are also called cash flow taxes because tax is only imposed when money flows out of investment and into consumption.
10. Freedom and Fairness Restoration Act of 1994, H.R. 4585, 103rd Cong. (1994) (proposed by Congressman Richard K. Armey, TX); the Flat Tax, S. 488, 104th Cong. (1995) (proposed by Senator Arlen Spector, PA); the Tax Simplification Act of 2003, H.R. 3060, 108th Cong. (2003) and S. 1040, 108th Congress (2003) (proposed by Congressman Nick Smith, MI, and Senator Richard C. Shelby, AL); the Flat Tax Act of 2003, S. 907, 108th Cong. (2003) (proposed by Senator Arlen Spector, PA); these proposals are for a business-level subtraction VAT with a yield-exemption (prepaid) type consumption tax at the individual level.

    The USA Tax of 1995, S. 722, 104th Cong. (1995) (proposed by Senators Sam Nunn, GA, and Pete V. Domenici, NM); the Simplified USA Tax of 2003, H.R. 269, 108th Cong. (2003) (proposed by Congressman Phil English, PA); these proposals are for a business-level subtraction VAT with a consumed income type (postpaid) consumption tax at the individual level.
11. Robert E. Hall & Alvin Rabushka, *The Flat Tax* (Stanford, CA: Hoover Institution Press, 1995).
12. David Bradford has written extensively on this subject. The foundation for his work can be found in his study for the US Treasury Department, *Blueprints for Basic Tax Reform,* 2nd ed. (Washington, DC; US Treasury Department, 1984) and many publications since; most recently, David Bradford, *The X Tax in the World Economy*, 3, 5 CSPS Working Paper no. 93, August 2003. <www.princeton.edu/~ceps/workingpapers/93bradford.pdf.>; and David Bradford, 'A System for the Twenty-First Century', in *Toward Fundamental Tax Reform*, eds. Alan J. Auerbach & Kevin A. Hassett (Washington, DC: American Enterprise Institute for Public Policy Research, 2005), 13–29.

subtraction VAT, the tax due is annually computed by multiplying the single VAT rate by the difference between the taxpayer's gross receipts and his deductible expenditures during the year. Typically, labor costs and return on capital are not deductible because they form part of the value added of a business. The innovation proposed by the Flat Tax and X-Tax is to allow deduction of wages at the business level but then to tax the same wages at the level of the individual wage earner.

Under the Hall and Rabushka Flat Tax, both business and individual income are taxed at a single rate, but the tax burden is graduated; therefore, progressivity is realized because the standard deductions allowed have relatively more value to low-income than high-income earners. As a result, higher-income groups are taxed more heavily than low-income groups. In this manner, the Flat Tax is able to counter the most important objection against the introduction of consumption taxes, namely that they would be regressive.

The X-Tax variant differs at the individual level by allowing more deductions, including charitable contributions and home mortgage interest; by accepting an earned income credit; by using the yield method for taxing savings and investment; and, last but not least, by employing graduated rates, that is, rates that rise with income, but only to a certain ceiling above which all income would be taxed at a flat rate equal to the rate applied for business income.

Alternative designs for a consumption tax in the United States apply the cash flow method to determine the individual tax base.[13] In other words, they combine the subtraction VAT for business income with a consumed income tax at the individual level. Under this approach, all income would be taxed when received, unless the funds are saved or invested.

Two legislative versions have been proposed over time: the USA Tax[14] and the Simplified USA Tax.[15] These proposals hinge on the unlimited ability for a taxpayer to use his income for savings and investments, and thus to postpone taxation, through the unlimited savings allowance (USA) deduction.

The two proposals deviate from the theoretical model. Under a consumed income tax, borrowing needs to be included in income whereas loan repayment is deducted from income.[16] The USA Tax allows individuals to save all new income and to finance all consumption through borrowing, thus providing opportunity to avoid taxation completely. In addition, savings predating the USA Tax can be used for tax-free consumption, while investing or saving current and future income. Under a true consumption tax, all consumption is taxed, regardless of how it is funded. The USA Tax departs from this model in that taxation depends on the source of the funds used for consumption. The USA Tax proposal tried to discourage borrowing for tax-free consumption through the application of Schedule S, but

---

13. Formulated for the first time by William D. Andrews, "A Consumption or Cash Flow Personal Income Tax," *Harvard Law Review* 87 (1974): 1113–1167.
14. *Supra*, n. 10.
15. *Supra*, n. 10.
16. Alvin C. Warren, "The Proposal for an Unlimited Savings Allowance," *Tax Notes* 68 (28) (1995): 1103 et seq.

that added significantly to its complexity. The Simplified USA Tax allows for a deduction of a savings allowance of current income only. In addition, it would repeal the estate and gift tax because these taxes are inconsistent with the imposition of a consumption tax. However, the Simplified USA Tax would allow for other inconsistencies such as deductions for charitable contributions, mortgage interest and certain tuition fees, which in fact constitute consumptive expenditure and should, therefore, be taxed.

One of the problems with federal tax reform is the inevitable coordination with the subnational sales and use taxes. None of the proposals discussed addresses this problem. In Chapter 11 we take particular aim at the complexity of tax coordination within a federal state.

7.4. THE MICHIGAN BUSINESS TAX

With effect from 2008, Michigan has replaced its SBT (an addition method VAT) with the MBT, in reality a package of four taxes consisting of the Business Income Tax, the Modified Gross Receipt Tax (MGRT), the Gross Insurance Premiums Tax and the Bank Capital Tax on Financial Institutions. For the purpose of this section, our interest rests entirely with the MGRT.

The MBT statute defines the tax base of the MGRT as worldwide gross receipts[17] reduced by worldwide purchases from other firms.[18] Deductible are materials, supplies, inventory and capital goods; the cost of services is not deductible unless purchased for resale.[19] For that reason, the tax is incorrectly identified in its name as a GRT. The tax is calculated at the aggregate level from the books and records of the business, but it is not a tax on gross receipts simply because total sales are reduced with the costs of procurement. For that reason, the tax can be classified as a (direct) subtraction method VAT (see Sections 3.2.2.2 and 7.1). This tax base is then apportioned between Michigan and the rest of the world using a sales-only apportionment formula.[20] The numerator of that formula is the total sales of the taxpayer in Michigan during the tax year, and the denominator is the total sales everywhere during that year, that is, Michigan sales divided by worldwide sales.[21] The basic rate is 0.8%,[22] increased by a surcharge of 21.99%,[23] bringing the total tax rate of the MGRT to 0.976%.

The Michigan apportionment formula uses unadjusted gross proceeds from sales, rather than sales reduced by purchases from other firms, in the apportionment formula. In other words, a specific purchase (input) is not directly allocated to a particular gross receipt (output) for the purpose of deduction; rather, deductions for

17. Mich. Comp. Laws Ann. s. 208.1111(1) (West Supp. 2007).
18. Mich. Comp. Laws Ann. s. 208.1203(3) (West Supp. 2007).
19. Mich. Comp. Laws Ann. s. 208.1113(6) (West Supp. 2007).
20. Mich. Comp. Laws Ann. ss 208.1301(1), (2) (West Supp. 2007).
21. Mich. Comp. Laws Ann. s. 208.1303(1) (West Supp. 2007).
22. Mich. Comp. Laws Ann. section 208.1203(1) (West Supp. 2007).
23. Mich. Comp. Laws Ann. s. 208.1281(1)(a) (West Supp. 2007).

purchases from other firms are allocated pro rata to domestic and to export sales, respectively.

Apportionment is required for the tax to be constitutional because without it Michigan would be taxing out-of-state consumption as well. Through apportionment the tax becomes destination based and it substitutes for the border tax adjustments found under the credit invoice method VAT.

Proper application of the apportionment rules require a definition of what constitutes a domestic (Michigan) sale, in other words, tax jurisdiction rules. As in all other VATs, a distinction is made between sales of goods and of services.

According to the statute, a domestic sale subject to the MGRT is a sale of tangible personal property where the property is shipped or delivered to any purchaser within the state based on the ultimate destination at the point that the property comes to rest regardless of the free on-board point or other conditions of the sale.[24]

For MGRT purposes, incoterms and contractual title transfer provisions are ignored and the physical flow of the product is the decisive factor in determining tax jurisdiction. Outbound sales, for example, under off-works terms are not taxable in Michigan if the seller can prove that the goods have left the state. Conversely, goods delivered outside Michigan for pick up, which are consequently transported by the buyer or on his behalf to the state, need to be considered as taxable sales in Michigan. Similarly, transshipments, that is, shipments of goods to and from the state are not taxable in Michigan because the ultimate destination is outside the state.

A reasonable interpretation of these rules would be that domestic sales only escape taxation if the seller knows the outbound destination at the time of sale. For reasons of practicality, over-the-counter retail sales in Michigan should be subject to the tax even if the customer takes the goods to his home in another state.

Services are taxable in Michigan if the recipient receives all of the benefit of the services in the state. If only some of the benefit is received in state, they are only included in the numerator of the apportionment formula to the extent the benefit is received in the state.[25] The law does not provide any further guidelines in this respect. This is regrettable because in practice there are many situations to which these rules cannot be applied easily or accurately. If a service is fully used or consumed in Michigan, clearly it will be subject to the MGRT, but some services are enjoyed over a longer period of time and others are difficult to allocate such as intermediary services. A practical rule would be to tax all services that are delivered by retail businesses, such as barber and hairdresser services, laundry and dry cleaning services and car repairs to name a few. Probably, a set of rules is needed to provide clarity, to ensure equal treatment and to prevent tax avoidance.

To be subject to the tax, nexus with Michigan is required.[26] Substantial nexus in Michigan exists if the taxpayer has a physical presence in Michigan for a period

24. Mich. Comp. Laws Ann. s. 208.1305(1)(a) (West Supp. 2007).
25. Mich. Comp. Laws Ann. s. 208.1305(2)(a) (West Supp. 2007).
26. Mich. Comp. Laws Ann. s. 208.1203(1) (West Supp. 2007).

of more than one day during the tax year or if the taxpayer actively solicits sales in the state and has gross receipts of USD 350,000 or more attributed to Michigan.[27] With this definition of nexus, the Michigan statute makes a reference to the criteria developed by the US Supreme Court in *Bella Hess*[28] and more specifically in *Quill*,[29] which I discuss in more detail in Section 9.6.1.3. For the first criterion, the statute does not provide a further qualification as to the nature or specifics of the physical presence but only provides a duration criterion. It is unsure, if not questionable, whether this is acceptable under *Quill*,[30] which requires that a physical presence is not *de minimis*. The second criterion for nexus is found in active solicitation of sales in the state above a monetary threshold, which can be satisfied without any physical presence in the state. If physical presence is a necessary condition for nexus, the economic presence standard would be unconstitutional. The question is whether the psychical presence test of *Quill* needs to be satisfied for other taxes than sales and use taxes. Because the US Supreme Court has not explicitly ruled on this issue, this remains unclear.[31] If the test is limited to sales and use taxes, the subsequent question arises as to whether the MGRT has sufficient similarities with RSTs to be viewed as belonging to the same group.[32]

The MGRT has adopted the concept of a unitary business. In general, commonly controlled firms – with the exception of foreign, that is, non-US, firms or domestic firms primarily engaged in out-of-state activities[33] – operating a unitary business are treated as a single firm, and all intragroup transactions are ignored for MGRT purposes.[34] This concept resembles the VAT grouping arrangements as applied in many countries with a credit invoice method VAT. The most important benefit from this arrangement is that it prevents tax cascading on intragroup services.

27. Mich. Comp. Laws Ann. s. 208.1200(1) (West Supp. 2007).
28. *National Bellas Hess v. Dept. of Revenue for the State of Illinois*, 386 US 753 (1967).
29. *Quill Corporation v. North Dakota*, 504 US 298 (1992).
30. See the comments of Michael J. McIntyre & Richard D. Pomp, "A Policy Analysis of Michigan's Mislabeled Gross Receipt Tax," *Wayne Law Review* 53 (2007): 1275–1319.
31. Opponents of this extensive view had some successes in the state courts, notably *Lanco, Inc. v. Director, Division of Taxation*, 908 A 2d 176 (N.J. 2006); *MBNA America Bank v. Tax Commissioner, State of West Virginia*, 640 S.E.2d 226 (W. VA. 2006), see s. 5.4.1.
32. McIntyre & Pomp, *supra*, 1303, hold that the similarity ends with the shared intention of taxing private consumption. I would contend that a retail sales tax is a close cousin to a subtraction VAT and, apart from the particulars of each state's sales tax, the main difference is found in single stage versus all stage tax collection, which is not a difference on principle.
33. Mich. Comp. Laws Ann. s. 208.1117(6) (West Supp. 2007).
34. Mich. Comp. Laws Ann. s. 208.1511 (West Supp. 2007).

Chapter 8
Credit Invoice Method VAT

8.1. INTRODUCTION

Like the general RST, the objective of the credit invoice method VAT is to tax the expenditure of private consumers. From an economic perspective, these taxes are equivalent. The VAT is imposed on each economic exchange along the manufacturing and distribution chain, and is collected from the seller who is assumed to shift the tax forward to his buyer as an add-on to the sales price. Business procurement is relieved from the tax by granting traders a credit for the tax paid on their purchases, which they can exercise against the tax due on their sales. If the input-tax credit exceeds the tax due on sales, generally, the difference will be refunded.

At the end of a tax period (generally a month or a quarter), a business will have to file a VAT return stating the total volume of sales and the tax due on those sales, from which the tax paid on purchases is deducted to arrive at the tax payable for the business.[1] In its simplest form a return would contain five boxes as shown in Figure 8.

The tax-from-tax methodology used provides an indirect way of approximating value added (see Section 3.2.2.3). Under this method of tax base computation, actual value added is never calculated; it is only the difference between tax liabilities on outputs on the one hand and inputs from other firms on the other hand that is computed. This system of providing tax relief for the business sector is fundamentally different from the one applied under the RST. Under the latter system, B2B sales are not taxed, provided that the buyer can show an exemption certificate issued by the taxing authority. Where RSTs are not collected until the final sale to the consumer, the credit invoice method VAT applies a fractioned

1. In case of multiple rates, a taxpayer, generally, will be required to differentiate sales accordingly, and it may be required as well to make a distinction between goods sold and services sold.

Figure 8. Simplified Periodical VAT Return

Total Sales	USD 500,000	Tax on Sales	USD 75,000
Total Procurement	USD 150,000	Tax Paid	USD 22,500-/-
		Tax Payable	USD 52,500

Assumptions: VAT Rate 15%
Sales: USD 500,000 (net of tax)
Procurement: USD 150,000 (net of tax)

collection system, that is, the tax is collected at each stage of the production and distribution chain, thus reducing the risk of noncollection for the taxing authority. In other words, under a RST, the tax liability is fully concentrated at the retail stage, generally perceived to be the most vulnerable from a tax administration and compliance perspective, whereas under a VAT, the tax liability is spread over each economic transaction, and the tax amount at risk is, therefore, smaller. However, the distribution of tax collection over the entire production process, as under the VAT, subjects many more transactions to tax and thus creates more opportunities for tax fraud. Under a RST, the taxing authority can also concentrate its auditing effort to a single stage, instead of spreading its resources (thin) over many more businesses. The problem lies primarily with small traders because large corporations, which make the vast majority of sales at the retail level,[2] are more likely to comply. Under either tax, the benefit of underreporting sales can be measured by the product of the tax rate and the amount not reported.[3]

Because businesses are relieved from the tax on their inputs through the credit system, accumulation of tax has been avoided. In principle, full expensing of the input VAT is allowed, which would classify the credit invoice VAT as a

2. Eighty seven percent of sales in the wholesale and retail trade sector are made by corporations with receipts of USD 1 million or more. According to Peter Mieszkowski and Michael Palumbo, "Is a National Retail Sales Tax Administrable? A Proposal for a Hybrid NRST," manuscript, Rice University, 1999, cited in George R. Zodrow, "The Sales Tax, the VAT, and Taxes in Between – or, Is the Only Good NRST a 'VAT in Drag'?," *National Tax Journal* 52 (3) (1999): 429–442. They also provide data indicating that the likelihood of tax evasion declines with firm size.
3. Provided that all tax credits are claimed under the VAT.

consumption type VAT. However, in most, if not all, countries real estate and durable moveable capital goods are subject to a form of pro rata temporis deduction system (see Sections 8.2.7.2.4 and 8.2.7.3), thus incorporating an element of the income type VAT into the deduction system. The tax qualifies, therefore, as an all stage tax, noncumulative, consumption type VAT. Since the tax credit is based and depends on an invoice issued by the seller, the system is commonly referred to as credit invoice method VAT.[4]

The invoice is the crux of the VAT system, but it is paradoxically also its Achilles heel. In order to qualify as an input-VAT credit, the tax needs to be stated on an invoice that meets the statutory standards and requirements. Where an invoice is absent (or incomplete), the purchasing business cannot exercise his right to deduct the VAT paid to the seller. The invoice has a direct monetary value for the buyer, and it is expected, for that very reason, that the latter will insist on the issuance of one. In this manner a paper trail is created allowing the taxing authority to check and control the correctness of input-VAT credit claimed and VAT due and VAT payable declared. Since at each stage the producer or distributor reclaims VAT paid on inputs, there is less (but not zero) incentive to evade. Therefore, it has been claimed that the credit invoice method VAT is self-enforcing or self-policing in nature, reducing the potential for evasion.[5] However, the built-in policing that the invoice method claims to provide is debatable. Even on transactions between registered traders, a buyer has, indeed, an incentive to ensure that an invoice is issued but none to ensure that tax is indeed paid. Moreover, such cross-checks by the taxing authority can only be made by first tracing all invoices issued by a trader when corresponding claims for repayment of input tax are made by any of the other registered taxpayers,[6] and then matching the totals of these to that trader's declared output, a task that is clearly impossible.[7] The experience with cross-border (carousel) fraud clearly demonstrates the limitations of the checks and controls of the invoice system (see Section 9.7). There exists not much research on VAT compliance. From the few studies that have been published, it appears that VAT evasion is widespread and involves significant revenue losses, though the extent varies considerably across countries. For the Netherlands it has been estimated that 34% of businesses actually evade VAT.[8] Of audited

4. Although other names are used instead, such as tax from tax method and tax deduction method.
5. See, for example, Ben Terra, *Sales Taxation: The Case of Value Added Tax in the European Community* Series on International Taxation, no. 8 (Deventer-Boston: Kluwer, 1988), at 38; and Joel Slemrod, "Which Is the Simplest Tax System of Them All?," in *Economic Effects of Fundamental Tax Reform,* eds. Henry J. Aaron & William G. Gale (Washington, DC: The Brookings Institution, 1996).
6. For example, at the start of the year 2007, 1,956.800 businesses were registered for VAT in the United Kingdom; see Department for Business Enterprise and Regulatory Reform, URN 07/111, 14 November 2007. <http://stats.berr.gov.uk/ed/vat/index.htm>
7. Richard Hemmings & John A. Kay, "The United Kingdom," in *The Value-added Tax: Lessons from Europe*, ed. Henry J. Aaron (Washington, DC: The Brookings Institute, 1981).
8. Sybren Cnossen, "The Netherlands," in *The Value-added Tax: Lessons from Europe,* ed. Henry J. Aaron (Washington, DC: The Brookings Institute, 1981).

French taxpayers, 66% have underreported the value of taxable sales (and about 17% did so fraudulently), and 40% had overstated the value of their creditable inputs.[9] In terms of revenue loss, studies suggest variations from 3% for France and the UK to 40% for Italy.[10] Tax evasion is a complex matter and is driven by more than short-term monetary gain, and depends also on chances of apprehension and punishment; audit probabilities; level of punishment; public embarrassment; the perceived fairness of a tax; dissatisfaction with the tax authorities; the perceived efficiency of a tax; the behavior of other taxpayers, notably direct competitors, whether real or perceived; and identification with community responsibilities. Behavioral studies may help in developing policies and approaches, fine-tuned to encourage compliance.[11]

The features of the credit invoice VAT are remarkably similar all over the world. The tax is broad based, including both the supply of goods and services. VAT is imposed on supplies made by registered businesses and, generally, small traders, that is, traders with annual turnovers below a certain threshold, are relieved from the obligation to register but are allowed to do so if this is more advantageous to them. Business purchases are relieved from the tax through a tax credit deductible from tax due on sales. All VATs apply the destination principle (see Section 9.1.2), that is, exports are relieved from tax through the application of the zero rate (see Section 9.4), and imports are taxed at the same rate as like domestic products to ensure a level playing field for goods and services produced domestically or, in other words, to ensure external neutrality (see Section 4.5). Most VAT systems have multiple positive rates, but more recently designed VAT systems, basically modifications of the European model VAT,[12] such as those of New Zealand, Australia and South Africa, generally, apply only one rate. Moreover, VAT systems often contain multiple exemptions, whereas the modified VATs have far fewer and much more tightly targeted exemptions. These differences hold a direct influence on key elements of a VAT. A lesser number of rates and exemptions will lead to lower administrative and compliance costs incurred by the taxing authority and businesses respectively, increased economic efficiency, increased ability to raise revenue and a lower overall rate for a VAT.

---

9. D. Duverne, "Coordinate Audits of Income Tax and VAT," presented at the Conference on Administrative Aspects of a Value-added Tax (Washington, DC, October 1990).
10. Ali Agha, Jonathan Haughton, "Designing VAT Systems: Some Efficiency Considerations," *Review of Economics and Statistics* 78 (2) (1996): 303–308.
11. See, for example, the effort by Paul Webley, Caroline Adams & Henk Elffers, *Value Added Tax Compliance,* paper presented at the conference Behavioral Public Finance: Towards a New Agenda, University of Michigan Business School (Ann Arbor, 23 April 2004–24 April 2004).
12. Some (Liam Ebrill et al., *The Modern VAT*, [Washington, DC: IMF, 2001]) present the VAT as developed by New Zealand as the modern VAT opposed to the traditional EU-VAT. It seems to me that such a distinction exaggerates the differences because New Zealand, and other countries following its lead, have, in fact, developed only an improved version of the EU model VAT, removing or reducing the disadvantages caused by multiple rates and extensive exemptions. In terms of efficiency, the New Zealand VAT is clearly superior, but others following its lead have remained within the bandwidth of EU-VATs efficiency rates, see s. 4.6.

In the following sections we take a closer look at several areas that are of concern from a VAT design perspective, including rate variations and exemptions, the agricultural sector, small traders, financial services, the government sector, the treatment of moveable capital goods and of land and real estate, adjustments of input tax credit in the case of bad debts, postsale price changes, mixed use and change of use (taxable/exempt) of inputs, and the treatment of composite supplies.

8.2. PROBLEM AREAS WITHIN THE CREDIT INVOICE METHOD VAT

8.2.1. Rates and Rates Variation

Of 157 countries, mentioned in the *International VAT Monitor* as having a form of VAT, 116 applied reduced rates and 22 applied increased rates.[13] Initially, multi-rate VATs were the standard, but it seems that over time lawmakers are developing a preference for a single rated VAT. The majority of VATs introduced before 1990 have multiple rates. Out of forty-eight countries, twelve applied a single rate on introduction and thirty-six had multiple rates. In the period from 1990 to 1994, forty-six countries introduced a VAT, thirty-one at a single rate and fifteen with multiple rates. From 1995 to 2001, thirty-one countries introduced a VAT, twenty-five with a single rate and only five with multiple rates.[14]

Necessities such as utilities, food items and clothing are generally subject to a lower or zero rate; luxury goods are generally selected for the application of increased rates.

8.2.1.1. Rationale for Rate Variation

From an administrative and compliance perspective, a single rate VAT seems the most effective. In actuality, this means two rates because a zero rate will be required to ensure that exports will be released from tax to allow them to compete on a level playing field in foreign markets. But the zero rate on exports is simply a technical mechanism to accomplish this, hardly complicating its administration, and does not lead to rate variation regarding domestic consumption.

If one rate is preferred, why introduce a variety of rates? Formulated from another perspective, if the objective is to tax private consumption, why make a distinction between components of consumption and tax them at different rates?

---

13. Fabiola Annacondia & Walter van der Corput, "Overview of General Turnover Taxes and Tax Rates," *International VAT Monitor* 19 (2) (2008): 2–11.
14. Liam Ebrill et al., *The Modern VAT*, 20–21. Confirmed by the findings of the International Tax Dialogue, 2005, the Value Added Tax: Experience and Issues, prepared for the ITD Conference on VAT, Rome, www.itdweb.org/VATConference/Documents/VAT%20-20Experience%20AND%20ISSUES.pdf, 15–16 March 2005.

This question is more pressing because consumption is also subject to product-specific taxes, such as excises.

Generally, three arguments are made for tax variation. The first reason for the introduction of rate variation is the perceived regressivity of a VAT. Lower-income groups pay relatively more VAT measured as a percentage of their income because they have less opportunity to save. In Section 4.4.2, we dealt extensively with this issue and concluded that the VAT, indeed, is regressive when measured on an annual income basis, but that it is more accurate to measure tax incidence on a life cycle income basis, in which case the tax would be proportional. Nevertheless, the perception of the VAT being regressive is a political reality for lawmakers who, to an extent, need to appease their constituents. A related argument is found for the application of increased rates on luxury goods presumably procured by high-income groups in an effort to make the VAT somewhat progressive. The reasoning is that higher rates on certain goods are justified to achieve a more equal distribution of the tax burden on the basis of the ability to pay principle. The problem with this argument is its weak philosophical foundation and the practical difficulty of determining the ability to pay of individuals and households.

Second, lower rates are supported for goods and services perceived to be meritorious, such as medical supplies and education. The same argument is used as regards exemptions.

The third reason to introduce lower rates can be found in existing concessional rates under preceding turnover taxes, leading to political pressure to continue the preferential treatment under the threat of withdrawing support for the change of tax system. This was the case in Europe when VAT was introduced to replace the existing turnover taxes.

8.2.1.2. Effect of Rate Variation

Most countries combine a standard rate with a reduced rate for goods and services presumably primarily used by lower-income groups and higher rates for goods and services presumably enjoyed more by higher-income groups. Whether lower rates are an effective tool in combating regressivity is questionable. The tax concessions do not only benefit the more affluent in the same way but also probably to a larger extent because they spend in absolute terms more on reduced-rate products and services. Public transportation, for example, is in most countries subject to a preferential tax rate under the apparent assumption that low-income households make more regular use of it, but commuters from the suburbs taking the train or subway to the commercial or financial districts derive the same benefit from that reduced rate. As I argued in Section 4.4.2.6.3, relative expenditure on certain reduced-rate goods and services increases as family income increases. Moreover, in absolute terms, the affluent spend far more on food than the poor because they purchase more expensive varieties, go to restaurants more frequently and are more likely to throw away food. The same is true regarding expenditure on children's clothing, another category of products that is blessed in many jurisdictions with a lower tax rate. As a result, preferential treatment of food and other necessities provides the better off with much more tax relief than low-income groups. In this sense, lower rates can be counterproductive when used to combat regressivity or, in other words, they are economically inefficient. The tax revenue lost as a result of the inherent extension of concessions to the rich probably outweighs the tax savings to the poor from the concessions. As I argued in Section 4.4.2.8, it would be more efficient to provide direct income support to the poor in lieu of tax concessions in the form of reduced VAT rates. If no concessions were to be made, the additional revenue collected from the affluent could be used to fund income support for the poor. New Zealand has opted for the broadest VAT base possible and a single tax rate, combined with increased income support payments for lower-income groups to offset the impact of the tax on the poor.

Nevertheless, where the political reality makes concessions unavoidable, it is essential to select goods and services that are, indeed, exclusively used by the poor, or to limit the concessions in terms of volume. For example, water is a necessity bound for preferential treatment, but it makes no sense to subsidize water used to wash the cars of the rich or to fill their swimming pools. A low tax rate on electricity has the side effect of subsidizing the use of electricity by the rich for running their air conditioners, home theaters, wine cellar climate controls and other gadgets. Limiting the amount of liters of water or the level of kilowatts of electricity that are subject to the preferential rate would remove these excess subsidies, but up to that limit the affluent still benefit as much as the poor. Identifying commodities that account for a high percentage of the consumption budgets of poor persons is not as straightforward as one may assume because consumption patterns of the different income categories tend to change over time. As a result, the impact of rate variations is much less than expected. In addition, the identification process would require the allocation of limited resources within the tax authority that can be more efficiently used in administrating the tax and for compliance auditing. Rate concessions also violate the principle of economic neutrality in that final consumers may substitute standard-rated goods and services for those subject to a reduced rate.

Given a certain revenue goal, the use of reduced rates as a means of countering any increase in the tax burden on the poor is a cost to the taxing authority that needs to be offset with a higher standard rate. This will result in a wider gap between concessionally taxed supplies and standard-taxed supplies, which will mutatis mutandis exacerbate the economic distortions from inconsistent treatment of different types of supplies.[15]

Higher rates for luxury items are sometimes applied to reduce the regressive effect of a VAT or to even make the tax progressive. However, because they relate to only a small section of the population, their distributive effect is equally small. Moreover, where these goods account for only a small proportion of total consumption, they generate only little additional revenue but at significantly higher administrative and compliance cost.

Market prices are, in the end, determined by the elasticities of supply and demand. Therefore, it will be uncertain whether a reduced rate will benefit a final

---

15. See Richard Krever (ed.), *VAT in Africa* (Pretoria University Law Press, 2008), at 19

consumer or whether an increased rate will be borne by the purchaser of a luxury item. Traders will adjust their prices to what the market can bear, regardless of the tax rate of an individual product or service. Their only commission is to collect a certain amount of tax from consumers. Given multiple rates, they will juggle their prices to market maximization level, lowering some prices (ex tax) and increasing others, which may result in items with reduced VAT rates cross-subsidizing standard rates and high rated items.[16]

Multiple rates may distort both consumer and producer choices. Final consumers may substitute standard-rated or higher-rated goods and services for those subject to a reduced rate, thus undermining the purpose of rate variation.

8.2.1.2.1. Classification Problems

The choice of which goods and services to subject to a lower rate and which to a higher rate than the standard rate of VAT is, to a large extent, arbitrary and open to constant debate and dispute. Moreover, multiple rates lead to classification problems regarding goods and services on the dividing line of definition, such as children's clothing which is difficult to separate from clothing for small adults. Rate variation may also reduce voluntary compliance by those traders who are discontent with the treatment of their products or services. Classification problems may lead to extensive litigation, requiring the allocation of valuable and scarce resources in terms of both people and funds that could be used more efficiently elsewhere.

8.2.1.2.2. Recouping Effect

A reduced rate only has an effect on the consumer price if it is applied to the retail stage. I will demonstrate this by comparing the taxation and price flow in a distribution chain when only a standard rate is applied (Table 17) with a distribution chain applying a reduced rate at the final stage (Table 18) and with a distribution chain applying a reduced rate at the intermediary level (Table 19).

Table 17. Distribution Chain with Standard Rate

VAT Rate 10%	Sales	Tax	To Treasury
Producer 1	1,000	100	100
Producer 2	2,000	200	200 – 100 = 100
Producer 3	3,000	300	300 – 200 = 100
Wholesaler	4,000	400	400 – 300 = 100
Retailer	5,000	500	500 – 400 = 100
Total			500

16. Alan A. Tait, *Value Added Tax: International Practice and Problems* (Washington, DC: IMF, 1988), at 42.

At every stage of the distribution chain, VAT is levied at a single rate. The seller is obliged to collect this tax from his customers (outputs) and to remit the tax to the government. However, the seller receives a credit for tax paid on his purchases (inputs). As a result, a business will only remit the difference between the VAT due on his outputs and the creditable VAT on his inputs to the treasury. In this way, VAT is more or less levied on the value added of each stage. No accumulation of taxes occurs as a result of the credit system, and the total tax accruing to the treasury (the balance between VAT due and VAT credits) equals the statutory rate applied to the final consumption price.

Table 18. Distribution Chain with Reduced Rate at Final Stage

VAT Rate 10%/5%	Sales	Tax	To Treasury
Producer 1	1,000	100	100
Producer 2	2,000	200	200 – 100 = 100
Producer 3	3,000	300	300 – 200 = 100
Wholesaler	4,000	400	400 – 300 = 100
Retailer	5,000	250	250 – 400 = 150
Total			250

The retail stage is subject to a reduced rate of 5% where all previous stages apply the standard rate of 10%. The retailer charges USD 5,250 to the final consumer, where in Table 17 the consumer had to pay USD 5,500. The total tax received by the treasury is USD 250 instead of USD 500 under a single standard rate VAT system as demonstrated in Table 17. A reduced rate applied at the final stage will lead to lower consumer prices and to a lower revenue intake or revenue loss for the treasury.

Table 19. Distribution Chain with Reduced Rate at Intermediary Stage

VAT Rate 10%/5%	Sales	Tax	To Treasury
Producer 1	1,000	100	100
Producer 2	2,000	200	200 – 100 = 100
Producer 3	3,000	150	150 – 200 = (50)
Wholesaler	4,000	400	400 – 150 = 250
Retailer	5,000	500	500 – 400 = 100
Total			500

Producer 3 is taxed at a reduced rate of 5%. Producer 3 paid 200 in taxes on the procurement from producer 2 but is due only USD 150 on the sales to the next stage. As a result, producer 3 receives a refund of USD 50. The wholesaler, however, can only deduct USD 150 (the tax paid to producer 3) and, as a result, must pay USD 250 in tax. However, if the statutory tax rate were applied on the value added of USD 1,000 (4,000 – 3,000), he would have paid USD 100. The lower rate in the prior stage results in higher taxation in the next stage. In other words, the tax lost in the reduced rate stage is recovered in the next stage. However, in the final stage, the application of the reduced rate at the intermediary level has had no effect on the total amount of tax paid to the treasury, which is still equal to the standard rate applied to the final sales price. This phenomenon is called the recouping effect.

This is important because it demonstrates the importance of applying the reduced rate only to goods and services actually sold to final consumers; otherwise, the rationale for applying reduced rates, as explained in Section 8.1.1, cannot be realized.

8.2.1.2.3. Administrative and Compliance Complexities

Higher rates on luxury items and concessions provided through lower rates lead to significantly higher compliance costs for businesses and administration costs for the taxing authority. As a result of rate differentiation, businesses must segregate their stock according to the tax treatment. This is easier for large department stores and supermarket chains that can automate this process and amortize the initial setup costs over high volumes of sales. The burden of distinguishing between fully taxed, higher-taxed and reduced-taxed products and services falls disproportionately on small businesses, which are rarely as automated and which are forced to amortize the costs of compliance over a much smaller sales volume. There exists a direct connection between the increase of compliance and administration costs and the number of rates and exemptions. According to Tait, the Irish tax return form, while only applying two rates, already requires thirty-eight entries. More rates mean a greater change of mistakes and error by both taxpayers and tax officials, and increase the potential for tax evasion,[17] or at least reduce tax compliance.[18]

8.2.1.2.4. Conclusions

As a result of the recouping effect, a reduced or elevated VAT rate will only affect the final consumer price when levied at the retailer level. Most economists and even policymakers agree that a single rated VAT is the most beneficial and practical. Differentiating rates (as with using exemptions) is an inefficient way to pursue equity objectives. However, political realities often make the ideal of a single rate on a broad base hard to achieve, and many policymakers feel obliged to appease constituents with lower rates.

---

17. *Supra.*
18. Webley, Adams & Elffers. See n. 11.

8.2.1.3. Optimum Efficient Rate for VAT

As a general statement, a tax rate increase will lead to a corresponding increase in revenue. Likewise, a tax rate cut would lead to a corresponding decrease in revenue. The economist Arthur Laffer has pointed out that there are limitations to the straightforwardness of this statement.[19] Increases in tax rates cannot indefinitely increase government revenue. High tax rates reduce the incentive to work, whereas low rates improve the incentive to work. If all income were taxed at a rate of 0%, logically revenue would be zero. The same zero revenue would be generated, however, with an income tax rate of 100% because the incentive to work would have diminished completely. Tax rates naturally affect people's choice between work and leisure. Laffer's theory is that there is a point on the line between 0% and 100% where the tax rate will have reached optimum efficiency, that is, where revenue would be maximized without affecting the work/leisure choice of taxpayers. Any increase in the tax rate beyond that point would, contrary to the general statement, lead to a reduction of revenue, and any tax reduction below that point would increase revenue.[20] This theory is true as an approximation of reality only. It seeks to predict human behavior to the demand of work in reaction to fluctuations in the level of taxation. At very high rates there seems, indeed, hardly any reason for a person to work more because it would lead to only a marginal increase of disposable income. If tax rates are cut, however, this would not necessarily lead to the choice to work more hours. The choice could be made to offset the increase of disposable income with more leisure. In other words, a person may decide to work less while maintaining the same income. When the income effect of a tax rate reduction outweighs the substitution effect, then the tax base would actually decrease and revenues would fall proportionally more than tax rates. Whether a reduction of tax rates would lead to an increase of tax revenues depends to a large extent on the elasticity of labor supply. An increase of revenue seems only feasible when average and marginal tax rates are very high and when the tax cut is significant.[21] Under a progressive income tax, the behavioral

19. Laffer does not claim to be the originator of this idea. The concept was well known by economists before him, but Laffer has popularized the notion, which has encouraged proponents of tax cuts. The idea of an optimum point of income tax rate was known to John Maynard Keynes, Alexander Hamilton (see Federalist Papers no. 21) and has been described by the fourteenth-century Islamic scholar Ibn Khaldun in his work *The Muqaddimah.*
20. The reemergence of this theory begins with a restaurant dinner in 1974 that included Arthur Laffer, then professor at the University of Chicago, journalist Jude Wanniski, Donald Rumsfeld, then Whitehouse chief of staff to President Gerald Ford, and his deputy Dick Cheney. According to the story, Arthur Laffer sketched a curve on his napkin illustrating the trade-off between tax rates and tax revenues. Wanniski named the trade-off "The Laffer Curve"; see Jude Wanniski, "Taxes, Revenues, and the 'Laffer Curve,'" *The Public Interest*, winter 1978. For more recent discussions on the Laffer curve, see Arthur B. Laffer, "The Laffer Curve: Past, Present, and Future," The Heritage Foundation, Backgrounder 1765, 1 June 2004. <www.heritage.org/Research/Taxes/bg1765.cfm>
21. David Henderson, "Limitations of the Laffer Curve as a Justification for Tax Cuts," *Cato Journal* 1 (1) (1981): 47, calculates that for revenues to remain unchanged when a tax cut of

response, as predicted by Laffer, will be manifest in particular among taxpayers subject to higher marginal rates. Even if a tax cut is not self-financing, it would come at a reduced cost; in this sense, a 10% tax cut may, for example, only correspond with a 3% to 5% loss of revenue. Recent research has found that the tax relief in the United States provided in 2001 and 2003 has induced taxpayers to report more income, to the extent that this positive behavioral response has roughly offset 25% to 40% of the static revenue loss of lowering the taxes.[22] Other benefits of tax reduction exist, such as an increase in saving and capital formation, reduced tax avoidance and evasion and a possible production shift from the shadow economy to the real (i.e., aboveground) economy.[23]

In principle, a sales tax affects decisions to work (the labor/leisure choice) much like the income tax because the tax is imposed on items purchased with earnings but is not levied on leisure. The question arises whether an optimal tax rate exists in the sense of the Laffer model for a VAT. In other words, is there a rate above which consumers reduce their procurement or redirect their consumptive expenditure to the shadow economy? In case of an excise tax, by its nature levied on a single product, consumers may switch their preferences (under ceteris paribus circumstances) to a similar nontaxed product, for example, from beer to wine, but such a substitution is not possible when a single rate general consumption tax, such as a VAT, is imposed.

Research into the relationship between changes in VAT rates and revenues has shown that rate increases produce diminishing increases in revenues but not an actual decrease for any country.[24] For Jamaica it has been estimated that the optimum rate is 18%,[25] and another study based on data from a number of developed countries suggests an optimum VAT rate of 20%.[26]

Where high income taxes may persuade taxpayers to simply work less and shift preference to leisure, in relation to consumption taxes, such as VAT, it is most likely that high rates would encourage consumers to redirect their procurement to the shadow economy.[27] This is especially manifest as regards labor-intensive

---

10% is introduced with a current average rate of 30% and a marginal rate of 40%, the labor supply elasticity needs to be 1.25, or people need to work 8.33% more.

22. Robert J. Carroll, *The 2001 and 2003 Tax Relief: The Benefit of Lower Tax Rates*, Washington, DC: Tax Foundation, Fiscal Fact, no. 141, 23 August 2008.
23. Max Moszer, "A Comment on the Laffer Model," *Cato Journal* 1 (1) (1981): 25.
24. C. Silvani & S. Wakefield, "The Relationship between Tax Rates and Tax Yield," paper presented at the thirty-sixth General Assembly of the Inter-American Centre of Tax Administrators (CIAT) (Québec, May 2002). They investigated twenty-two cases of changes of the standard rate in twenty-one countries in Latin America and Europe.
25. Kelly D. Edmiston & Richard M. Bird, *Taxing Consumption in Jamaica: The GCT and the SCT*, ITP Paper 0414, International Tax Program, Rotman School of Management, University of Toronto, December 2004. <www.rotman.utoronto.ca/iib/ITP0414.pdf>
26. Kent Matthews & Jean Lloyd-Williams, "Have VAT Rates Reached Their Limit? An Empirical Note," *Applied Economics Letters* 7 (2) (2000): 111–115.
27. The average size of the shadow economy in OECD countries is 17% of GDP with the highest relative extent in Greece (28%) and the lowest in the United States and Switzerland (9% each). In transitional and developing countries, it amounts to 38% and 41% of GDP respectively

services, such as hairdressers and house painters. However, the literature on tax evasion and its implication for optimal tax theory has concentrated on income tax evasion. The issue of commodity tax evasion has received relatively little attention even though it is important in many cases, especially in developing countries. A 2003 study[28] tries to estimate the VAT revenue maximizing rate of VAT for the EU for given conditions of noncompliance and other shadow economy transactions. The results confirm that the efficiency of the VAT system declines as the VAT rate increases. The decline in efficiency is due to a mixture of a reduction in the VAT base, and VAT evasion and avoidance. It estimates a Laffer curve for the standard rate of VAT using a pooled sample of data of revenue statistics for 14 countries in the EU. The revenue-maximizing rate of VAT for given conditions of noncompliance is in the range of 18.0% to 19.3%. Countries that have standard rates above this, such as Denmark and Sweden, could increase their revenue by lowering the standard rate.

In so far as consumers would respond to high rates of consumption tax by substituting leisure for labor, it is noted, that one way to influence the choice between consumption and leisure is through differential commodity taxation, that is, by imposing a higher rate of VAT (or excise tax) on goods and services associated with the enjoyment of leisure, such as vacation home rentals and sporting goods. It is important, however, to take substitution effects into account when selecting the leisure items to be subjected to higher tax rates. A higher tax rate on vacation home rentals may require a similar tax increase for campsite rentals to prevent or at least reduce the effect of substitution. Higher rates should preferably be imposed on goods and services with a high degree of price elasticity (see also Section 4.4.1).

8.2.2. Agricultural Sector

8.2.2.1. General Background

One would expect a broad-based general consumption tax to include the agricultural sector and then feel deceived by reality. The fact is that agriculture in almost all countries, developed or in transition, receives special treatment. There are several reasons for this.

---

during the period 1999–2000, according to Friedrich Schneider, *The Size of the Shadow Economies of 145 Countries All over the World: First Results over the Period 1999 to 2003*, Discussion Paper, no. 1431, Institute for the Study of Labor (IZA), 2004, and "Shadow Economies around the World: What Do We Really Know?," *European Journal of Political Economy* 21 (3) (2005): 598–642. As far as the VAT is concerned, for example, Chang Woon Nam et al., *Is the Completion of the EU Single Market Hindered by VAT Evasion*? CESifo Working Paper, no. 974, 2003, estimate that about 10% of it was not paid in Germany in 2001.

28. Kent Matthews, "VAT Evasion and VAT Avoidance: Is There a European Laffer Curve for VAT?," *International Review of Applied Economics* 17 (1) (2003): 105–114.

- Distributional concerns are particularly prominent regarding the agricultural sector since a tax on food would be borne by consumers in the form of higher prices. Where low-income groups spend a higher percentage of their incomes on basic food items, such a tax is widely perceived to be regressive. From the opposite angle, when demand is inelastic, the tax would be borne by agricultural producers, in many countries a sector of low individual incomes.
- A related argument is that agricultural products are already exempt in many countries because they are considered basic.
- Especially in developing countries, most farmers operate on the divide of the formal and informal economy, making mostly direct sales to consumers.
- Even in developed countries, smaller farmers often do not keep records, which complicates both compliance and auditing. In a number of developing and transitional countries, farmers generally are less educated or, in other words, their illiteracy rates are high, which makes it basically impossible to require them to keep books.
- The agricultural sector depends not on the labor and capital factors but primarily on the condition of the soil and on climate.
- The strength, organization and political influence of the agricultural sector as a special interest group.

From a long-term perspective, most economists contend that this sector should be fully integrated within a VAT system with relief only through the small trader threshold (as discussed in Section 8.2.3). Where special treatment is unavoidable, at least short-term, zero rating agricultural inputs or a special regime to provide credit for the tax incurred on agricultural inputs, appear to be preferred in practice. In the next section, a closer look is taken at the credit system as applied in the EU.

8.2.2.2. The EU Flat Rate Compensation for the Agricultural Sector

The VAT is a tool in realizing the EU common market, especially the free movement of goods and services. As a general tax, the sale of agricultural products and services should be included in its base.[29] Traditionally, however, the agricultural sector had received preferential tax treatment because it was less developed than other sectors of the economy, especially in terms of technology, management and its fragmented structure in many small economic production units. To a considerable extent that situation had changed at the time of the introduction of VAT in the EU; however, it was felt that the modernization of the agricultural sector was not structural and integral in nature, leaving the financial and economic situation for the agricultural sector unchanged in many geographically diversified areas in the

29. ABC Report, General Report of the Subgroups A, B, and C Appointed for the Study of the Various Possibilities for the Harmonization of Turnover Taxes (EEC, Commission, Directorate General for Competition, January 1962), at 113.

future Member States. Moreover, farmers had no need for keeping books since they were exempt from the GRTs and were, in all states but in the Netherlands, subject to a flat rate income tax.[30]

The challenge was to find a mechanism to include the agricultural sector in the VAT while also relieving the smaller farmer from the tax burden.[31] In its present form, the EU legislation provides the contours of the special regime for farmers, but full discretion is left to the Member States to decide whether to implement this facility in national law.[32] Farmers subject to the regime do not charge VAT on their sales (outputs) but are, in turn, not eligible to deduct the VAT incurred in relation to their procurement. Their input VAT becomes,[33] therefore, a cost to the farmer as is the case with any other business making exempt sales (see Section 8.2.4). The exemption on their outputs enables governments to exclude farmers from all their administrative obligations, and there is no need for them to register for VAT and to file returns or keep books in relation to VAT. The EU legislation provides two different ways to remove the input-VAT costs from farmers. Farmers will either be directly compensated for the input VAT by the state[34] or indirectly by the customers.[35] The latter method is based on the assumption of forward tax shifting, that is, the farmer receives compensation for the input VAT incurred from the buyer of his agricultural products through its sales price. The buyer cannot recuperate this "hidden" tax. Tax accumulation would still occur when subsequent stages of the distribution chain have to charge VAT on their sales,[36] the price of which includes the nonrecovered VAT, creating a tax-on-tax effect. The solution has been found in providing a credit to the buyer of agricultural products and services for the forward shifted tax. This credit has the form of a flat rate. The flat rate is not determined on the basis of the input VAT incurred by the individual farmer selling the products but reflects the average input VAT, as a percentage of the sales price, incurred by all farmers subject to the special regime.[37] The Member States are allowed to introduce varying compensation percentages for forestry,

30. Research showed that the agricultural sector in the original countries of the EU did not have an administration and lacked the proper education and skills for adequate bookkeeping; see Vermand-report, Series Competition-Harmonization of Legislation, no. 24, Brussels, 1973, 69
31. For a detailed overview of the discussion in Europe and the efficient integration of the agricultural interest within the legislative and executive branches as well as the main advisory commissions and committees, which provided a de facto decisive influence on the policymaking process as regards this economic sector, see R.F.W. van Brederode, *De bijzondere positie van de landbouw in de omzetbelasting* (VAT Treatment of the Agricultural Sector), (Deventer: Kluwer, 1993), 71–104.
32. The special regime for farmers is not available in Bulgaria, the Czech Republic, Denmark, Finland, Estonia, Malta, Portugal, Romania, the Slovak Republic and Sweden.
33. Article 302, Directive 2006/112/EC of 28 November 2006, O.J. L.347 of 11 December 2006.
34. Only France has chosen for direct payment by the state.
35. Article 301, Directive 2006/112.
36. As nonfarmers, the successive stages cannot share in the special regime and will need to add VAT to their sales.
37. Not, therefore, the average VAT cost of the whole agricultural sector, see Art. 298, Directive 2006/112.

Figure 9. Flat Rate Compensation

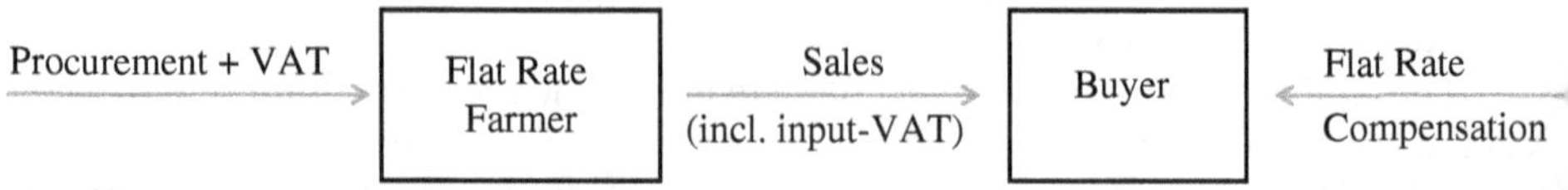

fishery and the different subdivisions of agriculture.[38] In this way, the nonrecoverable input VAT of the farmer is effectively removed from the distribution chain and tax accumulation is prevented as demonstrated in Figure 9.

The farmer's business customer is compensated for the VAT included in the price by allowing an input-VAT credit to the extent of the flat rate percentage to be deducted from the VAT due on his sales,[39] or will refund it.[40] All Member States allow farmers to opt out of the special regime and to be treated as any other business.

The underlying assumption has been that the introduction of the flat rate scheme was only a pyrrhic political victory for the agricultural sector. Like the Trojans who welcomed the Greek horse within their city walls unaware of the soldiers hidden inside, the flat rate farmers' scheme contains a poison pill that should eliminate the scheme automatically over time. The compensation reflects the average input-VAT burden of all participating farmers in a country. As a consequence, the rate will be too low for some farmers, who therefore would opt out of the regime to allow them to deduct the actual (higher) input VAT as any other business.[41] At the time of periodical recalculation, the compensation rate would then naturally become lower because the farmers with higher-than-average input VAT will have left the population. The new rate would, in turn, be too low for another group of farmers who would opt out of the regime, reducing the rate even further at the next recalculation, and so forth. In practice, however, the flat rate compensation scheme has not disappeared, and farmers make only sporadic use of the option to be subjected to the standard treatment.

The correct calculation of the flat rate compensation is crucial to avoid economic distortions between the Member States and to ensure that the EU receives its fair share of the revenue under the own resources arrangement.[42] Although the

---

38. Article 297, Directive 2006/112.
39. Article 303(1), Directive 2006/112.
40. Article 303(2), Directive 2006/112.
41. Spanish research shows that the VAT incidence on inputs can vary per type of farming from 1.1% to 5.7% as well as per region from 2.9% to 4.7%; see Tomas Garcia Azcárate, *El impuesto sobre el valor añadido y la agricultura española: unos primeros resultados* (The Value Added Tax on the Spanish Agricultural Sector: First Findings) (Hacienda Pública Española, no. 99, Madrid, 1986), 139–140.
42. Council Decision of 21 April 1970, regarding the replacement of financial contributions from the Member States by the community's own resources, Decision 70/243, O.J. 1970, L.94/19. From 1975 on, the budget of the community would include a certain percentage applied to an assessment basis, which is determined uniformly for all Member States. Although hidden in the

draft Sixth VAT Directive envisaged calculation of the flat rate for each country by the European Commission, the result of the political give and take was that the individual Member States would maintain their autonomy in this respect.[43] In some countries where the agricultural sector could exercise considerable political influence, the flat rate compensation was set at a rather generous level,[44] effectively removing the incentive of opting out of the regime, except for large, capital-intensive farmers.

Although the choice for a special regime for economic or developmental reasons is easy to understand and accept, policymakers need to realize how difficult it has proven to be, even in developed countries as those in the EU, to eliminate special treatment at some time in the future when conditions have changed. Therefore, special regimes should have an expiration date and should be accompanied by a strategic plan containing strict criteria to determine whether a regime should be continued or dissolved.

8.2.3. Small Enterprises

As a broad-based tax, it seems to make sense to include all taxable transactions, or at least as many as possible, within the scope of VAT. The broader the base, the lower the tax rate can be that is required to realize the revenue goal. However, in most countries, a small number of large businesses account for the vast majority of VAT collections.[45] The question arises whether it is worthwhile to include large numbers of small businesses into a VAT if they generate only a fraction of the revenue. On analysis, the issue is a bit more complex and contains several elements that need to be assessed individually as well as integrally. They are:

- the ratio between revenue generated by small traders and administrative costs for the taxing authority;
- the ratio between tax collected and compliance costs for small traders;
- the level of administrative sophistication of the taxing authority;
- the level of administrative capabilities of the taxpayer; and
- the access of small traders to the shadow economy.

---

national tax rates, this is a separate European tax in addition to the national VAT; see Terra, *Sales Taxation*, 74.

43. As a result, the basis for the calculation of the compensatory flat rate was not homogenous among the Member States; see Tait, 144–145, and European Commission, Report of the Commission to the Council (regarding the flat rate regime), Com. (83) 435 def., 12 July 1983.
44. For Germany, see Walter Hahn, *Steuerpolitische Willensbildungsprozesse in der Eurpäischen Gemeinschaft: das Beispiel der Umsatzsteuer-Harmonisierung* (Tax Policy Process in the EU: the Example of VAT Harmonization) (Frankfurt am Main, 1988), 187; for the Netherlands, see van Brederode, *De bijzonder positie van de landbouw in de omzetbelasting*, 169–174.
45. Liam Ebrill et al., at 117, give as a rule of thumb that the largest 10% of all firms generate about 90% of all revenue. Similar numbers are presented by Richard M. Bird & Pierre-Pascal Gendron, *The VAT in Developing and Transitional Countries* (Cambridge, 2007), 115.

The average administrative costs for OECD countries have been estimated at USD 100 per registrant and compliance costs at USD 500.[46] These numbers are averages for all taxpayers, and it seems reasonable to assume that these costs will be higher for the marginal taxpayer. Revenue is raised under the assumption that it is more beneficial for society as a whole when these resources are managed by the government instead of by the private sector. Including small traders in a VAT would only be rational if the value of the use to which the (additional) revenue is put is equal to or exceeds the amount of tax raised plus the administrative and compliance costs. Or, approached from the opposite angle, the decision whether to exclude small traders from the scope of VAT should depend on the outcome of a calculation consisting of revenue loss for the government on the one hand and reduction of administrative costs for the taxing authority and compliance costs for taxpayers on the other hand.

On such bases, gross turnover thresholds can be calculated below which a trader is excluded from the scope of VAT. If we were to ignore administrative and compliance costs, the accurate threshold would be zero because it would maximize revenue while minimizing distortions of economic neutrality between businesses of variable size. Balancing collection costs against the marginal value of additional tax revenues (given a certain tax base and rate) would arguably lead to rather high thresholds. On the basis of previous research and with corrections for inflation, Bird and Gendron suggest a threshold of about USD 100,000.[47]

Especially in poorer countries, but not exclusively, the taxing authorities have limited resources and skills, which means that they will need to make decisions about where to allocate these resources. In many instances the choice is made to concentrate on larger businesses that offer the potential of higher tax revenue. The crux, of course, is to draw the line between small and large businesses from an efficient tax collection perspective. Where limited resources are an issue, it may make sense to do this on the basis of the actual available administrative capacity of the taxing authority. The more capacity, the more taxpayers will be included in the scope of the VAT, that is, the lower the threshold. Taking the administrative capacity as a guideline also seems justified in light of the unfortunate experience in several countries of administering to too large a number of taxpayers due to a threshold that was set too low.[48]

A related issue is the capacity of the taxpayers to fulfill their compliance obligations under a VAT. Especially traders dealing with cash sales on street markets have difficulty keeping records of their gross sales.[49] Smaller traders

46. Sybren Cnossen, "Administrative and Compliance Costs of the VAT: A Review of the Evidence," *Tax Notes* 63 (1994): 1609–1626.
47. Bird & Gendron, *The VAT in Developing and Transitional Countries*, 115.
48. Albania, Croatia, Georgia, Ghana and Uganda report the low level of the threshold explicitly as a weakness of their VAT systems. In Ghana it is perceived as one of the reasons for the failure of the 1995 VAT, see Seth A. Terkper, "VAT in Ghana: Why It Failed," *Tax Notes International* 12 (1996) 1801–1816.
49. Tait, at 113.

also have more problems handling multiple rates. In addition, illiteracy[50] rates play an important role in determining whether to exclude certain groups of potential tax collectors.[51] Limitations in reading and writing capabilities will, as a consequence, negatively affect a person's ability to keep records and books. The highest illiteracy rates in UN and UNICEF studies were found in the less developed nations of Africa, Asia and South America; the lowest in Australia, Japan, North Korea and the more technologically advanced nations of Europe and North America.[52] This suggests that developing countries far more than economically advanced nations face taxpayer capability restrictions when determining the scope of transactions to be included in the VAT.

To an extent taxpayer, capacity to comply is in a balancing act with the administrative capacity of the taxing authority when assessing the correct threshold for small traders. In principle, both determine the threshold's minimum. In the same way as the threshold will depend on the number of taxpayers that the taxing authority has the capacity to administer to, it will depend on taxpayer compliance capacity because it makes no sense to include taxpayers within the VAT's scope that are unable to fulfill their obligations. Both the administrative and compliance capacity seem to correlate with the level of economic development of a country. A higher degree of economic development coincides with a higher literacy rate, a higher level of general education and, as a result, a more competent bureaucracy and, on average, more capable taxpayers. This suggests that developing countries need comparatively higher thresholds than developed countries.

Another restriction to including small traders in the VAT system is found in the possibility to escape into the shadow economy. The size of the shadow economy will differ from country to country, but it is likely larger in poorer countries, although it would be a mistake to underestimate its size and impact in developed countries. In developed countries, the shadow economy seems to have a particular attraction to labor-intensive service providers.

Businesses with annual turnover below the threshold should be allowed to register voluntarily to allow them to charge VAT and recover input tax when that is more beneficial for them, for instance, when they primarily sell to other registered businesses or are involved in zero rated export sales, or other sales at preferential rates. Without this option, competitive distortions may occur.

Views differ strongly as to the appropriate level of the VAT threshold, the level of turnover at which registration for the VAT becomes compulsory. Although most economists argue for a relatively high threshold so as to focus scarce

---

50. The United Nations (UN) defines illiteracy as the inability to read and write a simple message in any language.
51. Over the years, global illiteracy rates for the adult population (older than 15 years) have significantly dropped from 44% in 1950, 32.5% in 1978 to 16% in 1998. However, UNICEF predicts that the world illiteracy rate would increase in the twenty-first century because only a quarter of the world's children were in school by the end of the previous century.
52. Generally, only 1% in Western Europe, Australia, New Zealand and North America; between 3% and 15% in South and Middle America; and up to 52% in Bangladesh. Source: UNESCO, Institute of Statistics.

administrative resources on the most important taxpayers,[53] others believe that a low threshold holds a psychological advantage in fostering awareness of and compliance with the wider tax system. Both arguments have merit. However, when designing a tax one is limited by what is possible, not by what is desirable. It is inefficient to widen the scope of a tax to include a group of taxpayers for whom the collection costs would be higher than the tax revenue raised. Neither is it clear to me what the educational long-term benefit is when small traders decide to shift their activities to the shadow economy to avoid participation in and compliance with the very tax system they are supposed to be aware of.

A registration threshold can be perceived as discrimination against larger firms. The higher the threshold, the larger the incentive for a business not to cross the divide from being exempt to making taxed supplies.[54] The tax liability would reduce profits, so a large increase in gross turnover is needed to maintain the same profit level. This could also invoke the undesirable response by traders of underreporting their sales in an effort to stay below the threshold.

Most countries have introduced a threshold into their VAT legislation, which varies from zero[55] to more than USD 600,000.[56] Even within a harmonized VAT system of the common EU market, thresholds vary significantly, indicating the widely different views lawmakers hold regarding the correct level of the threshold.

The Netherlands offers a special regime for small traders, but it is limited to natural persons. Legal entities, such as corporations or limited liability companies, do not qualify for the facility, but partnerships do. However, eligibility is not determined by annual turnover thresholds, but by annual tax liability. That is an essential difference. Tax liability is determined by the difference between output tax on sales and input tax credit on procurements. Large businesses may owe a small amount of tax when their input tax in a given year is high, due to significant investments made, or because they are large exporters whose outputs are subject to the zero rate. The facility offers, in essence, a reduction in tax liability for traders with an annual tax liability equal to or lower than the threshold amount.[57] The rationale for the reduction is to provide financial compensation for the costs of tax collection, perceived to be a disproportional burden for small traders.[58]

53. Michael Keen & Jack Mintz, "The Optimal Threshold for a Value-Added Tax," *Journal of Public Economics* 88 (3, 4) (2004): 559–576.
54. This is also referred to as the poverty trap for small traders see Tait, at 118.
55. For example in Belgium, Chile, Hungary, Italy, Korea, Mexico, the Netherlands, Portugal, Spain, Sweden and Turkey. See Bird & Gendron, *The VAT in Developing and Transitional Countries*, Table 7.1, at 117–118.
56. In Singapore.
57. Article 25 (1) Wet op de omzetbelasting 1968 (Turnover Tax Act). The reduction is 2.5 times the difference between the tax payable (output tax – input tax) and the threshold but never more than the tax payable amount.
58. The argument has been made, on moral grounds, that all businesses, regardless of their size, should be compensated for the costs of their involuntary tax collection on behalf of the government. Otherwise, coerced tax collection would either constitute extortion, or be a form of taxation in kind that fails the moral standards of fairness and equality. See Robert F. van

8.2.4. Exemptions

8.2.4.1. Definition of Exemption under a VAT

VAT applies its own terminology. The general meaning of an exemption, in an economic sense, is that a certain supply of a good or service is fully relieved from tax. That is not the case under a VAT. Exemption within the context of VAT only means that no tax is due on sales of the exempt goods and services. However, tax paid on procurements (input VAT) is only creditable when and in so far as it relates to taxable outputs. Input VAT on procurements that relate to exempt sales can, therefore, under this approach not be recovered. Unrecoverable VAT becomes part of the cost base of the exempt business, and it is uncertain whether the exempt business will be able to shift the tax forward in his sales price. In this sense, the VAT is a paradox. A taxed business is, in fact, relieved from tax due the input-VAT credit system, whereas an exempt business is taxed because the credit system cannot be applied. Playing with the different meaning of the word *exemption* under VAT and in the general economic sense, we could formulate the VAT paradox as follows: those who are taxed are actually exempt, and those who are exempt are actually taxed.

So an exemption does not provide full relief from the tax. In fact, only the value added of the exempt business is relieved from tax, but all its procurements, including capital goods, are taxed. An exempt trader is put in a position similar to that of a private consumer. Exempt businesses are, generally, not required to keep records for VAT, which would simplify administration for the tax authorities and trader alike. However, no simplification will actually occur for businesses involved in both taxable and exempt transactions. Moreover, many of the book-keeping and recording requirements may be demanded anyway for income tax purposes.

In Section 8.2.4.3, the economic effect of exemptions is demonstrated on the basis of a numeric example.

8.2.4.2. Rationale for Exemptions

There exist only a limited number of arguments for exemptions under a VAT.[59] One group of goods and services are exempted for the purpose of combating the alleged regressivity of consumption taxes, casu quo to make the tax somewhat progressive. It does not matter whether the VAT actually is regressive, which is

---

Brederode, "The Morality of Coerced Tax Collection," *The Journal of Accounting, Ethics & Public Policy* (2009) (forthcoming). Interestingly, in the United States some states offer compensation to businesses for the costs of collecting sales and use taxes, see s. 10.3.8.

59. See, for example, Tait, 49–68; and Alan Schenk & Oliver Oldman, *Value Added Tax: A Comparative Approach* (New York: Cambridge University Press, 2007), 268–279.

questionable as we have seen in Section 4.4.2, but that it is perceived as such. Even if a VAT can be defined as a proportional tax in general terms, it may prove regressive in relation to specific goods.[60] Generally, goods and services that are primarily consumed by lower-income groups are selected for exemption under this rationale. Some countries choose to zero rate goods and services that fall under this heading. As we have briefly discussed, exemption does not really lead to a full relief of tax. Under a VAT, an exemption removes tax from sales (outputs) but does not allow recovery of tax paid on procurement made in relation to the exempt goods and services. As a result, these goods and services are still taxed through the nonrecoverable input tax. Only the value added of the business selling exempt goods and services remains untaxed, which, of course, is still a benefit for the final consumer. Under a zero rate, the sales are untaxed as well but input tax can be reclaimed, which leads to a larger benefit for the final consumer. In this category we find (children's) clothing, food, housing, public transportation and utilities.

The second justification is for goods and services that are found to be meritorious in the sense that they are in the public interest. In this category we find medical and veterinary services, education, cultural services, public broadcasting, postal services and services provided by nonprofits. Government services, depending on your approach, may fall into this category as well, and I deal with those separately in Section 8.2.9.

The last justification is found in certain goods and services being difficult to tax under a credit invoice method VAT, such as construction and real property leasing, to be dealt with in Section 8.2.7.3; financial services, see Section 8.2.6; and betting services.

The first and second justifications are used as well for the application of reduced rates when the choice is made not to exempt such a good or service.

8.2.4.3. Economic Effect of Exemptions

8.2.4.3.1. Recouping Effect within the Distribution Chain

In Section 8.2.1.2.2, we demonstrated the difference between a distribution chain where all stages are subject to the standard rate and one with a reduced rate at the final and at the intermediary stage. As a result of the recouping effect, a reduced rate at the intermediary stage has no effect on the final consumer price or on the total tax received by the treasury. The outcome is different when an exemption is applied at the intermediary level (see Table 20).

60. Such as fuel exclusively used by the poor. For example, kerosene in Indonesia and Tunisia and paraffin in South Africa.

Table 20. Distribution Chain with Exemption at the Intermediary Level

VAT Rate 10%/ Exempt	Sales	Tax	To Treasury
Producer 1	1,000	100	100
Producer 2	2,000	200	200 – 100 = 100
Producer 3	3,200	Exempt	0
Wholesaler	4,200	420	420 – 0 = 420
Retailer	5,200	520	520 – 420 = 100
Total			720

The sale of producer 3 to the wholesaler is exempt from VAT. The tax paid by producer 3 is not deductible because it is not related to taxable outputs and, therefore, becomes part of the sales price to the wholesaler. The wholesaler's price is higher than in Table 17 as a result of the nondeductible amount of VAT in the previous stage. The cost price of producer 3 has increased with the no deductible input VAT. In the next stages of the distribution chain, the nondeductible VAT forms part of the tax base. The aggregate tax burden on the final stage is not USD 500 + USD 200 (the original nondeductible VAT), but USD 500 + USD 200 + USD 20, the USD 20 being the amount of cumulated tax on the nondeductible VAT. This proves that the recouping effect does not work in the case of an exemption.

In other words, the exempt business's inputs will be built into the price and as such become part of the costs or inputs of the next trader in the distribution chain. Subsequent buyers cannot claim this built-in VAT as an input credit. As a result, part of the value added will be taxed multiple times, creating the same tax-on-tax effect or tax cascading that the VAT was designed to prevent.[61]

8.2.4.3.2. *Reduced Effective Rate with Exemption at Retail Stage*

The situation becomes different when the exemption is applied at the retail stage (see Table 21).

Table 21. Distribution Chain with Exemption at Retail Level

VAT Rate 10%/ Exempt	Sales	Tax	To Treasury
Producer 1	1,000	100	100
Producer 2	2,000	200	200–100 = 100
Producer 3	3,000	300	300–200 = 100
Wholesaler	4,000	400	400–300 = 100
Retailer	5,400	Exempt	0
Total			400

61. Tait, 30.

Because the retailer is exempt, he does not charge VAT on sales to the final consumer, but he also cannot recover the VAT paid to the wholesaler. The irrecoverable tax becomes part of the cost price and is shifted forward to the consumer. The consumer pays USD 5,400, which is USD 100 less than under a standard rated distribution chain, and the treasury collects less tax. The effective tax rate at the consumption level is 8% instead of the statutory rate of 10%.

In conclusion, when we compare Table 21 with the results of Tables 17, 18, 19 and 20, some striking observations can be made. A reduced rate at the intermediary stage of the distribution chain has no effect on final consumption price or revenue intake. Only a reduced rate applied at the final stage leads to a reduced consumer price and, consequently, reduced revenue intake. An exemption at the intermediary stage leads to a higher revenue intake or overcollection as well as a higher consumer price. Instead of USD 5, USD 500 under standard rating, the consumer pays USD 5, USD 720. However, if an exemption is applied at the retail stage, revenue undercollection is the result since the treasury receives USD 400 instead of USD 500 over the retail price of USD 5,000. As a result of the exemption the final consumption is in effect subject to a reduced rate.

8.2.4.3.3. Adverse Incentive of Self-production

Exemptions create an incentive for exempt businesses to self-produce goods and services in an effort to reduce their input-VAT costs, rather than purchasing these inputs from specialized firms, which ultimately leads to loss of economic efficiency. In other words, exemptions create an incentive for insourcing over outsourcing. Various degrees of integration will cause different levels of tax burden. The least integrated business will encounter the highest tax burden and will not be able to shift the tax (fully) forward, thus, it will have to absorb the tax in order to stay competitive. To the extent that a business absorbs the input VAT, the tax becomes in fact a business tax instead of a consumption tax. Insourcing can occur in many forms. An example is an exempt business running its own print division instead of using the services of a specialized outside contractor, or an exempt business building real property on its own land with its own personnel. VAT on labor and, in the latter case, on labor and the value of land would be avoided without countermeasures.

This problem is similar to vertical integration as discussed in Section 5.3.5. The countermeasures designed under GRTs are similarly applied under a credit invoice VAT. To discourage self-production by (partly) exempt businesses, the self-supplies are taxed and the exempt business is required to self-assess this tax and account for it in the periodical VAT return as a taxable output. Rules need to be developed to prevent double taxation in case certain elements of the self-produced goods or services have been procured with VAT from third parties. Either these elements need to be excluded from the tax base, or a refund needs be given for the VAT paid when the self-supply is made. Clearly, these special rules on self-supplies add to the complexity of VATs. In the next section we will take a detailed look at the self-supply rules as they are currently applied under EU-VAT.

Australia applies a special arrangement, the Reduced Input Tax Credit (RITC), to reduce the incentive of integration and encourage outsourcing, but only as regards financial institutions, by allowing those to recover 75% of tax paid on specified inputs.[62]

8.2.4.3.3.1. Self-supply Rules in the EU

The tendency to avoid tax accumulation by self-producing goods and services is not unique to VAT. A similar problem exists under a GRT and RST. The solutions to secure economic neutrality are similar as well: self-supplies are taxed (see Sections 5.3.5 and 6.2.12). Of course, there is no underlying sale when a business self-produces goods or services. Therefore, self-production is a deemed or fictitious supply, created by law for tax purposes.

Under EU legislation, Member States have the option to adopt self-supply rules.[63] Article 18 of Directive 2006/112 recognizes three situations in which Member States are allowed (but not obliged) to create a deemed supply of goods. They are:

> (a) the application . . . of goods produced, constructed, extracted, processed, purchased or imported in the course of a business, where the VAT in such goods, had they been acquired from another taxable person, would not be wholly deductible; (b) the application of goods . . . for the purposes of a nontaxable area of activity, where the VAT on such goods became wholly or partly deductible upon their acquisition . . . ; (c) the retention of goods by a taxable person or his successors when he ceases to carry out a taxable economic activity, where the VAT on such goods became wholly or partly deductible upon their acquisition. . . .

In addition, Article 27 of the directive contains a provision for the self-supply of services similar to the one for goods under letter (a).

The self-supply rule mentioned under letter (a), is not limited to self-produced goods but includes tax-free importation and production by a third person from materials provided by the customer. Therefore, self-supply would occur if a hospital manufactured its own hospital beds in an effort to save tax on labor, or when a flat scheme farmer built a new greenhouse from old materials, or when a contractor built a new wing to the hospital on land already owned by its principle.

The taxable amount for all these self-supplies is the purchase price of the goods or of similar goods or, in absence of a purchase price, the cost price, determined at the time when the application, disposal or retention takes place.[64] The purpose of the self-supply rules, as stated previously, is to prevent nontaxation of the items that are provided by the exempt business. However, in cases of

---

62. Peter McMahon, *Consumption Taxation and Financial Services*, vol. LXXXVIIIb, International Fiscal Association, 2003 Sydney Congress, Australian Branch Report.
63. See Joep J.P. Swinkels, "Scope of the Self-Supply Rule under EU-VAT," *International VAT Monitor* 19 (3) (2008): 175–181.
64. Article 74 of Directive 2006/112.

application as referred to in subitem (a), double taxation of elements that are procured with VAT also needs to be prevented. Under EU law, all the elements that make up such a self-supply are initially taxed. Double taxation, however, is prevented by granting a right to input tax credit that emerges in relation to tax paid on purchases from third parties,[65] but the total credit will always be lower than the tax due on the total value of the self-supply. For example, if an exempt business decides to erect an office building on its own land with its own personnel, it can deduct the VAT it pays on building materials and design, but it will pay the VAT over the total construction value including material, design, land and labor costs.

8.2.4.4. Classification Problems

As is the case with rate variation (see Section 8.2.1.2.1), the selection of exempt items is, to an extent at least, arbitrary and subject to political lobbying by those seeking preferential treatment or believing to be unjustly disadvantaged. Classification problems arise for those products and services on the borderline of definition. For example, the definition of medical services is not consistent among countries, and it is not clear whether chiropractors, acupuncturists and other providers of alternative medicine should be included. Classification problems may lead to extensive litigation, requiring the allocation of valuable and limited resources in terms of both people and funds that could be used more efficiently elsewhere.

8.2.5. VAT Adjustments

Commercial practice is never as straightforward as tax legislators would prefer. Because consumption tax collection piggybacks on commercial transactions, it has no choice but to take this reality into account. VAT is levied on transaction values, and where these values change ex post, this would affect both the output-VAT liability and the input-VAT credit entitlement. Values may change because of discounts or because of default on behalf of the buyer.

Input-VAT credit is only granted as regards taxable use of goods and services. Adjustments are required in the case of change of use, that is, when inputs are first used for generating taxable outputs and later for realizing exempt outputs or vice versa. Adjustments are also required when an input is used for both taxable and exempt outputs and the ratio between the components of the mix changes over time.

8.2.5.1. Bad Debts

Taxable persons under VAT serve as unpaid tax collectors for the government. From the perspective of the taxable business, the tax collected is a wash through.

65. Article 168(b) of Directive 2006/112.

A business, selling a good or a service, charges the VAT as an add-on to the sales price, and at the end of the tax period the business remits the thus-collected VAT to the taxing authorities. When the seller is a business that operates on a cash receipt basis only, VAT liability does not arise until the time payment is received, and bad debt relief is irrelevant from a VAT perspective. However, when operating on an invoice basis, the seller has to account for all VAT invoiced at the end of the tax period, regardless of whether the buyer has paid at that time. In many instances, there exists a time disparity between the points when VAT is due and when the buyer is obliged to make payment under the terms of the sale and purchase contract. Cash flow advantages and disadvantages arising from such disparities are part of the normal commercial risk of the seller. In circumstances where the seller accounts for VAT and the buyer defaults, the former will suffer not only a loss of the sales value but also of the VAT already remitted to the taxing authority. The question before us is whether the government should provide bad debt relief for VAT uncollected in case the buyer fully or partly defaults and, if so, to what extent and under what conditions. Taxing authorities are, naturally, cautious in reimbursing tax received. In the case of VAT, the invoice on the basis of which tax has been remitted by the seller to the taxing authority is also the basis for a legal claim by the purchaser for a tax credit. If the taxing authority reimburses the seller for VAT uncollected that is already deducted by the buyer as a credit against the VAT payable on sales, or has been rebated to the buyer in case total credits in the tax period exceed the amount of tax due on sales, the tax authorities incur a net cash loss.

From the position of the taxing authorities, the argument has been made that they do not choose their own debtors but have to follow the choice of a taxable business. In other words, the taxing authorities do not want to become the victims of bad choices made by sellers of goods and services. This argument has some merit but is overall not convincing because it has been the choice of the legislators to piggyback commercial transactions for the purpose of tax collection. By doing so, they also have accepted equally sharing the risk of default by buyers in a commercial transaction. In the end, it is a matter of balance of risks.

EU legislation provides for a reduction of the taxable amount in case of total or partial nonpayment,[66] but Member States may derogate from that provision,[67] which leaves discretion to the Member States as to the extent and conditions of such an adjustment.

In most jurisdictions, a shared risk for defaulting debtors has been acknowledged but not unconditionally. Before bad debt relief can be claimed, certain country-specific conditions must be fulfilled. Generally, the conditions will relate to the time frame for the relief request, the minimum age of the bad debt and minimum actions to be taken by the debtor to recover the debt prior to the relief request. Additional legislative protection for the fisc has been introduced in the UK and the Netherlands, for instance, by demanding repayment of a VAT credit

66. Article 90(1), Directive 2006/112.
67. Article 90(2), Directive 2006/112.

enjoyed by the buyer in relation to unpaid procurements.[68] Such a rule makes sense because it constitutes a direct claim by the taxing authority against the defaulter, and in most jurisdictions the taxing authorities will have a preferred position over other debtors in case of insolvency.

8.2.5.2. Treatment of Postsale Price Adjustments

A rebate, coupon or other form of price adjustment after the original sale is completed requires, as a consequence, an adjustment ex post of the amount of VAT due and the tax credit received by the buyer. In relation to sales between taxable persons, the most efficient way to account for these adjustments is for the seller to issue either a debit or a credit note to the purchaser, which has the additional benefit of creating an audit trail to verify the proper accounting of the adjustment by both seller and buyer. In the case of a previous understatement of VAT, a debit note is issued by the seller and additional output VAT needs to be reported on the next VAT return. The buyer can exercise an additional input-VAT credit on the next VAT return. In the case of a previous overstatement of VAT, the seller issues a credit note to the buyer. On the next return, the seller can deduct the overpayment from the output-VAT liability, and the buyer needs to deduct the amount from the input-VAT credit.[69]

A variation occurs when a discount is conditional on payment within a certain time frame; for instance, a 10% discount may be applied when payment takes place within 30 days. Since the grace period for payment in many instances will not concur with the statutory period for remitting tax returns, adjustments will be required at the time when it has become clear which price is actually received. There are two possibilities as to the initial position of the seller between which the legislator has to choose. Either the seller pays initially the tax over the gross sales price, thereby, disregarding the discount, or the seller pays the tax over the net sales price on the assumption that the buyer will pay within the grace period.

When the seller has remitted the tax on the basis of the gross price, and the buyer pays after the grace period, no adjustments are required. If the buyer pays within the grace period, the seller has remitted too much output tax, and the buyer has deducted too much input tax. The seller needs to issue an additional invoice for the discount as the basis for both seller and buyer to make adjustments.

---

68. Section 36 UK VAT Act 1994, and Art. 29 (2) Wet op de omzetbelasting 1968. The UK demands repayment where the supply has not been paid for within 6 months of the date of the supply or the due date for payment. The Netherlands demands repayment at the time when it may reasonably be assumed that the debtor will not pay for the supply, but in any event 2 years after the due date.
69. According to Schenk & Oldman, *Value Added Tax*, at 176, in case of an overstatement of VAT, New Zealand requires the seller to make the adjustment in the form of an input-VAT credit and the buyer has to correct his previous input VAT credit claim by reporting the adjustment as a taxable supply (New Zealand Goods and Services Tax, 1985, No. 141, s. 25 [4]).

When tax is remitted on a net sales price basis, and the buyer pays within the grace period, no adjustments are necessary. However, when payment takes place after the grace period, the buyer will lose the right to the discount. The seller has to pay an additional tax over the difference between the gross and net price (the discount) and needs to issue an invoice to the buyer to enable the latter to exercise his right to an input credit for the additional tax paid over the discount.

Rebates and discounts after the original sale to private consumers can be more complicated. The discount can be in the form of a coupon or voucher that entitles the consumer to obtain a discount on a subsequent purchase, which rather straightforwardly reduced the price of that subsequent sale and thus the output tax liability for the retailer. However, in many instances, the retailer will be eligible for a refund of the discounts he has provided to the consumers by remitting the collected coupons or vouchers to the manufacturer. The wholesaler is, generally, not involved in the rebate voucher procedure. Therefore, in the traditional chain of transactions, the sales price between manufacturer and wholesaler, and the sales price between wholesaler and retailer are not affected by the rebate. The manufacturer did not sell directly to the retailer but to the wholesaler, so the reimbursement paid to the retailer cannot, from a legal perspective, constitute a discount of the manufacturer's sales price to the wholesaler. The same is true in the situation in which consumers remit vouchers directly to the manufacturer and obtain rebates directly from the former. Nevertheless, from an economic perspective, the manufacturer did receive a lower price in relation to the sale of his product, and it seems that a correct theoretical result can only be realized when VAT legislation would allow the manufacturer to claim a refund of the tax included in the discount.[70] EU legislation, that is, Article 90 of Directive 2006/112, prescribes that "where the price is reduced after the supply takes place, the taxable amount shall be reduced accordingly," which seems to leave room for an interpretation as suggested here, but the provision is not specific on this point.

8.2.5.3. Mixed Use

A mixed business, that is, a business supplying both taxable and exempt services, is entitled to an input-VAT credit only in relation to taxable outputs. Therefore, a mixed business needs to allocate its inputs to the exempt and the taxable outputs in order to determine eligibility for credits.

A problem arises when a specific input is used in relation to both taxable and exempt outputs. In that case, a formula needs to be found to determine the percentage of tax credit. Normally, the formula will be related to the extent to which the input is used for either the exempt or the taxable outputs, but this is not always straightforward. The most common formula is based on revenue generated with

70. Where $r =$ rebate and $t =$ tax rate, the tax included in the discount can be calculated as follows: $r \times t/100 + t$.

taxable supplies relative to total revenue. The ratio between taxable and exempt outputs determines the percentage of input tax that will be recoverable, as follows:

$$\frac{\text{Turnover from taxable activities}}{\text{Total turnover}} \times 100$$

The numerator would be comprised of the total amount, exclusive of VAT, of turnover attributable to transactions in which VAT is deductible; the denominator is determined by the total turnover, exclusive of VAT, that is, turnover generated by taxable and exempt transactions.[71] This is not as straightforward as it may seem. Questions arise as to the inclusion in the formula of subsidies, turnover from incidental transactions, sale of capital goods and illegal activities, and turnover generated by transactions that are out of scope of the tax. To an extent this is a choice driven by the principle of neutrality and, of course, by common sense and practicality, but an element of arbitrarity will be unavoidable.

Under EU rules,[72] for example, subsidies directly related to the price are part of the turnover.[73] In principle, therefore, other subsidies will not be included in the formula. However, the directive provides Member States with the option to include subsidies not directly linked to the price in the denominator.[74] To ensure that the formula is sufficiently accurate, turnover generated by ancillary activities, such as sale of capital goods, incidental real estate and financial transactions is excluded.[75] It will not come as a surprise that the VAT directive does not provide a definition of or guidelines for when a transaction is incidental because it is virtually impossible to do so in any definite way given the factual and relative character of such an assessment. The EU directive does not provide rules for the apportionment of input VAT between economic and noneconomic activities. As a result, Member States have retained full discretion in choosing the appropriate formula.[76] A Member State needs to make a rather principle choice between including turnover from noneconomic transactions in the pro rata formula and excluding it. The reasoning for the first approach is that these noneconomic activities, regardless their characterization, form part of the business and should, therefore, be attributed to the taxable activities. The opposite approach seeks to eliminate any affect of the noneconomic transactions on the size of the input tax deduction. This requires a two-step apportionment procedure. Regarding input tax that cannot directly be linked to taxable, exempt and out of scope transactions, as a first step, allocation

71. See, for example, Art. 174(1) of Directive 2006/112.
72. For an overview of the EU position and issues, see Joep J.P. Swinkels, "Some Aspects of Input Tax Deduction under the Pro Rata of the EU-VAT System," *International VAT Monitor* 19 (5) (2008): 343–350.
73. Article 73 of Directive 2006/112.
74. Article 174(1) last paragraph of Directive 2006/112.
75. Article 174(2) of Directive 2006/112.
76. ECJ 13 March 2008, Case C-437/06, *Securenta Göttinger Immobilienanlagen und Vermögensmanagement AG v. Finanzamt Göttingen*, O.J. 8 May 2008, No. C116/7.

will be made to the out-of-scope transactions on the one hand and the taxable and exempt activities on the other hand on the basis of their respective turnover. Input tax allocated to the out-of-scope transaction will not be deductible. Next, the remainder input tax needs to be allocated between the exempt and taxable activities, again on the basis of their respective turnover, analogous to the normal pro rata rule.

Formulas related to the use of real property may try to determine the credit ratio on the basis of square footage in use for the respective outputs (actual use formula). For example, the rental of safe deposit boxes is taxed, which means that the input VAT on the purchase or lease of the building related to the space occupied by the area in use for the safe deposit boxes, including a percentage of general access areas, should be deductible. The standard formula is to divide the area in use for taxable supplies (*Xsf*) by the total square footage (*Tsf*) of the building to determine the percentage of input tax on the building that is creditable relative to the total input VAT incurred (*t*). For example, if we assume the input VAT on a building to be USD 200,000, the total square footage to be USD 10,000 and the square footage allocated to the taxable supplies to be USD 500, the creditable VAT can be calculated as follows:

$$\left\{\frac{Xsf}{Tsf} \times 100\right\} \times t \; or \left\{\frac{500}{10{,}000} \times 100\right\} = 5\% \times 200{,}000 = \text{USD } 10{,}000$$

When it relates to computers in use for mixed transactions, time spent on the computer relative to total time spent on the computer could create an appropriate formula, provided the business uses an electronic logbook.

In practice, many formulas may be applied, but they all share the same similarities as described afore in their approach.

8.2.5.4. Change of Use

Whereas a taxable business is entitled to a full deduction of input VAT incurred regarding its procurements, an exempt business is not. There exist many mixed character businesses, however, that is, businesses that make both taxable and exempt supplies. Apart from the mixed use complexities dealt with in the previous section, an issue arises when a good is initially used, for example, in relation to taxable supplies, and is at some later time used for making exempt supplies, or the other way around. Another complex situation occurs when an input is used in relation to both taxable and exempt supplies, and the ratio between them changes over time. The same problem arises when inputs are used for both taxable outputs and for private use by the business owner (sole proprietor). Consumption taxes are designed on the assumption that consumption is an immediate event, which is true for all perishable goods. The problem, just described, lies in the tax treatment of products that have a long, that is, not immediate, life cycle, in other words with capital goods. We deal with that situation in Section 8.2.7. More specifically, we explain the design chosen in the EU for adjusting input tax creditability for moveable and immoveable property in Sections 8.2.7.2.4 and 8.2.7.3, respectively.

8.2.6. Financial Services

The imposition of VATs on the financial services sector is a complicated subject. Most countries simply avoid the problem by exempting them. Unfortunately, exemptions, as we have seen, have significant economic side effects in terms of cascading and neutrality violation. The exemption of financial services also creates a bias towards the use of financial services, in the sense that it encourages consumers to take out loans rather than acquire fully taxed commodities. For these reasons, alternatives have been designed to tax financial services one way or the other. In this section, we first examine the arguments made pro and contra taxing financial services under a VAT as well as the practical problems encountered under the current exemption regime. Then, on the basis of an analysis of financial services, we evaluate several alternatives that have been developed for the purpose of bringing financial transaction within the scope of a VAT.

8.2.6.1. Arguments for Exempting Financial Services

There are several arguments for exempting financial services. Foremost is the argument that taxing financial services is difficult under a credit invoice method VAT because most financial services are rendered for an implicit fee where the VAT as a transaction tax is naturally oriented on explicit fees. Where implicit fees are charged, in other words when the value added is expressed in a margin, it cannot be identified on a transaction basis and, therefore, cannot be directly taxed under the credit invoice method VAT. Money inflows or gross receipts of financial institutions comprise both fees for the services rendered and simple transfers of funds. Only the former should be subject to VAT, which is possible only when they can be appropriately identified.

Some services by financial institution are, in fact, rendered for explicit fees, such as the rental of safety deposit boxes and the issuance of travelers' checks, and these services can, of course, be taxed as any other service delivered for an explicit fee. However, explicit fees do not always represent the actual value added of the service. For example, banks may offer low- or no-cost checking services to customers who maintain minimum balances in their checking accounts. Another example is premiums received by insurance companies that represent only partly a fee for the service of the insurer, the remainder covering the actuarial risk of payment under the policy, including any investment element.

Another argument for exemption is found in prevention of double taxation where other taxes, such as insurance premium taxes, are already in place.

A third argument, at least used in Europe at the time of the introduction of the VAT, is historical in nature. Neither the then-existing GRTs nor the VAT already in place in France applied to financial services, so it was deemed logical not to tax them under the VAT.

8.2.6.2. Arguments for Taxing Financial Services

Generally, there exist three main arguments for including financial services in the scope of VAT. First, because the VAT is a general, broad-based consumption tax, it should logically include the provision of all goods and all services, thus including financial services.[77] In other words, from the opposite perspective, it is fundamentally wrong to exclude an important economic sector from VAT.

The second argument, related to the first, is based on economic neutrality, the leading principle of VAT, which prohibits distortions that may arise from favoring financial services over other services by exempting them.[78] This is, however, not without debate. It has been argued that financial services should be free of all VAT because they are fundamentally inconsumable from the perspective of the final consumer. Most financial services are used not for direct consumption but to smooth consumption over time. The cost of such services is regarded as part of the price of acquiring the saving/investment instrument and not as part of the price of future consumption. Therefore, a consumption tax should not tax such services to avoid altering the relative prices between current and future consumption.[79] Others disagree because financial intermediation services require real resources and lower the transaction costs of intertemporal trade. Therefore, under this reasoning, taxing these services would have offsetting effects.[80] Auerbach and Gordon maintain that an efficient VAT should include financial services on the

77. Alan Schenk & Oliver Oldman, "Analysis of Tax Treatment of Financial Services under a Consumption-Style VAT: A Report of the American Bar Association, Section of Taxation, Committee on Value Added Tax," *Tax Lawyer* 181 44 (1991).
78. If the service is not taxed, its price will be too low, relative to the price of other, fully taxed goods and services. This price distortion will induce consumers to allocate too large a share of their income to untaxed financial services and too small a share to other, fully taxed goods and services. Consequently, according to this argument, financial services must be fully taxed in order to have an allocationally efficient, "neutral," consumption tax.
79. See Harry Grubert & James Mackie, "Must Financial Services Be Taxed under a Consumption Tax?," *National Tax Journal* 53 (1) (2000): 23–40.
80. See, Ngee-Choon Chia & John Whalley, "The Tax Treatment of Financial Intermediation," *Journal of Money, Credit, and Banking* 31 (4) (1999): 704–719. Nevertheless, they reach the conclusion that a broad-based consumption tax would be more efficient if financial services to consumers were exempted from the tax than if they were taxed at the same rate as consumer goods. An opposite conclusion is reached by Donald J. Rousslang, "Should Financial Services Be Taxed under a Consumption Tax? Probably," *National Tax Journal* 55 (2) (2002): 281–291, who argues that final financial services used to move revenue from the consumption tax over time are mostly wasted and that consumers do not use the services to move the associated fees over time. A tax on consumer goods raises the social cost of moving consumption over time but not the relative price of this consumption to consumers, whereas taxing the final financial services raises the relative price to consumers of this consumption, but it imposes no production-side distortion. In this case, the final financial services should be taxed at least as highly as the consumer goods.

basis of its equivalence to a labor income tax. A constant labor income tax (and tax on existing assets) ensures an efficient allocation of labor in all production (including financial-sector production) without distorting individual saving. The same holds for a comprehensive VAT that includes financial services. Thus, such a VAT ensures production efficiency.[81]

Third, as we have seen in Section 8.2.4.3.1, exemptions within the supply chain will result in tax cascading. Cascading provides an incentive to financial institutions to vertically integrate in an effort to reduce input tax costs (see Section 8.2.4.3.2), which can best be countered by eliminating the exemption that is at the root of the problem altogether.

The value of intermediate inputs, on which tax would cascade, has been estimated at 20% to 30% of the value of intermediation services.[82] In other words, financial institutions spend a fifth to a third of the value added they generate on purchases from other businesses. From a different perspective, on average 24.7% of the GDP in developed countries originates from the financial sector.[83] Exempting this sector, given its significant size, could easily generate serious economic distortions, paired with large loss of revenue.

8.2.6.3. Practical Problems with the Exemption Regime for Financial Services

8.2.6.3.1. General

When applying an exemption or special regime to a particular economic sector, such as financial services, it is essential to apply clear and incorruptible definitions and descriptions of the services and of the circumstances under which the special rules apply to prevent inequities and economic distortions. This is especially true in federal and common markets and in cross-border transaction situations. In practice, that is very difficult, if not impossible, to realize. In addition, there exist a number of specific problems associated with exemptions as discussed below.

8.2.6.3.2. Mixed Transactions

When a business makes a combination of taxable and exempt services for a single fee, theoretically, three options are open. First, the mixed transaction can be divided into its elements and each component will be treated separately and according to

---

81. Alan Auerbach & Roger Gordon, *Taxation of Financial Services under a VAT* (University of California at Berkeley: Mimeo, 2001).
82. Harry D. Garber & David G. Raboy, "Value-Added Taxation of Financial Services," in *VAT, Orthodoxy and New Thinking*, eds. Murray L. Weidenbaum, David G. Raboy & Ernest S. Christian, Jr. (Boston: Kluwer, 1989), at 172.
83. Alan Schenk & Howell H. Zee. "Treating Financial Services under a Value Added Tax: Conceptual Issues and Country Practices," in *Taxing the Financial Sector: Concepts, Issues, and Country Practices*, ed. Howell H. Zee (Washington, DC: International Monetary Fund, 2004), 60–74.

the applicable regime. Second, the mixed transaction can be treated as being one service sui generis and will generally be taxable at the standard rate. Third, the predominant component of the mixed elements may determine the tax treatment applied. Some countries apply rules that declare predominant the component rendering more than 50% of total fees received. Although this is a practical approach, it cannot altogether prevent infriction of economic neutrality. For instance, nonfinancial businesses, partially or incidentally providing exempt financial services, could easily avoid the consequences of exemption by combining them with a majority of taxable supplies. No limitation of input-tax credits would occur and tax accumulation in subsequent stages of the supply chain would be avoided. In case the buyer is a private consumer, the package could be structured to be dominated by exempt supplies. That would, indeed, reduce the input-tax credit for the seller, but ultimately a lower competitive sales price would be the result due to the avoidance of tax over the value added of the seller, as explained in Section 8.2.4.3.2. Businesses, generally rendering both taxable services and exempt financial services could, depending on whether their customers are entitled to a VAT credit, offer packages of supplies – one package being predominantly exempt and another package being predominantly taxable.

From a different angle, mixed transactions require a methodology to determine the input credit ratio for a financial institution. This is not as straightforward as it may superficially appear. Many different ratios have been developed for a multitude of situations (see also Section 8.2.5.3). In practice financial institutions are required to apply more than one ratio methodology to somewhat accurately determine their input credit, which only adds to the complexity and to their compliance costs.

8.2.6.3.3. Change of Use

One of the characteristics of capital goods is that they last over a long time period. With consumption taxes, the approach is to assume consumption to be an immediate event, and tax is levied when consumption expenditure is made. The input-VAT deduction is, therefore, determined on the basis of the (presumed) use of the good at the time of acquisition. If a good is used for making taxable supplies, the input VAT will be deductible. If a good is used for exempt supplies, the input VAT will not be deductible.[84] If a good is used for both taxable and exempt supplies, the input VAT will be deductible on a pro rata basis.[85]

Unless special rules are designed, adverse economic effects might occur in the case of a change in use of a capital good. A business should be partly refunded for VAT paid on the purchase of a good originally intended to be used exclusively for exempt activities when it is later used for making taxable supplies; otherwise, it will find itself at a competitive disadvantage compared with a business purchasing a similar good for direct use in relation to taxable outputs. However, the absence of

84. See Art. 168 of Directive 2006/112.
85. See Art. 173 of Directive 2006/112.

special rules would allow a business to deliberately exploit the tax credit system in an adverse way by simply using a good for taxable supplies during a limited time period, thus entitling it to a full credit, then changing to the intended exempt supplies-related use. The EU has developed special rules to deal with these situations, in essence a sort of depreciation rules for input VAT, which we will explore further in Section 8.2.7.2.4.

8.2.6.3.4. Sale of Used Business Assets

If an exempt financial institution sells business assets, this will constitute, in principle, a taxable sale. Under the assumption that the assets have been used in relation to the delivery of exempt services, no input VAT will have recovered and tax accumulation will occur on the residual value of the assets sold. As we will discuss in more detail in Section 8.2.7, it is important to find ways to avoid double taxation in these types of situations. If a financial institution has to charge VAT on the sale of a good for which it has not received an input VAT credit, double taxation would occur as regards the residual value of the good. For example, if a bank is purchasing 100 desktop computers for USD 300,000 plus USD 30,000 VAT (tax rate 10%), it will not be able to recover the VAT paid and the USD 30,000 would become a cost. A few years later the bank determines to sell these computers for USD 100,000. Without special rules the bank will have to charge USD 10,000 as regards the sale. Because the bank has paid irrecoverable VAT on the original purchase price, which was based on the total life cycle of the computers, the government has already been paid in full. The bank only used USD 200,000 of the total life cycle value of the computers but paid tax on the full life cycle value of USD 300,000. If tax is due again on the subsequent sale, double taxation could occur on the residual value depending on the tax status of the buyer. If the sale is made to another business which is eligible to full input-VAT recovery, double taxation is prevented. If the sale is made to an exempt business or to private persons, clearly such double taxation would occur. EU legislation tries to solve this problem by exempting the subsequent sale of goods wholly used for exempted activities.[86] However, this will not solve the problem in the case where the exempt vendor is able to (partly) shift forward the VAT costs to the buyer and would be able to sell for USD 110,000. In the case where the buyers are consumers, the total tax incurred on the goods would be accurate, but in the case where the buyer is a taxable business, tax accumulation may still occur because the recouping effect will not work as demonstrated in Section 8.2.4.3.1.

8.2.6.3.5. Sale of Repossessed Goods

Selling repossessed goods presents a similar situation to the one we dealt with in the previous section. Again the issue is one of tax overcollection by the government. If, for example, a bank sells a car that has been repossessed from a borrower/

86. Article 136(a), Directive 2006/112.

private individual, or an insurance company sells a car that has been stolen from a policyholder/private individual and has been returned by the police, the sale will be taxed. Because the original owner did not recover the VAT included in the purchase price, tax accumulation occurs unless special rules are formulated. One way to solve this issue would be to grant a tax credit to the bank or insurance company for the unrecovered tax incurred by the private individual/borrower or policyholder. However, if the financial institution received a full refund, that is, the VAT amount paid by the private consumer when he purchased the car, they would be overcompensated. The original purchaser paid VAT in relation to the full life cycle of the car. If we assume that he used the car for 1 year before he defaulted on the loan and the car was resold, tax related to that one-year "consumption" should accrue to the revenue. In other words, the credit allocation to the bank or insurer should be reduced with the time the car was used by the private consumer relative to the life cycle of the car. Let us assume that the retail price of the car was USD 20,000 exclusive of VAT (at 10%) of USD 2,000. The consumer borrows USD 22,000 to be repaid in equal annual installments over a period of 5 years at an interest rate of 8%. Assume further that the VAT legislation has fixed the economic life cycle for a car for tax purposes at 5 years. The revenue would refund to the bank/insurer 80% of the VAT paid at the original purchase, or USD 1,600. When the bank/insurer sells the car for, let us say, only USD 15,000, it has to charge VAT of USD 1,500 and remit this amount to the revenue. As a result, the revenue received in total is USD 1,900 in relation to the two subsequent sales. If the resale is made for USD 19,000, the VAT due on the sale would be USD 1,900, and the revenue received in total is USD 2,300 in relation to the subsequent sales.

An alternative would be to tax only the margin, similar to the margin scheme applied in the EU for the resale of used goods (see Section 8.2.7.2.2.1). In this case, however, the taxable margin would be calculated as the difference between sales price and unpaid loan amount. If we assume that the payments made by the borrower have been sufficient to pay all the interest due but that only half of the installment actually has been paid, the results for our examples are as follows. The outstanding principle is USD 19,800. In the first example, the resale price is USD 15,000, which leads to a taxable margin of (USD 4,800), and the bank/insurer would receive a refund of USD 480. The revenue receives in total USD 1,520 in relation to the subsequent sales. In the second example, the resale price is USD 19,000, which would set the taxable margin at USD 800, and the bank/insurer would receive a refund of USD 80. To the revenue would accrue a total of USD 1,920 in relation to the two subsequent sales.

8.2.6.3.6. Exported Services

Generally, the credit invoice method VAT applies the destination principle to determine tax jurisdiction regarding cross-border transactions. In other words, goods and services should be taxed in the country where they are used, consumed or enjoyed. Goods and services consumed outside a certain territory must, therefore, leave the territory untaxed. This also allows these exported goods and services to compete on equal terms in foreign markets with locally produced goods and services. Exported goods are, generally, untaxed under a VAT through the zero rating arrangement. We take a closer look at zero rating in relation to the export of goods in Section 9.4, but for now it is sufficient to conclude that zero rating is a legal mechanism to achieve full exemption of export sales. The export sale is subject to 0% VAT, and the exporter maintains full eligibility to input-VAT credit in relation to the exported goods. Through this arrangement, exported goods leave the country of origin free of tax and should be taxed on importation in the country of destination. Because the flow of goods can be physically followed, it is relatively simple to determine whether a good is exported. There exists no straightforwardness regarding export services because of their intangible nature. Designing rules on VAT jurisdiction for services has solved this. The country where a service is deemed to take place on the basis of these rules has jurisdiction for VAT purposes. I will not elaborate on these rules here because they are extensively dealt with in Section 9.5. It is sufficient to conclude that the destination principle is honored when the service is sourced to the country where the recipient of the service is located. Regarding the procurement of financial services by businesses, this has, indeed, been realized in the EU but not as concerns services rendered to private consumers. When a service is sourced to another country, the financial service provider typically is entitled to a full input-VAT credit in relation to the exported services.

In practice, determining the place of supply of financial services has, at times, proven to be quite difficult. Problems arise, for example, when a service is provided to several customers at the same time and for a single fee, where these customers have their business residences in different countries. In some Member States of the EU, an additional criterion for determining the place of supply of insurance services is the location of the risk covered under the policy. This criterion, however, is inefficient in the case of third-party liabilities and for international air and marine transportation. Furthermore, these criteria may be in conflict when the place of business of the policyholder and the location of the risk are in different countries.

8.2.6.3.7. Definition of Financial Services

Definition complexities make it more difficult to exactly distinguish between financial and nonfinancial services and lead to uncertainties regarding treatment by taxing authorities. Although clear and incorruptible definitions would be strongly preferred, in practice this has proven to be impossible to achieve. For example, the definition of exempt banking and insurance transactions in EU legislation are only described in general terms.[87] In the past, regulatory definitions of financial

87. Article 135(1) of Directive 2006/112: Member States shall exempt the following transactions:

    a. insurance and reinsurance transactions, including related services performed by insurance brokers and insurance agents;

services provided guidance for interpreting financial services for the purpose of value added taxation, at least in the EU. Due to the gradual broadening of the range of financial services which fall into the regulatory ambit, that is no longer the case. Financial services and products have increasingly become more complex, adding to the definition's divergence.[88] Where jurisdictions apply different definitions, competition distortions may occur in case of cross-border service supplies. In fact, a study for the European Commission found considerable differences in definitions applied by the then – twenty-five Member States to financial services.[89]

8.2.6.3.8. *Input Tax Allocation*

Financial institutions are not eligible for input-VAT credit in relation to their exempt financial services outputs. Generally, financial institutions are mixed businesses, providing exempt and taxable supplies. In addition, input VAT is recoverable in relation to exported services. The principle of neutrality, essential for the proper functioning of a VAT system, has consequences in the realm of mixed businesses, as well in the sense that a common and consistent methodology is needed to calculate the input-VAT credit for each individual financial institution to ensure that operators carrying on the same mixture of operations are able to recover equivalent levels of input tax. Basically, this would require a two-step approach. First, direct attribution of input VAT to either exempt or to taxable outputs. However, in the case, inputs are used for both exempt and taxable supplies, in other words, when direct attribution is not feasible, a pro rata apportionment computation needs to be performed.[90] It can be defined as a fraction whose numerator is the total annual turnover attributable to transactions in respect to which VAT is deductible and whose denominator is total annual turnover.[91] The difference

---

b. the granting and the negotiation of credit and the management of credit by the person granting it;
c. the negotiation of or any dealings in credit guarantees or any other security for money and the management of credit guarantees by the person who is granting the credit;
d. transactions, including negotiation, concerning deposit and current accounts, payments, transfers, debts, cheques and other negotiable instruments, but excluding debt collection;
e. transactions, including negotiation, concerning currency, bank notes and coins used as legal tender...
f. transactions, including negotiation but not management or safekeeping, in shares, interests in companies or associations, debentures and other securities, but excluding documents establishing title to goods, and the rights or securities referred to in Art. 15(2);
g. the management of special investment funds as defined by Member States.

88. PricewaterhouseCoopers, "Study to Increase the Understanding of the Economic Effects of the VAT Exemption for Financial and Insurance Services," Final report to the European Commission, 2 November 2006 (PwC report), 19.
89. *Supra*, 25.
90. In the EU, Member States are left the choice between the two. Several states rely on the pro rata rule alone, some of these requiring pro rata calculation on a sector basis. Others apply a mix of pro rata and attribution rules. See, IBFD Report, *Survey on the Recovery of Input VAT in the Financial Sector*, Amsterdam, December 2006.
91. See, for example, Art. 174, Directive 112/2006.

between the denominator and the numerator is equal to the level of turnover in relation to exempt transactions that do not give rise to a right of input-VAT recuperation. Measuring turnover, especially in relation to exempt transactions, on the basis of a consistent methodology is, of course, essential. In practice, within the EU, two different approaches have been developed that produce different recovery rates for a single set of data. For example, a bank acts as the intermediary between lenders and borrowers. It receives deposits on which it pays a certain interest and provides loans to borrowers against a higher interest rate. Regarding only this credit negotiation service, the question arises as to whether to measure turnover in terms of gross interest received or on the basis of gross margin. That constitutes quite a difference. Assume that a bank receives USD 1,400 in interest from borrowers and pays out USD 800 in interest to depositors; gross interest is USD 1,400 but the margin only USD 600. If the bank makes an additional USD 200 in taxable supplies, the pro rata would be 200/1,600 = 12.5% under the gross interest method and 200/800 = 25% under the gross margin method. The EU-VAT directive does not offer any guidance in this respect, but clearly applying two methods with significantly different outcomes creates competitive distortions and facilitates tax competition between states to attract inward investment.[92] In two cases, the European Court of Justice (ECJ) has indicated that it prefers the margin approach. In *Glawe*, it was held that the taxable consideration from a gaming machine is the net receipt over time because the full fees were never at the operator's disposal and need to be reduced with the proportion of the stake mandatorily required to be paid out as winnings.[93] In *First National Bank of Chicago*[94] the ECJ decided explicitly in favor of the margin method by ruling that "in foreign exchange transactions in which no fees or commission are calculated with regard to certain specific transactions, the taxable amount is the net result of the transactions of the supplier of the services over a given period of time." The reasoning in these rulings is also in line with our analysis of the value added of financial services in Section 8.2.6.4.

8.2.6.4. Analysis of Value Added of Financial Services

Although it is not possible to identify the value added of financial services on a transaction basis, determining the value added on an aggregate level seems feasible. Figures 10 and 11 demonstrate the identification of the value added on an aggregate level of simplified bank and insurance transactions.

---

92. The inconsistency in turnover measurement and casu quo recovery rate determination is not a new issue in the EU, and proposals have been made to create a common system but to no prevail. See the proposal for a nineteenth council directive on the harmonisation of the laws of the Member States relating to turnover taxes amending Directive 77/388/EC Common System of Value Added Tax, COM 84/648 final, O.J. C347 of 29 December 1984. Withdrawn on 14 December 1993.
93. ECJ 5 May 1994, Case C-38/93, *Glawe Spiel und Unterhaltungsgeräte Aufstellungsgesellschaft v. Finanzamt Hamburg-Barmbek-Uhlenhorst*, [1994] ECR I-1679.
94. ECJ 14 July 1998, Case C-172/96, *Commissioners of Customs & Excise v. First National Bank of Chicago*, [1998] ECR I-4387.

Figure 10. Value Added of Bank Services

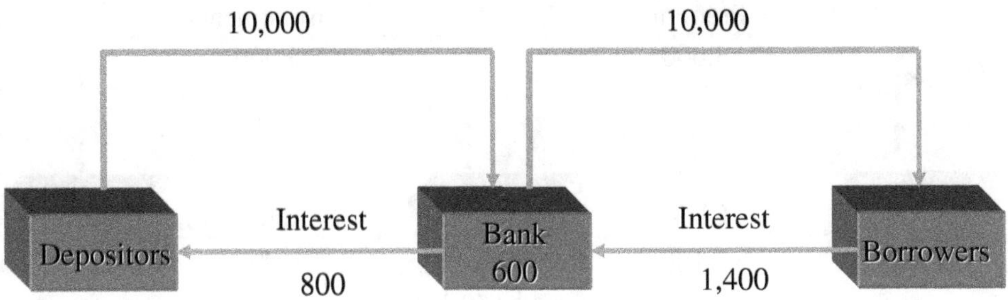

Costs: Wages
Equipment
Building
Loan default } (50)

$$\text{Value added} = \frac{\text{interest received (1,400)}}{\text{interest paid + costs (850)}} = 550$$

550 represents the value added of the bank's intermediation services

The bank provides intermediation services by pooling funds from depositors and making those available to borrowers. The transfers of funds in the form of deposits by savers and subsequent loans to borrowers, however, do not constitute any value added, nor do the payments of interest by the borrowers to the bank and by the bank to the deposit holders. Because the bank needs to pay for labor and capital, and incurs other costs including loan defaults, the value added, which should be subject to VAT, can be calculated as interest received (1,400) minus interest paid (800) and costs (50) = 550.

An insurer's service can be perceived best as the management of risk pooling. Neither the payment of premiums to the pool nor the payment of claims represents the value of the service rendered by the insurer; they are mere transfers of funds. Investment returns on the premiums will generally cover part of the claims paid to policyholders. The value added of the insurance intermediation service, which should be subject to VAT, can be identified as the premiums and investment earnings of the insurer (3,300) minus the claims and cash surrender paid, and costs (3,150) = 150.

Figure 11. Value Added of Insurance Services

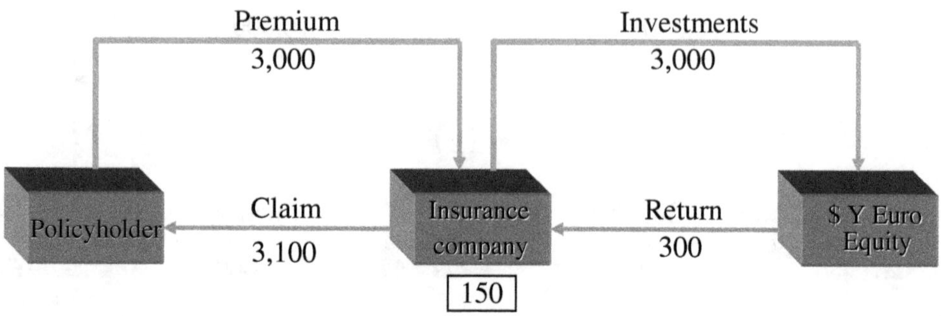

Costs: Wages
Equipment
Building
Dividends
} (50)

$$\text{Value added} = \frac{\text{Investments + return (3,300)}}{\text{Claims + Costs (3,150)}} = 150$$

150 represent the value added of intermediation services

8.2.6.5. Methods of Taxing Financial Services

Given the practical problems of the current exemption regime for financial services as described previously, it is evidently worthwhile to investigate alternative methods of taxation based on an aggregate-level determination of value added. We will distinguish between alternatives that are compliant with the credit invoice method, and alternatives that operate outside this system and are, in essence, separate regimes of value added taxation for financial services. The final section contains our evaluation of the many proposals.

8.2.6.5.1. Taxation under a Separate Regime

8.2.6.5.1.1. Addition Method

Under the addition method, value added is calculated as the sum of wages, rent, interest and profits. This system is not compatible with the credit invoice method and does not allow for input tax credits. The addition method, for that reason, could function as a general sales tax in relation to services rendered to private consumers. However, because the addition method is unable to determine the value added on a transaction basis, sales to taxable businesses cannot be invoiced with an add-on for the tax. As a result, credits cannot be identified or exercised. The addition method is origin based. It determines value added on an aggregate level without regard to the destination of the services. Excluding the value added in relation to export services is simply not feasible. Taxing financial services with an addition VAT is a possibility, but this would, in effect, turn the VAT into an accounts-based tax as it relates to the financial sector, which is inconsistent with the transaction-based VAT applied using the invoice-credit method to other (nonfinancial) sectors.

Israel is the only state that applies the addition method VAT to financial services, based on the computation of wages and profits. Interestingly, it is administered by the Income Tax Authority, and not by the VAT Administration. Applying an addition VAT for a single sector of the economy in conjunction with a credit invoice VAT for the other sectors leads to serious cascading as demonstrated by the practice in Israel.

8.2.6.5.1.2. Subtraction Method

Under the subtraction method VAT, as discussed in Section 3.2.2.2 and more extensively in Chapter 7, the tax base is computed by determining the value of total sales and then subtracting the value of total purchases and expenses. The tax base for an insurance company, typically, would be determined by deducting bad debt losses, claims paid, interest expenses, shareholder and policyholder dividends, and expenditures for supplies by other businesses from premiums received and investment income, including net realized capital gains, rent and other revenues.[95]

Several problems arise in connection with the application of the subtraction method VAT on financial services. In the first place, adjustments will be needed for investments in nonfinancial assets and in affiliated nonfinancial businesses. Because the subtraction method VAT for the financial sector would operate parallel to an overall credit invoice method VAT, it will be required to find a way to determine the input VAT credit for taxable customers. However, there exists no precise method of allocating the financial margin in relation to individual transactions. As a result, tax credits will have to be determined on the basis of an approximation formula with the risk of tax cascading where these formulas are too low. Last, but not least, the subtraction method is origin based, which implies that the tax base must be altered in order to eliminate the tax on financial services rendered to businesses outside the resident state of the bank or insurer; otherwise, a financial institution would find itself at a price disadvantage when it seeks to compete in foreign markets. However, under a subtraction VAT it is not possible to allocate net margin to domestic supplies of financial services and to exported services, respectively. Thus, allocation on a formula basis would be required.

These formula- or approximation-based adjustments complicate the application of a subtraction VAT from an operational perspective. Furthermore, they will lead to inequities because they give too much to one financial institution and too little to the other, thus violating the principle of economic neutrality.

On a different note, the question arises whether rebates of VAT related to services rendered to foreign customers are permitted under WTO rules. The subtraction VAT shares important features with direct taxes, the refund of which is not

95. See, for example, Thomas S. Neubig & Harold L. Adrion, "Value Added Taxes and Other Consumption Taxes: Issues for Insurance Companies," *Tax Notes* (22 November 1993): 1001–1011.

permitted under WTO rules. We will deal with this complicated question extensively, albeit in a different context, in Section 9.3.

8.2.6.5.1.3. Cash Flow Method

The cash flow method takes the financial inflows and outflows respectively to determine the tax base and the tax credit volume.[96] All cash inflows (e.g., deposits, interest received, loan repayments) are considered to be taxable sales and, therefore, tax has to be remitted on these inflows. Tax outflows (e.g., expenses, deposit repayments and interest paid) are treated as business expenses, allowing for tax credits. The cash flow method is demonstrated for a bank in Figure 12.

Figure 12. Cash Flow Method

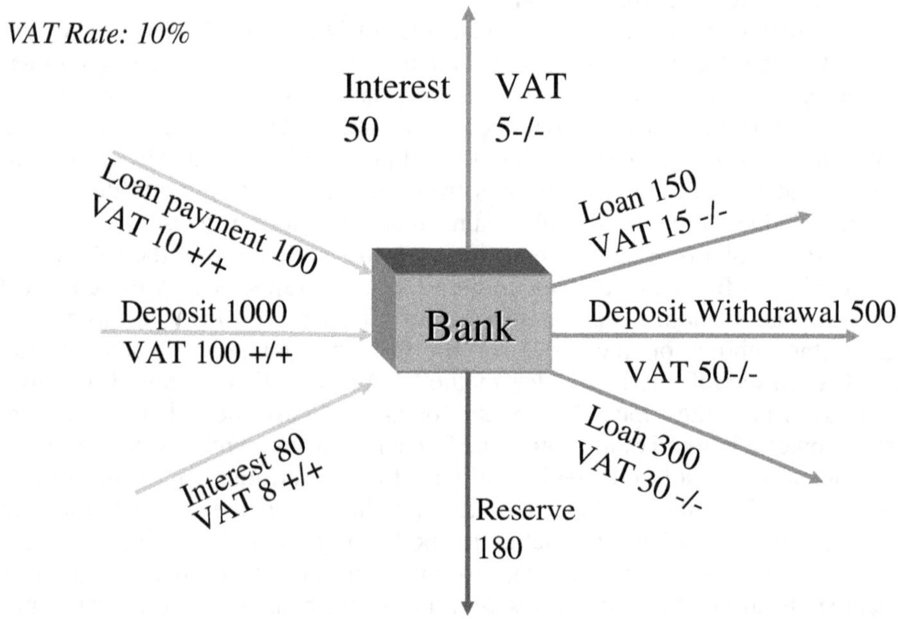

Inflows	1180
Outflows	1000
Value bank Service	180
VAT	18

Reservations are ignored for VAT because they constitute neither an inflow nor an outflow of funds. VAT payable + Vat due on inflows (118) minus VAT on outflows (100) = 18, which is 10% (the statutory rate) of the total value of the bank services.

96. Lorey Arthur Hoffman, Satya Poddar & John Whalley, "Taxation of Banking Services under a Consumption Type, Destination Base VAT," *National Tax Journal* 40 (1987): 547–554; and S. Poddar & M. English, "Taxation of Financial Services under a Value Added Tax: Applying

Loan repayments, deposits and interest received account for a total income of USD 1,180 (inflows), whereas loans, interest paid and deposit withdrawals amount to USD 1,000 of business expenses (outflows). Financial reservations made by the bank will be ignored for VAT because they constitute neither an inflow nor an outflow of funds. The VAT payable can be calculated as VAT due on the inflows (118) minus VAT on outflows (100) = 18, which is exactly 10% (the statutory rate in our example) of the total value (1,180 – 1,000 =) 180 of the bank's services.

The cash flow method seems to be fully compatible with the credit invoice method VAT. Tax cascading in relation to financial services will be eliminated under the cash flow method because registered businesses are eligible for tax credits regarding their outflows to financial institutions. No complicated formula of estimating the input-VAT credit for taxable customers is required as under the subtraction method VAT. The cash flow method is destination based; no tax will be due regarding financial services rendered to foreign customers.

Problems may arise with introduction of the cash flow method and when tax rates change. On its introduction, transitional rules will be needed to bring outstanding deposits and loans within the new system. Otherwise, a depositor would receive a tax credit on principle and interest when the funds are withdrawn despite never having paid tax on the cash inflows.

Business borrowers will be required to pay VAT on their outstanding debts and business lenders will receive a credit on their outstanding deposits. If the tax rate changes, adjustments need to be made. To operate accurately, the credit for a cash outflow should be at the same rate as that used for tax collection on the original cash inflow. In the case of a tax increase, borrowers will be required to pay an additional tax on their outstanding debts, including accrued interest, and lenders will receive an additional credit on outstanding deposits, also including accrued interest. In the rare case of a tax decrease, business lenders will be required to make restitution of an equivalent portion of their previously received credit, and business borrowers will receive an equivalent refund of tax paid. These adjustments would complicate the system and increase compliance and administrative costs.

This method also triggers a timing problem. When taking out a loan, a business would be required to pay tax that it would recover at a later time when the loan is repaid. As a result, the borrowing requirements would increase for the duration of the loan to finance the tax element associated with the loan. To mitigate this disadvantage the concept of Tax Collection Accounts (TCAs) have been suggested, which are managed by the financial institutions. Basically, the institution keeps a separate account for VAT purposes tracking tax due regarding of monetary inflows and tax credits regarding monetary outflows. In essence, it is a tax suspension account that allows for a deferral of tax due on inflows and of tax credit

---

the Cash Flow Approach," *National Tax Journal* 50 (1) (1997): 89–111. Earlier, Meade discussed this approach in the context of a replacement of the corporate income tax; see James Meade, *The Structure and Reform of Direct Taxation* (London: Allen & Unwin, 1978).

payments by the government due on outflows. The tax payable casu quo creditable is debited and respectively credited to the TCA and carried forward to when the capital transaction is reversed. At which time the balance will be settled. The account would bear interest at the government borrowing rate. The TCAs in the books of an individual business is the mirror image of the one held by the financial institution in relation to the same transaction. The TCA mechanism solves the cash flow issue through deferral of payments and compensates for losses or benefits resulting from the deferral period by indexing the outstanding balances by an interest rate. Transition issues can be resolved through the TCA as well by initial debiting or crediting of outstanding balances at the introduction of the new system, and by adjusting outstanding balances in case of rate changes.

A particular point of interest is the case of cross-border financial transactions, for example, when businesses borrow and/or lend in different jurisdictions. In principle, a business will be drawn into the VAT system of every country where it is engaged in financial services. When borrowing, it would have to pay VAT on its outstanding debt to the state in which the bank has residence; making deposits would give rise to a tax credit. This problem is avoided by simply zero rating exchanges with nonresidents. In other words, inflows from and outflows to nonresidents are neither taxable nor creditable. Under the destination principle this makes perfect sense. It also enables financial institutions to operate in foreign markets on a level playing field. For example, a bank would provide a loan to a foreign resident at a tax-exclusive interest rate.

Under the cash flow method, nonfinancial businesses would be required to conduct complicated calculations in order to exercise their right to input tax credits. Especially for smaller and medium-sized companies, this would constitute a significant additional administrative burden.

Conceptually, the cash flow method has been reviewed favorably regarding taxing margin services because it fully removes cascading on financial services rendered to business customers and avoids complications in cross-border situations. It is also perceived as very complex and leading to significant compliance and administrative costs. For that reason, financial institutions have shown no enthusiasm for the system, and, although it has been under consideration in the EU, it has not been adopted anywhere.

8.2.6.5.2. Taxation within the Credit Invoice Method

8.2.6.5.2.1. Option for Taxation

The option for taxation solution offers financial institutions flexibility to decide whether and in what situations to charge VAT on their services, and would lead to a recovery of input tax insofar taxable sales are made. EU legislation allows Member States to introduce the option solution in their national VAT legislation.[97] Only seven Member States[98] have included this provision in their legislation, but the

97. Article 137(1) (a) of Directive 2006/112.

98. Austria, Belgium, Bulgaria, Germany, Estonia, France and Lithuania.

application is far from uniform. Different treatment of financial services among Member States (option/nonoption) runs counter to economic neutrality.

In the EU the suggestion has been made to extend the scope of the option to all financial institution operating within the common territory and to make the option mandatory for all Member States. Under the option method, financial institutions will likely choose to tax their services rendered to business customers who will be entitled to a tax refund and prefer exempt treatment for services rendered to private consumers. The option method solves only partly the problems arising from exempting financial services. First, the value added of financial institutions would still remain untaxed in relation to sales made to private consumers. Second, the scope of its application is limited to fee-based services; the option method is not feasible in relation to margin-based transactions.

8.2.6.5.2.2. Zero Rating

Zero rating has the result that financial services will be totally relieved from tax. No VAT will be due on the supply of these services, whereas full input tax credit will granted to financial institutions regarding their purchases. Cascading, therefore, will be completely eliminated under the application of the zero rate, provided no compensating taxes are levied. The problems and complexities associated with the exemption of financial services, related to input tax allocation, mixed use and change of use, will automatically be eliminated as well, but definition complexities may remain when determining which services are subject to the zero rate.

Zero rating may lead to distortion of competition in cross-border situations. Financial institutions that are resident in a country that provide for a zero rating system have a competitive advantage when they operate in a foreign market that does not provide the same facility, unless an efficient system is in place to tax imported financial services. The latter is feasible where the recipient is a taxable business to whom the tax liability can be shifted but is unrealistic in relation to services provided to private customers.

Zero rating would result in financial institutions not being taxed at all, which seems counter to the objective of a VAT as a general consumption tax to include all consumptive expenditures. This is a very fundamental objection to zero rating, based on the principles of the tax itself, however, as explained in Section 8.2.6.2 the argument has been made that financial services should be free of consumption tax. Moreover, zero rating of financial services would create a difficult-to-justify preferential treatment that violates the principles of equality and neutrality.

The size of the tax base related to financial services is considerable, and zero rating would have negative budgetary consequences in terms of revenue lost because no tax would be collected on the outputs of financial institutions, whereas full refund must be paid in relation to their inputs. For this reason, zero rating may prove to be politically controversial.

A variation that addresses the problem of untaxing financial services rendered to private consumers is limiting the application of the zero rate to

B2B transactions[99] as is the current practice in New Zealand and Singapore. Since a VAT-registered business typically produces a mixture of taxable and exempt supplies, as a practical matter New Zealand's application of the zero rating of B2B transactions is restricted only to cases where the VAT-registered purchaser of financial services has taxable supplies that are at least equal to 75% of its total supplies. This would solve the problem of nontaxation that would arise when the zero rate were applied to all sales by financial institutions, including those to private consumers. However, this would require financial institutions to identify their sales to registered businesses and final consumers separately for apportioning their creditable input taxes, which may prove to be quite complicated and would certainly lead to a sharp increase in compliance costs.

Under an exemption, services rendered to private consumers are effectively taxed at a lower rate because the value added of the financial institutions remains untaxed. In other words, there is an element of undertaxation in relation to B2C sales of financial services. Partially zero rating, that is, zero rating of B2B transactions, does not provide a solution for that problem.

8.2.6.5.2.3. Modified Reverse Charge

As we have seen in Section 8.2.6.5.1.3 when we discussed the cash flow method, the value of the intermediation services rendered by, for example, a bank is the margin it makes between interest paid on deposits and the interest it receives on loans, or net interest. Deposits (or inflows) have to be considered as procurements from the banks position, and loans as sales. Consequently, depositors should charge VAT on the interest they receive because this is the remuneration for the deposit, and the bank should charge VAT regarding the interest charged to the borrowers. For the bank, VAT on interest received from borrowers would constitute output VAT and VAT paid on interest paid to depositors would be considered creditable input VAT. Taxing the loan and deposit interest on a transaction-by-transaction basis as described previously is theoretically correct and would be fully compatible with an invoice credit VAT.

There is no practical problem in tax collection as regards the bank's outputs, that is, the VAT on the interest received from borrowers, because the bank would be responsible for the collection. However, the vast majority of bank deposits are derived from private consumers, and it is inconceivable to recruit their vast numbers effectively as tax collectors.

To solve this problem Howell Zee[100] has suggested applying a modified reverse charge mechanism to financial services.[101] Normally, charging and reporting output VAT is a responsibility of the seller, and the deduction of input VAT is a

99. Harry Huizinga, "A European VAT on Financial Services?," *Economic Policy* 17 (35) (2002): 497–534.

100. Howell. H. Zee, "A New Approach to Taxing Financial Intermediation Services under a Value Added Tax," *National Tax Journal* 58 (1) (2005): 77–92.

101. Partly, this proposal also serves as an alternative for the cash flow method to reduce the complexity of the system and mutatis mutandis the compliance costs associated with it.

right of the purchaser. Under a reverse charge mechanism, these two elements are combined and are exercised by the same person. Especially when transactions originate with foreign suppliers, it is difficult to effectively enforce tax collection if they have no establishment in the taxing jurisdiction. For that purpose, tax collection is reversed to the business on the recipient side of the transaction. On the VAT return the recipient would account for both the output VAT (normally due by the supplier) but he would also include this amount in his in input VAT credit compilation.

When applied to bank intermediary services, the reverse charge would shift the collection of the VAT on deposit interest from depositors to banks. In effect, a bank would account on its VAT return for the tax paid on its deposits and claim the same as a credit against its output tax due on loan interest collected from its borrowers.

The interest in this context would be computed on a tax-inclusive basis. Borrowers, registered as taxable businesses, can deduct the VAT included in the loan interest as input VAT.

By applying the reverse charge, the bank's deposit-taking and lending activities are fully integrated into the invoice credit mechanism. The credit chain remains intact for businesses that purchase the bank's intermediation services, that is, borrow from the bank, because the tax on interest paid becomes creditable input VAT, and tax cascading has been prevented.

The reverse charge method would work well with a destination-type VAT. Foreign deposits are taxed under the reverse charge, as is the case with domestic deposits. Loans to nonresidents would simply be zero rated as exported services.

The application of the reverse charge to financial intermediary services is demonstrated in Table 22. The tax on deposits is accounted for by the bank under the reverse charge regardless of whether the depositor is a taxable business or a private consumer. The status of the depositor, therefore, is irrelevant in terms of tax burden because the bank will receive a tax credit for the same amount as the tax due on the deposit interest. However, the status of the borrower is relevant because it determines whether the taxing authorities would effectively collect any tax. If the borrower is a taxable business, it will receive a credit for the tax paid on the loan interest equal to the tax paid to and remitted to the taxing authorities by the bank. Only when the borrower is a final consumer, would tax accrue to the treasury.

A deposit of USD 1,000 is made to the bank that in turn grants a loan of the same amount to the borrower. The bank owes USD 50 in interest to the depositor, including USD 10 in tax. The bank pays the depositor USD 40 and accounts for USD 10 tax under the reverse charge but is eligible to an input tax credit for the same. As a result, no revenue accrues to the taxing authorities in relation to this transaction.

The borrower has to pay USD 100 in interest, including USD 20 VAT, which the bank will remit to the taxing authorities. If the borrower is a taxable business, it will receive an invoice from the bank on the basis of which it can claim a credit for the tax paid. No actual tax would accrue to the taxing authorities. However, if the borrower is a private consumer, no credit claim can be exercised and an amount of USD 20 in tax is effectively collected.

Table 22. Reverse Charge on Financial Intermediary Services

Depositor	Bank	Borrower	Output Tax	Input Tax Credit
1,000 →	1,000 →	1,000		
50 ← Interest			10	10
	100 ← Interest		20	0/20
Total Tax			20/0	

Assumptions: Principle amount 1,000
Deposit Interest Rate: 5%
Loan Interest Rate: 10%
VAT Rate: 20%

A problem with applying the reverse charge method to financial intermediary services is that in effect the outcome is a tax on gross interest where it should be a tax on net interest. The total tax amount due by the borrower is USD 20, which is equal to the statutory rate applied to the loan. The value of the intermediary service, however, is USD 50 (the margin between interests paid and received) and the tax burden should, therefore, be USD 10. This is immaterial for a borrower who has the status of taxable business because he will be able to recover the tax, but it is an issue, of course, when the borrower is a private consumer. Extending an invoice credit VAT to deposit and loan interest will lead to the overtaxation of final consumers as bank borrowers.

To overcome this problem a design is necessary by which the reverse charge on depositors can be used to reduce the VAT that is actually paid by borrowers. This is accomplished in Zee's model with a modified form of the reverse charge. The modification can be found in the application of a so-called franking account, which works exactly like a pooled account of depreciable assets under the declining-balance method. The bank maintains three running balances: (1) cumulated unlent deposits, (2) cumulated unclaimed reverse charges on the unlent deposits, and (3) unclaimed reverse charges per unit of unlent deposits. These balances are updated after each deposit or lending transaction, with the former giving rise to a credit entry and the latter to a debit entry.

Borrowing from Zee's examples, assume that two deposits are made, one for USD 1,000 and a second for USD 3,000 at deposit interest rates of 4% and 5%, respectively. The third transaction is a loan for USD 2,000 generating an interest of 9%. The three accounts would be computed as shown in Table 23.

Table 23. Franking Accounts

Cumulated Unlent Deposits (USD)	Cumulated Unclaimed Reverse Charges (USD)	Unclaimed Reverse Charges per Unit of Unlent Deposits (USD)
1,000	4	0.004
4,000	19	0.00475
2,000	9.5	0.00475

At a tax rate of 10%, the first deposit incurs USD 4 in tax and the second deposit USD 15, cumulating in a total of USD 19 in unclaimed reverse charges. The total tax per dollar of deposit is (19/4,000) = 0.00475. When the loan of USD 2,000 is made at an interest rate of 9%, a notional VAT of USD 18 (10% of USD = 180 in interest) is charged, but the borrower is granted a credit of USD 9.5 (computed by multiplying USD 0.00475 by the loan principal of USD 2,000) for the reverse charge that was levied on the deposits used to finance the loan. Hence, the net VAT payment by the borrower is USD 8.5, which the bank has to remit to the taxing authority. The tax amount should either be mentioned on an invoice issued by the bank or, alternatively, on the periodical bank statement. Either way, if the borrower is a taxable business, it will be able to recover the tax as an input VAT credit. For a more complete picture, we add an additional deposit of USD 2,000 at an interest rate of 3% and two loans of USD 1,000 and USD 3,000 generating loan interest of 7% and 8%, respectively (see Table 24).

Table 24. Franking Accounts Continued

Cumulated Unlent Deposits (USD)	Cumulated Unclaimed Reverse Charges (USD)	Unclaimed Reverse Charges per Unit of Unlent Deposits (USD)
4,000	15.5	0.003875
3,000	11.625	0.003875
0	0	0

The banks pays an interest of USD 60 on the last deposit, and accounts for USD 6 in reverse charge, and a cumulated total of USD 15.5, and a per unit amount of (15.5/4,000) = 0.003875. The first additional loan generates USD 70 in interest for which a notional VAT of USD 7 is charged, but the borrower receives a credit of USD 3.875, and pays a net VAT of USD 3.125. The second additional loan generates USD 240 in interest on which a notional VAT of USD 24 is charged. The borrower receives a credit for the reverse charge that was levied on the deposits used to finance the loan in the amount of (0.003875 times the loan principle of USD 3,000) USD 11.625 and pays a net VAT of USD 12.375.

To determine whether the franking system leads to the theoretically correct results, we make a computation in Table 25 of the total interest paid by the bank on the deposits and received in relation to the loans granted and the total net VAT paid by the borrowers and remitted by the bank to the taxing authorities.

Table 25. Total Tax Paid Relative to Value Intermediation Service

Total Deposit Interest	Total Loan Interest	Total Net Tax
40	180	8.5
150	70	3.125
60	240	12.375
Total: 250	490	24.00

In the sequence of three deposits and three loans each with a different principal and interest rate, the total net VAT paid by the borrowers is USD 24. The value of the intermediation bank service is determined by the difference of loan interest received (USD 490) and deposit interest paid (USD 250) or USD 240. At a statutory VAT rate of 10%, the tax remitted to the taxing authorities should be USD 24 and that is precisely what the franking system has accomplished.

Zee makes the observation that under the franking system only borrowers pay tax in relation to the bank's intermediation services. Because intermediation services benefit both depositors and borrowers, this is conceptually incorrect. To shift some of the tax burden to depositors, Zee suggests reducing the deposit interest paid to depositors with the tax that relates to it. If we assume that the interest rate should include a fee for the intermediation service of x, the first depositor would have received not 4% but $(4 + x)$. At a tax rate of 10%, the bank would collect as part of its output VAT $0.1x\%$ in VAT revenue on its deposits. The deposit interest paid would thus be $(4 - 0.1x)$. As a consequence, the reverse charge would increase as well from 4% to $(4 + x)\%$. Because any reverse charge is transferred to borrowers as a credit against the notional VAT on the loan interest through the franking mechanism described earlier, the net VAT paid by borrowers would be reduced by exactly the amount of the VAT paid by depositors.

Under the franking system the reverse charge on a USD 1,000 deposit would normally be USD 4 (10% of USD 40 in interest). The borrower would pay USD 90 in interest and be charged a notional VAT of USD 9 and receive a credit of USD 4. The franking credit under the allocation mechanism is increased with the VAT charged to the depositor for a total credit of USD 6. The total tax paid by depositor and borrower jointly is USD 5, which represents 10% of the total intermediation services of (USD 90 – USD 40) USD 50.

Table 26. Tax Allocation of Intermediation Services between Depositors and Borrowers

Gross Deposit	VAT Interest	Net Deposit Charged	Gross Loan Interest	National VAT	Franking Credit	Net VAT Charged
40	2	38	90	9	6	3

Assumptions: Deposit and loan amount: USD 1,000
Deposit interest rate: 4%
Loan interest rate: 9%
VAT rate: 10%
Depositor share of intermediation service (x): 2%

Although the modified reverse charge is designed as an alternative for the administrative complexities associated with the cash flow method and the TCA (see Section 8.2.6.5.1.3), it creates administrative complexities of its own through the franking and tax allocation systems.

8.2.6.5.2.4. Limited Credit to Financial Institutions

This solution, under the name Uniform Limited Input Tax Credit (ULITC), has been proposed by PricewaterhouseCoopers in their 2006 report to the European Commission.[102] Basically, it copies the Australian system to find input VAT relief for financial institutions (see Section 8.2.6.5.2.3). Either a fixed level of input tax recovery is applied to all purchases, or only to a predefined range of costs. This system requires a formula to determine or estimate the recovery rate. Under the Australian RITC system, the rate of recovery is linked to the wages and profit element of the outsourced service. The report suggests combining this with independent statistical surveys to determine the proportion of labor costs for each ULITC service, combined with simplified pro ratas for small and medium-sized financial institutions. We will refer to this method as the Limited Credit Method (LCM) and later we will examine the theoretical approaches that can be taken in determining the input tax recovery rate of financial institutions.

If the LCM would allow a full recovery of input VAT, it would have the same result as a zero rate, and financial services would not be taxed at all. As mentioned before, this would constitute a violation of the fundamental principles of VAT as a general consumption tax and is, therefore, not acceptable as a final solution.

It would make sense to allow input VAT relief for financial institutions in relation to their services rendered to taxable business customers. Because financial institutions provide mostly intermediation services, their value added would be incorporated in the cost base of the next stage of the distribution chain and taxed accordingly due to the recouping effect, demonstrated in Section 8.2.1.2.2. If the LCM rate was limited to sales to business customers, the services rendered to

102. PwC report, *supra* 88, 35.

private consumers would be taxed to the extent that the input VAT of the bank or insurance company is incorporated in their retail price. However, the value added of financial institutions would still remain untaxed.

The credit could be determined on the basis of the ratio of business sales to consumer sales. This would allow for a LCM rate per individual financial institution. For example, if a bank rendered 65% of its services to business customers and 35% to private consumers, it would be allowed a credit of 65% of the total input VAT in a year. However, this rate will probably not be exactly the same from year to year and would, therefore, require recalculations and adjustments, which would somewhat increase the compliance costs for the institutions and administrative costs for the taxing authorities. A recovery rate for the whole banking sector and the whole insurance sector is feasible as well, but a sector rate leads to economic inequities because the rate would never be accurate for each individual bank or insurance company. In reality, it would either be too high or too low for an individual institution, resulting in either under- or overcompensation.

Another method of determining the LCM rate is to provide relief of input VAT that is incurred only in relation to services that are exclusively rendered to business customers. This is feasible but would require precise identification and definition of these services. Financial services products are not static and are increasingly more complex. New products are under development that will require evaluation for VAT purposes. This methodology of rate determination would also require a format of international tax coordination, at least in common and federal markets, to synchronize identification and definition and to ensure that the same financial products are similarly relieved from input tax.

If the scope of the LCM is limited to encourage outsourcing or at least remove the disincentive of outsourcing, the rate would not be determined by all or certain outputs of a financial institution but rather by an approximation of the input tax on those particular procurements. Where the previous methods of recovery rate determination were based on a formula related to the outputs of a financial institution, this approach looks at the inputs. The selection of these procurements is, of course, rather arbitrary and open to prolonged and repeated discussions between taxing authorities and financial institutions either as a group or individually. Again, international coordination would be required, especially within a common or federal market, to ascertain a level playing field.

The assumption under the LCM system is that financial institutions would shift forward their tax credit through lower prices to their customers. This, however, is far from certain. There exits no incentive for a financial institution to lower its price if the market remains prepared to pay the previous higher price. The price will be determined by market conditions and price elasticity for financial services. Even if the credit were determined on the basis of services rendered to business consumers only, individual banks or insurance companies may decide to maintain their current price levels in the business market for all or some of their products and use the credit to improve their competitiveness in the private consumer market. If market conditions allowed either the sector as a whole or an individual institution to maintain its former price level, the system would only improve the overall profitability of either the sector or the individual bank or insurance company.

The LCM is feasible but far from perfect in solving the problems associated with exempting financial institutions. It adds an additional layer of complexity to the VAT system and leads to increased compliance and administration costs. A high level of international coordination and agreement will be required to ensure economic neutrality both in selecting the preferred method to determine the recovery rate and in the application of the chosen method.

8.2.6.5.2.5. Proxy Credit on Financial Services Procurement

Another, and in my opinion more practical, solution could be found in applying to financial services a system of tax crediting similar to the one used for the agricultural sector. As was discussed in Section 8.2.2, EU legislation provides for a special scheme to be applied at the discretion of the individual Member States to the agricultural sector. Within the system of taxing and crediting during the distribution chain, the agricultural sector is simply passed by or jumped over like the knights in chess can jump over other pieces. The input credit of the agricultural sector is shifted forward as a credit to the next stage in the chain.

Financial institutions subject to this special regime would not be eligible to a credit for the VAT they incurred in relation to their procurements as is the case under the current exemption system. Likewise, they would not charge VAT on their sales of financial services. Under the economic assumption that financial institutions shift the tax burden forward to their customers, they would be indirectly compensated for their input VAT through higher prices. To avoid tax accumulation, the business customer would be entitled to deduct the average input VAT burden of his financial services supplier, fixed at a percentage of the sales price. Whereas under the farmer scheme, the deduction is measured as the average input VAT burden of the agricultural sector, the input VAT credit for financial services would be determined by the average input VAT burden of the individual financial institution. This would allow for a fairly accurate calculation and avoid the inequities inherent in sector calculation. It is possible to do this because the total number of financial institutions is rather small, certainly compared to the number of farmers. The working of this system is demonstrated in simplified form in Table 27.

Table 27. Proxy Credit Method for Financial Services Rendered to Business Customers

Tax Rate 10%	Sales	Tax	To Treasury
Producer 1	1,000	100	100
Producer 2	2,000	200	200 – 100 = 100
Bank	3,200	0	0
Wholesaler	4,000	400	400 – 200 = 200
Retailer	5,000	500	500 – 400 = 100
Total			500

The bank's input VAT is USD 200, which it will forward in its sales price to the next stage. Instead of a sale price of USD 3,000 the bank sells for USD 3,200. The next stage receives a credit of USD 200, although the bank did not charge any VAT itself. The tax missed at the bank stage of the distribution is recovered by the treasury in the next stage. The wholesaler pays USD 200 instead of the USD 100 it would have paid if the statutory rate had been applied to this value added. This result is the same as under a reduced rate applied at the intermediary level (see Table 19). The total tax collected by the revenue is USD 500, which is the correct amount when we apply the statutory rate to the final consumer price of USD 5,000. This demonstrates that accumulation has been prevented, in contrast to an exemption system without input credits as shown in Table 20.

Financial institutions would simply mention their individual input credit percentage as well as the amount of credit on their invoice and a business customer can subsequently deduct this credit on his periodical VAT return.

Of course, the special regime could only be applied in relation to financial services. If a financial institution has nonfinancial outputs as well, these should be taxed in the same way as any other taxable business, and credits should be given for tax incurred on procurements exclusively associated with these taxable outputs. That would require a financial services supplier to make such a distinction in his administration, which would naturally increase the compliance effort. However, financial institutions already make those distinctions under the current exemption regime applied in most countries that have a VAT. If a financial institution uses certain inputs in relation to both taxable nonfinancial and financial services, our suggestion is to avoid complex allocation rules and instead to allow compensation for related input VAT only through the proxy method. That would lead to a simplification compared to the current situation and, therefore, to a reduction of compliance costs, whereas the compensation in monetary terms would be almost the same.

Cross-border transactions need careful consideration. Correct application of the destination principle would require a refund of the proxy input credit to foreign customers, regardless of whether they are businesses or private consumers. One way to accomplish this would be to have foreign customers file for a refund. From experience in the EU with refunds on the basis of the Eighth[103] and Thirteenth Directive[104] we can learn that such procedures are time consuming, leading to significant cash flow losses for applicants, and fraud sensitive. States are reluctant in rewarding rebates, sometimes because of budgetary restraints, and the procedures and execution are not uniform among countries even within such a harmonized system as that of the EU.

Most efficient would be to arrange for refunds to foreign customers at the time they make their purchase of financial services. This could be done by using the

103. Article 171(1) of Directive 2006/112 jo. Eighth Directive (79/1072/EEC) of 6 December 1979, OJ 27 December 1979, No. L 331/11.

104. Article 171(2) of Directive 2006/112 jo. Thirteenth Directive (86/560/EEG) of 17 November 1986, OJ 21 November 1986, No. L 326.

financial institutions as intermediaries in the refund process, acting on behalf of the taxing authority. In the case of services rendered to foreign customers, financial institutions would not only mention the input credit on the invoice but also actually deduct the credit from the amount due. For example, if a bank has an input credit proxy of 12% and sends an invoice for USD 1,000, the customer would pay the bank USD 880. Subsequently, the bank would claim a refund of USD 120 from the taxing authorities on a periodical VAT return.

The proxy method has the advantage of being straightforward and simple from an operational perspective. Administrative and compliance costs can remain at a relatively low level, even if the financial institutions administer the refunds. In addition, the method has been tested and proven to work in the EU. It is not a perfect system. The input credit is based on an average measured over a certain time period and corresponds, therefore, not exactly with the input tax related to each and every individual transaction. What is perceived as the most important faults of the current exemption for financial services, the economic distortions, especially tax cascading, and inequities, are solved under the proxy method. Financial services rendered to business customers will be relieved of VAT, but services rendered to private consumers will only be taxed insofar as no input VAT credit is allowed in relation to these services. They are input taxed only, which means that the value added of the financial institutions remains untaxed. The disadvantage of undertaxation of sales to private consumers under the exemption remains in place under the proxy method.

8.2.6.5.3. Evaluation and Conclusions

Financial services are generally exempt from VAT simply because it is difficult to tax this sector efficiently. Typically, the value added of financial intermediation services has the form of a margin, which cannot be identified on a transaction basis and, therefore, cannot be directly taxed under a credit invoice method VAT. Exempting financial services has a number of practical disadvantages and seems also wrong in its principle, where the tax is a broad-based consumption tax. Some, however, argue that financial services should not be subject to a consumption tax at all.

Exemption leads to overtaxation of business customers because the irrecoverable input tax of financial institutions will be incorporated in their price, resulting in tax accumulation effects. Sales to private consumers will be undertaxed because the value added of financial intermediary services will remain untaxed. Ideally, alternative solutions should solve these two problems without creating problems in terms of administrative complexity for taxpayers and taxing authorities alike.

On an aggregate level, the cash flow method seems to be quite promising because it solves most problems associated with the exemption of financial services. However, it comes at the price of increased compliance costs both for the financial institutions and for their business customers calculating their input VAT credit. Although the cash flow is compatible with the credit invoice method VAT, it remains a separate tax regime for one sector of the economy, but it does solve the problems both of over- and undertaxation.

The reverse charge option would be fully compatible with a credit invoice method VAT but leads to overtaxation of private consumers as borrowers, which can only be solved with a complex franking system. Further adjustments are required to ensure that both borrowers and depositors are equality subject to the tax, adding to the administrative complexity.

The LCM comes with many imperfections. The selection of the procurements that will give rise to an input tax credit is arbitrary, and the LCM would increase the compliance burden for financial institutions. Because only relief of the input tax incurred is given, the value added of financial institutions would still remain untaxed, and undertaxation of private consumers would not be solved.

The proxy method has the direct benefit that it is not only compatible with but also can be operated within the credit invoice method VAT. From an operational perspective, it is also fairly simple. Although towards a different economic sector, this method has been tested. In the version suggested previously with a credit tax rate calculated per service supplier and not per sector, it may prove to be the most practical solution to include the financial sector in the current VAT system. It solves the problem of overtaxation, but undertaxation of private consumers would remain.

Although the inclusion of the financial sector in the VAT sector is an important objective under a consumption tax, it should be noted that taxing financial services may have little impact on a state's revenue.[105] Actual payment would be restricted to the domestic consumer level, whereas financial services rendered to business customers as well as exported services would, in effect, be tax free. Financial institutions would be eligible to a full credit of their input VAT, whereas under the current exemption regime, input VAT can only partly be recovered. Recent research, however, concludes a significant increase of VAT revenues with little impact on overall welfare.[106]

8.2.7. Treatment of Capital Goods

8.2.7.1. Introduction and Scope

Consumption taxes are designed on the assumption that consumption is an immediate event. A good example is a father who buys his little girl an ice cream, which she expertly devours in minutes. The term *immediate* is relative; neither does it have to be the buyer who performs the actual consumption. If I were to order a 20-ounce Porterhouse steak at a local franchise, overestimating my digestive capabilities, and later on would take the remnants of my damaged culinary ego home in a doggy bag, either to eat myself at a later time or to feed to my Rottweiler, the sales

105. Ken Messere, *Tax Policy in OECD Countries* (Amsterdam, 1993), at 402.
106. Huizinga, 497–534.

tax or VAT paid in the restaurant would be appropriate because the steak is finally consumed.

For many products, immediate consumption is, indeed, the proper approach, and no economic distortions occur by doing so. The problem lies in the tax treatment of products that have a long, rather than immediate, life cycle, such as real estate, automobiles, clothing, boats, motorcycles, computers, furniture, photo cameras and other electronic equipment.[107] These (capital) goods are either used by the original purchaser until the end of their economic life cycle, sold during their economic life by the original purchaser to another private person, traded in when purchasing a similar new item, or sold to a dealer without purchasing a new item with the dealer reselling the item. To meet the principles outlined previously, the final result in terms of tax burden should be the same in all these situations.

Of course, it is not really the consumption that is being taxed, but rather the monetary value of consumption, reflected by the expenditure made to purchase an item, or the fair market value of the product. Consumption in the strict sense of the word is not required for taxation because tax is not reimbursed when, for instance, the little girl accidentally drops the ice cream in our earlier example. Taxation locks in at the time of consumptive expenditure. If a product is bought for the purpose of consumption, it is taxed. It does not matter who is actually consuming the product bought. It may be consumed by the buyer, his daughter or his dog. Essential is that an expenditure is made for the purpose of consumption. For these reasons, some argue that VAT and sales taxes should be characterized not as consumption taxes but as consumptive expenditure taxes. To a certain extent this is a matter of semantics because consumption itself can only be taxed if we can express its value in monetary units. The monetary value of consumption finds embodiment in the expenditure made to purchase it.

If a durable good is resold during its economic life cycle, that is, before it is fully consumed, its fair market value will be equal to the present value of the future consumption of that good.[108] Consequently, a consumption tax levied on the sales price (which represents the fair market value) of a durable good that is being resold in the course of its economic life is equal to the present value of the tax levied on the annual consumption of such good over the remainder of its life cycle.

Subsequent sales of a good during its life cycle, would lead to tax accumulation if each transaction is taxed without providing a form of relief for tax paid earlier. As mentioned earlier, some argue that under a sales tax or VAT, each transaction is considered to constitute consumption and is, therefore, rightfully taxed. Multiple taxation is simply consequential to taxing on a transaction basis. This approach is in itself correct if we consider VAT and RSTs to be levied on

---

107. In this section we limit our scope to moveable capital goods. Real estate is discussed separately in s. 8.2.7.3.

108. In the same way that an income-producing asset sells for a price equal to the present value of its future income stream.

consumptive expenditure and not on consumption itself. The philosophical divide hinges on whether one perceives consumption flows or consumption stocks to be the object of the tax.[109]

In my opinion, the principles of neutrality and fairness require that the total tax burden on similar goods (or services) is the same, regardless of the number of sales transactions. It should not make a difference whether consumption is immediate or subsequential. Durable goods are taxed at the initial sale over their total life cycle value in the same way as the ice cream in our example. In case a durable good is resold during its life cycle, each owner only "consumes" a part of it, and neutrality requires that each owner would incur a time equivalent part of the tax. For this reason, I support the idea that consumption taxes, such as VAT, should be levied on the consumption flow, and my further evaluation of the treatment of capital goods under VAT and US sales taxes departs from this view.

In Section 8.2.7.2, I compare the tax treatment of (used) goods under both a VAT as applied in the EU and a RST as applied in the United States at the sub-national level in regard to moveable tangible property.[110] Each section deals with a separate factual scenario. Section 8.2.7.2.1 looks at the situation in which a good is resold during its economic life by a business purchaser to another business or to a consumer, or between consumers. The treatment of secondhand goods is dealt with in Section 8.2.7.2.2, and trade-in sales are covered in Section 8.2.7.2.3. Where adequate, each section starts with an evaluation of the correct theoretical tax treatment and, then, provides an assessment of whether and, if so, to what extent, the VAT and sales tax arrive at the same or similar result as the theoretical model.

It is important to notice that VAT and sales tax are distinct in their calculative approach. Under a VAT, it is assumed (also in its legislation) that retail prices are tax inclusive, whereas under a sales tax, prices are supposed to be tax exclusive. To promote transparency in our calculations and numeric comparisons between the two subtypes of taxes, I have chosen to take all prices exclusive of tax unless otherwise indicated.

The questions arising in regard of real property are very similar to those addressed in respect of moveable tangible property. Real property has a long, if not indefinite, life cycle during which it may be sold, used for a purpose that is from a tax perspective different from its original use or even be traded-in when purchasing another property. We deal with the proper treatment for consumption tax purposes of this type of property in Section 8.2.7.3.

---

109. For a short treatise on both points of view, see Sybren Cnossen, "VAT Treatment of Immovable Property," in *Tax Law Design and Drafting*, vol. 1, ed. Victor Thuronyi (Washington, DC: IMF, 1996), 233–234.

110. An earlier study by Pomp and Oldman arrives at conclusions consistent with mine regarding sales tax but does not make comparisons with VAT. See Richard D. Pomp & Oliver Oldman, "A Normative Inquiry into the Base of a Retail Sales Tax: Casual Sales, Used Goods, and Trade-Ins," *National Tax Journal* 43 (4) (1990): 427–437.

8.2.7.2. Moveable Tangible Property

8.2.7.2.1. Resale of Goods during Economic Life Cycle

The principles of a consumption tax dictate that the lifetime use (consumption) of a good is taxed only once. The design of a consumption tax should be tailored at preventing overtaxation in case a product is sold multiple times during its economic life.

8.2.7.2.1.1. Business-to-Business (B2B) and Business-to-Consumer (B2C) Sales

A business (B1) bought a capital good, for example, a computer, for USD 2,000 and resells it after 2 years to either another business (B2) or a consumer (C1) for USD 800.

8.2.7.2.1.1.1. VAT Treatment

Under a VAT, B1 would have incurred VAT on its purchase of the computer at USD 400 (20% x 2,000), but could deduct that same tax as an input tax credit. As a result, there is no tax burden on the computer as long as it is used in the course of B1's business.[111] When B1 sells the computer, it will have to charge VAT over the sales price at USD 160 (20% x 800). If the purchaser is another taxable business, B2, the customer can deduct the same as an input tax credit because the computer will be used in the course of B2's business (see Table 28).

Table 28. VAT Treatment of B2B Resale of Used Goods

Seller	Buyer	Price	Tax	Credit	To Revenue
—	B1	2,000	400	–400	0
B1	B2	800	160	–160	0
Total			560	–560	0

The result is in accordance with the principles of a consumption tax. The computer remains untaxed (through the deduction mechanism) as long as it is used for business purposes. The VAT is not a cost factor, and the computer cost

111. In case a business uses a capital good for both taxable and nontaxable (called: exempt) purposes, or uses a good for taxable purposes entirely at first but changes its use to exempt purposes after some time and vice versa, most VAT regimes apply special rules to allocate the input VAT, or correct the input VAT credit over a certain adjustment period; see Art. 187(1), Directive 2006/112. In the context of this section, I ignore these special rules to avoid unnecessary complexity and confusion, but reference is made to s. 8.2.7.2.4.

of B1 is USD 2,000 – 800 = 1,200. If the customer is a final consumer, C1, he will incur the tax he is not entitled to tax credits (see Table 29).

Table 29. VAT Treatment of B2C Resale of Used Goods

Seller	Buyer	Price	Tax	Credit	To Revenue
—	B1	2,000	400	400	0
B1	C1	800	160	0	160
Total			560	–400	160

When purchased by a business and later resold to a private consumer, it is taxed only for the value of the remaining lifetime of the product, the value of which is determined at arm's length (i.e., the sales price of USD 800).

8.2.7.2.1.1.2. Sales Tax Treatment

Since B1 bought the computer for use in the furtherance of his business but not for resale, the seller will charge him with sales tax. The statutory rate of sales tax is generally lower than the VAT rates applied in Europe. For reasons of calculation simplicity, we assume a sales tax rate of 10%. The seller will charge and B1 will incur USD 200 in sales tax. If B1 sells the computer after 2 years to B2, unless B2 buys for resale purposes, sales tax will be charged again at USD 80. It makes no difference whether B1 sells to a business or to a consumer, such as C1; in both cases a sales tax will have to be charged (see Table 30).

Table 30. Sales Tax Treatment of B2B or B2C Resale of Used Goods

Seller	Buyer	Price	Tax	To Revenue
—	B1	2,000	200	200
B1	B2/C1	800	80	80
Total			280	280

As a result tax is levied twice and the total tax burden on the computer is USD 280. Although the tax rate is 10%, the total revenue received by the revenue service is 14% of the initial value of the computer.

We may expect B1 to try recuperating the sales tax initially paid, at least partially, by increasing the sales price. This will depend, of course, on market conditions. If B1 is unable to do so and, therefore, absorbs the tax as a cost, the total cost price of the use ("consumption") of this computer is USD 2,200–800 = 1,400.

Let's assess the situation in which B1 is able to fully shift the tax burden forward, in which case the resale price will be USD 1,000 (see Table 31).

Table 31. Sales Treatment of Resale of Used Goods with Tax Shifting

Seller	Buyer	Price	Tax	To Revenue
—	B1	2,000	200	200
B1	B2/C1	1,000	100	100
Total			300	300

In our example, additional tax revenue of USD 20 is generated as a result of B1's ability to shift forward the tax burden, which is exactly 10% (the statutory tax rate) of the tax amount. The same effect as demonstrated in Table 20. In essence, the state will collect more in tax revenue relative to the total "consumption" of the product as reflected by its original price. The magnitude of the tax cascading effect will be determined by the length of the chain of transactions in combination with the relative ability of sellers to shift forward the tax burden.

8.2.7.2.1.2. Consumer-to-Consumer (C2C) Sales (Casual Sales)

Under a consumption tax, immediate consumption is assumed. Unless the product in question has a longer-than-immediate life cycle, taxing a product at initial sale would be final and appropriate. In the case of C2C sales of used durable goods, there exists no reason for correction either because the resale price would be a fraction of C1's tax-inclusive cost price. Assume C1 buys a photo camera for USD 1,000 plus 10%, USD 100, in taxes. The total cost is USD 1,100. After 4 years C1 resells the camera to a neighbor for USD 750. C1's cost is USD 350, including USD 32 in sales tax on 4 years of "consumption," while C2 pays USD 68 in tax on C2's "consumption" over the remainder of the camera's life cycle.[112] The state has received the tax due over the full length of the product's lifecycle (i.e., the "consumption" of the product) at the initial sale. Exempting C2C sales is normatively correct because it leads to an economically correct result (see Table 32).

Table 32. Exempt C2C Resale of Used Goods

	C1		C2	Revenue	
Sale	Out	In	Out	In	Out
To C1	1,000				
Tax	100			100	
C1–C2		750	750		
Total	1,100 –	750 = 350	750	100	

112. Because these are tax inclusive sales prices, the tax amount can be calculated with a tax rate of 10% as follows: 10/110×350 = 32; and 10/110×750 = 68.

In principle, it would be possible as well to construct this exemption through a refund to the original buyer, C1, of a proportion of the tax paid, and subsequently tax the resale.

In this example, C1 would buy the camera for USD 1,000 plus USD 100 in tax and receive USD 682 from C2 as payment for the camera and a refund of USD 68 from the revenue service. C2 would buy for USD 682 and pay a 10% tax at USD 68, incurring a total cost of USD 750 (see Table 33). The revenue service would still receive USD 100.

Table 33. C2C Resale of Used Goods with Tax Refund

	C1		C2	Revenue	
Sale	Out	In	Out	In	Out
To C1	1,000				
Tax	100			100	
C1–C2		682	682		
Tax		68	68	68	68
Total	1,100 –	750 = 350	750	168 –	68 = 100

The financial and normative results are the same, but obviously the latter solution is impractical and would lead to exceptionally high administrative costs for the revenue service.

8.2.7.2.1.2.1. VAT Treatment

VAT is due when a sale is made by a taxable trader. According to the legal definition of a taxable person and its accepted interpretation,[113] a consumer involved in occasional sales does not fulfill the definition of taxable person under the EU-VAT law and as a result all his sales remain outside the scope of VAT, regardless of the kind of products he sells. There is one explicit exception in the legislation,[114] namely for C2C sales of new means of transport, such as motor vehicles.[115] However, the exception applies only to cross-border sales to other Member States when that means of transport is, indeed, transported to the other Member State.

Therefore, a sale of a car between two Belgian consumers is not subject to the exception, neither is a sale by a Belgian consumer to an uncle in Switzerland.

113. See Art. 9 of Directive 2006/112. This directive is a recompilation of the Sixth Directive without any significant material changes, see further Paul Quigley, "The New European VAT Directive," *International VAT Monitor* 18 (2) (2007): 158–164.
114. Article 9(2), Directive 2006/112.
115. Article 2(2) (b), Directive 2006/112. This article contains precise definitions for what constitutes "new" for land vehicles, aircraft and seacraft, respectively. Land vehicles, such as cars, are considered "new" when they are less than 6 months old from the date of first use, or have been used for traveling for no more than 6,000 kilometers.

If, however, our Belgian consumer sells his car to a nephew in Germany, he is considered to be an incidental taxable person but only in regard to this single sale and only at the time of this sale. When C1, bought the car, he acted as a private consumer and paid the tax on the purchase price without any right of deduction or credit. This is correct, because his future status as incidental taxable trader was not anticipated at the time, not even by himself.

Let us assume C1 bought a Honda Accord for EUR 25,000 plus EUR 5,000 in VAT. Later on C1 sells the car to a nephew in Germany, C2, for EUR 20,000. This incidental sale changes C1's status from private consumer to taxable trader. However, because the sale entails a cross-border, intracommunity transaction, in other words, it originates in one EU Member State's tax jurisdiction and ends in another EU Member State's tax jurisdiction, the sale is exempt through the application of the zero rate in the country of origin, Belgium. C1 does not charge any VAT on the sale, but the recipient of the car, C2, has to pay German VAT on the purchase price. This is a correct application of the destination principle underlying VAT legislation in Europe. Where C1 paid tax over the full purchase price and C2 has to pay tax over the remainder value, an element of double taxation remains. However, under the exception rules, C1 is entitled to a credit of part of the tax paid on the original purchase that corresponds with the use or "consumption" of the car. C1 can recuperate[116] the input tax paid to an amount that equals the tax rate applied to the selling price of EUR 20,000, or EUR 4,000.

8.2.7.2.1.2.2. Sales Tax Treatment

In the United States, occasional sales are exempt from the RST in most states, not so much because this would be the correct thing to do from a tax normative perspective, but basically for reason of the administrative difficulties taxation of informal sales of used goods between neighbors and during garage sales would invoke. The C2C resale of durable goods that need registration, such as automobiles, motorcycles, boats and campers, however, are taxed in the majority of states for the single reason that this is a simple matter from an administrative perspective. Payment of sales tax is a precondition for registration, and payment can be made in many states on registration with the Department of Motor Vehicles. Assume C1 buys a Chevrolet Impala for USD 23,000 and sells the car after 5 years for USD 10,000 after advertising it in the local newspaper. C1 would have incurred sales tax over the full purchase price in the amount of USD 2,300. C2, however, needs to pay an additional USD 1,000 (10% × 10,000) sales tax when he registers the car. Obviously, the car has not reached the end of its useable life yet.

As explained previously, C2 should not be taxed at all since he takes the place of C1 as consumer, or C1 should receive a refund, because he is paying for a consumption of a car that is no longer available to him. By taxing the full purchase price at the initial sale and retaxing the residue value on resale, the state

116. Article 172, Directive 2006/112. This tax can be recouped only at the time of supply of the new means of transport.

overcollects; it receive a total of USD 3,300 in taxes or 14.34% instead of the statutory 10%. Some states accept the resale price of the car, but others take the stated price of the *Kelley Blue Book*, a used car catalog, based on make, model, year and mileage, or apply another method of value objectivation, such as the standard presumptive value, used in Texas.[117] Some defend the use of the catalog or presumptive value by claiming that this guarantees equal treatment. The opposite is true, however, because these objective standards are based on generalizations to indicate an average price of a used car and cannot take the particulars of an individual car into account. In other words, it provides equal treatment to nonequal situations.

Connecticut, at least in the past, used both the *Kelley Blue Book* and the agreed sales price, applying whichever price was the highest as the taxable amount.[118] There is no normative justification for legislation that ignores a market price reached between unrelated parties, except in the case of fraud,[119] or between related parties as long as the price is at arm's length. Neither can a system of arbitrary taxation be accepted for the purpose of maximizing revenue.

8.2.7.2.1.2.3. Conclusions

Because of the input tax credit system, the VAT achieves the goal of single taxation under the scenario of multiple sales during the life cycle of a good when the seller is a business. This is not the case with the US sales tax where the limitations of the exemption system lead to tax cascading and, thus, to overtaxation.

Generally, incidental C2C sales remain out of the scope of both VAT and sales tax, preventing overtaxation. However, C2C sales of registered vehicles are taxed in the United States, leading to overtaxation. Under the EU-VAT, such sales are only within scope in cross-border (but within the EU) situations and when the vehicles are new, but the seller receives a refund of remainder tax to eliminate double taxation.

8.2.7.2.2. Treatment of Secondhand Goods (Sale to Dealer with No Trade-In)

Second-hand goods sales occur when a private person (C1) sells a used good to a dealer (B1), who resells it to another private consumer (C2). Again, the principles

117. Tex. Tax Code Ann. § 152.0412 (Vernon 2007).
118. *See* Conn. Gen. Stat. § 12-431 (2008); Conn. Agencies Regs. § 12-431(b)-1 (2009). Connecticut now uses the N.A.D.A. Official Used Car Guide as its source for used car valuations. Conn. Agencies Regs. § 12-431(b)-1 (2009).
119. The adoption of valuation benchmarks is, indeed, motivated by fraud. The problem is that even unrelated parties may account for a lower price on the bill of sale than the price actually agreed on, especially in cash deals. However, it is not a fair system when bad faith is assumed, unless margin fluctuations from the benchmark value are allowed and a taxpayer has the opportunity to provide evidence that the sales price is reasonable and at arm's length given the condition of that particular car.

of a consumption tax would require a design that warrants single taxation, or prevents double taxation.

Assume the following example that was examined above. A camera is purchased for USD 1,000 and later resold for USD 550 to a dealer, who in turn sells it to C2 either for USD 550 or for USD 600. At the initial purchase, C1 paid tax relative to the total economic life of the camera, or on its total consumption. Since C1 sells the good at some point during its economic life, C1 has overpaid in tax relative to the use made of the camera. From an economic perspective, C1 is compensated through the sales price for the tax on the remainder of the camera's economic life. In other words, the sales price includes a reimbursement for the (remainder) tax on the consumption that C1 did not enjoy. Assume the camera is halfway through its economic life and the tax rate is 10%, the price C1 receives consists of USD 500 for the remainder value of the camera and USD 50 represents the present value of the tax levied on the annual consumption of the camera over the remainder of its life cycle.

To meet the requirements of economic neutrality, additional tax should only be levied on the value added by the dealer, B1. If the dealer resells the camera for the same price (USD 550) and does not generate a profit, the government has no entitlement to additional tax. It received USD 100 at the original purchase, which represents the total tax on its entire economic life. C2 paid the tax due on his part of consumption through compensating C1 for the overpayment. However, if the dealer resells for a higher price, for example, USD 600, the margin realized represents the value added to the efficiency of the distribution chain,[120] and the government is entitled to tax over the extra USD 50 because it represents future consumption. In that case, B1 should charge USD 605 to C2, the USD 5 representing the consumption tax over the dealer's value added.

8.2.7.2.2.1. VAT Treatment

The private consumer making the original purchase incurs a 20% surcharge, or USD 200, in VAT on the camera. The consumer's sale to the dealer remains out of scope of VAT because he is not a taxable person. Although the sale price may include compensation for the tax on the remainder of the consumption, the dealer cannot deduct this "hidden" tax under the normal tax credit rules because it is not separately charged. The subsequent sale by the dealer to C2 would be subject to tax, and, as a result, tax cascading would occur. To avoid this, special rules have

120. From an economic perspective, the dealer fulfils a brokerage function between sellers and buyers of used goods. However, the dealer has not entered into an agency relationship with either of the parties. In fact, the dealer operates as a buy – sell. Instead of trading directly with each other and to avoid the complexities associated with the sale and purchase of used goods, consumers often prefer to make use of the intermediary function of the used-goods dealer. A seller may be willing to accept a lower price selling to a dealer than he would selling to another consumer, and/or the buyer may be prepared to pay more buying from a dealer than from a private seller. Either way, the dealer adds value not directly to the used good itself, which remains unchanged in nature or quality by his actions, but to the efficiency of the market for that product, and as that is reflected in the price, it should be taxed.

been adopted,[121] generally referred to as the margin scheme or margin arrangement. This set of special rules applies not only to secondhand (used) goods but also to works of art, collector's items and antiques.

To avoid tax cascading, a dealer is allowed to remit VAT on the margin the dealer makes on the sale, the margin being defined as the difference between the dealer's purchase and selling price.[122] Three situations can, in practice, occur. The dealer either makes a profit, breaks even or sells at a loss. Under the profit scenario, indeed, under the EU-VAT rules, the dealer, using the numbers applied previously, would be obliged to remit tax on the difference of the sales price of USD 600 minus the purchase price of USD 550. The dealer would have to pay 20% on the margin of USD 50 that is USD 10 to the revenue service, which is the tax at the statutory rate over the gross profit or value added generated with this sale.

In the case the dealer breaks even, he would not remit any tax to the revenue service because he apparently did not create any added value, but the sales price does include the "hidden" tax paid by the dealer to C1.

Although the dealer is compensated for the tax included in his purchase price, his treatment is not completely equal to purchases made from regular businesses. If a business buys a product from another business, the seller would charge VAT on the sales price, and the buyer would be eligible to an input tax credit in the same tax period. In principle, therefore, a business' inventory is tax free. Traders in secondhand goods, however, receive their input tax credit only at the time of resale. In other words, inventory is taxed until sold, and a secondhand goods dealer has to finance the input tax on inventory where a dealer in "regular" goods does not.

In case the dealer makes a resale at a loss, however, the margin scheme does not provide for a reimbursement of the residual VAT included in the purchase price the dealer paid to C1. If, for example, the dealer would resell the camera for USD 540, the dealer would not only make a loss of USD 10 compared to the purchase price of USD 550 but also would be unable to recuperate the "hidden" VAT, included in the original purchase price. Because both the purchase price of USD 550 and the sales price of USD 540 are tax inclusive prices, the dealer should be entitled to a tax refund over the price difference.

To demonstrate the difference in treatment, in Table 34 we look at a dealer buying from a taxable business supplier and consequently selling to a consumer. In situation 1, the dealer sells at a profit; in situation 2, the dealer breaks even; and in situation 3, the dealer sells at a loss. In Table 35 we encounter the same three

121. Articles 311–325 of Directive 2006/112. The margin arrangement applies to used goods, antiquities, collector's items and objects of art. For the purpose of this section, the description of the EU rules for used goods is presented in simplified form.

122. Article 315, Directive 2006/112. Although for reason of simplified comparison, we use tax-exclusive prices in our examples, the VAT directive considers prices to be tax inclusive. Where both purchase and selling price include the VAT, the margin will naturally be tax inclusive as well, and the amount of tax (assuming a rate of 20%) to be remitted to the revenue will be calculated by multiplying 20/120 × Margin. For example, if the inclusive purchase price is USD 550 and the inclusive selling price is USD 720, then the tax due is 20/120 (720 – 550) = 28.

situations, but this time the dealer buys from a consumer and applies the margin arrangement.

Table 34. Dealer Buys from B and Resells to C

B1	B2 (Dealer)	C	Tax
1,000 (+200 tax that is recovered as input tax credit)	500 + 100 (tax)	(1) 600 (2) 500 (3) 490	120 – 100 = 20 100 – 100 = 0 98 – 100 = –2

B1 buys a camera for business purposes at USD 1,000. The VAT charged at 20% (USD 200) is recoverable as an input VAT credit. After 5 years, B1 sells the camera to dealer B2 for USD 500 and has to charge VAT at USD 100 over the sales price. Assuming that B2 sells the camera in the same tax period, B2 will deduct the VAT paid on the purchase from the VAT charged on the subsequent sale. In situation 1, 20% tax is due on the profit margin of USD 100, which is realized by deducting the input VAT of USD100 from the output VAT of USD 120. In situation 2, the dealer breaks even on the transactions and the tax due on the sale equals the input VAT credit on the purchase. As a result B2 incurs a zero tax obligation. In situation 3, the dealer sells at a loss. By deducting his input VAT credit from the VAT due on the sale, the dealer receives a refund of USD 2.

Table 35. Dealer Buys from C and Sells under Margin Arrangement

C1	B1 (Dealer)	C2	Tax Margin Scheme
1,000 + 200	600 (including tax)	(1) 700 (2) 600 (3) 590	$(700 - 600)t = 20$ $(600 - 600)t = 0$ 0

C1 buys a camera for USD 1,200 and cannot deduct the VAT of USD 200. After 5 years, C1 sells the camera to the dealer for USD 600 (including original tax). B1 subsequently sells the camera to C2 and has to remit tax over the margin realized, that is, the difference between sales price and purchase price. In situation 1, the margin is USD 700 – 600 = 100 at 20%, so the tax due is USD 20. In situation 2, the dealer breaks even and there is no taxable margin. In situation 3, the dealer makes a loss and remits no tax on the sale and is not eligible to a partial refund of input VAT.

From a comparison between Tables 34 and 35, it is clear that the margin scheme fails to provide compensation under scenario 3 where the dealer sells at a loss. As a result, the VAT becomes a business tax on the negative margin realized on the resale.

The margin scheme offers an adequate (albeit not perfect) solution when goods are purchased and sold individually (with the exception of sales at a loss) but fails when goods are purchased in lots and resold in different lots or individually, which may occur in the case of stamp or coin collections. In those instances, it is practically impossible to determine a purchase price for an individual item, and, henceforth, a taxable margin cannot be identified. As a solution, EU legislation allows Member States to introduce a globalization rule under which tax would be due not on the margin of an individual sale but on the margin realized on total sales within a certain tax period.[123] Under this special arrangement, problems with resales of used goods at a loss are resolved as well.

8.2.7.2.2.2. Sales Tax Treatment

C1 paid 10% sales tax at USD 100 when purchasing the camera. The sale by C1 to the dealer, B1, is not taxed because the sale for resale exemption applies. In nearly all states the subsequent sale by B1 to C2 is subject to sales tax.[124] The sales tax legislation of the respective states do not provide for a system comparable to the margin arrangement. For a good comparison with the treatment under VAT, in Table 36 we employ the same situations as in Section 8.2.7.2.2.1 and explain the tax consequences in the case of resale by the dealer with a profit, at break even, or at a loss.

Table 36. Sales Tax Treatment of Dealer Sale

C1	B1 (Dealer)	C2	Tax
1,000 + 100	550 (including tax)	(1) 600	100 + 60
		(2) 550	100 + 55
		(3) 540	100 + 54

C1 bought the camera for USD 1,000 and paid additional USD 100 in sales tax at 10%. After 5 years, C1 sells the camera to a dealer for USD 550, of which USD 50 represents compensation for the tax on the remainder of the camera's economic life. Subsequently, the dealer resells the camera for USD 600 plus USD 60 in tax, for a total of USD 660. The revenue service receives a total of USD 160 in relation to the sale of the camera. From a theoretical perspective, the tax due should be 10% × USD 1,000 = USD 100 for the consumption of the camera and 10% over the margin realized by the dealer (USD 50), which represents the value of the dealer' service, consumed by C2, leading to a total amount of USD 105. The same

123. Article 318 of Directive 2006/112. This is a legislative option for Member States, and some have and others have not incorporated the globalization rule into their national VAT legislation.

124. Arkansas and Oklahoma provide an exemption for the sale of used goods by a dealer, on the condition that the original purchaser paid the tax.

result, overpayment of tax, occurs when the dealer sells at break-even (USD 155 instead of USD 100) or at a loss (USD 154 instead of USD 99).

In addition, economic distortions occur where the resale of a used good by a dealer is subject to sales tax, and the sale of a used good by one consumer to another consumer remains outside the scope of tax as a casual sale.

Apart from a margin arrangement, a correct theoretical solution could be found in reimbursing the original purchaser (C1) for the present value of the tax levied on the annual consumption the camera over the remainder of its life cycle. In that event, C1 would receive USD 500 as payment from the dealer, B1, and an additional USD 50 from the revenue service as a tax refund. Subsequently, B1 would sell the camera for USD 550 (realizing the same margin of USD 50) to C2 and would charge sales tax over the full price. The USD 55 represents the tax over the remainder of the camera's life cycle, including the additional value added by the dealer's services. Exempting the subsequent sale by the dealer to C2 would provide a solution only to the extent that it would eliminate the double taxation; however, it would incorrectly leave the dealer's margin untaxed and lead, in other words, to an undercollection of tax.

8.2.7.2.2.3. Conclusions

When a consumer sells a used good to a dealer, the sales price will include compensation for the tax on the remainder of the consumption, which tax the dealer cannot recuperate. Where the subsequent sale by the dealer will be taxable, tax cascading would occur. Only VAT offers a solution for this problem by taxing only the margin realized by the dealer. The margin scheme is an acceptable solution but is not perfect because it does not provide relief in the case of a subsequent sale at a loss. In that case, the VAT becomes a business tax on the negative margin realized on the resale. Moreover, the dealer only receives compensation for the hidden tax at the time of resale and, therefore, has to finance the tax on his inventory unlike traders in new goods.

8.2.7.2.3. Treatment of Trade-Ins

The trade-in situation occurs when a retailer accepts personal tangible property from a consumer as part payment towards the purchase of a (generally like-kind) item. To prevent overtaxation, the principles of consumption tax would require a design that allows a credit for the tax paid on the remainder value (the unused portion) of the traded-in property.

Returning to our previously used example, assume C1 wants to buy a new top-of-the-line digital camera for USD 1,500 and to trade in the mirror-reflex camera purchased 5 years earlier for USD 1,000. The dealer values the trade-in at USD 550 (including tax) and resells it later to C2 for USD 600. Basically, between C1 and the dealer two sales take place that are executed simultaneously. Instead of the dealer first paying USD 550 to C1 for the old camera and then receiving USD 1,500 back as payment for the new one, parties simply exchange cameras and C1 pays an additional USD 950.

From the analysis in previous sections, it is clear that the revenue service should collect tax (at 10% for sales tax and 20% for VAT) over the life cycle consumption of the old camera (USD 100 or USD 200), tax on the value added of the intermediary function in relation to the resale of the old camera (USD 5 or USD 10) and tax over the life cycle consumption of the new camera (USD 150 or USD 300), for a total amount of USD 255 under a sales tax and USD 510 under a VAT.

Crucial in this respect is the reimbursement either directly or indirectly of the tax on the nonconsumed portion of the old camera. If the revenue service would refund the present value of the remainder tax directly to the original purchaser (C1), all subsequent trades would simply be taxed to arrive at the correct theoretical treatment. The dealer would pay C1 only USD 500 instead of paying a tax inclusive price. C1 would receive USD 50 (or USD 100 under a VAT) from the revenue service as tax reimbursement, receiving a total of, indeed, USD 550 (or USD 600). Subsequently, the dealer would add a margin to the price and resell the used camera for USD 550. The sale of the new camera is subject to tax under the normal rules. This is demonstrated in Table 37.

Table 37. Treatment of Trade-Ins

Product Sale	C1	B1 (Dealer)	C2	Sales Tax	VAT
Reflex camera	1,000			100	200
Trade-in		500		–50	–100
Resale Trade-in			550	55	110
Digital camera	1500			150	300
Total				255	510

The total value of consumption is 1,000 + 50 + 1,500 = 2,550 × 10% = 255 or 2,550 × 20% = 510

Clearly, direct reimbursement has the result that the total tax paid equals the statutory rate applied to the total consumption value.

To my knowledge, direct refund of remainder tax to the original purchaser is not applied in any country. The trade-in allowance of USD 550 (or USD 600) granted by the dealer to the consumer includes an implicit reimbursement of the present value of the tax over the remainder of the used camera's life cycle. It is in fact the dealer who reimburses C1 for the remainder tax. Consequently, the question arises how to compensate the dealer for the tax paid to C1 in order to avoid tax overpayment. The easiest way to achieve this is by permitting the trade-in allowance to be deducted against the purchase price of the new item, and remit tax over the difference. Where the dealer effectively pays over the margin, the original consumer is indirectly compensated for the remainder tax on the traded-in item. This system is discussed in more detail in Section 8.2.7.2.3.2.

8.2.7.2.3.1. VAT Treatment

The VAT legislation at the EU level does not contain provisions exclusively tailored for traded-in goods. Basically, the sale of the new item is subject to the normal rules of taxation, and the margin arrangement applies to the traded-in item (see Table 38).

Table 38. VAT Treatment of Trade-Ins

Product Sale	C1	B1 (Dealer)	C2	VAT
Reflex camera	1,000			200
Digital camera	1,500			300
Trade-in		500	550	$(550 - 500)t = 10$
Total				510

If we compare Table 38 to Table 36, it is demonstrated that the VAT treatment has the correct theoretical result.

8.2.7.2.3.2. Sales Tax Treatment

Most states have provisions that permit a dealer to deduct the trade-in allowance against the selling price of the new item (see Table 39).[125]

Table 39. Sales Tax Treatment of Trade-Ins

Product Sale	C1	B1 (Dealer)	C2	Sales Tax
Reflex camera	1,000			100
Digital camera	1,500			$(1,500 - 500)t = 100$
Trade-in		500	550	55
Total				255

If we compare Table 39 to Table 36, it is clear that the treatment system under sales tax leads to the correct theoretical result. Under the EU-VAT, the compensation is accomplished by reducing the tax as regards the resale of the trade-in item, whereas under sales tax, the same compensation is realized by reducing the tax due on the sale of the new item. However, most, but not all, states allow the trade-in deduction methodology to avoid overcollecting. The rules vary per state. Some states permit it only for certain items, such as cars, boats, motor homes, farm tractors, aircraft and snowmobiles. This limitation may be the result of assurances

125. According to CCH (900-830), eleven states and the District of Columbia tax trade-ins by not allowing a credit for the trade-in on the sale of the new item and by taxing the full sales price when the trade-in is resold. The states taxing trade-ins are Alabama, Arkansas, California, Maine, Maryland, Massachusetts, Michigan, North Carolina, Ohio, Oklahoma and Rhode Island.

the states seek that tax was paid on the original purchase of the trade-in, which is the case with the vehicles mentioned here, as payment of sales tax is a precondition for registration. Nevertheless, the limitation is incorrect and leads to overcollection of tax and violates the principle of production and distribution neutrality because C from C purchases offer a price advantage over purchases from a dealer as a result of tax cascading.

Other states, for instance Connecticut, accept the trade-in arrangement for all products but require that the traded-in item is of the same category or classification as the property being purchased without regard to its grade or quality, but it is not required to be of the specific type within the class. In other words, the distinction is made on the basis of genus not on species.[126] Most states require that the traded-in item is used and is not new.[127] Depending on the specific rules for a state, a used item may be traded in for only a new like-kind item, or for either a new or another used like-kind item. Some states allow more than one item to be traded in for a single item as long as all these items fall into the same category of goods. Connecticut requires that the (fair market) value of the traded-in item and thus the trade-in allowance is for an amount less than the original purchase price, which would mean that the trade-in arrangement cannot be applied for items that tend to appreciate over time, such as collectibles and objects of art. In all probability, the latter rule has been inspired by budgetary considerations and Connecticut tries to avoid engagement in scenarios under which sales tax has to be, in fact, paid back.

8.2.7.2.3.3. Conclusions

Both the VAT in the EU and the US sales tax arrive at the correct theoretical result of providing relief to the dealer for the tax hidden in the price paid for the trade-in item but through different methodologies. Under the VAT, the compensation is accomplished by reducing the tax of the resale of the trade-in item, whereas under sales tax, the same compensation is realized by reducing the tax due on the sale of the new item. However, the rules among US states vary, and trade-ins are subject to all forms of limitations, which violate the general principles of production and distribution neutrality and lead to overcollection of tax on products excluded from the compensation system.

8.2.7.2.4. Pro Rata Temporis Credit for Capital Goods

As a consequence of applying different VAT regimes, that is, the distinction between taxable and exempt supplies, a problem arises when the use of fixed assets

---

126. Example of acceptable exchanges: clothing for clothing, but also footwear for clothing or women's clothing for men's clothing. Also, a sofa for a table, or a guitar for a clarinet. See State of Connecticut, Dept. of Revenue Services, Information Publication IP 2006 (13), Sales and Use Taxes Returned Merchandise, 19 May 2006.
127. Connecticut considers the trade-in of a new item for another new item as an exchange of goods, subject to its own specific rules.

fluctuates over time. Contrary to the general practice for income tax, capital inputs are expensed under a credit invoice method VAT to ensure neutrality as regards the choice between capital and labor or investment and consumption.[128] That would mean that the initial use of a capital good, exempt or taxable, would determine whether and to what extent the VAT paid on the purchase of the good is recoverable. If the initial use is for the production of exempt supplies, no VAT would be creditable, even if the same good were used for making taxable supplies at a later point during its economic life cycle. On the flip side of the coin, if the initial use were in relation to taxable outputs, all VAT would become recoverable, regardless of later use for exempt supplies. An expensing regime for capital goods would not only encourage manipulation as regards their initial use but also could easily lead to economic distortions.

The VAT legislation in the EU contains specific rules for input VAT adjustments in the case of capital goods, basically determining the extent of tax expensing over a longer time period. The choice would be between expensing over a time period that more or less represents the economic life cycle of a specific good, which would have the result of different expensing periods depending on the type or qualification of a good,[129] or to set a time period for all goods, ignoring difference in life cycles. The EU has chosen for the latter method, and Article 187(1) of Directive 2006/112 determines that the adjustment shall be spread over 5 years including that in which the goods were acquired or manufactured.[130] Initially, the amount of input VAT that can be recovered is determined at the time of purchase of a capital good. Subsequently, at the end of each year, an assessment is made as to the percentage of creditable VAT for that year. Adjustments shall be made on the basis of the variation in deduction entitlement in subsequent years in relation to that for the year in which the goods were acquired or manufactured. Therefore, if the percentage is different from the initial ratio, an adjustment is made on the portion of tax allocated to that year, which is one-fifth of the total input VAT.[131] The adjustment system of the EU is hybrid in character where it allows immediate expensing at the time of acquisition and combines this with a pro rata temporis method of adjustments. The system is demonstrated in Table 40.

128. The result of expensing, generally, is that a business will generate a significant excess input tax claim when major investments are made. To avoid paying out huge rebates, Art. 11(3) of the Second EU-VAT Directive allowed Member States, as a temporary measure, to exclude purchases of capital goods from the right of input VAT deduction, or to spread the deduction over time (pro rata temporis) similar to depreciation under income tax.
129. To an extent comparable to the depreciation periods under most corporate income tax regimes.
130. The Member States are allowed, however, to base the adjustment on a period of 5 full years starting from the time at which the goods are first used; see Art. 187(1) second sentence, Directive 2006/112. Only Finland does not apply adjustment rules but subjects movable assets to self-supply rules that are not limited in time.
131. Article 187(2), Directive 2006/112.

Table 40. Input VAT Adjustments over a 5-Year Period

	Year 1	Year 2	Year 3	Year 4	Year 5	Totals
Ratio tax/ exempt use	80%	70%	90%	60%	85%	
Initial tax credit as annual share	3,200	3,200	3,200	3,200	3,200	16,000
Annual eligibility	3,200	2,800	3,600	2,400	3,400	15,400
Correction payable	0	400		800		} 600
Correction credit	0		400		200	

Assumptions: Investment amount: 100,000
Tax rate: 20%
Total tax: 20,000
Annual tax portion: 4,000

A manufacturer buys a new machine for USD 100,000 plus USD 20,000 in VAT. At the time of purchase, the manufacturer assumes that he will use the machine for both taxable and exempt outputs at a ratio of 80/20. For that reason, the manufacturer receives a refund of 80% of the total input tax, or USD 16,000. At the end of the year, it is determined to what extent the machine has been used for the production of taxable and exempt supplies, respectively. In our example, the machine has, indeed, been used for 80% in relation to taxable outputs, and no adjustments need to be made. At the end of year 2, it appears that the machine is used for only 70% for making taxable supplies. The annual share of total input VAT is USD 4,000 (1/5 × USD 20,000). The manufacturer is only eligible for a tax credit of 70% of USD 4,000, or USD 2,800. Since the manufacturer has initially received a credit of USD 3,200 for the year (80% × USD 4,000), he needs to make a repayment of USD 400. In year 3, the input VAT eligibility is 90%, or USD 3,600, where only USD 3,200 has been recovered in relation to that year's portion, and the manufacturer is entitled to an additional credit of USD 400. In year 4, only 60% of the machine is used in relation to taxable supplies, which leads to an input VAT eligibility of USD 2,400. In relation to year 4, the manufacturer has to pay additional tax of USD 800. In year 5, input VAT is eligible for credit at 85%, or USD 3,400, which is USD 200 more than initially received for the year. Over the whole 5-year period, the manufacturer had an average percentage of taxable use of 77%, which would make it eligible for an amount of USD 15,400 in tax credits. Initially, it had received USD 16,000, and over the adjustment period the manufacturer on balance makes a repayment of USD 600.

This system denies significance to disparities between the initial use at the time of acquisition and actual use in later years. Although the statutory length of the adjustment period is in itself arbitrary and not an exact representation of the actual economic life of each capital good, it has the benefit of being relatively simple to administer for both businesses and taxing authorities. From a cash flow perspective, it remains beneficial to somehow ensure that the initial use to the largest extent possible is related to the production of taxable outputs.

In most instances, a change of use of a capital good – from taxed to exempt or vice versa – will have been triggered by an action of the taxpayer. However, if the change in use of a capital good is caused by legislative action, the pro rata temporis rules apply as well,[132] provided the measure is not introduced with retroactive effect[133] and the Community principles of legal certainty and legitimate expectations are not violated.[134]

8.2.7.3. Immoveable Tangible Property (Real Property)

8.2.7.3.1. Outline of the Theoretical Problems

The problems posed by immoveable property are very similar to those discussed in respect of other capital goods (see Section 8.2.7.2). The consumption of the asset is not immediate and complete, but the use is spread over many years. The consumption of a durable good, whether moveable or immoveable, is the flow of services derived from the durable good in a given time period. When a VAT system applies exemptions, then mixed use and the change of use or change of the ratio of use will become issues that need attention. Theoretically, since the consumption or use of a capital asset takes place gradually during its life cycle, taxation should also occur over time. However, in most instances, the same result can be achieved by collecting the tax upfront at the time when the asset is purchased because the initial tax represents the net present value of tax collected over time. Either way, if the same person uses an asset during its whole life cycle, the correct amount of tax will be collected and no distortion will occur. Problems arise with intermediate sales. VAT is irrelevant, of course, for sales between fully taxable persons because the credit system will remove the actual tax burden. As previously discussed, when VAT is

132. ECJ 29 April 2004, Joint Cases C-487/01 and C-7/02, *Gemeente Leusden and Holin Groep BV v. Staatssecretaris van Financiën* [2004] ECR I-5337. In this case, the Netherlands withdrew by legislative amendment the right to opt for taxation of certain lettings of immoveable property.
133. ECJ 6 August 2000, Case C-400/98, *Breitsohl* [2000] ECR I-4321.
134. These principles form part of the Community legal order and must be observed by the Community institutions (ECJ 14 May 1975, Case 74/74 *Comptoir national technique agricole (CNTA) SA v. Commission* [1975] ECR 533), but also by the Member States when they exercise the powers conferred on them by Community directives (ECJ, 12 March 1998, Case C-381/97, *Belgocodex* [1998] ECR I-8153; ECJ 8 June 2000, Case C-396/98, *Schlossstrasse* [2000] ECR I-4279; and ECJ 11 July 2002, Case C-62/00, *Marks & Spencer* [2002] ECR I-6325).

levied on the initial purchase of long-life consumer products, subsequent sales from one private individual to another do not require any adjustments. The initial VAT will be incorporated in the future sale price of an asset and, as a result, subsequent buyers will each bear an amount of VAT equivalent to the time they had the asset in use. This is different, however, with intermediate sales of immoveable property. Immoveable property is unique[135] in that it, generally, appreciates in value over time, whereas most other capital assets depreciate. If tax is only imposed on the initial purchase, no tax would be collected from and be incurred by subsequent owners in respect to the increased value of the property. As is the case with moveable capital goods, intermediate sales between by consumers or other nontaxable entities to the taxable sector would lead to tax accumulation. This could be resolved by taxing all subsequent sales of immoveable property, including those by private individuals, but registering all private homeowners for incidental sales is neither practical nor politically feasible. Most jurisdictions simply allow the increase in property value to escape taxation and only tax the initial purchase of new construction. The rental of residential property clearly constitutes consumption and should, therefore, theoretically be subject to VAT. To ensure neutrality in treatment, the "rental value" of owner-occupied property should also be taxed. However, where subsequent sales of residential property remain untaxed, jurisdictions generally opt to also exempt home rentals from VAT.

Another problem area is self-construction of real estate by private individuals where they, in effect, avoid taxation on the labor component. In relation to exempt businesses, such as hospitals or financial institutions, most jurisdictions apply complex self-supply rules to mitigate the advantage of self-production, but these rules cannot be applied to private consumers without also mandating registration.

The main problem areas under VAT in relation to immoveable property (real estate) can be summarized as follows:

- mixed use and change of use of real estate;
- treatment of owner-occupied property;
- trades between consumers or the nontaxable sector to taxable persons;
- dual character of real estate transactions, constituting both consumption and investment;
- treatment of small traders; and
- self-construction.

In practice, the rules governing the VAT treatment are quite complex and diverse because of many definition problems and borderline issues. The context and purpose of this book do not allow discussing these issues and problems in detail, but we will touch on them briefly in the next section when we take a closer look at the rules set out in the EU-VAT Directive. Many of these problems do not originate in tax law but belong to the realm of common law or civil law. When is property residential and when is it commercial? Are mobile homes and

135. A quality shared with perhaps art, antiques and some other collectibles.

houseboats real estate? Is a prison or a cemetery lot residential? Civil law has the complicated concept of immoveable property or real estate by destination under which property that by itself is perfectly moveable becomes immoveable because of its physical attachment to or its exclusive and subservient use for a particular real estate. Under common law this is generally referred to as fixtures. Telephone cables, water or sewer pipes, satellite dishes, plants and trees, unharvested fruits and crops, and also farm animals or the fish in a pond can all be immoveable depending on circumstances.

Designing an efficient and equitable way of taxing housing is relevant because expenditure on housing is significant, especially in developed countries. The expenditure on housing in the United States in terms of rental values for the year 2007 was USD 1.46 trillion, and the value of new construction, the only expenditure subject to VAT in most jurisdictions, was USD 0.6 trillion.[136] Household units spent 15.97% of their annual gross income in 2006 on shelter, and their total expenditure on housing, which includes shelter, equipment, furnishings, services, utilities and so on, was 27% of gross income.[137]

The correct theoretical treatment of real estate transactions is not under much debate and most, if not all, economists agree with this. The theoretical views and insights are covered in Section 8.2.7.3.3 and conclude in Section 8.2.7.3.4.

8.2.7.3.2. The Current Treatment in the EU

There are a large number of options when deciding on how to tax the sale, resale or rental of real estate, but mainly the choice is between taxing, exempting or zero rating. The choice is not exclusively driven by revenue requirements but also by neutrality and fairness considerations, practicality and social policy. In this section we will focus on the treatment of real property in the EU, not to suggest that their choices represent the optimal and best, but merely as an example to demonstrate the complexity of the issues.[138]

The EU rules regarding VAT treatment of immoveable property are complex because they mandate taxation of certain supplies but include exceptions to the rule of taxation as well as derogations that individual Member States may choose to introduce at their discretion. The main rule is that the supply of a building or parts thereof, including the land on which it stands, shall be exempt from VAT,[139] unless the supply takes place before first occupation. In other words, the sale of existing buildings is exempt and that of new buildings is taxed. Similarly, unimproved land is exempt and building lots are taxed.[140,141] In addition, the leasing or letting of

136. Source: U.S. Department of Commerce, Bureau of Economic Analysis.
137. U.S. Bureau of Labor Statistics, Expenditure Survey 2004–2006.
138. For a comparative study, see Schenk & Oldman, *Value Added Tax*, 408–432.
139. See Art. 135(1) (j) of Directive 2006/112.
140. See Art. 135(1) (k) of Directive 2006/112.
141. Only in Malta are supplies for new buildings and building land exempt, and in Greece new buildings are exempt where they serve as the owner's main residence.

immoveable property is exempt as well,[142] with the exception of the provision of accommodation in hotels or sectors with similar function, holiday camps and camping sites,[143] parking lots,[144] permanent installed equipment or machinery[145] and safe deposit boxes.[146] Member states, however, are allowed to apply further exclusions to this exemption.[147] At their discretion, Member States may allow taxable persons a right to opt for taxation, in the case of otherwise-exempt sales of land or buildings or exempt lease of immoveable property.[148] This allows Member States to prevent nondeductible input VAT (and thus tax pyramiding) to emerge within the production and distribution chain. Member States also have the right to restrict the scope of the right of option and to determine detailed rules governing its exercise.[149] The directive does not provide definitions of first occupation, building land or permanent installation. Explicitly, it refers to the laws of the Member States to define hotel and similar accommodation. With the EU rules as they are, it will come as no surprise that the treatment of real estate varies considerably among Member States. Because the tax jurisdiction as regards real estate transactions accrues to the country where the property is located, and cross-border transactions are physically impossible, different rules and interpretations are not a concern from the perspective of equal treatment, or external neutrality, but they are important from the perspective of legal certainty.

Although rule variation among Member States is consequential to the design of the EU regime for real estate as laid down in the directive, terms and definitions are European in nature. With the inception of the ECs, a separate legal regime has been created that has precedence over national law and applies its own concepts and definitions. Terminology such as transfer of ownership, lease or letting, first occupation, new building, and so on are not defined under national law nor are they concepts of either common or civil law, but they are concepts of European law. The ECJ has, therefore, a distinct role in clarifying terminology. However, the directive allows the Member States extensive latitude in that it permits them to lay down detailed rules to apply the concept of first occupation in the case of conversion of

142. See Art. 135(1) (l) of Directive 2006/112.
143. See Art. 135(2) (a) of Directive 2006/112.
144. See Art. 135(2) (b) of Directive 2006/112. Although mandatory, Italy and Lithuania have not excluded parking lots from the exemption.
145. See Art. 135(2) (c) of Directive 2006/112. Although mandatory, not implemented in Lithuania.
146. See Art. 135(2) (d) of Directive 2006/112. Although mandatory, not excluded from the exemption in Germany, Italy and Lithuania.
147. See Art. 135(2), last sentence of Directive 2006/112.
148. See Arts 137(1) (b), (c), and (d) of Directive 2006/112. Twenty-one Member States provide taxable persons with the option to tax regarding the lease of immoveable property, thirteen states allow the option for the sale of existing buildings, and eleven states provide the option for the sale of unimproved land. Many states limit the exercising of the option to property that will be used by the buyer or lessee exclusively or almost exclusively for making taxable sales. Generally, these conditions have been introduced to ensure exemption of residential property and to block tax-avoidance schemes by exempt entities regarding commercial property.
149. See Art. 137(2) of Directive 2006/112.

buildings and essentially delegates to them the authority to determine the meaning of "the land on which a building stands"[150] and of "building land."[151]

Although buildings, in principle, are to be considered "new" until the time of first occupation, Member States are allowed to apply different criteria based on the time period between the date of completion and that of first occupation, or between the latter and the date of subsequent supply.[152] Certainty in respect to whether a building is considered to be "new" is important because it has major financial consequences. The status of the building determines whether VAT has to be charged on the sale and whether the seller is eligible to input VAT credit on construction or acquisition costs. Without certainty in this respect, it will be hard to determine whether a building project is financially viable.

Although Member States have been empowered to develop their own criteria in this respect, the ECJ has provide some guidance in a case about a moveable tangible property. The question raised was whether the restoration and rebinding of an antique book constituted a "new" good. The ECJ ruled that this can only be the case when the result of contractor's work is an article whose function is different from that of the materials provided.[153] Applied to immoveable property, a total renovation of, for example, an office building, which remains an office building after completion of the work, would probably not constitute a "new" building, but the conversion of a factory into apartment units probably would.

Other problems arise when a newly constructed building remains unsold or unleased. In some jurisdictions, the property would remain new because the event of a first occupation would not have taken place, but in other jurisdictions a building loses its status as "new" when a certain number of years have passed since the start of the construction. It is feasible that even during the construction period a building becomes "old," as a consequence of which the subsequent sale would be exempt and the builder would not be able to recover any input VAT, unless the legislation allows the builder to opt for taxation.[154]

Difficult borderline issues arise when immoveable property is used for both residential purposes and commercial purposes, subject to different VAT treatment, or when an exempt residential lease is combined within itself taxable services, such as cleaning or grooming services. In such an event, should the consideration paid be split between a part paid for the exempt lease and a part paid for the taxable services and, if so, how exactly should the input tax be allocated?

To add to the confusion, Member States are permitted to consider as tangible property certain interests in immoveable property, rights in rem that provide the holder thereof with a right of use, and shares or interests equivalent to shares giving the holder thereof either de iure or de facto rights of ownership or possession over

150. See Art. 12(2), para. 2 of Directive 2006/112.
151. See Art. 12(3) of Directive 2006/112.
152. See Art. 12(2), para. 3 of Directive 2006/112.
153. ECJ, 14 May 1985, Case 139/84, *Van Dijk's Boekhuis BV v. Staatssecretaris van Financien* [1985] ECR 1405.
154. This situation could occur in the Czech Republic where a building switches status 3 years after the start of construction and where no option for taxation is available.

immoveable property.[155] Some states have done so and others have not. In conclusion, it can be said that the rules among the Member States of the EU are diverse if not simply chaotic.[156]

In many instances, the use of real estate will vary over time. Relevant for VAT, use is either for taxable or for exempt purposes. In the case of mixed use, or change of use, or a change in the ratio of use rules need to be in place by which to determine input VAT credit eligibility, over- or undertaxation would occur, and simple opportunities for tax avoidance would emerge. The EU has introduced an adjustment period for capital goods during which input VAT will be recategorized in case the use of the good changes in subsequent years compared to the use in the year of acquisition. For immoveable capital goods, Member States can set the adjustment period between 5 and 20 years,[157] with most Member States taking a 10-year period.[158] The mechanics of the adjustment scheme for immoveable and moveable capital goods are basically identical (see Section 8.2.7.2.4) The adjustment period for immoveable property is demonstrated in Table 41.

Table 41. Input VAT Adjustments for Immoveable Property

	Y1	Y2	Y3	Y4	Y5	Y6	Y7	Y8	Y9	Y10
Ratio tax/ exempt use	70%	60%	80%	65%	85%	90%	100/0%			
Initial tax credit as annual share	140K	140K	140K	140K	140K	140K	140K	140K	140K	140K
Annual eligibility	140K	120K	160K	130K	170	180K				
Correction payable	0	20K		10K						
Correction credit	0		20K		30K	40K				

Assumptions:

Investment amount: 10,000,000
Tax rate: 20%
Total tax: 2,000,000
Annual tax portion: 200,000

155. See Art. 15(2) (a) (b) (c) of Directive 2006/112.
156. For a more detailed overview of the treatment of real estate in selected Member States, see Christian Amand, Gottfried Schellmann & Rob Vermeulen, "Immovable Property and VAT: Lessons from Past Experience," *International VAT Monitor* 16 (5) (2005): 325–334.
157. See Art. 187(1), para. 3 of Directive 2006/112.
158. The Czech Republic, Finland and Greece apply a 5-year period; Belgium uses 15 years; and Bulgaria, France, Ireland, Malta, Portugal, Romania and Slovenia apply the maximum period of 20 years.

A business buys a new machine for USD 10,000,000 plus USD 2,000,000 in VAT. At the time of purchase, the business assumes that it will use the machine for both taxable and exempt outputs at a ratio of 70/30. For that reason, the firm receives a refund of 70% of the total input tax, or USD 1,400,000. At the end of the year, it is determined to what extent the machine has been used for the production of taxable and exempt supplies, respectively. In our example, the machine has, indeed, been used for 70% in relation to taxable outputs, and no adjustments need to be made. At the end of year 2, it appears that the machine is used only 60% for making taxable supplies. The annual share of total input VAT is USD 200,000 (1/10 × USD 2,000,000). The manufacturer is only eligible for a tax credit of 60% of USD 200,000, or USD 120,000. Because the manufacturer has initially received a credit of USD 140K for the year (70% × USD 200,000), it needs to make a repayment of USD 20K. In year 3, the input VAT eligibility is 80%, or USD 160K where only USD 140K has been recovered in relation to that year's portion and the business is entitled to an additional credit of USD 20K. In year 4, only 65% of the machine is used in relation to taxable supplies, which leads to an input VAT eligibility of USD 130K. In relation to year 4, the business has to pay additional tax of USD 10K. In year 5, input VAT is eligible for credit at 85%, or USD 170K, which is USD 30K more than initially received for the year. Regarding year 6, 90% of input tax is deductible, which gives rise to an additional refund of USD 40K. At the end of year 7, the business sells the property for USD 2,5MM. Because the property is older than 2 years, it is considered to be "old" and, therefore, the sale is exempt from VAT, unless the option to tax is being exercised. The remainder of the adjustment period is allocated to the point of sale. In other words, if the sale is exempt, the business is supposed to have used the building for the remainder adjustment period for exempt purposes. This would mean in this case, that the business has to repay to the revenue the tax initially recovered in relation to years 8, 9 and 10, or 3 × USD 140K = 420K. However, when the sale is taxed through the option, the business is supposed to have used the building for the remainder of the adjustment period exclusively for generating taxable output and will be eligible to an additional refund of 3 × USD 60K = 180K.

8.2.7.3.3. *A Practical Solution for Incorporating Immoveable Property in a VAT System*

Over the past decades, no new insights have been offered as to the theoretically correct treatment of immoveable property (real estate) under a VAT. Most economists agree that a broad-based consumption tax, such as VAT, should include all economic transactions regarding immoveable property. Taxation of all transactions would also remove the problem, incurred under current treatment, of defining what precisely constitutes a new building, especially when a renovation is sufficiently significant to transform an old building into a new one for tax purposes, and would avoid all the other definition problems. To fully comprehend the problems associated with taxing all transactions of immoveable property down the supply chain, we need to distinguish between types of transactions, that is, sales and rentals, on the one hand, and between the VAT status of the persons involved in the transactions, that is, taxable persons and private individuals on the other hand.

8.2.7.3.3.1. Sales of Commercial Property

Taxing all sales of commercial property would lead to the least difficulty, and would, one might suspect, be welcomed by taxable businesses that are eligible to full input VAT credits. Taxable businesses are already registered for VAT, and reporting immoveable property sales and deducting input tax in relation to their purchase and maintenance would be a rather straightforward process for them. If only sales of commercial property would be taxed, a clear definition to distinguish commercial from residential property would still be needed. This problem could be avoided by taxing sales of residential property as well.

8.2.7.3.3.2. Sales of Residential Property

All initial and subsequental sales of residential property should be brought within the realm of taxation as well. Where sales from a taxable person, such as a lessor, to a private person, that is, an owner-occupier, is subject to tax, equal treatment requires taxing sales from one owner-occupier to another private person as well. In most jurisdictions, these sales would exceed the threshold for small traders. It seems neither practically nor politically feasible to register all individuals who sell residential property and charge them with collecting tax from other private individuals. Sales of residential real estate occur only irregularly and are generally mediated by legal professionals, such as attorneys, solicitors or notaries, involved in title verification and the disbursement of moneys. In most jurisdictions they are already responsible for the collection of transactional taxes, such as transfer or conveyance taxes. It makes practical sense to also charge these mediators with the withholding of VAT due as regards a sale of real estate on behalf of the seller. In this model,[159] a private individual would pay tax on the purchase of either new construction or existing housing but would be assumed to use it exclusively for consumptive purposes until an intermediate sale occurs. This sale would trigger a fiscal metamorphosis and transform the individual from a nontaxable into a taxable person. Because the taxable person is making a taxable supply, he would become eligible for the deduction of any tax incurred in relation to his residence prior to the sale. That is not so much a problem with the tax paid on the initial purchase if we assume that the tax originally paid would be registered in the real estate registers that most jurisdictions require either at the local or regional level. For all other costs, such as maintenance and renovations, private individuals would need to keep and maintain records in order to be able to exercise their right of deduction at the time of closing.

159. See in more detail, Robert Conrad & Anca Grozav, "Real Property and VAT," in *VAT in Africa*, ed. Richard Krever (Pretoria University Law Press, 2008), 81–112.

Another complication is that most home purchases are predominantly financed by a third party (bank). If home sales are taxed, this would require owners to finance the tax due on purchase (in essence to pay interest over the tax) as well, which would add to the problem of public acceptability and political feasibility.

8.2.7.3.3.3. Commercial Rentals

Taxing commercial rentals, again, would be straightforward, and the tax charged by the lessor on the monthly or quarterly payments will be deductible as input tax credit by the lessee. If residential rentals are not taxed, again a clear definition would be needed to distinguish between the two types of property.

8.2.7.3.3.4. Residential Rentals

Short-term residential rentals (hotel rooms, camping sites, and so on) are already taxable in many jurisdictions, but long-term rentals generally are not. Taxing long-term residential rentals would be logical from the perspective that such a use of real estate clearly constitutes a form of consumption. Neutrality, however, would require also taxing the rental value of owner-occupied property. Otherwise, ownership would receive preferential treatment over renting. Cnossen is correct in his assumption that taxing rental value of owner-occupied real estate would be difficult politically where these values are also taxed under an income tax and would give rise to the suspicion of double taxation.[160] If owner-occupiers are taxed on the rental value of their property, all homeowners would be elevated to the status of taxable person. As a consequence, they would be eligible to deduct input VAT related to this "self-rent," including tax paid on its purchase, maintenance and repair. However, in most cases the annual taxable output of a homeowner, that is the total rental value of his owner-occupied home, would remain below the small trader threshold, unless the "self-rent" is excluded from the small trader exemption. Moreover, if rental value is taxed, the consequence would be that the tax paid on the purchase of the property would become immediately creditable at the time of purchase instead of at the time of subsequent resale, which may raise the question as to why intermediate sales of residential property should be taxed at all. In other words, if both the sale and "self-rent" of residential property are taxed, it appears that no tax would actually be collected on the sale of residential property since owner-occupiers would be eligible for an input VAT credit as a result of their obligation to remit tax on the "self-rent." If the "self-rent" would escape taxation because of the small trader exemption, then only the sales of residential property would lead to actual taxation.

8.2.7.3.4. Conclusions

As we have seen, in the EU (and in many other jurisdictions for that matter) only the initial sale of real estate, whether commercial or residential, is subject to VAT. Increases in value over the lifetime of a property, therefore, escape taxation.

160. Cnossen, "VAT Treatment of Immovable Property," 231–245.

However, Member States are permitted to allow contracting parties to opt for taxation in relation to the sale and rental or commercial property. Long-term residential rentals are exempt from tax, but short-term rentals, such as rentals of hotel rooms, camping sites, and so on, are taxed. As a consequence, all the problems associated with exemptions emerge in relation to the exempt sales and rentals of real estate. In addition, because real estate is effectively used over a long period of time, taxing it only at the initial sale requires adjustments of input VAT whenever the use of the property changes. Taxing real estate transactions, whether sales or rentals, may theoretically be most correct and would solve many of the practical and definition problems. Especially in regard to the rental of residential properties, political problems may be expected where equal treatment would require taxing the rental value of owner-occupied property as well. However, it seems that the rental value of a house in almost all cases would remain below the small traders' threshold and, therefore, would remain untaxed.

8.2.8. Composite Supplies

The VAT systems of most countries apply multiple rates and make a distinction between supplies of goods and of services. It would be a mistake to assume that these distinctions are under all circumstances separate compartments. A composite supply is a transaction consisting of several elements that, if supplied separately, would be subject to different treatment. This could be a combination of a good and a service, or of supplies subject to different rates or subject to different jurisdiction rules, or a combination of taxable and exempt or out of scope supplies. The question arises how such a composite supply should be treated. Which rate should be applied when the elements of the combined supply are subject to different rates? Which jurisdiction rule should be chosen when a good is bundled with a service? When exempt and taxable supplies are merged, which regime applies?

Basically, there are three theoretical possibilities:

(a) The composite is considered to be a supply sui generis, treated according to its own characteristics.
(b) The treatment of the composite is determined by the dominant element.
(c) The composite is dissected into its elements and each element is treated on the basis of its own characteristics.

The question arises whether any guidance exists as to which of these approaches has priority. Jurisdictions, of course, may have different views in this respect. The ECJ has taken the position in a 1999 ruling that the main rule should be that a supply is regarded as distinct and independent and that no artificial division should be made into individual elements of a supply that comprises a single service from an economic perspective.[161] There is a single supply where one or more elements

161. ECJ 25 February 1999, Case C-349/96, *Card Protection Plan Ltd v. Commissioners of Customs and Excise* [1999] ECR I-973.

of the bundle of supplies constitute the principle service, and the remainder elements have to be regarded as ancillary or incidental to the principle service. This needs to be judged from the perspective of the customer. If the customer's purpose is to receive a particular element, this constitutes an individual supply. A service element is ancillary if the customer's aim is not directed at receiving this element in particular; the element only serves to improve or enhance the delivery or enjoyment of the principal service. Canada and Australia have adopted very similar approaches.[162]

If someone drops his car off at the local garage to replace the brake pads, the aim will be directed at receiving both the parts as well as the service of having them installed. Therefore, it makes sense to distinguish between the two if and when they are subject to a different treatment. However, in the case of the repair of a flat tire on a bicycle, the supply of the little rubber pad used to cover the pinch hole and the glue needed to adhere the pad to the inner tire is absorbed by the overall repair service because the aim of the customer is to have the flat tire repaired and the pad and glue are just ancillary to performing this service.

Another example is a scenic antique train ride that can be found in many a tourist destination. Sometimes the ride is advertised together with an offering of dinner and drinks. The reasoning could be that the catering is an aim in itself for the customers and should, therefore, be treated as a separate supply. This could be relevant when different rates for food and transportation apply, or in case of exempt international travel.

In the United States, bundled transactions have arisen as an issue especially in regard to telecommunication services. Most telephone and cable companies offer a diversity of services packaged together, including local and long distance phone services, cable television service, Internet access service, and wireless voice and data services, all for a single price that is lower than when the same services are purchased individually. The tax issues created by bundles are largely governed by federal and state tax and regulatory statutes. For example, at the federal level, the Internet Tax Freedom Act (ITFA) as amended[163] and the Mobile Telecommunications Sourcing Act (MTSA)[164] both provide guidance for the taxation of bundles. Specifically, the acts both provide that where separate elements of a bundle are taxed differently, the entire sales price can be taxed at the highest applicable rate unless the service provider can reasonably identify the portion of the sales price attributable to products and services taxed at lower rates or not taxed at all based on its books and records kept in the regular course of business.[165] At the state level, the treatment varies considerably. Some states follow the federal rules;[166] others require nontaxable services to be separately stated in order to enjoy tax exempt

---

162. See Schenk & Oldman, *Value Added Tax*, at 135–136.
163. ITFA, Pub. L. no. 105-277 (1998) as amended by Pub. L. no. 107-75 (2001) and Pub. L. no. 110-108 (2007) (codified as amended at 47 U.S.C. § 151 n.).
164. Mobile Telecommunications Sourcing Act, 4 U.S.C. §§ 116–126 (2008).
165. ITFA § 1106; Mobile Telecommunications Sourcing Act, 4 U.S.C. § 123(b) and (c).
166. See, e.g., 35 ILL. COMP. STAT. 636/5-7 (10) & 636/5-20 (2008).

status;[167] others again treat the bundle as tax exempt but apply tax to taxable elements (as a result unbundling will be necessary);[168] and finally some states have their own unique rules requiring, for example, preapproved agreements as regards the tax treatment of bundled services, or creating so-called safe harbor tests that effectively unbundle the charges for tax purposes.[169]

What remains unclear is what constitutes a reasonable standard for unbundling, based on a company's books and records. It seems that the taxing authorities will not prima facie accept a segregation of the price made by the service provider, but no objective criteria have been introduced in the federal legislation to provide guidance in this matter.

Moreover, the individual services of the bundle may be subject to different state jurisdiction rules, which in turn may lead to diverse interpretation among the states as regards the taxation of the bundled service and thus potentially to multiple taxation.

8.2.9. Public Sector

8.2.9.1. Theory and Background

One of the main policy decisions to be made when designing a VAT (or any other type of consumption tax for that matter) is how to treat government procurement and supplies made by public bodies.[170] Where the central government is concerned, the VAT incurred on its purchases is, in essence, a wash through because the seller will remit the tax paid by the government to the same government. The same is true for local and intermediate levels of government, evidently to the extent that they are funded by the central government, but also when they have other sources of income because an increase of their procurement cost price due to VAT would inevitably increase the funding needed from the central government.[171] That does not lead, by consequence, to the conclusion that government procurement should be relieved from tax but only that it does not matter from a budgetary perspective.

The activities of the public sector can be divided into three groups:[172]

(a) redistribution of income and wealth;
(b) provision of public goods and services; and

---

167. See, e.g., LA. ADMIN. CODE tit. 61, pt. I, § 4301- Sale of Services (b) (2008).
168. See, e.g., COLO. REV. STAT. § 39-26-104(1)(c)(IV) (2007).
169. See, e.g., KAN. STAT. ANN. § 79-3603(b)(3) (2006) (amended 2007).
170. Charities and not-for-profit organizations perform similar functions and, consequently, the same VAT issues arise in respect to their outputs and inputs.
171. In China, local governments receive, in effect, a refund of 25% of input VAT incurred on their procurement because 25% of all VAT collected in their jurisdiction is allocated to them; see Xiaoqiang Yang, "VAT Treatment of Government Procurement: A Comparative Analysis," *International VAT Monitor* 16 (5) (2005): 342–348.
172. Michel Aujean, Peter Jenkins & Satya Poddar, "A New Approach to Public Sector Bodies," *International VAT Monitor* 10 (4) (1999): 144–149.

(c) provision of goods and services similar to those supplied by the private sector.

In many instances, government supplies are made for only nominal or nil consideration because they are financed partly by direct fees but mostly from taxes and borrowings. Often, there exists no direct link between the supplies made and the means of financing. The first category does not constitute consumption or create any value added but is effectively a transfer of funds between different income groups via the intermediation (taxation and subsequent redistribution) of the government. As such, it should remain out of the scope of VAT and, consequently, within the current VAT system, no (direct) recovery of input VAT would be possible. The provision of goods and services in competition with the private sector should ideally be taxed to meet the requirement of economic neutrality. The tax base should include any grants and taxes directly received as consideration for these supplies, and public bodies should be eligible for full credit of input VAT incurred in relation to the provision of private goods and services.

There is no reason, in principle, to exempt the supplies of public services and goods and to treat public bodies as final consumers in regard of these. In effect, exemption means that tax will be due on the procurement by public bodies because input tax will not be deductible. This appears to be incorrect because VAT should apply to the value of consumption, which is negligible where the marginal cost is nil. In any event, the final consumers of public goods and services are the individuals receiving them.

There is no economic rationale for the current exemption system with no or only partial input tax recovery. So why do most countries provide a special regime for government output? The answer is both political and practical in nature. It is believed that government activities are hard to tax, especially because of their diversity, which makes it difficult to determine a single treatment. Moreover, political consensus has it that not taxing public sector supplies serves the realization of generally accepted social and distributional objectives.

Special treatment for public bodies,[173] whether by exempting or through zero rating their output, is currently the norm, but naturally this complicates the VAT system.[174] Although zero rating is generally the preferred method of providing tax relief, it also presents opportunities for fraud where traders fake sales or overstate their sales to public bodies.[175] Economic distortions may occur when public bodies are involved in activities that compete with the private sector and would be allowed to make tax-free supplies. Such situations are rather frequent. Public bodies are active in many areas where private enterprises operate as well. Most notably are education, health care and social services, but also transportation, waste management, car parking, air traffic control, radio and television broadcasting, recreation,

---

173. In this section, we use the single term *public body* to refer to states, regional and local government authorities, and other bodies governed by public law, mentioned in Art. 13(1) of Directive 2006/112.

174. See, for a general description of the issues, Ebrill et al., *The Modern VAT*, 91 et seq.

175. Tait, *Value Added Tax*, at 76.

and utilities. The competition is not always immediately clear, especially when the government seems to be the exclusive supplier of certain services as is the case in some countries with the railway system. Distortion may still occur insofar as railroad transportation competes with privately owned bus lines for passenger transportation or with trucking companies and river barges for the transportation of commodities. Public postal services compete with private businesses such as UPS, FedEx and DHL. Semimonopolies supported by beneficial tax treatment may prevent private companies from entering the market. In many instances, a level competitive playing field is created by providing similar relief to private providers rendering the same services as public bodies. This is typically the solution chosen for services considered to be meritorious in nature, such as educational and health care services. However, this only enlarges the scope of the derogations from the general VAT system.

Exempting government output is another, almost traditional, form of preferential treatment, chosen, for example, by the EU and by many other countries. Unsurprisingly, it evokes the same adverse effects as exempting the private sector. As a consequence of an exemption, public bodies are not eligible for input VAT credit. For that reason input VAT is perceived as a cost. As discussed, for the central government, the tax is a wash through because the supplier charging them VAT is actually collecting that tax on the same government's behalf. Lower-level public bodies are funded on the basis of their costs, which will include the input tax incurred by them. However, this does not change perception, and production and investment decisions are distorted where public bodies are focused on cost minimization. In addition, classification problems may likely arise between what constitutes a commercial activity and a public service. Similar to the effect of exemptions in the private sector, outsourcing is discouraged and insourcing (self-supply) preferred, leading to economic inefficiencies. Input tax allocation issues may arise where a public body is engaged in both commercial and government activities. Moreover, the ineligibility to input tax recovery leads to tax cascading when subsequent supplies are made to the business sector. Finally, the perceived burden of input tax had led public bodies to engage in tax-avoidance planning, which is not only budgetarily costly for the central government but also undermines the moral standing and authority of the government in general when it tries to combat tax avoidance by the private sector.

Several countries have responded to these difficulties by reimbursing public bodies for the VAT incurred on input related to their exempt activities.[176]

176. Canada, Austria, Finland, France, Luxemburg, the Netherlands, Portugal, Sweden and the UK. See on these refunds more in general: Harpert van Dijk & Guido Lubbers, "The VAT Compensation Fun(d)?," *International VAT Monitor* 11 (1) (2000): 6–9.

In Canada the size of the refund depends on the type of organization and the type of tax (federal GST, the Harmonizes Sales Tax and the Quebec Sales Tax, and varies from 0% to 100%; see Pierre Pascal Gendron, "Value-Added Tax Treatment of Public Bodies and Nonprofit Organizations," *Bulletin for International Fiscal Documentation* 59 (11) (2005): 514–526.

Full refund of input VAT, in effect, converts the exemption to zero rating.[177] Potentially, however, these refunds may worsen the existing distortions of competition, depending on the scope of the refund. All countries, with the exception of the Netherlands, limit the refund to VAT incurred on domestically sourced procurement, thus creating inequality between domestic and foreign suppliers. Some countries, notably the UK and the Netherlands, provide VAT refunds only on costs related to the activities that are out of scope of VAT, which leaves the incentive for self-supplies over outsourcing in place as regards exempt activities. However, if the refund is extended to exempt activities, as is the case in Denmark, Finland and Sweden, private companies providing similar exempt supplies find themselves at a competitive disadvantage to the extent of the input VAT incurred.

Exempting government procurement from state and local sales and use taxes is also the method chosen in the United States.[178]

The lesson to be learned is that it is best from both a theoretical and a practical perspective to include government in the VAT system to the widest extent possible. New Zealand and Australia are the only countries that apply a VAT system that includes the provision of goods and services by the public sector.[179] Government procurement is taxed in the same way as sales made to regular taxable businesses, and all supplies made by public sector entities for consideration (including both direct fees and general funding through local taxation) are taxed, including supplies made between different sectors or departments of the government. As a consequence, these taxable supplies lead to an entitlement to input VAT credits on procurement that relates to these taxable supplies. The rationale for taxing pubic bodies can be found in administrative simplicity, accountability and transparency of government operations; comprehensiveness of coverage; and sound economic management.[180] Nevertheless, the example set by New Zealand and its positive experience has not created a general following among countries that have introduced a VAT at a later date.

When VAT was introduced in the EU, the role of the government and its participation in the marketplace was different from today's. In other words, what constituted typical public activities 40 years ago may now be performed by the private sector as well. Moreover, many public activities are increasingly outsourced to realize efficiency objectives. As a result, the determination of which supplies of goods and services should be subject to VAT has become more urgent to prevent distortion of competition with private enterprises supplying the same. In the next section, a closer look is taken at the practice and problems that have arisen as regards the chosen treatment of the public sector.

---

177. Ebrill et al., 95.
178. Article 21 of the US Federal Acquisition Regulation. This regulation also provides for relief of other taxes. See further, Yang, "VAT Treatment of Government Procurement," 343–344.
179. As well as to the nonprofit and charitable sector. See, for a short overview, Bird & Gendron, *The VAT in Developing and Transitional Countries*, 93–97.
180. Peter Barrand, "The Taxation of Nonprofit Bodies and Government Entities under the New Zealand GST," *International VAT Monitor* 10 (1) (1991): 2–3.

8.2.9.2. The EU Treatment of the Public Sector

Under the main rule, public sector bodies are not regarded as taxable persons, that is, their supplies are out of the scope of VAT regarding activities or transactions in which they engage as public authorities, regardless of whether payment, dues or fees are received in return.[181] Many exceptions to this general rule are formulated in the directive, and a public body is deemed to make a taxable supply in case:

(a) they engage in activities as public authorities but their treatment as non-taxable persons would lead to significant distortions of competition;[182]
(b) they provide the activities listed in Annex I of Directive 2006/112, unless negligible in scale;[183]
(c) they make intracommunity acquisitions above a certain threshold.[184]

As a consequence of being out of the scope of VAT under the general rule, public bodies are not eligible to input VAT credit on their procurement because this privilege is reserved for taxable persons insofar and to the extent that they make taxable supplies of goods and/or services. Public bodies acting in their official capacity are treated as final consumers and must pay VAT on all their purchases.[185]

In practice, however, determining a public body's VAT liability is far from an easy exercise.[186] Supplies made by a public body may be outside the scope of VAT under the general rule, or they may be inside the scope because the government entity is not acting in the capacity of a public authority or its activities are subject to one of the exceptions mentioned previously. When they are within the scope of VAT, these supplies may either be taxable or exempt. Taxable supplies of goods and services made by a public body must be charged with VAT at a standard rate or at a reduced rate. However, no VAT is chargeable on supplies that are made in the context of a public body's activities outside the scope of VAT or on supplies designated as exempt supplies.

The variable positions held by public bodies under VAT also complicate the determination of their input VAT credit entitlement. Input VAT in direct connection to taxable output will be recoverable, whereas input VAT incurred in relation to exempt output[187] and government activities will not give rise to a credit

181. Article 13(1), Directive 2006/112.
182. Article 13(1), para. 2, Directive 2006/112.
183. Article 13(1), para. 3, Directive 2006/112.
184. Articles 2(1) (b) (i) and 3(2) (a), Directive 2006/112.
185. However, there are some exceptions in which supplies to public bodies are either exempt or zero rated, such as gold for central banks (Art. 152, Directive 2006/112); supplies of warships and provisioning of and maintenance and other services to those ships (see Art. 148(b), Directive 2006/112); supplies to international bodies (Art. 151(b), Directive 2006/112); supplies under diplomatic arrangements (Art. 151(a), Directive 2006/112); and supplies within the context of NATO (Arts 151(c) and (d), Directive 2006/112).
186. Rita de la Feria, *The EU-VAT Treatment of Public Sector Bodies: Slowly Moving in the Wrong Direction,* (Oxford University Centre for Business Taxation, Working Paper 08/08).
187. Pursuant to Arts 131–137 of Directive 2006/112.

entitlement. As is the case for taxable persons other than public bodies, pro rata allocation will be required for input tax relating to both taxable and nontaxable or exempt activities (see Section 8.2.5.3).

The distinction between taxable and exempt supplies may be complicated when the activities performed navigate near the borderline of definitions. In this respect, however, public bodies will find themselves engaged in the same disputes as other taxable persons, which was discussed in Section 8.2.4.4.

The first paragraph of Article 13(1) of Directive 2006/112 contains two cumulative conditions for the provision to apply.[188] The first condition is found in the qualification of the supplier, who has to be a body "governed by public law" and the second condition refers to the context within which the activities are conducted, namely "as public authorities." Because the treatment of public bodies derogates from the main rule that supplies are taxed, a strict interpretation is necessary, requiring both conditions to be simultaneously fulfilled.[189]

The main problem is found in the textual vagueness of Article 13 of the directive. It remains unclear and undefined when a public body is engaging in activities "as a public authority" and what constitutes a "significant distortion of competition."

The ECJ has ruled that it is for the national courts to determine which activities or transactions fulfill the conditions set out in Article 13(1), first paragraph of the Directive,[190] but it has also provided some guidelines. According to the ECJ, a body acts as "public authority" when its activity is subject to a "special legal regime" which differs from the general regime applicable to private economic operators. Activities that would normally fall within the prerogatives of a public authority will no longer share in the facility of Article 13(1) of the Directive, when they are outsourced to an independent third party.[191] In a recent case, the ECJ has shed some light on the exception rule for activities that lead to a significant distortion of competition. The first issue was one of benchmarking, or how competition should be evaluated. The ECJ ruled that competition must be evaluated by reference to the activity in question and not by reference to any particular local market. As to the degree of distortion, the court explained that the word *significant* in the concept of "significant distortions of competition" means something that must be more than negligible, but does not mean a "materially adverse or exceptional effect" on competitors.[192]

---

188. ECJ, 26 March 1987, Case 235/85, *Commission v. the Netherlands* [1987] ECR 1471, where the public services of notaries and bailiffs were treated as out of the scope of VAT, although rendered by persons in private capacity within the context of a liberal profession.
189. ECJ, 17 October 1989, Joint cases 231/87 (*Commune di Carpaneto Piacentino*) and 129/88 (*Commune di Rivergaro*) [1989] ECR 3233.
190. For a critique to this approach, see Servaas van Thiel, "EEC: Public Authorities as Taxable Persons for VAT," *International VAT Monitor* 9 (2) (1990): 28–34.
191. ECJ, 25 July 1991, Case C-202/90 (*Ayuntamiento de Sevilla)* [1991] ECR I-4247, at paras 19 & 20, and recently in ECJ, 12 June 2008, Case C-462/05 (*Commission v. Portugal*), O.J. 5 August 2008, No. C209/3 at paras 38–42.
192. ECJ, 16 September 2008, Case C-288/07 (*Commissioners of HMRC v. Isle of Wight Council and Others*), O.J. 22 November 2008, No. C301/9. In dispute was whether off street parking

Article 13(2) provides Member States with the option to treat activities that are exempted under Articles 132, 135, 136, 371, 374–377, 378(2), 379(2), and 380–390 of the VAT Directive as activities outside the scope of VAT when carried out by public bodies.[193] The result, of course, is an increase in the diversity of treatment of public sector activity among the Member States. It also adds to the complexity of the system, where the status of a public body as taxable (but exempt) or nontaxable person is unclear to other participants in the supply chain. That status may be relevant, for instance, to determine tax jurisdiction, or the place of supply, of certain services.[194]

The relationship between the different sections, (1) and (2), of Article 13 is also not clear, adding another element to the legal uncertainty surrounding the treatment of the public sector under VAT. It seems reasonable to assume that the option granted in Section 2 is subject to the restrictions formulated in Section 1.[195] In other words, a Member State cannot exercise the option to treat a listed exempt activity as out of the scope of VAT when this would lead to a significant distortion of competition.

The rationale for this provision is somewhat obscure because the switch from exempt to nontaxable status has no influence on the tax base, since in both cases the directly related input tax is irrecoverable. However, it does make a difference for the calculation of the pro rata deduction because nontaxable turnover is not included in the denominator where exempt turnover is.[196] As a result, public bodies will increase their overall VAT recovery on overhead and other costs that cannot directly be associated with taxable or exempt output, when a Member State decides to exercise the option to treat exempt activities as nontaxable activities.

The EU Commission is aware of the complexities and potential distortions inherent to the current treatment of the public sector and started an internal assessment of the social and economic impact of possible legislative changes. The main considerations for the commission are including certain public sector activities within the scope of the VAT, providing input tax credit in relation to out-of-scope activities and reducing the number of exemptions.[197] It is unlikely, however,

---

offered by a public body was subject to VAT because it would constitute significant distortion of competition. In an earlier case, ECJ 14 December 2000, Case C-446/98 (*Fazenda Pública*) [2000] ECR I-11435, the ECJ had ruled that off street parking was not per se or necessarily subject to VAT, which triggered the UK local authorities to request for repayments of VAT remitted in the past.

193. Mainly activities in the areas of medical and hospital, welfare, sports, educational, and financial services.
194. See, for example, Art. 56(1) of Directive 2006/112 where the status of the customer determines whether the origin or destination principle applies to listed services, in other words whether the services are deemed taxable in the country where the supplier is located or the country where the customer is located.
195. Rita de la Feria, *The EU-VAT Treatment of Public Sector Bodies: Slowly Moving in the Wrong Direction,* Oxford University Centre for Business Taxation, Working Paper 08/08, (2008) at 13.
196. See Art. 174 of Directive 2006/112.
197. See Michel Aujean et al., at 79.

Figure 13. VAT Treatment of the Public Sector

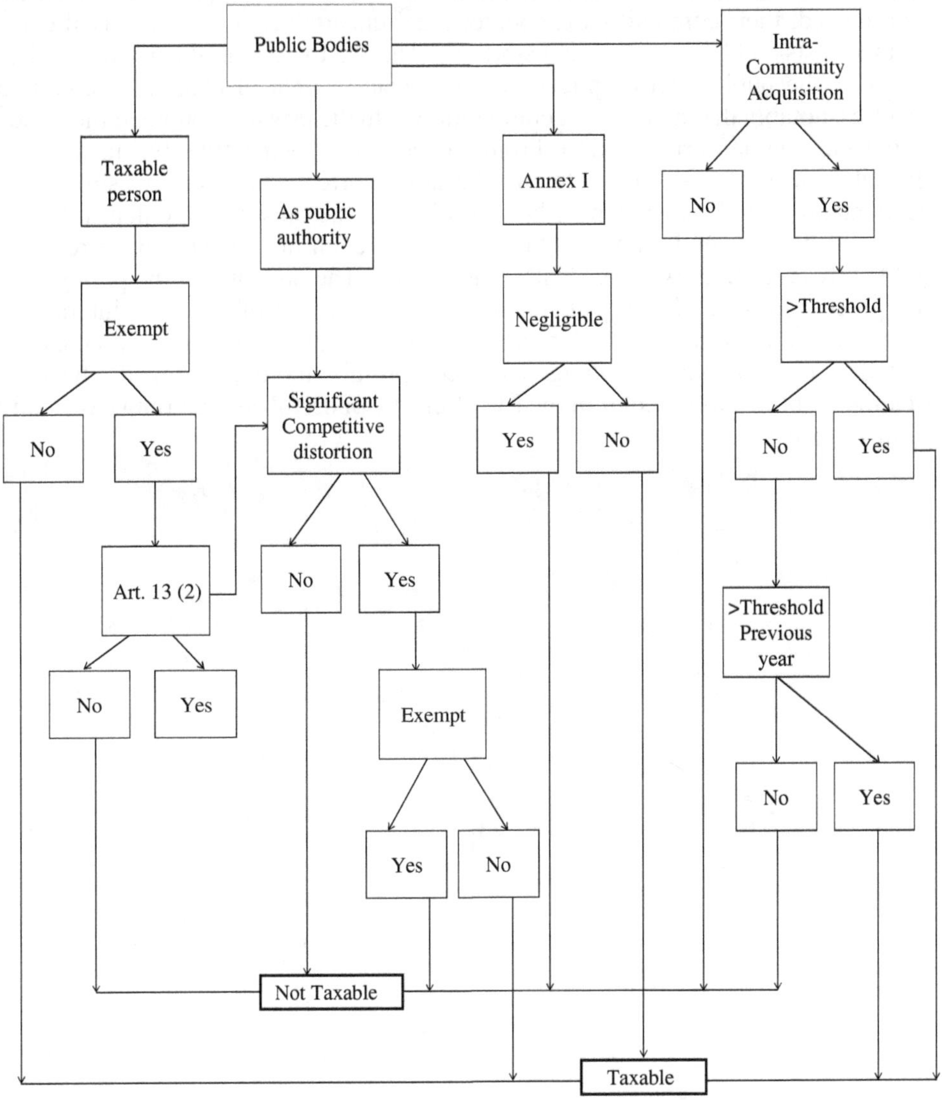

that the commission would propose full taxation of the public sector, given the reality of the small-steps-only policymaking process in the EU.

Figure 13 summarizes the current VAT treatment of the public sector.

8.2.9.3. Conclusions

Practical experience in the EU demonstrates the problems created by applying a special VAT regime to public sector activities. These activities may be exempt, out of scope, nontaxable or taxable under the VAT, depending on many, and rather vaguely defined, criteria. As a result, public bodies, their suppliers, their customers and, indeed, their competitors encounter legal uncertainty, incur increased compliance costs and face economic distortions. The EU treatment of activities undertaken by the public sector appears to be archaic in light of changing economic realities, notably the intensifying competition with the private sector and the trends to outsourcing and privatization. From an economic perspective, full taxation of the public sector has strong preference because it offers administrative simplicity, accountability and transparency. New Zealand is the only country that has fully accomplished the optimum structure. For most countries, what can be realized politically is far from what is ideal economically. The outcome of the policymaking process in general, not just for tax law, is the result of complex interaction between competing visions and interests, a constant give-and-take within the context of traditional political trading, until a compromise has been reached. The VAT treatment of the public sector in the EU offers a wonderful and ongoing case study of this process.

Chapter 9
Cross-Border Transactions

The issue with cross-border transactions, obviously, is to develop universal rules of tax jurisdiction to prevent double taxation or nontaxation of a certain supply of a good or service. Treaties regarding the prevention of double taxation do not cover indirect tax and are focused exclusively on direct taxes. The concept of double taxation for direct taxes is also different from the one applicable to indirect taxes. In the case of direct taxes, the focus is on the same tax subject being taxed more than once, whereas under consumption taxes, the concern is with the same tax object being taxed by more than one jurisdiction.

Most countries apply the territoriality principle, which limits the capacity of a state to tax transactions taking place within its borders or within its national territory, regardless of whether the supplier is a domestic or foreign business. Consequently, foreign transactions are outside a state's jurisdiction, even when performed by a domestic firm. This principle provides a guideline for the allocation of tax jurisdiction, but there are instances where a transaction can be allocated to more than one jurisdiction. Territoriality is one of the founding principles of EU-VAT[1] and also regulates interstate commerce within the federal market of the United States (see Section 9.6.1.3).

To prevent double taxation or nontaxation of cross-border transactions the choice is between taxing the supply of a good or service either in the country of production (origin principle) or in the country of consumption (destination principle). We take a closer look at the practical implications of these principles in Sections 9.1.1 and 9.1.2.

Under WTO rules, a choice is made for the destination principle, including the possibility of rebates of indirect taxes paid in the country of origin. This may put countries that rely more on direct taxes than indirect taxes for government funding

1. Articles 2 and 3 of Directive 2006/112.

at a competitive disadvantage when engaging in international trade, a prominent issue among US policymakers (see Section 9.2).

The tax allocation principles under a territorial, destination-based VAT can be summarized as shown in Table 42.

Table 42. Tax Allocation Principles of a Destination VAT

Transaction	Taxable	Exempt
Domestic sale of goods and services	X	
Exported goods and services		X
Imported goods and services	X	

Under the destination principle, imports of goods and services must be taxed, and exports must be relieved from tax. As a consequence, border tax adjustments are required. For goods, the entry into and exit from a country can be physically verified at the border by customs. Allocating the use of services to tax jurisdictions is accomplished solely on the basis of legal assumptions.

The physical verification of goods, however, depends on the presence of a customs service. That will be the case at the outer borders of a state and verification of the traffic of goods with third countries will be possible, but no border controls generally exist, nor should they exist, at interstate borders within a federal state or a common market. Goods can cross the border between Michigan and Ohio or between New York and Massachusetts freely without being subjected to inspections and verifications. Border controls are considered to be economically disadvantageous and hinder the proper functioning of a federal or common market. For that reason, border controls have been fully abolished per 1993 within the EU as part of the process of economic integration (see Section 9.2). Before that date, cross-border sales of goods within the EU were treated for VAT purposes in the same way as imports and exports with third countries. The abolition of border controls required the introduction of a separate regime for intracommunity supplies of goods, which is explained in some detail in Section 9.5.1.

The principle of economic neutrality requires that imported goods and services are taxed at the same rate as similar goods and services produced domestically because the purpose is to create a level playing field and not to protect the domestic market.

VAT applies its own terminology, which may at times be confusing to the nonspecialist. The jurisdiction rules are generally referred to as place-of-supply rules whereby a distinction is made between supplies of goods and supplies of services.[2] We explain these rules, taking the EU legislation as an example, both in relation to transactions with third countries and with other Member States of the common market (see Section 9.5).

---

2. For an in-depth treatise, see Ben Terra, *The Place of Supply in European VAT* (London-The Hague-Boston: Kluwer Law International, 1998).

Although these rules are generally satisfactory in realizing taxation in the country of destination for B2B transactions, cross-border sales to private individuals pose their own specific challenges, especially with the emergence of e-commerce and the Internet. Section 9.6 is dedicated to the treatment of distance sales in both the United States and the EU.

9.1. ORIGIN VERSUS DESTINATION PRINCIPLE

The traditional approach towards cross-border trade is that it can be taxed only by one of two jurisdictional principles, namely the origin principle and destination principle. Simply stated, under the origin principle, a good is taxed where it is produced, and under the destination principle it is taxed where it is consumed. An important aspect of the principles is that of tax allocation. Under the origin principle, the tax should accrue to the country of production; under the destination principle, the tax should accrue to the country of consumption.

9.1.1. Origin Principle

In essence this means that the tax on a certain article or service applies equally to all domestically produced values regardless the ultimate destination of the product. Values produced abroad are not subject to the tax. Exports are taxed up to their export value similarly to domestically sold products, and imports are exempt from tax up to their import value.[3] No border tax adjustments are required when the origin principle is applied (see Figure 14).

A trader in country A sells a certain product to a customer in the same country as well as to a customer in country B. In both cases, the trader will add to the price the tax applicable in country A, collect the tax from the customers and remit it to the taxing authority of country A.

As a result, however, distortions of competition may occur due to tax rate differences among countries. Under ceteris paribus circumstances and assuming that tax rates are reflected in prices, a good produced in a low-rate country may undercut the prices of their competitors in countries that apply a higher rate. Only small differences in tax may be offset by higher transportation costs.[4] These distortions of competition would likely lead to trade deficits and force the import country to take countermeasures either to reduce the real costs of domestic production or to reduce its currency exchange rate. In addition, the import country suffers reduced tax revenue when imports are favored over domestically produced

---

3. Clara K. Sullivan, "Indirect Taxation and Goals of the European Economic Community," in *Fiscal Harmonization in Common Markets*, vol. II, ed. Carl S. Shoup (New York and London: Columbia University Press, 1967), 21.
4. William M. McNie, "The Origin Principle and Transport Costs," in *Fiscal Harmonization in Common Markets*, vol. I, ed. Carl S. Shoup (New York and London: Columbia University Press, 1967), 265–311.

Figure 14. Origin Principle and Cross-Border Transactions

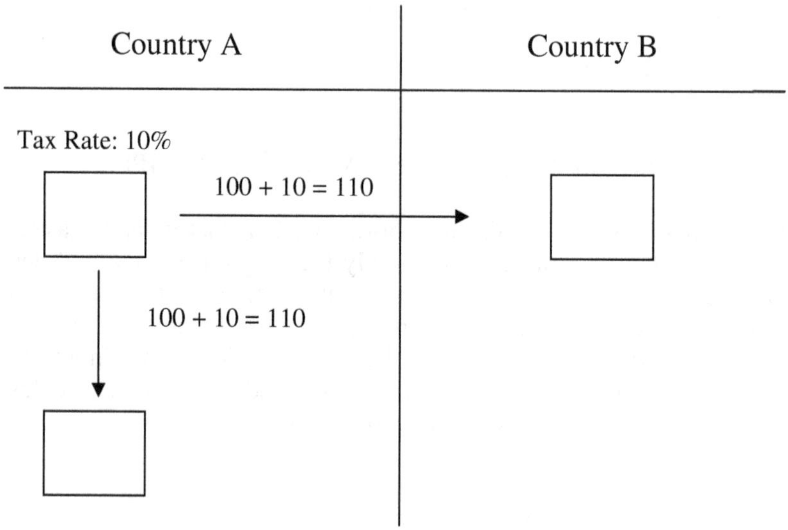

items and services. It is generally accepted that the origin principle should only be applied between countries with identical or closely similar tax systems and rates.[5]

9.1.2. Destination Principle

The opposite principle taxes all products alike in the jurisdiction where they are consumed, regardless of their country of origin. In other words, imported goods are taxed in the same way as domestically produced products. On the flip side of the coin, the production state will not tax a product that is destined to be exported. As a result, all goods when sold for final consumption will bear the same tax burden, namely that imposed by the country of destination (see Figure 15).

A trader in country A sells to a customer located in the same country, adding local VAT, which is remitted to the taxing authority of country A. Sales to a customer in country B are not taxed in country A, or are subject to a 0% rate. On importation in country B, VAT will be due by the importer at the rate applicable in country B, and the tax will be remitted to the taxing authority of country B.

Under the destination principle, the competition between domestic products and imported products is not distorted by tax differences; however, border tax adjustments will be required. If a good is exported, the country of production

5. Alexander J. Easson, *Tax Law and Policy in the EEC* (London: Sweet & Maxwell, 1980), at 60.

Figure 15. Destination Principle and Cross-Border Transactions

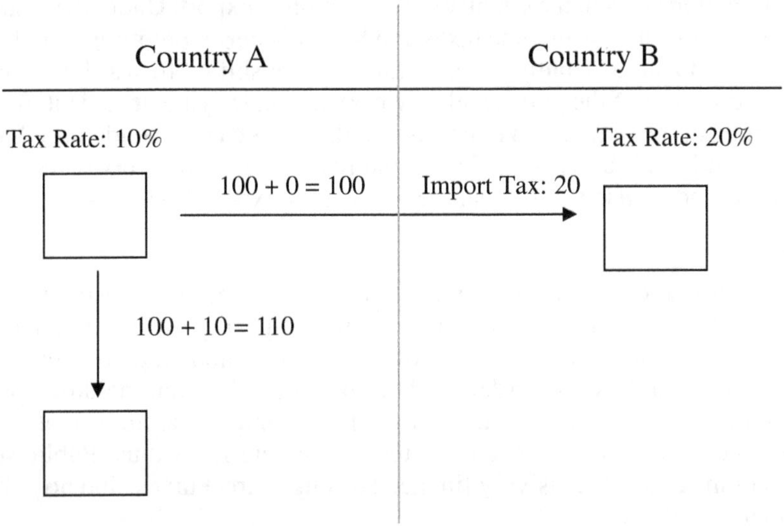

will need to refund the tax already borne by the product. On importation, a compensatory tax needs to be imposed to equalize the tax burden on the imported goods with that borne by similar domestically produced goods.

9.2. WTO RULES FOR BORDER TAX ADJUSTMENTS AND THEIR ECONOMIC EFFECTS

In an effort to accommodate fairness in international trade and prevent double taxation, the WTO and its predecessor, the General Agreement on Tariffs and Trade (GATT),[6] have adopted rules that determine which country has the power

6. The GATT was first signed in 1947. The agreement was designed to provide an international platform that encouraged free trade among Member States by regulating and reducing tariffs on traded goods and by providing a common mechanism for resolving trade disputes. As an international agreement, GATT is similar to a treaty. The agreement is based on the "unconditional most-favored-nation principle." This means that the conditions applied to the most-favored trading nation (i.e., the one with the least restrictions) apply to all trading nations. The WTO came into being on 1 January 1995, as part of the Uruguay Round of negotiations (1986–1994), and is the successor to the GATT. Whereas GATT was a set of rules agreed on by nations, the WTO is an institutional body. The WTO has expanded its scope from traded goods to trade within the service sector and intellectual property rights. The WTO deals with the rules of trade between nations at a near-global level; it is responsible for negotiating and implementing new trade agreements and is in charge of policing member countries' adherence to all the WTO

to tax goods that are traded across borders. The choice went for the destination principle, including the possibility that goods crossing borders would be exempt from transaction taxes in the country of production or export. Under the assumption that direct taxes, such as income taxes and Social Security premiums, are borne by the production and distribution sectors (and are not shifted forward to, in the end, the final consumer of the goods and services), the underlying argument to prohibit rebates of this type of taxes on export is that the taxes cannot be identified with the exported goods and services. Under similar reasoning, indirect taxes are explicitly identifiable and, consequently, can be rebated on exportation.

Example 1

A simplified example can demonstrate how border tax adjustments of indirect tax would theoretically support economic neutrality of international trade.[7] Assume that we have two producers of computer components, one based in the United States and the other in Japan. The cost of production, including profit, of one component is USD 100 in both countries and we assume that all other circumstances, including exchange rates, are at ceteris paribus. Public services in both countries are exclusively financed through direct taxes, and no border tax adjustments are made.

Now assume that Japan decides to increase overall taxation by introducing a credit invoice method VAT levied at the rate of 20%, which is entirely shifted forward into a higher selling price. The domestic price of the components would increase to USD 120 in Japan, whereas it would remain USD 100 in the United States. Where the Japanese component producer decides to export the components to the United States, the exported components are not subject to Japanese VAT and the producer receives a rebate of all the VAT paid in relation to his procurements (input VAT). In other words, the components leave Japan free of any VAT. On arrival in the United States, no tax would be levied because, in example 1, the United States only applies a direct tax. The Japanese components would sell in the United States for USD 100, which is the same price as prior to the introduction of the VAT. If the US manufacturer would decide to export to Japan, the US manufacturer would, of course, receive no rebate in the United States but would pay an import VAT of USD 20, increasing the price to USD 120, which is the same as the

agreements, signed by the bulk of the world's trading nations and ratified in their parliaments. More than 150 countries participate in the WTO. See John H. Jackson, *The World Trade Organization: Structure of the Treaty and the Institution, Sovereignty, the WTO and Changing Fundamentals of International Law* (Cambridge University Press, 2006); Bernard Hoekman, "The WTO: Functions and Basic Principles," in *Development, Trade, and the WTO: A Handbook*, eds. Bernard M. Hoekman, Aaditya Mattoo & Philip English (Washington, DC: World Bank Publications, 2002).

7. See, for an extensive analysis of border tax adjustments, William P. Orzechoski, *Border Tax Adjustments and Fundamental Tax Reform*, Background Paper no. 39 (Washington, DC: Tax Foundation, November, 2001); and Gary Clyde Hufbauer & Carol Gabyzon, *Fundamental Tax Reform and Border Tax Adjustments*, Policy Analysis in International Economics 43 (Washington, DC: Institute for International Economics, 1996).

competing Japanese product. As a result of the border tax adjustments, both manufacturers are able to trade in each other's markets under tax-neutral conditions. The US company can compete under equivalent market circumstances in Japan, and the Japanese manufacturer is protected in its home market against the cheaper US products through the import tax.

In the United States, the WTO rules have come under increased criticism, and US corporations are believed to be placed at a competitive disadvantage as a result of these rules. Basically, the reasoning is that taxes based on the destination principle and those based on the origin principle, regardless of whether they are labeled as direct or indirect taxes, have the same economic result. Where, in example 1, no border tax adjustments are made, that is, where the goods exported from Japan are not relieved of Japanese VAT and goods imported into Japan are not subject to Japanese VAT, the Japanese products would, indeed, be more expensive. At a price of USD 120, they would not be able to compete in foreign markets, where similar domestic products cost USD 100. Similarly, imports of US products into Japan would be cheaper and would price the Japanese products out of the Japanese market.

Economists reason that, in a perfectly flexible model of the economy, price adjustments would occur when the domestic price for goods is higher than the world market price. If, in example 1, we assume that, in Japan, both labor and capital receive pretax factor incomes of 50% of the price of the goods, each would receive USD 50 and the government would receive USD 20. To compete in the world market, the factor prices would have to fall to restore the pretax price. A decrease of factor incomes of 16.66% would accomplish this, and labor and capital would each receive USD 41.67, and the government would receive USD 16.66 (20% × 83.34). The government, labor and capital receive the same share of total price, but the price is reduced to allow the producer to compete in the world market.[8]

Economists also contend that, apart from adjustment of factor incomes, price differences between countries would be compensated through an adjustment of the currency exchange rate.[9] In example 1, the Japanese components are USD 20 more expensive in Japan than their US counterparts. In other words, Japanese final consumers could save that amount by buying goods imported from the United States, instead of Japanese goods. As a result, the demand for dollars would increase and, over time, the yen would depreciate relative to the dollar by 16.66%, leveling out the price difference. If that adjustment would actually occur, it can only be the result of a long-term process. For businesses, the short-term (the "here-and-now") disadvantageous effects of changes to the tax system are more important than the comforting prospect of a theoretical long-term equilibrium. The business community always perceives border tax adjustments as an advantage to local businesses. If, indeed, the exchange-rate effect would be immediate, why would exports be relieved of VAT in the first place?

8. The lower returns on capital and labor have, of course, real economic effects.
9. Jane G. Granville, *Corporate Tax Reform and International Competitiveness*, Congressional Research Service Report no. 86-42E (Washington, DC, 25 February 1986), 1–2.

In the end, justification of border tax adjustments comes down to the interpretation of the concept of tax incidence. There are economists who reason that businesses will always attempt, to the extent allowed by the market circumstances, to shift the tax burden forward to their customers. As a result, all taxes would, in the end, be borne by the final consumers. On the opposite side of reasoning, all taxes are supposedly borne by the businesses because the world market prices would leave no room for shifting taxes forward. The WTO follows a traditional approach to tax incidence, on the basis of which all direct taxes are presumed to be borne by businesses and all indirect taxes by final consumers. Under that approach, the distinction between direct and indirect taxes seems justified. However, under either of the other approaches, regardless of whether the taxes are borne by businesses or final consumers, the distinction seems to have a discriminatory effect. By all probability, the economic reality is more complex and all taxes are borne by final consumers, labor and capital together, albeit that there is no certainty as to what extent each group ultimately bears the burden of the tax. Even if it were possible to establish the proportions, they are likely subject to constant change.

Valuable as the economic nuances may be, they are irrelevant where a certain economic viewpoint has been accepted as the correct approach and has become a legal axiom.

In essence, economic truth has been replaced by perceived legal truth. Where economists challenge the economic presumptions of lawyers, and rightfully from their perspective, at the same time they ignore that what are assumptions in economics have become accepted premises in the legal context of affairs. Basically, we deal with parallel worlds that seem to have no means of effectively communicating with each other, creating Babylonian discussions at best. The assumptions that direct taxes are borne, both legally and economically, by the person who is liable to remit the tax to the government, and that indirect taxes are borne, not by the person who is legally liable to remit the tax to the government but, instead, by the consumer buying the goods or services have become legal axioms. The criticism of economists that they are based on an oversimplified economic theory may be justified. However, it will not have legal bearing unless and until the legal, but economically based, premises on the effect of direct and indirect taxation are being revised. Economic criticism and research is nevertheless of essential importance because it offers the legal community the opportunity to reassess its legal assumptions. However, it is a misunderstanding to believe that economic scholarly criticism will have an immediate impact and result on legal reasoning.

In the past, the United States has tried to support exports through its Foreign Sales Corporation (FSC) provisions – in essence an income tax rebate on US exports. However, those provisions were rejected by the WTO as a prohibited export subsidy. Their replacement, the Extraterritorial Income Exclusion Act (ETI) was also challenged before the WTO and found to be noncompliant as well.[10]

10. Gary Clyde Hufbauer, *The Foreign Sales Corporation Drama: Reaching the Last Act?* Institute for International Economics, Policy Brief no. PB02-10 (Washington, DC, 2002).

9.3. US TAX PROPOSALS TO MITIGATE CROSS-BORDER DISADVANTAGE

The unsuccessful efforts by the US government to create a somewhat more level playing field by introducing vehicles for income tax rebates in relation to exports, even though they were rejected on dubious economic grounds, have made it necessary to search for legislative alternatives. In this Section, we take a closer look at two approaches. First, we investigate the feasibility and economic effects of a replacement of the US corporate income tax by an indirect tax. The second approach, which is embodied in the Border Tax Equity Act, is more confrontational in nature.

9.3.1. Replacement of Income Tax by a Federal Indirect Tax

9.3.1.1. General

For a country that relies more on direct than on indirect taxation, the most straightforward way to avoid competitive disadvantages is to change that reliance. Introducing an indirect tax while, at the same time, reducing the rate of the corporate income tax would achieve that result in a budget-neutral way. A federal sales tax or federal VAT are the first to come to mind because almost all other countries that levy a VAT also have a corporate income tax (albeit that they may rely on it to a lesser extent). Another option would be to replace the US corporate income tax altogether with either a federal VAT or a federal RST, as proposed in the Fair Tax Act, which would turn the competitive situation around and provide US exporting companies with an comparative advantage.[11] This is the situation to be evaluated next.

9.3.1.2. The Economic Effects of Substituting an Indirect Tax for a Corporate Income Tax

Realization of trade benefits is the most important argument to replace the US federal corporate income tax with an indirect tax, such as a VAT. Border tax adjustments, that is, taxation of imports and relief of exports of internal taxes, would presumably improve the trade balance of the United States. Indeed, to a considerable extent, corporate income taxes seem to constitute an additional cost, reflected in the price of goods and services. Therefore, because of the incorporated income tax burden,[12] US exports may be relatively more expensive than domestic products in importing countries that have a VAT. Were the income tax to be replaced by a VAT-type of tax, or any other indirect tax for that matter, export

11. Replacing the corporate income tax with a consumption tax would remove a large portion of the distortionary tax burden on capital formation in the United States. The lower cost of capital would increase investment, improve productivity and enhance the competitiveness of US exporters in foreign markets.
12. Under the assumption that the country of destination of the goods does not apply a corporate income tax or applies it at a lower rate.

sales would be relieved of the tax burden incurred, generally through zero rating the export transactions (where there is no rebate of direct tax), thus reducing the price of US exports or, in other words, improving their competitiveness[13] abroad. Imports into the United States would become more expensive relative to domestically produced goods because the latter would no longer include the burden of domestic corporate income tax, while prices of imported goods would still include income tax incurred in the exporting country.[14] The VAT or other indirect tax itself would be neutral in this respect because both domestic and imported goods would be subject to the same rate of US indirect tax.

Example 2

If, in example 1, in which the public services in both the United States and Japan were initially financed through direct taxes only, instead of increasing its overall taxation by introducing an additional VAT, Japan would replace its corporate income tax by a credit invoice method VAT, generating the same revenue, the price of the domestically produced product in the Japanese market would remain USD 100. Initially, this price included income tax, now it includes VAT. From a competitive perspective, this replacement would make a big difference. The zero rating of exports would enable the Japanese manufacturer to compete in international markets at a lower price of USD 83.34, while the production cost of the components produced in the United States remain USD 100 (including income tax). Where they are imported into Japan, the US components would be subject to 20% import VAT, raising their price to USD 120. Replacing income tax with an indirect tax, therefore, provides a competitive advantage to exporting companies to the amount of the replaced tax.

Even if it is true that any direct price effect resulting from the change of the tax system will be reduced over time by an adjustment of either the competitors' sales prices or the currency exchange rate, the adjustment of the exchange rate will be extremely slow. In addition, the value of a currency also depends on other constantly changing macroeconomic variables[15] and noneconomic and monetary factors, which makes it virtually impossible for economists to predict exchange rate movements, short term and long term, especially in the context of a fundamental tax reform.[16] There is no empirical evidence that confirms that exchange rates are an equilibrating factor.[17]

13. Dan Throop Smith & Bertrand Fox, *An Analysis of Value Added Taxation in the Context of the Tax Restructuring Act of 1980* (Washington, DC: The Financial Executives Research Foundation, 1981), 20–21. This is true under the assumption that exporters would, indeed, attempt to increase their export volume by reducing prices to reflect reduced costs.
14. The underlying assumption of tax incidence is that both corporate income tax and VAT are reflected in the prices, that is, are shifted forward, at least to a large extent, to the final consumer.
15. Philippe Bacchetta &S Eric Van Wincoop, "A Scapegoat Model of Exchange-Rate Fluctuations," *American Economic Review*, May 2004, 114–118.
16. J.D. Foster, *International Aspects of Tax Reform* (Washington, DC: Tax Foundation, April 2000).
17. David G. Raboy, "International Implications of Value-Added Taxes," in *The Value Added Tax: Orthodoxy and New Thinking*, eds. Murray L. Weidenbaum, David G. Raboy & Ernest S. Christian Jr. (Boston: Kluwer Academic Publishers, 1989), 150.

In other words, any expansion in net export as the result of replacing the US corporate income tax with a VAT would, certainly for the medium term, be economically beneficial to US businesses, although that benefit may in the long run be reduced by an appreciation of the dollar relative to other currencies.[18]

9.3.2. The Border Tax Equity Act

In order to address the perceived imbalance between the United States and its trading partners that apply a VAT, the bipartisan member group of the House of Representatives that has proposed legislation[19] under the heading "Border Tax Equity Act of 2007" follows a totally different approach. The proposal has the effect that US exporters receive a rebate and that goods imported into the United States are subject to taxation not on the basis of the domestic tax burden in the United States but on the indirect tax burden in the importing or exporting country concerned.

The Border Tax Equity Act clearly states that its supporters perceive the WTO distinction between direct and indirect taxes to be arbitrary and to be to the disadvantage of countries, such as the United States, that rely primarily on direct taxes for revenue, rather than on indirect taxes. The supporters also observe that US exporters are subject to double taxation by paying direct tax on the production of the exported goods in the United States and indirect taxes on those goods in the importing country, whereas imports into the United States remain untaxed in the United States and are subsidized in the exporting country through VAT rebates. This assumed disadvantage for US companies is estimated at USD 239 billion in the form of VAT rebates in the exporting countries and USD 140 billion in the form of nontaxation of imports into the United States. Supporters of the act conceive this VAT-induced tilted playing field as the cause for the US trade deficit of USD 836 billion and the loss of USD 3.2 million manufacturing jobs across the country. The objective of the legislation is to create leverage for the US trade representative in negotiations with the WTO to remedy this discrepancy in treatment.

In the absence of an agreement with the WTO, the Border Tax Equity Act authorizes the imposition of a tax on goods and services imported into the United States in an amount equal to the VAT rebated or refunded by the exporting country, and in payments to US exporters to neutralize the (perceived) discriminatory effect of border taxes levied by importing countries (import VAT). If, for example, China applies a 17% VAT on US imports, the United States would apply a 17% tax on goods imported from China and provide a 17% rebate to manufacturers of US goods being exported to China.

The disadvantages incurred by US exporters as described by the proponents of the Border Tax Equity Act are an extraordinary exaggeration due to a

18. US Department of the Treasury, *Tax Reform for Fairness, Simplicity, and Growth, vol. 3, The Value Added Tax* (Washington, DC: US Department of the Treasury, November 1984), 22.
19. House of Representatives (HR) no. 2600.

misrepresentation of fact. The proponents of the act ignore the fact that the competitors of US businesses are subject to corporate income tax in their home country as well. Furthermore, they seem to miss the fact that VAT levied on the importation of goods serves the objective of creating a level playing field between imported and domestically produced goods that are also subject to VAT. Exports are, indeed, relieved of VAT, which may have the effect that the exporter receives a refund of input VAT but that refund is inherent to the VAT system. It simply ensures that, under the destination principle, exported goods are free of VAT, just like goods exported from the United States are in principle free of state sales tax, albeit that the US sales taxes are not federal taxes. Finally, it is true that goods imported into the United States are not subject to tax at the federal level. However, under the same destination principle, imported goods are subject to use tax in the state of destination. In other words, the economic distortion is much smaller than the proponents of the Border Tax Equity Act suggest.

In my assessment, the supporters of the bill realize perfectly well that their proposal, if it would become law, would not survive a challenge before the WTO. The impressive rhetoric demonstrates not only the sensitivity of the subject but it is also directed towards a domestic audience. Whether the proposal fails in Congress because of its alleged violation of the WTO rules, or it becomes law and is later shipwrecked before the WTO, either way, it will generate domestic pressure for tax reform. In other words, failure of the Border Tax Equity Act may trigger wider support for other proposals for tax reform, such as the Fair Tax Act, which were actually introduced by some of the same legislators.

However, although their analysis of the VAT system is incomplete and simplistic, the supporters of the Border Tax Equity Act have a point in their basic notion of the unfairness of the WTO rules, as was indicated in Section 9.2. It is, however, unlikely that the other WTO Member States will concede to US pressure and allow rebates of income taxes on exports. The distinction between direct and indirect taxes regarding export rebates was clear from the beginning of the GATT negotiations in which the United States participated. If the United States is dissatisfied with its inability to make rebates on exports and/or levy import taxes, the question arises as to why it continues to rely on taxes that are not and have never been eligible for border tax adjustments.

9.3.3. The Alternative: Change the Character of the Corporate Income Tax

To replace the current US corporate income tax with an indirect tax, whether it be a federal sales tax or a European-style VAT, would not only constitute a fundamental change but also one that will be perceived as radical. Both taxpayers and legislators prefer to stay within the comfort zone of that which with they are familiar. That is exactly the reason that tax reform is such a sensitive political issue. There is always a group of constituents who believe to be disadvantaged by the change. This is particularly true in the American context where, to a large extent, the tax system has been corrupted by special interests. For this reason, it would make sense to examine whether the current tax system could be changed in such a way that border tax adjustments under WTO rules would be permissible to a larger extent. Clearly, this would mean a metamorphosis of the corporate income tax from a direct tax into an indirect tax. The idea of changing the corporate income tax into a WTO-compliant indirect tax has been suggested by several economists,[20] and the particulars of this solution are considered later.

Once the US corporate income tax has been qualified as an indirect tax, export and other foreign income can be relieved of US tax. A truly territorial tax system[21] would be the result, allowing US companies to invest and compete directly in foreign markets.[22] Indirect tax status is imminently obtainable within the framework of current law and within the framework of the American tax tradition because an income tax has a base that is more or less equal to the taxpayer's value added. Contrary to a general belief, an indirect tax does not have to resemble a sales or turnover tax.

In fact, value added is conceptually very similar to net income under the US corporate income tax. In essence, only two amendments are required to change its base to value added. First, the interest that a corporation pays to its debt holders must be made nondeductible in the same way that the dividends it pays to its equity shareholders are presently nondeductible. As a result, all the income from both debt and equity capital would be included in the corporation's income tax base.[23] The next step to complete the value added base would be to include the income from labor. The measure of this income is the amount of wages paid to the corporation's employees.[24]

---

20. David Bradford, *Untangling the Income Tax* (Harvard University Press, 1986), and *Blueprints for International Tax Reform* (American Enterprise Institute, 2001); and Ernest S. Christian, Testimony before the Subcommittee on Select Revenue Measures of the House Committee on Ways and Means, 9 May 2002. An earlier proposal by a study group of the Department of the Treasury for the Comprehensive Business Income Tax also takes value added as the tax base; see also US Department of the Treasury, *Integration of the Individual and Corporate Tax Systems – Tax Business Income Once* (Washington, DC: GPO, 1992).
21. A territorial tax system subjects to tax only income, whether earned by residents or nonresidents, derived from sources within the territory of the taxing authority, whereas the United States currently applies a system that taxes worldwide income, that is, derived from sources located both within and outside its territory.
22. Devices such as FSC and ETI would be unnecessary.
23. A deduction for interest paid is not an inherent characteristic of a corporate income tax. Indeed, allowing a deduction for interest (the cost of debt capital) but not for dividends (the cost of equity capital) is a major distortion under present law with negative effects on GDP growth, see Department of the Treasury, *Integration of the Individual and Corporate Tax Systems – Tax Business Income Once* (Washington, DC, GPO, 1992).
24. Under the present law, gross wages are deductible for corporate income tax purposes. However, below a certain threshold (USD 97,500 in 2007), they are subject to employer social insurance contribution (called FICA taxes). In essence, FICA taxes (based on the Federal Insurance Contributions Act) are taxes on corporate income, albeit under a different name and at a much lower rate (7.65% versus 35% CIT).

By disallowing deductions for interest, dividends and wages, the base of the corporate income tax would be significantly broadened, which would allow for a lower rate of between 12% and 15%. To avoid double taxation of the wage component of the new tax base, corporations would be allowed a credit for the employer FICA[25] tax.

The new tax base would remove distortion caused by imperfections in the current tax. All cost of capital would be taxed, and the discriminatory distinction between debt and equity capital would be eliminated. Moreover, all business income would be taxed in the same way, thus eliminating the existing difference of taxation of incorporated and unincorporated businesses. In addition, it has been suggested to treat capital equipment as a current expense ("first-year expensing"), instead of depreciating it, and treat business expenses on a transaction basis, instead of on the basis of inventory accounting. Those new features are common features of the standard VAT system but not a requirement per se to qualify it as an indirect tax.

Example

A simple example may clarify how a value added income tax would work. Assume that ABC Corp. in a given year has a gross income of USD 120 from the production and sale of computer components. ABC Corp. bought parts from another company for USD 40, purchased an assembly machine for USD 20, paid USD 2 for interest on a loan to finance that machine, paid USD 60 in wages and USD 9 in dividends to its shareholders. The value added income tax base would be determined as demonstrated in Table 43.

Table 43. Taxable Income under Value Added Income Tax

Gross income		120
Deductible purchases:		
– Parts	40	
– Machine	+20	
Total	60	–60
Taxable income		60

The purchases from other producers of goods and services are deductible for value added income tax purposes because these inputs are included in the taxable income of those suppliers. Without this method of deduction of business inputs, the tax would not qualify as a tax on value added but would be a GRT and tax accumulation would be the result. Interest, dividend and wages are not deductible.

25. The FICA taxes are payroll (or employment) taxes imposed by the federal government on both employees and employers to fund federal Social Security and Medicare programs that provide benefits for retirees, the disabled and children of deceased workers. Social Security benefits include old-age, survivors, and disability insurance (OASDI) and Medicare provides hospital insurance benefits.

Under the current corporate income tax regime, net income can be estimated as shown in Table 44.

Table 44. Taxable Income under Current Corporate Income Tax Regulation

Gross income		120
Deductibles:		
– Parts (allowed under inventory accounting rules)[26]	30	
– Depreciation of machine (5 years)	4	
– Salaries	60	
– Interest	2	
Total	96	–96
Net income		24

The income tax would be 35% on a net income of USD 24, which is USD 8.40. The same revenue could be generated under the value-added-based income tax with a tax rate of 14%.

Compared to the present situation, the value-added-based corporate income tax seems to offer several significant advantages. To exempt exports from taxation, export-related income (and other foreign-sourced income as explained in Section 9.3.4.2) would simply be deducted from gross income. In our example, if ABC Corp. would generate USD 10 in export and foreign income, its gross income would become USD 110, instead of USD 120.

Although it is not necessary to tax imports to arrive at the desired characterization of this income tax as one based on value added, it would be easy to do. Assume that ABC Corp. would import in a given year for USD 5, then its gross income would be (120 – 10) + 5 = USD 115. It would not only level the playing field for US exporters but also provide a competitive edge because US exports would be relieved from all tax, whereas imports into the United States would only be relieved of the VAT burden in the country of exportation and their prices would still include the exporting country's corporate income tax burden. Indeed, when combined with first-year expensing, the United States could become a location of choice for manufacturing and sales. The value-added-based income tax would probably reduce the tax incentives that trigger corporate, asset or capital migration, and would remove the arbitrary distinction between debt and equity financing. Moreover, repatriation of foreign income would no longer be discouraged, thus improving the investment climate in the Unites States.[27] The proponents of the

26. We assume that not all parts were used in the same year as they were purchased because, in a typical real-life scenario, businesses have some costs that would be perpetually deferred under the inventory accounting rules.

27. Under the current law, repatriated income (including income that is deemed to be repatriated under the provisions of Subpart F of the US Internal Revenue Code regarding Controlled Foreign Corporations) is taxed (albeit with a foreign tax credit). As a result, reinvestment of

value-added-based income tax believe that their proposal is politically feasible because there exists, in principle, bipartisan support to cure the fundamental defects of the current corporate income tax and international tax rules. Action in the past was halted by the conviction that this could only be done by repealing the income tax and replacing it with a form of sales tax. Whether the proposed tax meets the criteria of the WTO under which exports rebates are allowed is investigated in the next section.

9.3.4. Feasibility of the Value-Added-Based Corporate Income Tax

Essential for the success of the tax reform is to determine whether the proposed change of character of the US corporate income tax from a direct tax into an indirect tax based on value added, as described in Section 9.3.3, would be acceptable under the WTO rules as explained in Section 9.2. To do this, we first take a closer look, in Section 9.3.4.1, at the legal reasoning of the WTO appellate body in the case against the provisions of the Foreign Sales Corporation (FSC) Act and the ETI Act. Then, in Section 9.3.4.2, an analysis is made of the feasibility of the proposed value added corporate income tax against the criteria applied by the WTO.[28]

9.3.4.1. WTO Arguments against FSC and ETI

To fully appreciate the WTO rulings discussed here, some historic background may be useful. In 1960, the GATT basically codified the distinction between permissible and nonpermissible border tax adjustments based on the origin and destination principles for direct and indirect taxes, respectively. Indirect taxes can be levied on the importation and rebated on the exportation of goods, but direct taxes cannot, based on the economic assumption that indirect taxes are shifted forward in the form of higher prices for goods, and direct taxes are shifted backward to the capital and labor factors.[29] What was true in the past is not

---

capital from a low-tax country in the United States is penalized and investment abroad is supported.

28. General references for this section are as follows: Hufbauer, *The Foreign Sales Corporation Drama: Reaching the Last Act?*; Hufbauer & Gabyzon, *Fundamental Tax Reform and Border Tax Adjustments*; Michael Daly, "The WTO and Direct Taxation," *The World Economy* 29 (5) May 2006, 527–557; Johann Wagner, *Direkte Steuern und Welthandelsrecht – Das Verbot ertragsteuerlicher Exportsubventionen im Recht der WTO* (Direct Taxation and International Trade Law: The Prohibition of Export Subsidies under WTO Law) (Baden-Baden: Nomos, 2006).
29. This distinction goes back to the nineteenth century when excise duties were the leading, if not the only, indirect tax, and property tax was the dominant direct tax. The distinction made sense in that context but is debatable in the contemporary context of globalization; complex tax structures, including a multitude of different type of taxes, such as social security taxes, income taxes and various types of sales taxes; and very competitive market conditions.

necessarily true for the present and, especially in the United States, these economic assumptions are vigorously challenged.[30] The new types of taxation that emerged in the twentieth century required their classification for the purposes of the GATT rules, and a working party classified VATs as indirect taxes. Interestingly, from an economic perspective, a VAT amounts[31] to a combination of direct taxes: a direct tax on profits earned by the corporation, a direct tax on interest and rent paid by the corporation, and a direct tax on wages. A series of direct taxes are transformed into an indirect tax, but the true magic is that the indirect tax is eligible for border tax adjustment where the very similar direct taxes are not. In other words, border tax adjustments based on the destination principle are prohibited for the corporate income tax on export earnings but permitted for the VAT.

In the past, US companies were able to defer payment of income tax on foreign earned income if they structured it through a subsidiary based in another, preferably low-tax, country. Income tax would be due only when the income was repatriated to the United States, which could be postponed for decades. As a result of compound interest, deferred tax payment over such a long time is close to tax forgiven. However, in 1962, the United States enacted Subpart F of the Internal Revenue Code. Basically, this was an antiabuse rule aimed at preventing the possibility of infinite deferral of corporate income tax. In those days, US companies were globally dominant and the United States had a persistent trade surplus. This situation changed in the 1970s, when the United States was facing a more competitive world market and incurred significant trade deficits. Political pressure led the United States to introduce legislation that allowed the establishment of Domestic International Sales Corporations (DISCs), which offered partial tax deferral for export earnings.[32] The idea was to soften the self-inflicted damage to US exporters caused by Subpart F. The EU challenged the DISCs claiming that they constituted a prohibited export subsidy under Article XVI of the GATT.[33]

30. In a modern open economy, the actual incidence of taxes (whether shifted forward in the form of higher prices for goods and services or backward in factor earnings) depends on the uniformity of the tax, competitive conditions in the marketplace and, importantly, whether the tax is adjusted at the border. In other words, tax incidence is as much a result of border adjustment rules as a reason for adopting any particular set of rules. See Hufbauer, *The Foreign Sales Corporation Drama: Reaching the Last Act*? n. 28, at 2.
31. This description fits particularly well with a subtraction method of VAT. However, credit invoice method VATs are not very different. In both cases, the tax base essentially consists of wages, interest (rent) and profits.
32. DISC tax relief amounted to about 12% points on export profits earned by the parent corporation and its DISC. The normal corporate tax rate then was 48%.
33. Article XVI (Subsidies) of the GATT provides:

    Section A – Subsidies in General

    1. If any contracting party grants or maintains any subsidy, including any form of income or price support, which operates directly or indirectly to increase exports of any product from, or to reduce imports of any product into, its territory, it shall notify the contracting parties in writing of the extent and nature of the subsidization, of the estimated effect of the subsidization on the quantity of the affected product or products imported into or exported from its territory and of the circumstances making the subsidization necessary. In any case in which it

In its defense, the United States argued that Article XVI forbids tax exemptions on exports but not tax deferral, and that the EU had not demonstrated that goods exported through DISCs were sold at lower prices than comparable goods in the US home market, in other words, the bilevel pricing test of the provision had not been violated. In turn, the United States challenged Belgium, France and the Netherlands for exempting the export earnings of sales subsidiaries located in tax havens. All defendants lost, which resulted in negotiations between the parties involved. The appeal panel's reasoning was politically overruled by a council decision during the Tokyo round negotiations in 1981, culminating in the Code on Subsidies and Countervailing Measures (SCM Code), which was affirmed in the Uruguay round. It was concluded that economic processes (including transactions involving exported goods) located outside the territorial limits of the exporting country need not be subject to taxation by the exporting country and should not be regarded as export activities in terms of Article XVI(4) of the GATT. In addition, transactions between related companies must be based on the arm's length pricing standard.[34] The distinction between direct and indirect taxes was preserved, and VAT was explicitly recognized as an indirect tax.

---

is determined that serious prejudice to the interests of any other contracting party is caused or threatened by any such subsidization, the contracting party granting the subsidy shall, upon request, discuss with the other contracting party or parties concerned, or with the contracting parties, the possibility of limiting the subsidization.

Section B – Additional Provisions on Export Subsidies

2. The contracting parties recognize that the granting by a contracting party of a subsidy on the export of any product may have harmful effects for other contracting parties, both importing and exporting, may cause undue disturbance to their normal commercial interests, and may hinder the achievement of the objectives of this Agreement.
3. Accordingly, contracting parties should seek to avoid the use of subsidies on the export of primary products. If, however, a contracting party grants directly or indirectly any form of subsidy which operates to increase the export of any primary product from its territory, such subsidy shall not be applied in a manner which results in that contracting party having more than an equitable share of world export trade in that product, account being taken of the shares of the contracting parties in such trade in the product during a previous representative period, and any special factors which may have affected or may be affecting such trade in the product.
4. Further, as from 1 January 1958 or the earliest practicable date thereafter, contracting parties shall cease to grant either directly or indirectly any form of subsidy on the export of any product other than a primary product which subsidy results in the sale of such product for export at a price lower than the comparable price charged for the like product to buyers in the domestic market. Until 31 December 1957 no contracting party shall extend the scope of any such subsidization beyond that existing on 1 January 1955 by the introduction of new, or the extension of existing, subsidies.
5. The contracting parties shall review the operation of the provisions of this Article from time to time with a view to examining its effectiveness, in the light of actual experience, in promoting the objectives of this Agreement and avoiding subsidization seriously prejudicial to the trade or interests of contracting parties.

34. In essence, this means that prices for transactions between related parties should be similar to pricing for transaction between unrelated parties.

The United States repealed the DISCs and enacted the FSC in 1984, which allowed partial exemption for income of a foreign corporate subsidiary derived from handling US export sales.[35] In 1997, the EU challenged the FSC before the WTO as a violation of the SCM Code.

At that time, the WTO had come into existence. The WTO Agreement includes, inter alia:

> (a) the provisions in the General Agreement on Tariffs and Trade, dated 30 October 1947 . . . as rectified, amended or modified by the terms of legal instruments which have entered into force before the date of entry into force of the WTO Agreement;
>
> (b) the provisions of the legal instruments set forth below that have entered into force under the GATT 1947 before the date of entry into force of the WTO Agreement:
>
> . . .
>
> (iv) other decisions of the contracting parties to the GATT 1947;[36]
>
> . . .

The WTO Panel Report, which was affirmed by the Appellate Body in February 2000, decided against the United States. First, it did not recognize the 1981 council decision as a legal instrument within the meaning of Annex 1A to the WTO Agreement.[37] That opened the door for assessing the legality of the FSC against the provisions of the SCM Code. It was found that the FSC was a prohibited export subsidy because tax revenue is foregone, which violates Article 1 of the SCM Code,[38] and because exports are taxed more favorably than production abroad. Moreover, the Panel gave an important interpretation of footnote 59 to the SCM Code.[39] In respect of the FSC, the Panel Report conceded that footnote 59 recognizes that territorial tax systems do not amount to per se export subsidies but then

---

35. The FSC benefit usually amounts to about 15% of the corporate tax rate on export profits earned by the parent corporation and its FSC.
36. Annex 1A to the World Trade Organization Agreement.
37. Under Art. II(2) of the WTO Agreement, the agreements and associated legal instruments included in Annexes 1, 2 and 3 [. . .] are integral parts of this Agreement, binding on all Members.
38. Article 1(1) of the SCM Code provides:

    For the purpose of this Agreement, a subsidy shall be deemed to exist if:

    (a)(1) there is a financial contribution by a government or any public body within the territory of a Member (referred to in this Agreement as "government"), i.e. where:

    (i) . . .

    (ii) government revenue that is otherwise due is foregone or not collected (e.g., fiscal incentives such as tax credits);

    (iii) . . .
39. Insofar relevant in our context, footnote 59 to the SCM Code provides:

    ". . . Para. (e) is not intended to limit a Member from taking measures to avoid the double taxation of foreign-source income earned by its enterprises or the enterprises of another Member." In this footnote, "Para. e" refers to the Illustrative List of Export Subsidies laid down by Annex 1 to the SCM Code, of which Para. e reads: "The full or partial exemption

distinguishes between a territorial system that provides a "broad exemption of income deriving from foreign economic activities" and a territorial system that provides an exemption "specifically related to exports." The former system does not constitute an export subsidy, whereas the latter does. In other words, a territorial exemption that applies solely to export earnings is not permitted.

This interpretation has been highly criticized, at least in the United States, because the distinction exceeds the discussions and agreements reached during the Tokyo and Uruguay round negotiations. From a US perspective, it is incomprehensible that a partial territorial system, such as the FSC that exempts about 30% of export profits, is prohibited, whereas a full territorial system, as applied in many EU countries, which exempts a much larger share of export profits, is permitted.[40]

The ruling that the FSC was prohibited because exports were taxed more favorably than production abroad seemed to provide an opening to essentially save the FSC by extending its scope to the foreign production of US businesses.

By the end of 2000, the US Congress adopted the ETI, which excluded from taxable gross income a portion of export earnings and a portion of earnings from production abroad. However, the EU initiated a second round of WTO litigation, and the ETI failed the benchmark. In essence, and to the extent relevant in this context, it was found that the ETI violated Article1 of the SCM Code because it offered taxpayers the alternative to elect a foreign tax credit instead of the extraterritorial income exclusion. Under the assumption that a rational taxpayer would only elect the ETI when this is beneficial, "revenue otherwise due" had been foregone. Moreover, the ETI exclusion was unacceptable because it was limited in scope to exports and selected production abroad. The ETI conditioned its benefits on the use of less than 50% foreign inputs of goods and services, which was perceived to be an infringement of the national treatment requirement embodied in Article3 of the GATT.[41]

9.3.4.2. Evaluation of a Value-Added-Based Income Tax against WTO Rules

The Appellate Body in the previous cases acknowledged that a territorial system that exempts foreign income and exports from tax is, in principle, permissible

---

remission, or deferral specifically related to exports, of direct taxes or social welfare charges paid or payable by industrial or commercial enterprises."

40. Hufbauer, *The Foreign Sales Corporation Drama: Reaching the Last Act?*, 5.
41. Article 3 of the GATT provides:

    1. ...
    2. The products of the territory of any contracting party imported into the territory of any other contracting party shall not be subject, directly or indirectly, to internal taxes or other internal charges of any kind in excess of those applied, directly or indirectly, to like domestic products. Moreover, no contracting party shall otherwise apply internal taxes or other internal charges to imported or domestic products in a manner contrary to the principles set forth in Para. 1.
    3. ...

under WTO rules, provided that the exemption is not limited and includes all, or nearly all, foreign-source income. Any new tax that seeks to relieve export and other foreign income needs to be carefully designed to ensure it would sustain WTO scrutiny. The value-added-based income tax should be a compulsory system that applies to all US corporations and not feature any election options. Otherwise, it may be argued that the US government has foregone revenue "otherwise due." Also, foreign-content limitations are unacceptable, which should not cause a problem because they are basically redundant. Last but not least, the definition of foreign income has to be sufficiently broad to comply with the Appellate Body's interpretation of footnote 59. This can all be done rather simply with the value-added-based income tax described previously.

At the core of the issue is whether such a tax escapes the prohibited export subsidies definition, used by the WTO. According to the SCM Code, prohibited export subsidies include "the full or partial exemption, remission or deferral specifically related to exports, of direct taxes. . . ." In this framework, "direct taxes" are defined as taxes on wages, profits, interest, rent, royalties, and all other forms of income, and taxes on the ownership of real property, whereas indirect taxes are described as sales, excise, turnover, value added, franchise, stamp, transfer, inventory and equipment taxes, border taxes and all taxes other than direct taxes and import charges.

The proposed income tax resembles a subtraction method VAT. As such, it seems to be acceptable as an indirect tax, which can be adjusted at the border because VAT can unquestionable be adjusted at the border. However, when the definition of indirect tax was extended to VATs, only the EU applied a VAT, which was based on the tax-from-tax method. Because the negotiations at the time took place primarily between the EU and the United States, it is conceivable that the WTO would reason that the inclusion of VATs in the definition of indirect taxes only refers to the latter and not to the subtraction method of VAT.

9.3.5. Conclusions

The tax rules as regards international trade are complicated. Although the distinction between direct and indirect taxes may seem somewhat archaic, it is unlikely that it will be abandoned. For its revenue, the United States relies more heavily on direct taxes than its major trading partners. As a result, US businesses believe that they have to operate on a tilted playing field. The US proposal to change the features of the existing corporate income tax to the effect that it resembles a subtraction method VAT seems legitimate and WTO compliant, although there is no absolute certainty on this point. It seems to make sense for the United States to abstain from a confrontational approach, and to negotiate at the WTO council level on the details of this altered tax to ensure its acceptance. There exist a sufficient number of EU subsidies and tax practices that are questionable under WTO rules to provide the United States some leverage in the negotiations. If the subtraction method VAT is found to be non-WTO-compliant, the United States could always simply replace the income tax with either a national sales tax or a federal tax deduction type of VAT.

9.4. IMPORTATION AND EXPORTATION OF GOODS

9.4.1. Importation

According to the destination principle, goods should be taxed in the country where they are used or consumed. Imported goods are, therefore, taxed regardless of whether the importer is a registered business or a private consumer.[42] However, taxable businesses can, in principle, deduct the import VAT as a credit on their periodical VAT return.[43] Taxation takes place upon the entry of a country for Customs purposes.[44] It is important to note, that customs procedures apply to the goods for VAT purposes, even when no duties are actually due. Import VAT will become due when the goods are brought into free circulation within a state (as defined by customs law). Goods placed in a bonded (customs) warehouse, or that are imported into a duty-free zone or under a duty-suspension regime, or that are in transit remain out of scope of VAT until they are released for free circulation within the territory.[45] If they leave the warehouse, free zone or regime with a foreign destination, no importation will have taken place and consequently no import VAT will be due.

The VAT will be calculated on the customs value, which generally includes any import duties due and certain costs for services directly related or associated with the importation, such as insurance and freight.[46]

Most states follow the rules for customs debt to determine the liability for the import VAT. The tax needs to be paid by the importer of record, which could be the seller or the buyer or a third party, such as a freight forwarder, the postal service, UPS, FedEx or DHL, acting as a customs agent on behalf of either of them.

Some countries allow the payment of import VAT to be deferred. The rules and conditions vary per jurisdiction, but it means that in effect the import VAT is not paid to customs at the time of importation; instead the recipient of the goods will account for the import VAT on a periodical VAT return. This is generally referred to as postponed accounting.

In the US, customs are not involved in the collection of subnational or state taxes. The recipient of imported goods, whether a private consumer or a business, is responsible for the remittance of use tax over the value of the good. The taxable amount for use tax on imported goods varies by state but will at least be the

42. Article 2(1) (d) of Directive 2006/112.
43. Article 168 (e) of Directive 2006/112.
44. See, for example, Art. 70 of Directive 2006/112.
45. See, for example, Art. 71 of Directive 2006/112.
46. See, for example, Art. 78 of Directive 2006/112.

purchase price with or without add-ons for freight,[47] insurance[48] and cost of handling.[49]

9.4.2. EXPORTATION

Under the destination principle, goods that are exported should leave the country of dispatch without VAT. Tax relief has two aspects. In the first place, the sale of the exported product should not be taxed in the country of origin or dispatch. Second, all input tax incurred by the seller in relation to the exported product must be creditable.

Under the US sales and use taxes, the export sale is either out of the scope of or exempt from the tax, while the seller would also have purchased the product without tax under the sale-for-resale exemption rule.

Under VAT, there are two ways to achieve the objective of full tax relief in the exporting country. The export sale could be exempt from VAT while maintaining the eligibility to a credit for tax paid on inputs related to the export sale. This is referred to as "exempt with credit" and contrasts with the general rule under VAT that excludes input tax credits related to exemptions. Another method is zero rating. Under this approach, exports are taxable but subject to a tax rate of 0%. Because the export sales technically constitute taxable supplies, the exporter fully retains the right to deduct input tax. Although the legislative formatting is different, the two approaches arrive at the same material result and full VAT relief of the exported product is realized.

Although the EU applies the exempt-with-credit method in its legislation both for export sales to third countries[50] and for cross-border sales to other Member

47. Shipping costs are included in the value and thus taxed in twenty-four jurisdictions. Georgia excludes the costs only if transport occurs after the title has passed to the buyer, and West Virginia only if by common carrier and directly paid by the customer. The costs are excluded when separately stated in Alabama, Arizona, California, Colorado, the District of Columbia, Florida, Idaho, Illinois, Iowa, Louisiana, Maine, Maryland, Massachusetts, Michigan, Missouri, Nevada, Utah, Wisconsin and Wyoming; see CCH Tax Research Network, Multistate Sales Tax, 61–150.
48. Mandatory insurance charges are generally included in the value of the goods (taxed), except for Georgia and Maine. Arizona, Indiana, North Dakota, Tennessee, Utah, Virginia and Wisconsin exclude insurance from the value only when separately stated. Optional insurance charges are excluded or excluded when separately stated in twenty-seven jurisdictions, but taxed in Alabama, Arkansas, Connecticut, Hawaii, Illinois, Kansas, Kentucky, Louisiana, Mississippi, Nebraska, New Jersey, New Mexico, Pennsylvania, South Carolina, South Dakota, Texas, Washington and West Virginia; see CCH Tax Research Network, Multistate Sales Tax, 61–110.
49. Cost of handling is not included without further conditions in Utah and Wyoming. It is excluded when separately stated in Arizona, Colorado, Florida, Idaho, Illinois, Iowa, Massachusetts, Michigan, Missouri and Oklahoma. These costs are taxed in all other jurisdictions. See CCH Tax Research Network, Multistate Sales Tax, 61–150.
50. Export sales are exempt under Art. 146 of Directive 2006/112 while retaining eligibility for a tax credit ex Art. 169 (b) of Directive 2006/112.

States,[51] most Member States have chosen for the zero rate arrangement to materialize this result in their national legislation.[52]

9.5. TAX JURISDICTION RULES

Tax jurisdiction rules serve to determine which country is allowed to tax a certain supply of goods or services in a manner that prevents said supply to be taxed twice or not at all. These rules are only relevant in situations of cross-border transactions. When a supply is made within the borders of a single state, that is, within the same tax jurisdiction, it will be taxable in that state, and the locations of the seller and buyer respectively are irrelevant. Some states in the United States, however, allow surcharges by subnational governments and localities, in which case rules are required to adequately allocate the tax to each jurisdiction.

Under a VAT, a distinction is made between the supply of goods and the supply of services. The reason for this distinction can be found in the intrinsic difference between the two: goods being physical and services being intangible. The flow of goods, physical as they are in nature, can be followed when they move across borders and from one country into another. That opportunity is not available when dealing with services and, therefore, services require a different set of jurisdiction rules to arrive at the desired result, that is, taxation in the country of destination.

Now that the underlying principles and main objectives regarding cross-border transactions have been clarified, we will further examine the specific jurisdiction rules for VAT in the EU.

9.5.1. Place of Supply of Goods Under EU-VAT

Under EU law, a distinction is made between goods that are transported and those that are not. A supply of goods without transport is taxable where the goods are located at the time when the supply takes place.[53] This would include most domestic sales and would exclude sales of goods located outside the borders of a jurisdiction. When goods are transported, the supply will be taxable where the goods are located when transport begins, or in the country of importation.[54] This rule is only material in the case of cross-border transactions because the movement of goods within the same tax jurisdiction would not alter the tax treatment. It may seem that taxing the supply in the country of departure constitutes the application of the origin principle. However, this sale is either exempt with credit or zero rated and, as a result, no actual tax will accrue to the country of departure. Taxation will take place in the country of arrival. If the goods arrive from a third country, that is, a country outside the EU, VAT will be due on

51. Intracommunity supplies of goods are exempt ex Art. 138 of Directive 2006/112, but with credit ex Art. 169 (b) of Directive 2006/112.
52. See, for example, the Netherlands VAT Act (Wet op de omzetbelasting 1968), Art. 9(2) (b) jo. Tabel II (a)(2) for the zero rate and Art. 15(1) (a) for the right of input tax deductions.
53. Article 31 of Directive 2006/112.
54. Article 32 of Directive 2006/112.

importation; if they arrive from another Member State, VAT generally will be due by the recipient (if a registered person) as an intracommunity acquisition.

Without also identifying the country of importation as an alternative place of supply, in the case of chain transactions,[55] all sellers could claim that the supply had taken place in the country where transport begins and thus avoid VAT because that country would have exempt the export sale.

Moreover, this rule only applies to supplies that have triggered the transportation. Goods sold during transportation are not supplied in the country of departure because that would violate the territoriality principle, but on board of the transporting vessel, and therefore remains out of scope of VAT until they are imported.[56]

Separate rules have been designed for cross-border transactions between Member States. The rules are similar to those applied to the trade in goods with third countries, but the terminology used is different. The sale is called an intracommunity supply which takes place in the Member State where the transport begins. As discussed, this sale is exempt with credit. Subsequently, an intracommunity acquisition takes place in the Member State of arrival[57] with tax liability shifted to the recipient of the goods. The recipient has to self-assess for the VAT but will normally deduct the same as a creditable input tax.[58]

Table 45. Overview Treatment of Cross-Border Transactions in the EU

	Third Country	EU	EU-1		EU-2
Name of transaction	Export	Import	Intracommunity supply		Intracommunity acquisition
Treatment	Exempt with credit/ zero rated	Import VAT	Exempt with credit/zero rated		Domestic VAT
Paid by	n/a	Importer of record	Registered recipient	n/a	Registered recipient
Paid when	n/a	At time of importation	Via VAT return (postponed accounting)	n/a	Via VAT return
Input credit	n/a	Via VAT return	Via VAT return	n/a	Via VAT return

55. Subsequent sales of the same goods may occur, which are eventually physically transferred directly between the first supplier and the ultimate buyer.
56. Ben Terra, *Sales Taxation: The Case of Value Added Tax in the European Community*, Series on International Taxation, no. 8, (Deventer-Boston: Kluwer, 1988), at 21.
57. Article 40 of Directive 2006/112.
58. Article 168 (c) (d) of Directive 2006/112.

The treatment of cross-border sales to third countries (import–export transactions) is essentially the same as the treatment of cross-border sales within the European common market (intracommunity transactions). The seller receives full input VAT credit while the sale itself is not subject to tax because it is either zero rated or exempt. When a good reaches the country of destination, it will be taxed as an import or as an intracommunity acquisition. The real material differences are who has to pay the tax and when. Import VAT is due by the importer of record at the time the import takes place. A taxable importer will be able to recover this import VAT via its periodical return but will suffer a cash flow disadvantage, unless the country of import applies the so-called postponed accounting system, allowing the recipient of the goods to account for the import VAT on its periodical VAT return while deducting the same as a credit, thus realizing full cash flow neutrality. In relation to intracommunity cross-border transactions between taxable persons, taxation is always shifted to the recipient who will accounts for it via a return and deduct the same as a credit. Postponed accounting and cash flow neutrality are incorporated in or immanent to the EU system of taxing intracommunity sales of goods.

Another supply requiring special rules in the case of cross-border implications is the sale of goods to be installed or assembled. An installation sale is a composite supply (see Section 8.2.8 for a general treatise) consisting of a supply of goods; the sale of parts and components; and a supply of services, the assembly or installation. Without a special provision, the service element and the goods element would be subject to different jurisdiction rules. Arguably, under the correct circumstances, the whole transaction could be allocated to the country of exportation and would thus escape taxation, or the service element would remain untaxed. To avoid this, a special provision has been introduced in EU legislation, creating tax jurisdiction for the country where the installation or assembly takes place.[59] As a result, the distinction between goods and services has disappeared, the latter being absorbed by the former, and the law only acknowledges a supply of goods.

9.5.2. Place of Supply of Services Under EU-VAT

9.5.2.1. Current Rules

The main jurisdiction rule for services is that services are deemed to take place where the supplier of the service has established his business or has a fixed establishment from which the service is supplied.[60] The origin principle, therefore, has primacy in relation to the provision of services.

There exist several exceptions to this rule. Services connected to immoveable property, including services of estate agents and experts, and services of architects or for the preparation and coordination of construction work, are deemed to be

59. See Art. 36 of Directive 2006/112.
60. Article 43 of Directive 2006/112.

performed where the property is located.[61] This situs rule is in compliance with the destination principle because these services are directly connected to and, therefore, evidently will be used or enjoyed where the real property is located.

Transport services are, generally, taxed where the transport takes place with jurisdictional appropriation on the basis of distances covered,[62] except for intra-community transport which takes place in the country where the customer is registered for VAT or, otherwise, in the country of departure.[63] Services by intermediaries, generally, follow the rule of the underlying service.[64]

A number of services are deemed to take place where they are actually performed, such as ancillary transport services;[65] cultural, artistic, scientific, educational, entertainment and similar services;[66] and valuation of moveable property.[67] Regarding most of these services, it could, indeed, be argued that they are enjoyed or consumed where they are performed, but this is not necessarily correct for all of them or under all circumstances. Some of these services may be enjoyed at multiple locations at the same time, such as entertainment and cultural performances when they are, for example, broadcasted. The benefit or results of scientific or educational services can be simultaneously or consequently enjoyed or used anywhere. A single jurisdiction rule solves this dilemma.

Finally, EU legislation applies the destination principle to a number of miscellaneous services.[68] Transfers of copyrights, patents, licenses and trademarks; advertising services; the services of consultants, accountants, lawyers, engineers and so on; banking, insurance and other financial services; the hiring of tangible moveable property with the exception of means of transport; telecommunication services; radio and television broadcasting services; and electronically supplied services are deemed to take place where the customer is located but only if the customer, regardless of his or her status, is located outside the EU, or within the EU if the customer is registered but in another country than the supplier. Broadcasting and electronically supplied services by a taxable person established outside the EU to a nontaxable person inside the EU takes place where the residence state of the customer is.[69]

In order to avoid double taxation or nontaxation or distortion of competition, Member States have the option to introduce use and enjoyment rules as an additional but overriding criterion to determine tax jurisdiction.[70]

61. Article 45 of Directive 2006/112.
62. Article 46 of Directive 2006/112.
63. Article 47 of Directive 2006/112.
64. See Arts 44 and 50 of Directive 2006/112.
65. Article 52(b) of Directive 2006/112.
66. Article 52(a) of Directive 2006/112.
67. Article 52(c) of Directive 2006/112.
68. Article 56 of Directive 2006/112.
69. Article 57 of Directive 2006/112.
70. Article 58 of Directive 2006/112.

9.5.2.2. Future Rules (2010–2015)

The tax jurisdiction rules for services will change fundamentally in 2010 and in 2015.[71] A shift will be made from origin to destination principle. Under the current main rule, services are taxed where the supplier is located; under the new main rule, services are taxed at the situs of the business customer. In this respect, nontaxable customers who are registered for VAT and customers who make both taxable and nontaxable sales will be considered as taxable persons for the purpose of the tax jurisdiction rules. Where services are supplied to nontaxable persons (B2C sales), the general rule will continue to be that tax jurisdiction accrues to the situs state of the supplier. Most services, however, will be subject to an overriding use and enjoyment rule, which Member States have the option to implement.

Several existing exceptions to the main rule remain in place. Services connected with immoveable property remain taxed where the immoveable property is situated. Unchanged as well remains the rule for cultural, artistic, sporting, scientific, educational, entertainment and similar services, which allocates tax jurisdiction to the place where they are physically carried out. However, from 1 January 2011 this rule will change and jurisdiction will be allocated to the situs of the customer. Passenger transport will be taxable where such transport takes place according to distance covered.

In most countries, the taxable customer will be liable for the VAT under the reverse charge rule. To enhance reverse charge reporting by the customer, the supplier will be required to submit a recapitulative statement or electronic sales listing (ELS) for these services, which constitutes an additional compliance burden. The ELS information is exchanged between Member States.[72]

The new rules will affect the effectiveness of current tax planning in terms of outsourcing of services by exempt persons to countries that either do not have a VAT or that do have a VAT but apply an opposite tax jurisdiction rule. Under current rules, these services would escape VAT; under the new rules, they will be drawn into the VAT system of the country where the customer is located.

From 2015, telecommunication, broadcasting and electronically supplied services will be taxable where the customer resides, and different treatment for telecommunication and e-services, and between EU and non-EU suppliers, will be eliminated. As a result, however, a supplier may face VAT liabilities and registration requirements in multiple jurisdictions. To reduce the compliance effort of businesses engaging in activities in Member States where they are not established, a so-called mini-one-stop-shop scheme will be introduced, which allows VAT registration in a single state, that is, the Member State where the supplier is established. The supplier is obliged to invoice the customer with VAT at the rate in force in the Member State of the customer. Under this scheme, a supplier only needs to

---

71. Directive 2008/8/EC of 12 February 2008, O.J., 20 February 2008, L44/11-22.
72. The exchange will take place electronically on the basis of Regulation 143/2008 of 12 February 2008, O.J., 20 February 2008, L44/1-6, amending regulation 1798/2003.

submit (electronic) VAT returns to the taxing authorities in the state of registration but has to indicate the VAT due in the state of consumption. Total VAT is paid to the taxing authorities in the state of registration.[73] If it is administratively more convenient, suppliers will have the option to register in each individual country where they conduct business.

9.6. DISTANCE (MAIL-ORDER) SALES AND E-COMMERCE

An issue arises with cross-border shopping by private individuals in federal states and common markets when there are no border controls. Consumers may be tempted to do their shopping in states that offer lower prices induced by lower consumption tax rates. However, the price advantage to be gained is counterbalanced by additional transportation costs consumers will incur when traveling to shops located further away. Therefore, the effect of cross-border shopping will generally be limited to a narrow geographical area close to the border.[74] These limitations disappear when goods and services are purchased from a catalog or ordered over the Internet and are subsequently shipped to the consumer or delivered electronically. When a retailer sells a product over the counter, he has no choice but to charge local consumption tax because the retailer can neither determine the residency of the customer nor have any control over the final destination of the product. Mail-order and e-commerce sellers (also jointly referred to as distance sellers), however, are aware of the final destination as far as goods are concerned because they deliver to a shipping address, but the situation is less straightforward regarding services. The main questions are whether and, if so, under what circumstances and conditions, to require mail-order and e-commerce sellers to account for destination tax. These main questions interact with practical concerns and with matters of legal principle and economic neutrality. Where states have legitimate concerns about revenue loss, distance sellers worry about undue compliance costs, and brick-and-mortar retailers complain about the competitive disadvantage created by tax rate differences in combination with the absence of border tax adjustments.

In this section we concentrate on comparing the situation in the United States with that in the EU. For the purpose of consumption taxes, a distinction needs to be made between the supply of goods and the supply of services. Although the discussions in the United States and in the EU progress along similar lines, the legal context is different. The EU has introduced a special regime for distance

73. The one-stop scheme only applies to output VAT. If a supplier incurs input VAT in another Member State, regardless of whether he makes sales there, an individual refund claim needs to be filled under the Eighth Directive procedure.

74. The size of this area will depend on the ratio between gasoline prices and the fuel efficiency of the consumer's car on the one hand, and the price advantage to be realized on the other hand. A consumer in country A, incurring a tax on a certain good of T, will shop across the border in country B if the tax due in country B, t, combined with transportation costs, (δs, where s denotes the distance from the border, is smaller than the tax paid in his home country A, or $T > t + \delta s$.

sales (Section 9.6.2), whereas the United States is still searching for a solution (Section 9.6.1).

9.6.1. The American Debate

9.6.1.1. Introduction

In the United States, a total of forty-five states and the District of Columbia, and about 7,500 local jurisdictions (such as counties and cities) levy sales and use taxes. Sales taxes are limited in their scope to domestic sales, that is, to sales made within the state borders. For constitutional reasons (see Section 9.6.1.3), the states are unable to tax out-of-state sales. Therefore, exports to another state are exempt from sales tax, and imports from another state cannot be taxed under a sales tax. To compensate for this inability, all states that levy sales tax have introduced an equivalent system of use tax, which applies to imports.[75] Use tax is due by both businesses and private consumers purchasing goods from out-of-state vendors. Businesses have to report the use tax due on out-of-state purchases on their monthly sales tax return; private consumers must either file a separate use tax return or account for use tax on their out-of-state purchases via their annual state income tax return. Except in the case of purchases of goods that require registration, such as motor homes, cars, boats and airplanes, compliance by private consumers is extremely low.[76]

The idea that, in practice, goods purchased in another state are effectively tax free is increasingly tempting for consumers. Although buying from remote sellers is not a new phenomenon in the United States, where mail-order companies started their activities in the middle of the nineteenth century,[77] the impact of distance sales has taken unconscionable proportions since the invention of the Internet and the development of e-commerce, and the loss of revenue has increased accordingly.[78]

75. As accepted by the Supreme Court in *Henneford v. Silas Mason*, 300 US 577 (1937).
76. Kentucky reports that about 1% of filers report something with an average tax liability of USD 37. Maine, with the highest compliance rate, estimates that 10% of income tax filers report use tax due for a total amount of USD 1.6 million on total use tax revenue of USD 78.6 million. It further estimates a USD 30 million to USD 100 million loss as a result of underreporting (Maine Dept. of Revenue 2006).
77. Alfred Hammacher established the first mail-order company in 1848 in New York. Aaron Montgomery Ward is credited with issuing the first mail-order catalog in 1872 for his Chicago based company. Sears issued its first catalog around 1894.
78. In relation to remote sales, the US General Accounting Office estimates the revenue erosion at between USD 2.6 million and USD 20.4 billion. The midpoint of that range, USD 11.5 billion, is about 4% of total revenue that states expect to receive from sales and use taxes; see *Sales Taxes: Electronic Commerce Growth Presents Challenge, Revenue Losses Are Uncertain*, GOA Report OCE-00-165 (Washington, DC: GAO, 30 June 2000), 21. Estimates by private researchers of the loss range from USD 15.4 billion to USD 16.1 billion for 2003, and they project a revenue loss ranging from USD 21.5 billion to USD 33.6 billion for 2008; see Donald Bruce & William F. Fox, *State and Local Sales Tax Revenue Loss from E-commerce: Estimates as of July 2004* (University of Tennessee, July 2004), 5.

Indeed, loss of revenue is a growing concern for the states and local jurisdictions, but equally important are the detrimental economic consequences of nontaxation, at least by prevailing practice, of distance sales. Nontaxation of distance sales violates the principle of neutrality that should exist between different methods of production and distribution of goods, and should apply to consumer preferences as well. Clearly, traditional retailers are placed at a competitive disadvantage when distance sales of similar goods remain untaxed. Although, from a legal perspective, distance sales are taxed through the imposition of use tax, in practice, because of the significant lack of compliance, no taxation effectively takes place. The use tax system could be improved by requiring vendors to withhold use tax on "export" sales to another state. However, under the current judicial interpretation of the constitutional prohibition for states to impose an "undue burden" on interstate commerce, only vendors with adequate physical presence (called nexus) in a state are required to register as use tax collectors. Without nexus, remote sellers, such as Internet vendors and mail-order retailers, cannot be required to charge to their out-of-state customers the use tax applicable in the state of destination. The constitutional issues and relevant leading case law is discussed in Sections 9.6.1.3 and 9.6.1.6.

The current treatment of out-of-state remote sellers is a thorn in the sides of the state and local governments for reasons of increasing revenue loss, as well as for traditional retailers, facing what they perceive as unfair competition. The economic repercussions of nontaxation of distance sales is reviewed in Section 9.6.1.4. A solution can only be found at the federal legislative level by eliminating or substantially altering the physical-presence rule or by authorizing the states to collect use tax from out-of-state vendors (see Section 9.6.1.6). A more prominent role for Congress in the matter of state sales taxation does, however, have implications for the tax autonomy of the states and, as a consequence, for federalism itself.

Retailers are pressing for Congress to somehow create a level playing field for all retailers, regardless of whether they sell out of brick-and-mortar buildings or through virtual shops on the Internet.[79] They also make another important point, namely that it is essential to reduce the complexity of the sales and use taxes and, henceforth, reduce the severe compliance costs before requiring distance sellers to collect use tax on behalf of the states. That issue is discussed in Section 9.6.1.5.

A separate issue is the taxation of Internet access, which is currently under a moratorium, as well as other online services. In this respect, the political viewpoints are very diverse, and the task to develop a common policy seems Herculean in nature (see Section 9.6.1.8). Recent case law seems to indicate that, in respect to the sale of intangibles, a nonphysical-presence test can be applied to determine nexus, which would be a significant departure from the approach taken in respect to tangible products. Nevertheless, to avoid double taxation and nontaxation, as well as to realize the objective of simplification, a common definition standard for

---

79. National Retail Federation, *The Level-Playing Field and Beyond: Position Paper on the Framework for a Fair, Workable, and Simplified Sales and Use Tax System* (Washington, DC, March 2001).

nexus in relation to sales of intangibles, and common rules to determine the tax jurisdiction of the states, will be required.

As a consequence of the trend towards globalization, transaction taxes, such as sales and use taxes cannot be addressed as a national issue only. The international aspects to be considered in the United States when contemplating a change of the tax rules are summarized in Section 9.6.1.9.

9.6.1.2. Scope of the Debate

Regarding the taxation of electronic commerce, the participants in the political debate hold different views as to what the scope of the discussion should be.[80] Some accept the current tax treatment of distance sales of tangible products and prefer to limit the discussion to taxation of digital content sales and of Internet access. Others believe this is too narrow a base for a useful discussion because digital content downloaded from the Internet is a substitute for tangible products. Moreover, e-commerce sales of tangible products compete with other distance sales, as well as with traditional sales. Still others would like to seize the opportunity to rationalize and streamline the state sales and use taxes and, in the process, establish equal taxation for Internet access and telecommunications services.

The focus of this section is on sales and use taxes in respect to goods and services purchased over the Internet, as well as on Internet access taxation. Reform and harmonization of the sales and use taxes is discussed only in the context of the proposed solutions for the problems encountered with the current method of (non) taxation of e-commerce sales.

9.6.1.3. Legal Environment

The two clauses of the US Constitution determining the scope of state taxes are the due process clause, introduced by the Fourteenth Amendment, and the commerce clause.[81]

Generally, the due process clause relates to the fairness of the tax burden and to the question of whether a business has minimum contacts with the taxing jurisdiction. The primary goal of the commerce clause is to secure a unified, national market unimpeded by obstacles imposed by the states on cross-(state) border trade. However, under the federal system, the states have a legitimate interest in taxing business activities within their own borders. The commerce clause is designed "to make the delicate adjustment between the national interest in free and open trade and the legitimate interest of the individual states in exercising their taxing powers."[82] In *Bellas Hess*,[83] the Supreme Court ruled that the state of Illinois

80. Charles E. McLure, "Achieving a Level Playing Field for Electronic Commerce," *State Tax Notes* 14 (1998): 1767–1783.
81. Article I (8), clause 3 of the US Constitution.
82. *Boston Stock Exchange v. State Tax Commission*, 429 US 318, 329 (1977).
83. *National Bellas Hess v. Dept. of Revenue for the State of Illinois*, 386 US 753 (1967).

could not require out-of-state mail-order companies to collect a use tax from resident customers where their only contact with the state was via the US Postal Service or common carriers, such as UPS or FedEx. The Supreme Court found those contacts to be insufficient to establish physical presence, or nexus, under either the due process or commerce clauses. For both clauses, the Supreme Court uses criteria based on physical presence.

Twenty-five years later, the Supreme Court reaffirmed in *Quill*[84] that, in the absence of substantial nexus, a state cannot force the seller to collect use tax. At issue was whether an out-of-state seller had nexus where in-state contacts were confined to licensed software and common carriers delivering office equipment to customers. The facts of that case were very similar to those of *Bellas Hess*. However, and this is a significant difference, the Supreme Court based its decision in *Quill* predominantly on the commerce clause. The minimum physical contacts to establish nexus under the due process standard, as formulated in *Quill*, are easily met. In that respect, the Supreme Court only requires that a company purposefully directs activities towards residents of the state imposing the tax. As a result, since *Quill*, efforts of the states to collect tax on distance sales from out-of-state vendors will be measured only under the commerce clause.

The policy concerns underlying the commerce clause differ from those of the due process clause and, therefore, a different and more comprehensive standard is applied when considering state taxes under the commerce clause. It seems appropriate to take a closer look at the requirements for nexus under the commerce clause.

In *Complete Auto Transit*,[85] an earlier ruling, the Supreme Court imposed a four-part test to determine whether a state is eligible to tax certain activities under the commerce clause. For a state tax to be applied to an activity:

- there must be substantial nexus with the taxing state;
- the tax must be fairly apportioned to activities carried out in the state (internally consistent);
- the tax must not discriminate against interstate commerce (externally consistent); and
- the tax must be fairly related to the services provided by the state.

9.6.1.4. Economic and Competitive Distortions

Apart from the significant and increasing loss of revenue for governments, the de facto inability of the states to enforce use tax compliance distorts economic decisions, including consumers' choices on where and how to make purchases, and business decisions on the location of their activities and their corporate structure. Price-sensitive consumers with no intent to pay use tax find it cheaper to buy over the Internet than from a local brick-and-mortar store.[86] It is estimated that effective

84. *Quill Corporation v. North Dakota*, 504 US 298 (1992).
85. *Complete Auto Transit v. Brady*, 430 US 274 (1977).
86. A consumer might choose to purchase a product over the Internet for USD 100, inclusive of shipping cost, pay no sales tax, and fail to remit use tax, rather than purchase the same product

application of sales and use tax to Internet sales would reduce the number of online shoppers by 24%.[87, 88]

To minimize the tax they have to collect from their customers, vendors have an incentive to locate their activities in low-population and low-tax jurisdictions. Internet seller Amazon has strategically located more than half a dozen warehouses in low- and no-sales-tax states around the United States.[89] To create a more level competitive playing field with Internet vendors, traditional brick-and-mortar vendors (such as Barnes and Noble Booksellers, Gateway Computers, Borders Books and Music) with retail outlets in almost every state have created separate companies for virtual sales (e.g., barnesandnoble.com) in an effort to avoid nexus with the customers' states and, consequently, the obligation to collect use tax.[90] However, to secure the envisioned result, the commercial procedures need to be construed carefully, as Borders Online found out to its detriment when its noncollection of use tax was challenged in court by the tax authorities of California.[91] Borders Online had no physical presence in the state of California in terms of offices, tangible property or employees. However, Borders Books and Music, its sister company with many bookstores in the state, allowed Borders Online customers to return merchandise and receive cash refunds at their stores, and promoted the online sister company through general in-store advertising. The California Court of Appeal concluded that Borders Books and Music acted as an agent for Borders Online and, henceforth, that Borders Online had physical presence in the state.

The *Borders Online* case takes its place in a growing number of state court decisions regarding nexus for state sales and use tax purposes. However,

---

from a local store for USD 102, inclusive of local sales tax at USD 5. The real resource cost of the product, including profit, bought from the Internet seller is USD 100. The real resource cost of the same product from the local store is USD 97. The sales tax portion of USD 5 is a mere transfer of funds from the consumer to the government and uses no resources. The tax differential that results from the consumer's noncompliance with the use tax causes an increase in production cost of USD 3. That amount represents a loss of economic well-being to society because those USD 3 in resources could have been used to produce a USD 3 value in other goods or services. Example taken from a report by the Congressional Budget Office (CBO), *Economic Issues in Taxing Internet and Mail-Order Sales* (Washington, DC: CBO, October 2003).

87. Austan Goolsbee, "In a World without Borders: The Impact of Taxes on Internet Commerce," *Quarterly Journal of Economics* 115 (2) (2000): 561–576.
88. Where access to the Internet seems to increase with income, nontaxation of Internet sales has a regressive effect as well; see The Federal Reserve Bank of Chicago, Letter no. 154, June 2000.
89. According to an article on its founder, Jeff Bezos, Amazing Person.com, *Time*, 27 December 1999.
90. The following example illustrates how tax differentials may also affect location decisions: an Internet seller has a distribution center in jurisdiction A, in which the distribution cost for the product in note 86 is USD 10, rather than in jurisdiction B with more potential buyers and lower distribution costs (USD 7). By choosing A as its location, the vendor avoids nexus in jurisdiction B and the obligation to collect B's USD 5 sales tax from domestic customers. In other words, the vendor uses USD 10 of resources for distribution and charges a customer in B USD 100 (no tax), rather than using USD 7 of resources and charging USD 102 (including sales tax). Example taken from a report by the Congressional Budget Office.
91. *Borders Online v. State Board of Equalization*, 129 Cal. App. 4th 1179 (Cal. Ct. App. 2005).

the physical-presence requirements, as defined by the respective courts, vary considerably.[92] This disharmony at the state level strengthens the arguments of those who seek a strict federal definition of what constitutes physical presence and/ or binding legislative measures by Congress.

9.6.1.5. Complexity and Costs of Withholding Use Tax

Administrative costs are the cost incurred by the (federal, state or local) tax authorities that are charged with collecting taxes. Compliance costs are the cost borne by the taxpayers in the case of income tax, or by businesses in the case of sales and use taxes, where they act as tax collectors. Taken together, the administrative and compliance cost of taxation represent a considerable social cost. Similar to the cost of economic distortion, they are a cost on top of what is collected from the private sector and transferred to governments for public use. As a consequence, these costs should be kept at the lowest level possible.

To a certain extent, tax systems seem to be designed to take into account these costs. Some services are excluded from the tax base because they are supposed to entail higher than usual administrative costs per dollar of revenue collected. For the same reason, states avoid enforcing use tax collection on business-to-consumer distance sales.[93] If distance sellers were required to collect use tax for the states of destination, administrative cost certainly would be reduced significantly and perhaps distortion cost as well. However, the reduction in administrative costs would be accompanied by rising compliance costs for remote vendors. A recent study conducted by PricewaterhouseCoopers and the University of Chicago[94] found a national average of sales tax compliance costs for the year 2003 of 3.09% of tax collected for all retailers, 13.47% for small retailers (turnover between USD 150,000 and USD 1 million), 5.20% for medium-sized retailers (turnover between USD 1 million and USD 10 million) and 2.17% for large retailers (more than USD 10 million in turnover). This study, however, does not distinguish between single state and multistate collection. It seems logical to expect that compliance costs would increase for distance sellers operating in multiple jurisdictions because such vendors would face different tax bases, tax rates and audit rules. The conclusion of a study conducted by Ernst & Young in 1999 was that, as a share of revenue collections, the compliance costs would rise as the number of states in which a firm did business increased and the size of the firm decreased. Estimates ranged from 1% of revenue collected for large firms

92. For an overview of these cases, see Chris Atkins, *Establishing Physical Presence: Borders Online Case Reveals Court Disharmony in Applying Physical Presence Rules to State Sales Taxes*, Fiscal Fact no. 67 (Washington, DC: Tax Foundation, 26 September 2006).
93. The Operation Equity program in Connecticut pays other states 50% of first year's use tax collected as a result of information provided by those states' sales tax audits, a number suggesting that the cost of enforcing compliance by other means, like auditing individual taxpayers, is prohibitive.
94. PricewaterhouseCoopers, *Retail Sales Tax Compliance Costs: A National Estimate*, 7 April 2006.

collecting the tax in a single state to 48% and 87% for medium-sized and small firms, respectively, doing business in forty-five states.[95] In other words, for every tax dollar collected, a medium-sized company would incur 48 cents in costs, and a small business would spend 87 cents to collect a single dollar in tax. Size, indeed, seems to matter. Where, in the past, companies operating in multiple or all states would necessarily be relatively large, the Internet enables even the smallest enterprise to conduct business in multiple states. The latter study seems to indicate that, once out-of-state distance sellers were required to collect use tax, the tax compliance costs could be prohibitive for medium-sized and smaller businesses to either enter this market or maintain their position. The main issue is the complexity of compliance as a result of the diverse rules and definitions applied by the forty-five states and the District of Columbia, and the approximately 7,500 different local jurisdictions. Even if distance sellers collect the home addresses of their customers, correct appropriation of the tax is not guaranteed because zip code boundaries do not coincide with local tax jurisdictions. Moreover, there exists no sales tax template or standard on which states could model their sales tax legislation. As a result, tax rules differ considerably in respect to tax base, definition of goods and services, exemptions, rates, bookkeeping obligations and audit procedures. There are software programs on the market to calculate the appropriate tax for each jurisdiction; however, their effectiveness in reducing compliance costs depends on their accuracy in respect to the specific tax rules, rates and definitions for each jurisdiction, as well as on their speed in updating the ever-changing information.

9.6.1.6. The Role of Congress

In principle, the taxing power of a state is limited to domestic transactions. A state may tax a transaction if there is some connection between the transaction and the state. If both the seller and customer are located in the same state, the state has the authority to require the seller to collect and remit sales tax. However, where the transaction is purely one of interstate commerce and where the seller does not have the requisite nexus to the customer's state, Congress is the only entity that may regulate the activity or authorize the states to do so.

In *Quill*, the Supreme Court reversed its *Bellas Hess* ruling that taxation of distance sales by a state violates both the due process clause and commerce clause of the Constitution. The Supreme Court dropped the physical-presence test for nexus under the due process clause, requiring only that the seller's efforts be "purposefully directed toward the residents of the taxing State." Therefore, the due process clause was no longer an impediment to requiring use tax collection by out-of-state sellers. However, the Supreme Court also reaffirmed the physical-presence standard or

95. Robert J. Cline & Thomas S. Neubig, *Masters of Complexity and Bearers of Great Burden: The Sales Tax System and Compliance Costs for Multistate Retailers* (Washington, DC: Ernst & Young, 8 September 1999). See also Lorrie Jo Brown, "Sales Tax Compliance Costs for E-tailers Revisited: A Critique of the Ernst & Young Study," *State Tax Notes* 18 (4) (2000): 315–317, who suggests that those estimates grossly overstate the likely compliance cost but does not herself provide comparable estimates for multistate vendors.

substantial nexus under the commerce clause. This is important because Congress could not authorize the states to collect a tax that violates the due process clause, whereas it has explicit constitutional authority to regulate interstate commerce.

In other words, the removal of the due process clause as a roadblock opened the door for Congress to undertake action. Whereas the issues involved in-state taxation of distance and e-commerce sales might not appear to raise federal questions, Congress's power under the commerce clause brings these issues into the federal arena. Under its commerce powers, Congress can legislatively empower the states to require out-of-state sellers to collect use taxes from their customers and remit the revenues to the customers' home states. In fact, in *Quill*, the Supreme Court specifically invited Congress to undertake action in this respect.[96] That policy role is the only involvement of the federal government in the e-commerce debate; the issue has no direct federal budgetary implications.

There are competing demands made and arguments offered in the congressional debate on whether or not Internet sales should be subject to taxation. Depending on which side of the debate is supported, requiring remote sellers to collect use tax will have different effects that can be summarized as follows:

- decrease of revenue loss;
- increase of the compliance costs for businesses;
- elimination of a tax advantage that is instrumental in enabling the Internet to grow to its full potential;[97]
- enhancement of the equal distribution of the tax burden, or compliance with the principle of equal treatment;
- compromise of the tax autonomy of the states and local governments, if taxation of interstate transactions would require standardization of use tax legislation; and
- imposition of a tax burden on remote sellers who, unlike local sellers, derive no compensating benefit from the public services financed by the tax.[98]

Crucial in the discussion are the compliance costs for remote vendors, which seem to be excessive (see Section 9.6.1.5), and the tax autonomy of the states and

96. The Supreme Court noted that the issue of taxing remote sales was "not only one that Congress may be better qualified to resolve but also one that Congress has the ultimate power to resolve."

97. This argument is only true for a new industry in its infant years. In view of the fact that, in 2001, 56% of the population in the United States was using the Internet, the online industry has amply passed that stage, at least in my opinion; see US Dept. of Commerce, *A Nation Online: How Americans Are Expanding Their Use of the Internet* (February 2002), Table 2-2, 26.

98. This latter argument seems less valid to me where the tax is actually borne by the consumer and the vendor is only acting as the tax collector. Because the tax would accrue to the state of destination or use of the goods or services, the consumers, as the actual taxpayers, would benefit from the public services in that state. The argument can only be accepted from the perspective of the Austrian school of economic thought that all taxes are borne by businesses because price maximization leaves no room for shifting taxes forward. It is true that tax collection also has an impact on remote vendors in the form of compliance costs, which, as could be argued, is unfair because remote vendors receive no benefits from the states for which they collect the taxes. This burden could be reduced or mitigated by offering compensation for the cost of collection.

local governments. As to the latter, the business community, as well as the state and local governments, generally oppose federal efforts to codify nexus standards, which they view as an undue restriction of the ability of the states to levy an (income) tax on business activity, as well as sales and use taxes.[99] Federal legislation that would permit the state and local governments to collect use tax on remote sales from the vendors is perceived as imposing high compliance costs on these remote vendors, which may offset the gains in economic efficiency derived from a reduction of the current cost of distortion. To date, Congress has chosen not to enact legislation granting the states the authority to require out-of-state sellers to collect and remit use taxes, mainly for the reason of excessive compliance costs. In this respect, the approach by Congress is in line with the Supreme Court's decision in *Quill* where it explicitly cites the high compliance cost and legal complexity of the state and local sales and use taxes as causes of an unacceptable burden on interstate commerce.

There appears to be widespread agreement in and outside Congress that the states need to simplify and standardize their systems of state and local sales and use taxes if they hope to improve collection of the use tax on interstate sales, whether through the Internet or by mail order, telephone or face-to-face methods of distribution to their residents. The perceived need for administrative simplification applies, regardless of whether collection by the remote sellers is to occur on a voluntary basis or under a legal obligation imposed by the states authorized to that effect by Congress.

In the United States, sales taxation is assigned to the subnational governmental (state) level. Basically, elementary questions, such as which taxes to levy, how to define the tax base, how many rates to apply and at what level, and what administrative obligations to impose, are all decided at the subnational level. As evidenced by the present sales and use tax systems, total subnational tax autonomy can easily lead to unnecessary complexities, inequities, economic distortions, and duplication of compliance and administrative efforts. From an economic perspective, the United States is a common market; however, for a common market to function appropriately, a minimum level of sales tax coordination is required.[100]

That the rights of the states as regards sales and use taxation are absolute, and that any reduction in their taxing power should be conceived as an unconstitutional usurpation of power by the federal government seems to be a rather questionable interpretation of the Constitution. The founding fathers assigned the regulation of interstate commerce to the federal government, indeed, because they were concerned about the tendency of the states to pursue parochial interests.[101] Moreover, economic reality disavows the claim of the states on absolute

99. Martha Kessler, *FTA Opposes Nexus Change Bill, Favors Expansion of Sales Tax Collection Duty* (Bureau of National Affairs, Daily Tax Report, no. 113, 12 June 2000), G-5, and Lee A. Sheppard, "Business Taxpayers Resist State Tax Nexus in Courts and Congress," *Tax Notes* 87 (6) (8) (2000): 740–747.

100. A truth demonstrated by the success of the EU. However, there exists no institutionalized forum with legislative authority in which the states can take multilateral decisions.

101. Charles E. McLure, "Electronic Commerce, State Sales Taxation, and Intergovernmental Relations," *National Tax Journal* 50 (4) (1997): 731–749.

sales tax autonomy. With the coming of globalization and the information age, marketplaces become more integrated by the day. Thinking of marketplaces as simply a local phenomenon is increasingly becoming archaic. This does not mean that local marketplaces have ceased to exist but only that, to a large extent, the local marketplace has integrated into a larger market unit. Local markets are now statewide markets, state markets have lost their boundaries and have emerged as nationwide markets and national markets have evolved into global markets. In addition, boundaries between industries have faded. The extension of market scales does not correlate with a subnational level of tax authority, in the same way that the reality of economic presence does not correlate with taxable nexus. For this rather simple reason, federal legislation or substantial tax coordination between the states will be required to break the status quo. In the absence of such coordination, Congress could claim jurisdiction over nonconsenting states, arguing that globalization and market integration evidently elevate sales taxation to the realm of federal, that is, national, interests.[102] In view of its case law, the Supreme Court appears to accept federal rules, determined by Congress under the commerce clause of the Constitution, that prohibit the states from imposing sales and use tax on cross-border transactions, unless they:

- limit the tax to a single rate per state;
- adopt uniform definitions of taxable supplies;
- simplify their administrative procedures for collecting taxes, as specified by Congress; and
- only require out-of-state sellers to collect use tax, if their (in-state) sales exceed a certain *de minimis* level.

In addition, it seems acceptable for Congress to permit the states to require distance sellers to collect use tax, regardless of their nexus with a state.[103] Because electronic commerce invariably constitutes a regular commercial transaction (e.g., the purchase and/or transfer of a digital or nondigital product over the Internet), there can be no doubt that it forms part of the interstate stream of business, which is sufficient reason to support a congressional regulation.[104]

102. *Houston E&W Tex. Ry v. United States*, 234 US 342 (1914), generally known as the *Shreveport rate* case, in which the Supreme Court stated: "It is unnecessary to repeat what has frequently been said by this court with respect to the complete and paramount character of the power confided to Congress to regulate commerce among several States. It is of the essence of this power that, where it exists, it dominates. . . . By virtue of the comprehensive terms of the grant, the authority of Congress is at all times adequate to meet the varying exigencies that arise and to protect the national interest by securing the freedom of interstate commercial intercourse from local control."

103. See the analysis of jurisprudence by Walter Hellerstein, "Federal Constitutional Limitations on Congressional Power to Legislate Regarding State Taxation of Electronic Commerce," *National Tax Journal* 53 (4) (2000): 1307–1325

104. In *United States v. Lopez*, 514 US 549 (1995), the Supreme Court distinguished three broad categories that Congress may regulate under the commerce clause:

9.6.1.7. Possible Solutions

Several bills are pending in Congress that propose guidelines for simplifying state and local sales tax regulations. Indeed, some of the proposals pursue tax simplification as a means of encouraging a system of voluntary compliance by remote sellers. Other bills provide a formal mechanism in the form of an interstate compact under which Congress would grant the states the authority to require out-of-state sellers to collect and remit use tax if the states comply with certain criteria for sales tax simplification.[105] However, on one hand, the states are strongly opposed to any guidelines or criteria set at the federal level because they perceive those measures as an infringement of their rights. On the other hand, the states do realize that they cannot expect Congress to give them carte blanche authorization for remote seller collection of use tax without taking measures to reduce the complexity of the tax system and the sellers' compliance costs.[106] For this reason, the states have initiated the Sales Tax Streamlining Project, which is essentially an effort to harmonize sales and use taxes on a voluntary basis. In a sense, that project is a political preemptive strike to render federal guidelines obsolete in lieu of considerable streamlining of the existing legislation of the participating states and, henceforth, significant reduction of compliance costs.

In theory, apart from Congress, the Supreme Court could also approve an obligation for remote sellers without nexus to collect use taxes if the states were successful in their multilateral simplification and harmonization efforts because the essence of *Quill* is that the current complexity caused by the diversity of the state and local sales and use taxes imposes an unacceptable burden on interstate commerce. However, for the Supreme Court to overturn an earlier decision is no small feat given the emphasis on precedents embodied in the stare decisis doctrine.[107]

- the use of the channels of interstate commerce;
- the instrumentalities of interstate commerce, or persons, or things in interstate commerce; and
- activities that substantially affect interstate commerce.

105. Dennis Zimmerman, *Economic Issues in Taxing Internet and Mail-order Sales*, Congressional Budget Office (CBO) paper (Washington, DC, October 2003).
106. See Steven Maguire, *State and Local Sales and Use Taxes and Internet Commerce*, CRS Report (28 January 2005); and John L. Mikesell, "Remote Vendors and American Sales and Use Taxation: The Balance between Fixing the Problem and Fixing the Tax," *National Tax Journal* 53 (4) (2000): 1273–1285.
107. The term is derived from the Latin *stare decisis et non quieta movere* (stand by decisions and do not move which is quiet). The stare decisis doctrine is a common law concept under which judicial institutions abide or adhere to previously decided cases. Although the doctrine does not prevent the courts from reexamining and overruling prior decisions made by themselves or other courts, it a fundamental juridical policy that, in view of the assumption that certainty, predictability and stability of the law are the major objectives of the legal system, prior applicable decisions must normally be followed by the courts.

In addition, the streamlining project anticipates offering remote sellers financial compensation for the compliance costs they incur as tax collectors. From a macroeconomic perspective, this would not reduce the social cost of taxation but merely shift the cost from the vendors to the taxpayers. However, that compensation seems fair and reasonable, given that currently only certain sectors of the economy have to act as sales and use tax collectors.[108]

The states will lobby to obtain authorization to require use tax collection from remote vendors when sufficient progress is made by the participating states regarding harmonization of the tax base, terminology, administrative procedures and so on.[109] It seems likely that the states will be successful in their effort if, indeed, their harmonization of the sales and use taxes turns out to be successful. In politics, progress is defined in terms of a workable compromise between opposing views and objectives. Congress will, in my assessment, seize any reasonable opportunity to avoid opening the constitutional Pandora's box of conflict between state rights and federal authority.

9.6.1.8. Taxation of Internet Access and Other Online Services

The ITFA was enacted on 21 October 1998, placing a 3-year moratorium on the ability of the state and local governments to impose new taxes on Internet access[110] but grandfathering existing taxes on Internet access. This initial moratorium was extended by 2 years under the Internet Tax Nondiscrimination Act,[111] and further extensions of the moratorium, until 1 November 2007,[112] and until 2014.[113]

---

108. Mikesell, "Remote Vendors and American Sales and Use Taxation," 1281.
109. Interestingly, the harmonization process in the United States is developing according to a model that is the reverse of the European model. In the EU, tax harmonization is initiated at the central administrative level and enforced through directives that are binding on the Member States, whereas, in the United States, the states are initiating the harmonization process on a voluntary basis to avoid legislative initiatives at the central (federal) level.
110. The ITFA defines Internet access service to be a service "that enables users to access content, information, electronic mail, or other services offered over the Internet."
111. Public Law (PL) 107-75 of 28 November 2001. At that time, ten states and the District of Columbia applied sales tax to Internet access services, according to the National Conference of State Legislatures, "Which States Tax Internet Access?," (25 March 1998). Subsequently, Connecticut, Iowa, Tennessee and the District of Columbia eliminated their tax and South Carolina decided not to enforce its collection. As a result, New Mexico, North Dakota, Ohio, South Dakota, Texas and Wisconsin impose a sales tax on Internet access. However, according to the CBO, several local jurisdictions in Colorado, Ohio, South Dakota, Texas, Washington and Wisconsin collect taxes on Internet access; see CBO, *Cost Estimate of Senate Bill (S) 150, the Internet Nondiscrimination Act, 9 September 2003*, contained in 108th Cong. 1st Session Report 108-155 (Washington, DC: CBO, 29 September 2003).
112. PL 108-435, which was approved by the Senate on 29 April 2004, by the House on 19 November 2004 and signed by the president on 3 December 2004. The act also clarified that the prohibition of taxation of Internet access applies, regardless of whether the tax is imposed on the provider or customer of the Internet access.
113. H.R. 3678 of 30 october 2007. The legislation also clarifies that services related to Internet access, such as instant messaging, e-mail and personal online storage, are not taxable.

Congress is facing several principle questions regarding taxation of Internet access. The most important question is whether the moratorium should be extended, temporarily or permanently, or, in other words, whether and, if so, when and under what conditions, the states should be allowed to impose use tax on Internet access.

The intent of the moratorium was to prevent multiple state jurisdictions from taxing the same Internet access service and to ensure that commerce over the Internet would not be singled out for discriminatory tax treatment. Proponents of the moratorium believed that the Internet should be shielded from the burden of taxation to encourage the development of the Internet technology and associated economic activity. Opponents contended that a federal moratorium infringed the states' tax autonomy and that Internet transactions should not benefit from a preferential treatment compared to traditional transactions.

A further temporary extension of the moratorium would enable Congress to periodically reassess developments in computer and software technology, the effects of nontaxation of Internet access and e-commerce on state revenues, as well as allow the states more time to further streamline their sales and use taxes. A permanent moratorium (that is a tax exemption) would provide immediate certainty as to state taxation and would eliminate the necessity for Congress to evaluate the issues surrounding the Internet, but it would not resolve the issue of state tax autonomy.

In the United States, the discussion on tax jurisdiction in relation to electronic services and other intangibles mainly revolves around the concept of nexus and two decisions of the Supreme Court.[114]

The first significant case to address the modern commerce clause standard in the context of a tax on services was *Goldberg*.[115] In *Goldberg*, the Supreme Court considered the constitutionality of an Illinois statute that imposed a tax on the gross fee for interstate telecommunications services that either originated or terminated in Illinois and which were also charged to an Illinois service address, understood by the Court as meaning the address where the telephone equipment was located and to which the telephone number was assigned, regardless of the address to which the call was invoiced or from which the invoice was paid. The Court concluded that, in *Goldberg*, each of the four prongs of the test laid out in *Complete Auto Transit*[116] was satisfied. The Court's discussion of the substantial nexus criteria is of particular significance to taxation of e-commerce services. According to the Supreme Court, only two states can have a sufficiently substantial nexus to tax a consumer's purchase of an interstate telephone call. The first is the state (in this case Illinois) that taxes the origination or termination of an interstate telephone call charged to a service address within its territory. The second is the state that

114. For an economic approach towards the case law, see William F. Fox & Matthew N. Murray, "The Sales Tax and Electronic Commerce: So What's New," *National Tax Journal* (19) 50 (3) (1997): 573–592. For a legal analysis of the implications of e-commerce, see Martin I. Eisenstein, "The Constitutional Limits on Sales Taxation of Cyberspace," *State Tax Notes*, 24 February 1997, 601–605.

115. *Goldberg v. Sweet*, 488 US 252 (1989).

116. See n. 85.

taxes the origination or termination of an interstate telephone call invoiced or paid within its territory. Therefore, substantial nexus of an activity with a state to permit taxation of a service requires that:

- first, the service originates or terminates in the state;
- second, the fee for the service is charged to a service address within the state; or
- third, the service is invoiced to or paid in the state.

This nexus standard is a significant departure from the physical-presence test applied in *Quill*. Apparently, in the event of a service, there must be a connection between the state and the activity itself, rather than between the service provider and the state that seeks to impose the tax,[117] as was the case in *Quill*, where the question was whether the state had the authority to tax the corporation at all.

In *Jefferson Lines*,[118] the state of Oklahoma required the collection of sales tax on interstate bus transportation purchased in that state. On the basis of the Supreme Court's ruling in *Central Greyhound*,[119] the lower courts ruled that the tax violated the commerce clause. However, the Supreme Court pointed out that there were significant differences between the two cases. In *Central Greyhound*, the Court declared that the New York GRT did not apply because of a lack of apportionment of the service to New York on the basis of the mileage traveled within the territory of New York and that within the other states involved. In principle, Central Greyhound could be subject to GRT in each state through which it traveled, and, therefore, New York's GRT was not externally consistent in terms of the third prong of *Complete Auto Transit*. The cases were similar as to the type of services provided but different in respect to the tax levied and the identity of the taxpayer. The Court perceived the GRT as a type of income tax, whereas the sales tax is a transaction tax. In *Central Greyhound*, the tax was levied on the service provider, and in *Jefferson Lines*, on the customer. In the latter case there was no risk of multiple taxation.

As the Court stated in *Jefferson Lines*: "The taxable event comprises agreement, payment, and delivery of some of the services in the taxing state; no other state can claim to be the site of the same combination." On that ground, the Court rejected Jefferson Lines's argument that the sale of services does not occur until delivery is made for the portion of the trip that occurs outside of Oklahoma. The sale occurred in Oklahoma, because "the combined events of payment for a ticket and its delivery for present commencement of a trip are commonly understood to suffice for a sale." Interestingly, the nexus reasoning applied in both *Goldberg* and *Jefferson Lines* transforms the sale of electronic services into a domestic, that is, a single state, supply.[120] Therefore, the seller is responsible for collection of sales

117. *Allied-Signal Inc. v. Director*, Division of Taxation, 504 US 768, 778 (1992).
118. *Oklahoma Tax Commission v. Jefferson Lines, Inc.*, 514 US 175 (1995).
119. *Central Greyhound Lines Inc. v. Mealey*, 334 US 653 (1948).
120. Also: Scot R. Grierson, "State Taxation of the Information Superhighway: A Proposal for Taxation of Information Services," *Loyola of Los Angeles Entertainment Law Journal* 16 (3) (1996): 603–655.

tax, rather than use tax. The purchase of the ticket and the start of the bus trip in *Jefferson Lines* correlates to the *Goldberg* situation of charging a call to a service address in the taxing state and the origination or termination of service in that state.

Since cyberspace is a world without geographical boundaries, tax jurisdiction rules based on the significance of national borders have in fact become anachronisms. Although academic discussion focuses on the application of the *Goldberg* and *Jefferson Lines* criteria to e-commerce transactions, including Internet access, it is an illusion to believe that the judicial branch of the government can rescue laws that neither reflect the differences between goods and services, nor the nature of the online services industry and the circumstances under which it operates. Whereas online services and tangible goods supplied by distance sellers have in common that they can easily be sold across state borders, they also display substantial differences. Although there are examples of online services of which the tax jurisdiction can easily be determined on the basis of the nexus standard set by the Supreme Court, there are more cases in which the efforts to determine the tax jurisdiction will prove to be as futile as the Internet is virtual, certainly with the ever-changing technology, and with the speed of these changes, more and higher hurdles are being added for the legal athletes to clear.

All aspects that helped determine the previously discussed court cases, more specifically the place of origination and termination of the service, invoice and payment address, and place of connection, are extremely difficult to substantiate for Internet access and online services. The very nature of Internet access and online services is their mobility. Whereas, in respect to typical mail-order sales, or other interstate sales of goods, the destination of the goods can easily be determined, such is not the case for Internet access and online services. A person can access the Internet or receive an online service from virtually anywhere in the world. The service provider simply cannot determine from where the communication commenced and, mutatis mutandis, he will be unable to establish to what extent the services must be attributed to a given state.

Unlike the telephone service at issue in *Goldberg*, there is no service address for Internet access or online services. The "equipment" is the software package provided by the provider to its customers, which is inherently moveable. The equivalent to the telephone number, which was used to site the service address in *Goldberg*, is the password or another log-on code, which cannot be exclusively sourced to a specific state, as is the case for telephone numbers.

Similarly, the invoice address may not offer a simple answer to the tax jurisdiction question either. Providers and customers generally do not know each other's locations or addresses. Most online transactions will be paid by credit card, and it could be argued that the provider invoices the card company (American Express, Visa, Master Card and so on) or the payment processor (such as PayPal), which in turn invoices the customer. Very unlike the case of a landline telephone service, the invoice address for online services can hardly be regarded as a viable indication of the state in which the services are enjoyed or used because of the mobility of these services and the customers.

As a result, it may be cumbersome for a state that seeks to tax an out-of-state service provider to establish that the provider meets the physical-presence test of *Quill* or that the four-part nexus requirements of *Complete Auto Transit*, as interpreted under *Goldberg* and *Jefferson Lines*, are satisfied. Moreover, and as a consequence of the difficulties for a state to establish all these requirements satisfactorily, it may find itself compromised in its ability to pass the internal consistency requirement, that is, the prohibition from taxing an activity if another state is also eligible to tax the same activity with an identical tax.[121]

The states could try to strengthen their position by arguing that, for out-of-state service providers, nexus can be established through the activities of a third party, such as an Internet access provider or payment processor. This would not be an easy argument to make and support with facts because it will be necessary that the activities of the third party are instrumental for the out-of-state service provider to establish and maintain the in-state market position. However, even if successful, it would not contribute to the transparency of the tax system and would only lead to more uncertainty for firms and endless and costly litigation. Some indicate that *Jefferson Lines* may have opened the door for sales taxation of Internet access and other online services based on the origin principle. This would not result in a fair distribution of revenue over all states relative to the expenditure on online services by residents of each state. More importantly, in their effort to gain a competitive edge, taxation under the origin principle would enable service providers to locate their business in states without sales tax or even outside the United States, in order to avoid the obligation to collect sales tax. In the end, one can only predict a deluge of litigation when, facing a significant loss of revenue, the states introduce a new, and no doubt creative, line of nexus-like arguments to reason that a service provided to a resident in his state in fact originated in that state.

In essence, the issue of taxing Internet access and other online services is similar to that associated with taxing distance sales of tangible goods. The main issues are again nexus and simplification. It is a federal issue only in terms of authority, not in terms of revenue. It seems that the concept of nexus does not work well in respect to electronic services. Instead of using a myriad of evolving nexus theories in an effort to put intangible e-commerce activities, including Internet access, into a tax policy envelope in which they clearly do not fit, it would make more sense to think outside the legislative box and abandon the concept of nexus altogether as a tool to determine tax jurisdiction. Where sales and use taxes are considered consumption taxes to be levied in accordance with the destination principle, it is essential to develop simple and practical rules to determine which state is entitled to tax the services, that is, in which state are the services deemed to be used or enjoyed. These rules can be fictitious, provided that they are consistent. The states seek permission to tax Internet access and to require access providers

121. See *Radio Common Carriers*, 601 NYS2d 513 (1993), in which the New York Supreme Court declared that a law imposing a tax on pagers used in New York, Connecticut and New Jersey was unconstitutional because New Jersey and Connecticut could levy a similar tax and, therefore, the standard of internal consistency had not been met.

and other online service providers without nexus to collect the use tax for them. As with use taxes on distance sales, federal permission will, in all probability, depend on harmonization and simplification of the sales and use taxes, resulting in a significant reduction of the compliance costs for vendors. For this reason, progress with the Streamlining Project will prove to be essential regarding the taxation of Internet access and other online services.

9.6.1.9. International Aspects

Assuming that, under the most likely scenario, legislation will be introduced that will require distance sellers to collect use tax for the state of consumption, consideration must be given to sales made by distance sellers from outside the United States. It seems that US-based distance sellers would find themselves at an economic disadvantage relative to non-US sellers and may potentially lose business to the latter.

In addition, if distance sales by vendors abroad would remain outside the scope of the US use taxes, domestic suppliers could potentially avoid the tax by creating subsidiaries abroad through which they channel their distance sales to the US market. This situation would raise the same economic issues that are part of the current discussion on interstate distance sales and would generate an additional loss of revenue. The size of that loss is difficult to assess. For tangible goods, the shipping costs may partly offset or even exceed the avoided use tax but, regarding digitized goods and services, additional delivery costs would not play a role. To avoid the necessity for nonresident traders to register in each state in which they have customers, the United States may consider allowing them to register with, and remit the tax to, a central collection agency, which, in turn, will redistribute the revenue to all the states. Although the system of central registration would still require nonresident vendors to collect data on the state of destination and charge the tax at the rate applicable in that state, it would significantly simplify their compliance commitment. In addition, a *de minimis* threshold would prevent registration of nonresident vendors only making distance sales or providing online services to US customers on an occasional basis.

9.6.1.10. Conclusions

Taxation of distance sales and online services is a thorny problem for the states because of low consumer compliance with the use tax rules, and the legal inability of the states to require sellers to collect the tax on their behalf. It is unlikely that this problem can be solved satisfactorily on the basis of the nexus doctrine as developed by the Supreme Court in *Quill* for goods, and in *Goldberg* and *Jefferson Lines* for intangibles. Congress, which has exclusive authority to regulate interstate trade, holds the key to the solution. However, it seems that Congress is reluctant to adopt legislative measures that would enable states to require distance sellers and online service providers to collect use tax because of the excessively high compliance costs associated with meeting the diverse and complex rules in more than 7,500 different jurisdictions. Because they are strongly opposed to any guidelines or criteria set at the federal level, which they perceive as an infringement of their rights, the states are left with the option to harmonize their sales and use taxes on a voluntary basis in an effort to simplify the rules and regulations and, henceforth, realize a significant reduction in the compliance costs for businesses collecting the tax.

The states will lobby to obtain authorization to require use tax collection from remote vendors when sufficient progress is made between the participating states as regards harmonization. It seems likely that the states will be successful in their efforts because they have has political merit for Congress and should prevent conflict between state rights and federal authority.

9.6.2. European Practice

The EU legislators realized that the rules applicable to cross-border B2B sales would be impossible to enforce in the case where the recipient of the goods was a private consumer or another nonregistered entity. Potentially millions of private individuals would need to be registered to account for intracommunity acquisitions, invoking excessive administrative costs for tax authorities as well as high risks of tax evasion by consumers. The experience in the United States with low compliance numbers for use tax due by consumers on cross-border purchasers provides a reasonable basis for the latter assumption. The need was felt to contain cross-border shopping and the inherent loss of economic neutrality, while at the same time protecting distance sellers from excessive compliance costs when making only occasional sales to a certain jurisdiction. The result is a potentially complex and hybrid system, applying the origin principle below and the destination principle above a certain sales threshold.

According to the main rule, cross-border (distance) sales are subject to VAT in the country of arrival of the goods[122] in accordance with the destination principle. However, the main rule does not apply, and, as a consequence, the sales are taxable in the country from which the goods are dispatched if the total sales of the distance seller to the country of arrival have not exceeded EUR 100,000 in the current calendar year[123] or in the previous calendar year.[124] Member States, however, are allowed to limit this threshold to EUR 35,000.[125]

The concept of distance sales is limited to cross-border sales within the EU to private individuals and to a group of entities that is generally treated as a final consumer; in the sense that they are taxed on their inputs, namely flat rate farmers, fully exempt persons and nontaxable legal persons, but only if and as long as the total value of their intracommunity acquisitions does not exceed a threshold of

122. Article 33, Directive 2006/112.
123. Article 34(1) (b), Directive 2006/112.
124. Article 34(1) (c), Directive 2006/112
125. Article 34(2), Directive 2006/112. The threshold is EUR 100,000 or the equivalent in local currency in Austria, France, Germany, Luxemburg, the Netherlands and the United Kingdom; and EUR 35,000 or the equivalent in local currency in Belgium, Bulgaria, Cyprus, the Czech Republic, Denmark, Estonia, Finland, Greece, Hungary, Ireland, Italy, Latvia, Lithuania, Malta, Poland, Portugal, Romania, the Slovak Republic, Slovenia, Spain and Sweden.

EUR 10,000 in the current or previous calendar year[126] and provided such an entity has not opted for treatment as a taxable person.[127] Moreover, the distance sales rules do not apply in case of the cross-border sale of new means of transport or goods supplied after assembly or installation[128] because these sales are already subject to special treatment.

Figure 16. VAT Treatment of Distance Sales

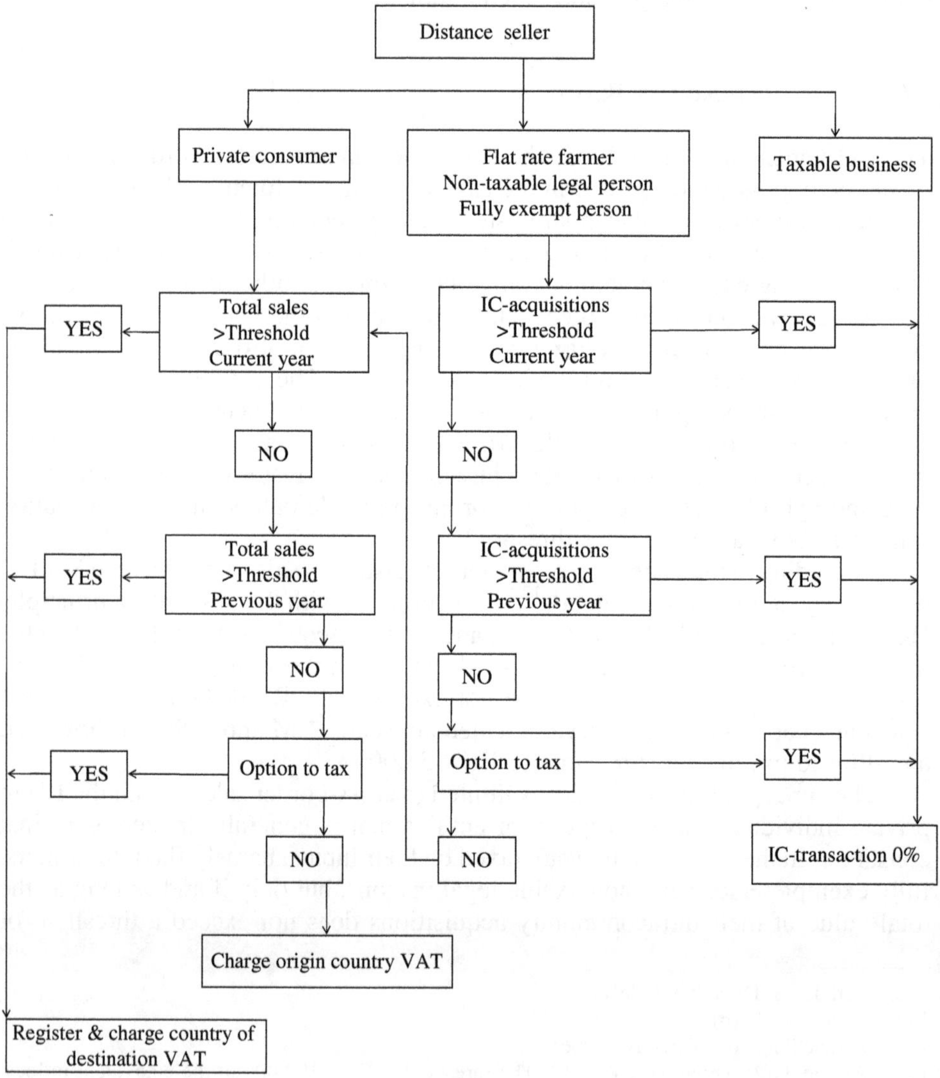

126. Article 33(1) (a) jo. Art. 3(2) (a) and (b), Directive 2006/112.
127. Article 3(3), Directive 2006/112.
128. Article 33(1) (b), Directive 2006/112.

All in all, it seems to be quite an exercise for a business engaging in distance sales to determine the correct VAT treatment of sales. Figure 16 demonstrates the decision model as a step-by-step process.

A distance seller needs first to determine whether his customer falls within the category to which the distance sales regime is applicable. Although this appears to be quite complex on paper, in practice the buyer will indicate his VAT status as a taxable person by providing his VAT registration number to the seller, which the latter can verify through the tax authorities in his country of residence. If the number is valid, the seller will assume that the customer with regard to this particular procurement is acting in the capacity of a taxable person. In that event, the distance sale rules do not apply, and the transaction constitutes an intracommunity supply for the seller subject to 0% VAT in the country of dispatch and an intracommunity acquisition for the buyer subject to the VAT rate in the country of arrival.

If no VAT number is submitted, or if it proves to be invalid, the seller will treat the buyer as a private consumer, located in another Member State. The correct treatment depends solely on the seller's situation in terms of sales volume, or on his choice for taxation in the destination country. Although it is conceivably a compliance burden to keep track of sales volume to twenty-seven different countries, automation significantly reduces the pain and effort.

9.7. THE CHALLENGE OF FRAUD SCHEMES

9.7.1. Introduction and Summary

VAT fraud is becoming more and more of a universal problem. Most taxpayers quite legitimately deduct VAT on the basis of VAT shown on invoices issued by their suppliers. In case the total amount of input VAT exceeds the total amount of output VAT, a taxpayer is entitled to a refund. A problem arises when these refunds are based on counterfeit invoices, or when fraud schemes are designed with the purpose to avoid payment of tax by the supplier while the recipient exercises his refund entitlements. In principle, it is true that tax uncollected in one stage of the distribution chain will be made up at the subsequent stage as a result of the recouping effect. However, fraudsters only appear to be part of the distribution chain, issuing invoices, submitting returns and claiming refunds. In reality, most sophisticated fraud schemes avoid real transactions of goods and only create a paper trail as a means to collect the VAT. In such a situation, the recouping effect does not work, and the treasury will incur a real loss of revenue. The first defense is, of course, a solid policy framework backed up by an efficient risk-based auditing system that is able to distinguish between legitimate and fraudulent transactions. That is no sinecure; as we see later, the fraud schemes are not only sophisticated and tend to mutate quickly but also hide within legitimate distribution chains.

Although fraud is a universal phenomenon, we will concentrate on the European theater because it offers excellent context and examples of the issues. Fraud is an issue of growing concern for the tax authorities in EU countries because the zero rating system of relieving intracommunity sales from VAT helps in creating fraud opportunities. This concern is fueled by the size and frequency of fraud, its increased sophistication, the inherent difficulty of combating it and its financial significance. We also take into account the delicate position of a third party that somehow gets entangled in the myriad of transactions that form what is generally referred to as carousel fraud. First, a basic description is provided of the design of a carousel fraud, and then a closer look is taken to how some individual Member States of the EU have tried to combat this type of fraud. Finally, the latest developments in case law of the ECJ, the acceptance of the principle of abuse of law, and of joint and several liability are discussed, especially the severe consequences these concepts have on the position of a third party entangled in such a fraud scheme but acting in good faith.

9.7.2. Description of Carousel Fraud

From an economic perspective, the VAT as applied in the EU is a consumption tax. It is charged at each stage of the production and distribution chain (output VAT), but by allowing taxable traders a credit for tax paid on their purchases (input VAT), the tax is in effect imposed on the final consumption of taxable goods and services. Under the destination principle, its aim is to tax domestic consumption only. In international transactions, therefore, border tax adjustments are required. In relation to third countries, imports will be subjected to domestic VAT when released into free circulation and exports should leave the country VAT free, which is realized by not charging output VAT on the export sale while the trader retains its right of input VAT credit. For intracommunity transactions[129] a similar system is in place. The supply is not taxed (zero rated) and the recipient makes a taxable intracommunity acquisition in the country of arrival for which he has to account on a periodical VAT return. In principle, the recipient can claim the same tax as an input credit.

The VAT is a significant part of total revenue for the EU Member States, accumulating to 13% to 22% of total annual revenue.[130] With standard rates varying between 15% and 25%, the VAT also embodies a significant cash flow that has a fatal attraction to some operating in the shades of regular trade. The size of the refund claims made in a jurisdiction can be substantial. In a recent study it

129. The EU is based on a customs union and is a single customs territory. Imports and exports, therefore, refer to cross-border transactions with countries outside the EU. Cross-border transactions within the EU are technically not imports and exports and are called intracommunity transactions.

130. Source: OECD, Revenue Statistics of OECD Member Countries.

was found that refunds measured as a percentage of gross VAT collections averaged almost 30% in the countries surveyed, with the average for the EU being 38.1% (see Table 46).[131]

Table 46. Value of VAT Refunds (Average Refund Level Over a 4-Year Period, 1998 to 2001, in Percent of Gross VAT Collections)

Advanced Economies		Transitional Economies		Emerging Economies		Others	
Canada	50.3	Bulgaria	21.5	Chile	28.8	Algeria	24.3
France	21.2	Hungary	48.2	Colombia	4.1	Bolivia	10.4
Ireland	24.9	Latvia	49.1	Indonesia	12.4	Cambodia	2.8
Netherlands	50.0	Romania	24.7	Mexico	32.1	Cameroon	8.8
New Zealand	35.5	Russia	44.6	Morocco	5.1	El Salvador	9.6
Sweden	48.6	Slovak Rep.	53.9	Peru	19.8	Kenya	7.2
UK	40.9	Ukraine	24.1	South Africa	39.5	Mozambique	2.7

Source: IMF, WP 05/218, November 2005

The first cases of what are generally referred to as carousel fraud occurred in the 1980s regarding transactions between the Netherlands and Belgium, but they have, unfortunately, proven to be contagious. The cost of carousel fraud has been estimated at about EUR 2.1 billion in Germany for the year 2005 and between GBP 1.12 billion and GBP 1.9 billion in the UK.[132] The trade tends to be in high-value, low-volume consumer goods, such as mobile phones, computer components or other electronics. The fraud is usually carried out quickly, with the fraudsters disappearing before the tax authorities follow up with regular assurance activities.

In its most basic form, the carousel fraud scheme is construed as shown in Figure 17.

All parties participating in this scheme are registered as taxable persons, A in the United Kingdom, and B and C in Belgium. A imported a certain quantity, let us assume 10,000, I-pods from the United States. The VAT paid on importation is subsequently deductible as a tax credit on A's monthly VAT return. A sells the I-pods to company B in Belgium and charges 0% VAT because it is an intracommunity supply. B needs to account for the intracommunity acquisition, but the VAT due in that respect is immediately and on the same return deductible as a tax credit. In turn, B sells the I-pods to company C for let us assume EUR 100 each.

131. Graham Harrison & Russell Krelove, *VAT Refunds: A Review of Country Experience*, IMF Working Paper, WP/05/218 (Washington, DC, November 2005).

132. "HM Revenue and Customs: Measuring Indirect Tax Losses," *The Economist* (2005); and "A Tax Net Full of Holes," *The Economist* (13 May 2006).

Figure 17. Carousel Fraud

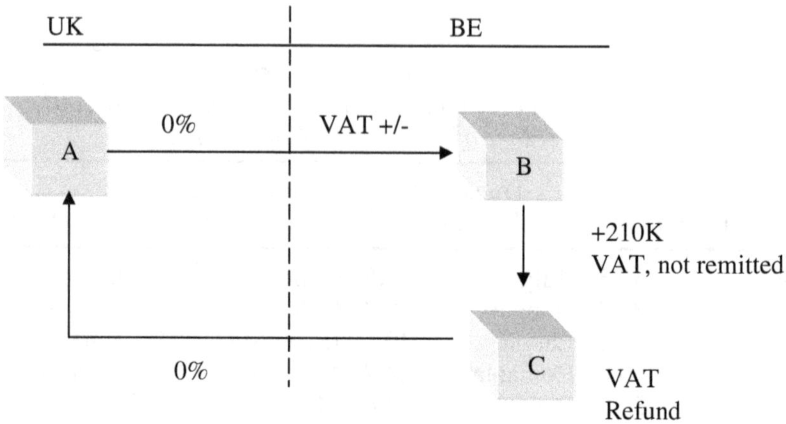

This constitutes a domestic supply in relation to which the seller has to charge Belgium VAT at 21%, that is, EUR 210,000. Company B does not remit this VAT to the tax authorities, but C who in turn sells the I-pods back to the UK with zero VAT, files a claim for refund of the EUR 210,000 invoiced to him by B. Thus, a circular chain of transactions (carousel) has been created whereby the goods start and end up with the same trader. The carousel is repeated several times, each time leading to a tax claim of EUR 210,000, after which the I-pods are sold in bulk for cost price on the local UK market. The VAT collected on this domestic sale will, naturally, not be remitted to the tax office. Several variations of this basic scheme have been applied in practice. Clearly, no real transactions take place between the three related companies; the I-pods stay in the United Kingdom and only a paper trail, suggesting transactions between them, is created. The only real transaction is the final bulk sale to an unrelated party. No money is transferred between the three parties, and after a while the "businesses" will be closed and the companies dissolved. New companies are set up and the fraud scheme will be repeated. In case the authorities catch the scent of such a carousel before the companies are terminated, they will find the bank accounts empty and the directors to be mere fronts. Over time, the tax authorities have become more aggressive in investigating this type of fraud, and the carousel schemes have become more and more sophisticated. Smoke screens have been created to make it more difficult for the authorities to discover the fraud. For instance, by mixing low-volume legitimate transactions with high-volume artificial ones, by expanding the chain with bona fide unrelated traders and by increasing the chain's geographical complexity, that is, adding more cross-border transactions, spread over more jurisdictions, including jurisdictions located outside the EU, such as Switzerland and Dubai.

For the purpose of this subject, we are also interested in the position of third parties who get involved in a carousel, and who may either be aware of this or may be acting in good faith. As we will see, this distinction may be relevant. Assume that company C in our example is a third party, a subsidiary of an American parent company. Again, company A sells the I-pods to B, who in turn sells to C, who consequently sells to A. C may not be aware that B purchased the I-pods from the same party as he (C) is selling to. In this case the goods are actually transported from the UK to Belgium and back to the UK. Payments take place for the B–C and the C–A transactions. Again, B does not remit the VAT it has charged to C, and the latter files a refund claim for the same VAT. There is a difference though. In the first scenario, all parties involved being related, no payments were made between them, and C collects an input VAT refund for VAT it did not actually pay to B. In the second scenario, C being an unrelated party did pay the input VAT to B.

C's position is precarious in this respect. Where the tax authorities are unable to collect the VAT from B, they may seek to mitigate the risk for the revenue by denying C's refund, which would be particularly painful in the case where C is acting in good faith.

9.7.3. COUNTERMEASURES TO FRAUD

9.7.3.1. Civil Law Defense

Until recently, the Belgian tax authorities applied civil law rules in the fight against tax abuse and avoidance. According to the Belgian Civil Law Code, contracts without a legal basis or with a false or unlawful legal basis are considered to be null and void.[133] Transactions prohibited by law, violating good faith or public order have an unlawful basis.[134] Defrauding the Belgian State of tax is conceived of as a violation of public order. The tax authorities, supported by Belgian's Supreme Court,[135] took the position that all sale contracts embodying the totality of the carousel transactions were null and void[136] and, therefore, no transfer of ownership had taken place between either of the parties. As a result, neither party could legitimately claim an input VAT credit.

The legal reasoning by the Belgian authorities is questionable. Its emphasis on domestic Belgian law seems to ignore the primacy of EC law.[137] Concepts of

133. Article 1131 Belgian Civil Code.
134. Article 1133 Belgian Civil Code.
135. Cour de Cassation, 12 October 2000, No. C.99.0136.F, Pasicrisie 2000, I, No. 543.
136. Where the public interest is concerned, it is sufficient that one of the parties involved in the complexity of transactions has unlawful intentions, and good faith of one of the other parties involved does not lead to exoneration of that party.
137. ECJ, 15 July 1964, Case 6/64 (Costa/Enel), [1964] ECR.1255. See, on the relationship between national law and community law, Robert F.W. van Brederode, "Justice and Judgement, Methods of Judicial Interpretation in Value Added Taxation," *International VAT Monitor* 10 (1990): 13–20.

national civil law are, in fact, irrelevant because European legislation constitutes a separate system of law, which has its own concepts and context.[138] Interpretation of community concepts on the basis of national law is, therefore, prohibited. In defining taxable transactions, the Sixth VAT Directive does not rely on contract law concepts, but instead employs an economic approach. A taxable supply of a good is the right to dispose of a good as owner,[139] which is much broader than the mere transfer of legal title.

Effective November 2005, Belgium has introduced a general anti-VAT avoidance provision.[140] Under that provision, the tax authorities for VAT purposes can recharacterize a contract or series of contracts if they suspect or have established that the purpose of those contracts is avoiding VAT, unless the party or parties involved prove or sufficiently demonstrate that these contracts serve legitimate economic or financial purposes. Again, there is no basis for the recharacterization in European law, which avoids civil law concepts.

9.7.3.2. Noneconomic Defense

During 2006, the ECJ decided several cases involving carousel fraud brought by the UK High Court. In the *Optigen* case,[141] the revenue service had taken the position that under a carousel scenario the chain of transactions should be considered in its entirety and the fraudulent intentions of one of the traders would derive all transactions from being qualified as economic transactions in terms of Article 5 of the Sixth Directive and, as a result, would remain outside the scope of VAT. As a consequence, under such reasoning, company C in our example would lose its right to deduct or reclaim the VAT it paid to company B.

The UK High Court asked for clarification regarding whether a transaction, which in itself was not fraudulent and where the trader was acting in good faith, should be regarded as supply and an economic activity within the meaning of the Sixth Directive, when the transaction formed part of a chain in which another prior or subsequent transaction was vitiated by such fraud and whether the trader under such circumstances is entitled to input VAT recovery.

The ECJ rejected the approach taken by the UK revenue service to consider the chain of transactions in its entirety. Each transaction must be considered objectively and on its individual merits and characteristics, which cannot be altered by earlier or subsequent events in the chain. In line with earlier rulings,[142] the ECJ

138. ECJ, 4 October 1995, Case C-291/92 (Ambrecht), ECR 1995, I-2775; ECJ, 16 January 2003, Case C-315/00 (Maierhofer), [2003] ECR, I-563; ECJ 6 February 2003, Case C-185/01 (Auto lease Holland), [2003] ECR, I-1317; ECJ 18 November 2004, Case C-284/03 (Temco), [2004] ECR, I-11237.
139. Article 5(1), Sixth Directive.
140. Article 59(3) Belgian VAT Code.
141. ECJ, 12 January 2006, joint cases C-354/03 (Optigen), C-355/03 (Fulcrum), and C-484/03 (Bond House), O.J. 25 March 2006, No. C74/1.
142. ECJ 8 February 1990, Case C-320-88 (Safe), [1990] ECR 285; ECJ 4 December 1990, Case C-186/89 (van Tiem), [1990] ECR 4363.

noted that the terms *economic activity* and *supplies of goods and services* are wide in scope and objective in character, in this sense that activities are considered per se and without regard to their purpose or results. The ECJ also rejected the view that carousel transactions should remain outside the scope of VAT because of their unlawful character. A general distinction between lawful and unlawful transactions would infringe the principle of fiscal neutrality of the tax. In line with earlier rulings,[143] the Court pointed out that such could only be the case in limited cases, where no competition between a lawful economic sector and unlawful sector can exist. Finally, the ECJ observed that the right to recuperate input VAT may, in principle, not be limited. Each transaction should be considered individually, and a party that acted in good faith should not be deprived of its right to recover VAT as a result of fraudulent activities by others.

Nevertheless, there seems some room left for the revenue services of the Member States to maneuver, where the ECJ conditions its ruling on the absence of mala fides on the part of the trader (in our example, company C). The Court states that:

> transactions as those at issue . . . constitute supplies of goods and services and an economic activity . . . , regardless of the intention of a trader other than the taxable person concerned . . . and/or (regardless) the possible fraudulent nature of another transaction . . . of which the taxable person has no knowledge and no means of knowledge. The right to deduct input value added tax . . . cannot be affected by the fact that in the chain of supply . . . another . . . transaction is vitiated by . . . fraud, without that taxable person knowing or having any means of knowing.

In many cases the UK revenue service has permanently disallowed input VAT recovery when a transaction appeared to be involved in a carousel, the total amount withheld being estimated to approach GBP 1 billion.[144] Following the *Optigen* decision, in the majority of instances the withheld amount has been reimbursed, but the revenue service has refused to do so in a handful of cases where it believes it can reasonably make the argument that the trader in question had knowledge or means of knowledge of the fraudulent carousel trade.

---

143. ECJ 28 February 1984, Case C-294/82 (Einberger II), [1984] ECR 1177 regarding import VAT on illegal drugs; ECJ 6 December 1990, Case C-343/89 (Witzemann), [1990] ECR I-4477 regarding import VAT on counterfeit currency; ECJ 5 July 1988, Case C-269/86 (Mol), [1988] ECR 3627 and ECJ 5 July 1988, Case C-289/86 (Happy Family), [1988] ECR 3655 regarding VAT on domestic supplies of illegal drugs. See also, Paul Farmer & Richard Lyal, *EC Tax Law* (Oxford: Clarendon Press, 1994), 130–132. This does not mean, however, that illegal activity will remain out of the scope of VAT under all circumstances. Where legal and illegal transaction circuits of the same or similar products compete within the territory of a single Member State (for instance sales of fire arms) or activities are legal in one state but illegal in another (as with some forms of pornography), it seems appropriate to levy VAT on both.

144. See Colin Woodward, "The New UK Approach to Carousel Fraud," *International VAT Monitor* 17 (4) (2006): 240–241.

The Belgian Court de Cassation has referred preliminary questions in four cases in 2004[145] and 2005[146] regarding carousel fraud. The 2005 cases have been suspended by the ECJ until delivery of the earlier cases, which the Court decided to combine.

The *Recolta* and *Axel Kittel* cases of 2004 are mirror images, in the sense that the appellant in the first case alleged to have had no knowledge of the carousel, whereas in the second case awareness of the ongoing carousel remained undisputed. Although the Court has not as yet ruled in these cases, the advocate general has delivered his opinion and it is worthwhile to take a closer look at his approach. In summary, the advocate general concludes as follows.

(1) National law and qualifications of a contract are irrelevant.
(2) A recipient of goods will not loose his right of input VAT recovery if he entered into a contract in good faith.
(3) A recipient of goods will not loose his right of input VAT recovery even if he knew about the supplier's fraud, provided he did not himself participate in or benefit from the fraud.
(4) A recipient of goods will loose his right to recover input VAT when he is knowingly involved in a transaction set up for the sole purpose of tax fraud.

In light of earlier jurisprudence by the ECJ, notably the *Optigen* case, the opinion of the advocate general is no surprise as to conclusions 1 and 2. Conclusion 3, however, exceeds the ECJ ruling in *Optigen* in that it offers protection to the recipient even if he has knowledge of the fraud scheme as long as he does not participate in or benefit from it.

The criteria developed here are not totally clear, but it seems to me that the advocate general is trying to find a balance in risk allocation. The right of input VAT recovery is essential for the proper functioning of the VAT because this guarantees that the tax is a consumption tax and not a business tax. For this reason, the input VAT recovery can only be denied under special circumstances. Businesses acting in good faith clearly need protection where they unknowingly get involved in a fraud scheme. The advocate general, however, does not elaborate as to why businesses need protection when they know that they are included in a fraud scheme. The distinction between knowledge and participation seems very thin in my opinion. If a business knows it is participating in a fraud scheme, does that not automatically imply it is involved? Carousel fraud is not simply a tax law issue; it is also, and perhaps primarily, a criminal law issue.

---

145. ECJ 15 June 2006, joint Cases C-439/04 (Axel Kittel) and C-440/04 (Recolta), O.J. 2 September 2006, No. C212/4.
146. Case C-42/05 (Ring Occasions) and Case C-378/05 (Samotor), both cases removed from register by order of the president of the Court of 14 September 2006, O.J. 2 December 2006, No. C294/35.

In other words, culpability should play a role in determining the consequences of being involved in carousel fraud. From this perspective, there exists good reason to protect a business that is part of a carousel transaction scheme without knowing or having means of knowing of the existence of this scheme. But knowledge establishes a degree of guilt. The word *involvement*, in this context, includes the sense of knowledge. Participation may be passive; involvement, by its mere definition, assumes active collaboration. In my opinion, on the one hand, there exists no rationale for protecting a party involved in fraud, regardless of whether this party benefited from it. And, on the other hand, a party acting in good faith, that is, without knowledge, should be protected even if it derived a benefit from the scheme. The advocate general seems to be trying to make a fine distinction in relevant degrees of culpability. No knowledge of fraud intention and mere participation exonerates a trader under all circumstances; knowledge without participation will exonerate as well, even if the trader benefited from it; but knowledge and involvement removes protection when the scheme is set up for the sole purpose of tax fraud. The advocate general, however, seems to offer more latitude than the ECJ did in the *Optigen* case and it will be interesting to see whether the Court will agree with the advocate general's opinion and approach.

In any event, issues of definition remain. What exactly constitutes knowledge in this context? And under what circumstances is a scheme set up solely for the purpose of tax fraud?

9.7.3.3. Abuse of Law Doctrine

In February 2006, the ECJ rendered judgment in three cases, commonly referred to as *Halifax*,[147] in which it recognized the principle of abuse of law in the context of VAT.

Abuse of law exists where specific transactions, notwithstanding formal conformation to provisions of VAT legislation, result in a tax advantage that is contrary to the purpose of those provisions, and where the essential aim of the transactions concerned is to obtain that tax advantage.

In essence, this is a substance over form rule that a number of Member States already apply in the fight against tax avoidance and, especially, tax evasion. The prohibition of abuse rule is limited, however, by community law per se, the effectiveness of which may not be undermined by national legislation. The national antiabuse regulations as well as national rules of evidence may not, in effect, prohibit or make it excessively difficult to exercise rights (such as the right of input VAT reclaim) conferred by community law. Moreover, the antiabuse rule cannot be applied when other explanations than tax advantage can be provided for the alleged set up of transactions.

---

147. ECJ 21 February 2006, Case C-255/02 (Halifax), [2006] ECR I-1609; Case C-419/02 (Bupa), [2006] ECR I-1685; and Case C-223/03 (Huddersfield), [2006] ECR I-1751.

In its application, the abuse of law doctrine covers not only tax evasion (fraud) but also tax avoidance. Belgium has changed[148] its antiabuse rules to conform to *Halifax.* Interestingly, in the explanatory memorandum examples are given of unacceptable transactions, for example, sales and lease back transactions, which have been found legitimate by the Netherlands Supreme Court under very similar antiabuse regulations. For tax lawyers and consultants engaged in designing VAT planning for tax exempt entities, the challenge will be to ensure the design has sufficient substance to withstand the scrutiny of the revenue service and the courts.

When in a framework of transactions the two conditions of *Halifax* (as to result and as to aim) are fulfilled and, therewith, it has been established that an unjustified tax advantage has occurred, the transactions must be redefined in order to create the situation that would have prevailed in the absence of the abusive practice, including reimbursement to the State of VAT improperly obtained in the furtherance of such an abusive practice.

In addition, it is possible, if not likely, that penalties will be imposed in abuse of law situations, ranging from 5% or 10% of the tax amount to, in case of fraud, 100% (in the Netherlands), 200% (in Belgium) and 300% (in France). Fiscal penalties constitute criminal prosecution in the meaning of the European Human Rights Convention[149] and must, therefore, meet the criteria of fair trial laid down in that same convention.[150] It is beyond the scope of this book to elaborate on this aspect, but clearly an entity unknowingly entangled in carousel transactions can counter the fiscal penalty on the basis of absence of culpability.

Although the abuse of law rule could be a strong weapon in combating tax evasion and avoidance, as a principle of community law it could easily collide with other community law principles, especially the principle of legal certainty. Certainly, the Member States have good reason to seek protection against loss of revenue in cases of tax avoidance and evasion. However, a trader who gets entangled in carousel transactions must be allowed input VAT recovery on the basis of the principle of legal certainty when he is acting in good faith. It is for the courts to sail between the Scylla of abuse of law principle and the Charybdis of protecting good faith traders. Finding the precarious balance between the legitimate interests of the treasuries in protection against loss of revenue through applying the abuse of law rule (*Halifax*) and of legal certainty for third-party traders acting in good faith (*Optigen*) will turn out to be quite an acrobatic tour de force, and it is my prediction that we will witness a number of legal saltos mortales.

---

148. Article 1(10) Belgium VAT Code, introduced by law of 20 July 2006, Staats Gazette 28 July 2006, in effect as of 7 August 2006.
149. Netherlands Supreme Court (Hoge Raad), 19 June 1985, BNB 1986/29. See: R.F.W. van Brederode, "De rechten van de mens in het belastingrecht" (Human Rights in Tax Law), *Weekblad voor Fiscaal Recht* 5779 (1987): 749–759.
150. Such as, the right of a public hearing by an independent tribunal within a reasonable time, dual jeopardy and the presumption of innocence.

9.7.3.4. Joint and Several Liability

Another way to protect the treasury's interests is to hold a third party liable for the tax lost. This is certainly a simple way, but whether this approach is ethically acceptable depends, in my view, on how broad it is applied. The ECJ in the *FTI*[151] case held that Member States are able to introduce joint and several liability in their respective legislations, provided the principles of legal certainty and proportionality are not breached. In essence, this condition is in line with earlier rulings by the Court discussed previously, especially *Optigen*. In the case of carousel fraud, this means that any party involved in the framework of transactions can be held liable for the VAT lost, unless he has been acting in good faith. That means that trader C in our example could be held liable for VAT that company B has failed to remit to the tax authorities, even if C had been invoiced properly and paid that same VAT himself to B, unless C has been acting in good faith. A liable person is defined by the ECJ as a person to whom a supply of goods or services has been made and who knew, or had reasonable grounds to suspect, that some or all of the VAT payable in respect to that supply or of any previous or subsequent supplies would not be remitted to the tax authorities. In short, a party involved in carousel fraud could be held liable for any unpaid VAT in the chain of transactions. Indeed, good faith becomes a valuable asset in VAT. Crucial in this respect is the part of the sentence that reads "reasonable grounds to suspect." It remains unclear when that is the case. Obviously, there is reason for suspicion for a third party when the purchase price offered to him is significantly below market value, or when the supplier normally does not trade in that specific type of goods, or the quantities offered are much higher than justified by the supplier's size. When a third party has reason to believe that his supplier is related (legally, economically or otherwise) to the subsequent purchaser, there is a strong reason for suspicion as well. Certainly there will be cases where grounds for suspicion are obvious. However, the sophistication of carousel schemes is found in the deliberate engagement of third-party traders by the fraudsters, who will, naturally, make efforts to hide their criminal intentions from the third-party trader. The liability, in principle, can be a multitude because it is not limited to VAT unremitted by a direct supplier. When a third-party trader is so unfortunate as to become engaged in carousel transactions, and VAT in regard to each of the individual transaction has remained unpaid, the third-party trader may, as the only genuine business, end up being held liable for all VAT payable on the total of transactions, previous and subsequential. Without doubt, in my mind at least, an element of overkill has found its way into the liability rules.

The concept of good faith seems to offer a degree of protection, but the rules of evidence in tax law are not as strict as in criminal law. Generally speaking, as the rules of evidence are determined on the national and not on the EU level, the tax authorities have the initial burden of proof. If the authorities are able to offer at least initial proof that a third party should have been aware of the fraud scheme, the

151. ECJ 11 May 2006, Case C-384/04 (Federation of Technological Industries and others), O.J. 15 July 2006, No. C165/7.

burden of proof can easily be reversed, and the third party will have to prove that he neither knew nor had reasonable grounds to suspect that he was somehow engaged in a fraudulent carousel.

Interestingly, subsequent to *FTI*, the British tax authorities have developed a strategy of notifying third-party traders when they suspect they are engaged in suspicious trade cycles. Ignoring such notification bears the risk that the recovery of input VAT on future transactions with suppliers from the chain will be denied. Moreover, by issuing the notification the authorities believe to have established "knowledge" or "reasonable ground for suspicion" in the meaning of *FTI*, and, as a result, the third-party trader is exposing himself to severe liability risks.[152] Even though the urge for the revenue to prevent or reduce tax loss is understandable and justified, this practice is, however, questionable. It is unclear why, from a legal perspective, the notification by the tax authorities has to be accepted on face value and would shift the risk completely to a third-party trader when he does not immediately discontinue trading with parties identified by the tax authorities as suspect. Such notification could prove to be extraordinarily disruptive of business when parties, who cannot bear the financial risk of third-party liability,[153] terminate business relationships on their basis. However, the tax authorities render the risk of being sued for damages in case their notification bears insufficient grounds and leads to loss of business revenue, termination of a legitimate business activity, bankruptcy, or loss of good standing and reputation.

Ultimately, it will be up to the national courts and the ECJ to develop, on a case-by-case basis, a doctrine to clarify the extent of third-party liability, balancing the interest of revenue loss with the interest of free conduct of business.

9.7.3.5. Alternative Solutions

The approaches taken by national tax authorities seem to be rather rigid and to contain an element of overkill. In my opinion, feasible alternative solutions exist, although none of them may win the fiscal beauty contest. First, either on the EU or on the national level, a *butoir* rule could be introduced. A *butoir* is a term coming from French legislation, and basically it limits the total input VAT credit to the total output VAT. In essence, a business cannot deduct more input VAT than it is required to pay in tax over its sales. For example, when sales in a tax period are 100 at a tax rate of 20%, and purchases are 300, a seller will only be able to deduct input VAT to the amount of VAT due on sales in the same tax period. Normally, a business would have a tax payable of 20 (20% of 100) and deduct 60 in input tax credit (20% of 300), receiving a refund of 40. Under the *butoir* rule, the tax credit would be limited to the amount payable on sales. In other words, the seller would only be able to exercise his right to input VAT credit to the extent of VAT due on sales. As a result the tax credit would be maximized at 20, and no refund

---

152. See n. 143.
153. Please bear in mind that Mr. Axel Kittel, in the case that bears his name, is the receiver in bankruptcy.

would be paid. The remainder of the tax credit would be shifted forward to the next tax period. In effect, the seller would never receive an actual refund in monetary terms. So, in tax period 1, the seller would have output VAT of 20 and input VAT credit of 60. The maximum deduction would equal the tax due on sales (20) and the remainder of the input VAT claim (40) would be applied to the output tax due on sales in the next tax period. If the seller would make sales at 400 in the next tax period and incur purchases at 200; in period 2, the seller would have a tax payable account of 80 and a credit account of 40 + 40 input tax from period 1. As a result the seller would pay zero in tax in period 2 and would not receive a refund.

This system works perfectly, except for net exporting firms. In Italy, net exporting firms are subject to a deterred refund rule to the extent of 12 months. Basically, this provides the tax authorities with a 12-month window to determine whether the input VAT claim is legitimate. In view of the serious tax fraud schemes, the application of these rules would not seem unreasonable. In addition, two more rules could be introduced to provide for an equal balance of risk distribution. First, there would be a system of recognition for approved economic traders, who would be eligible to a full and immediate input VAT credit deduction based on their proven bona fide tax payer reliability. This rule would protect established traders with sound track records and exonerate them from the tax credit limitation rules. New companies applying for this status would be held to strict benchmark standards. If a start-up company is unable to meet these standards, input VAT credit would be limited according to the *butoir* rule or postponed according to the 12-month rule, but the state would be required to pay a reasonable interest at the time a final refund is made to compensate the company for their cash flow disadvantage.

As a second alternative, the European Commission is contemplating a different approach.[154] Although the operation and management of tax systems is primarily the responsibility of Member States, the commission plays a role in the free circulation of goods and services within the internal market, and the globalization of the economy makes it practically impossible for a Member State to act individually against this particular type of tax fraud. The strategy is threefold. First, it envisions enhancing cooperation between Member States in combating fraud. The other two alternatives imply substantial changes in the current VAT system. The commission contemplates either taxing intracommunity supplies, which would eliminate the net exporting position for a firm and would render the carousel fraud scheme obsolete, or extent the reverse charge rule. The first option is feasible[155] but ignores the fact that fraud schemes involving sales to third countries (non-EU Member States) such as Switzerland would replace the current ones. Extending the reverse charge rule makes more sense. Basically, under

154. Opening speech of Commissioner Kovács at the conference "Tackling VAT Fraud: Possible Ways Forward" (Brussels, 29 March 2007).

155. This would, however, require either full harmonization of VAT rates among Member States, or the introduction of a separate rate on intracommunity supplies, perhaps based on a design similar to the C-VAT concept, see s. 11.4.3.

the reverse rule, a purchaser is liable for the output VAT on its purchases instead of the supplier. Because the purchaser is also eligible for an input VAT credit, no actual obligation to remit tax to the treasury would ever occur. In effect, this would change the EU-VAT system from a multistage consumption tax into a single stage retail consumption tax, albeit while maintaining a paper trail to previous sales. This would be a remarkable policy change when one bears in mind that the VAT was chosen as the preferred consumption tax system in the EU, inter alia, for its ability for fractioned tax collection, that is, collecting of tax on the value added of each stage instead of over the total value added at the final retail stage to reduce, indeed, the risk of underreporting and tax fraud.

9.7.4. Conclusions

Revenue loss is a genuine concern for the tax authorities whether as a result of tax avoidance or tax evasion. In monetary terms the stakes are significant. National law approaches, as taken by the Belgian authorities, are ineffective because they are simply irrelevant. The British defense of declaring certain transactions noneconomical, although European in essence, fails because it is too broad and insufficiently specific. The community concept of abuse of law as well as the introduction of third-party liability in the case of tax fraud provide ample tools to the authorities for combating avoidance and evasion of VAT. The financial risks for third parties are considerate and third-party liability, in my opinion, contains an unacceptable element of overkill. The ECJ has provided some balance by exonerating from responsibility and liability third parties acting in good faith. The concept of good faith, however, is still too vague and needs to be further defined in future case law to offer business transactions protection against zealous assumptions by the tax authorities. There exist alternative approaches, however, that seem to offer a more balanced risk distribution. The approach recently suggested by the European Commission seems to entail a significant departure from the very reason the current VAT system was introduced.

Chapter 10

Harmonization of Indirect Tax in Federal or Common Markets

10.1. INTRODUCTION

Harmonization of taxes is, generally, triggered by economic necessity. States treasure their independence, including tax autonomy, and resist federal or supernational authority. The advantages of harmonization, however, may be too attractive, or the disadvantages of refraining from harmonization too severe. In either or both cases, there exist strong incentives, whether formulated in positive or negative terms, for states to arrive at a certain level of tax coordination.

In this chapter the focus is on the harmonization process in the EU and the United States, but the intention is not to make in-depth policy process comparisons. The objective is merely to provide an overview of the motives to seek harmonization, to describe the process and the content of harmonization. Nevertheless, there exist some striking similarities and clear differences. In the United States, the harmonization of sales and use taxes is the initiative of the states and entirely based on voluntary participation. In the EU, the initiative rests with the European Commission, that is, at the central level, although unanimous agreement of all Member States is required for a legislative measure to become binding law. Both in the United States and the EU, states are protective and reluctant to accept infringements of their autonomy. As a result, the harmonization process, generally, is slow and dependent on political compromise. This is particularly true for VAT harmonization in the EU, which can be described as a step-by-step process. In many instances, the reluctance of Member States to accept further harmonization is not based on principle but caused by domestic political circumstances.

It is interesting to compare the EU with the United States regarding harmonization. In the EU, the main purpose of tax harmonization is to enable and support the creation of a single or common market. In the United States, such a common market already exists and streamlining the state sales and use taxes is intended to simplify compliance for businesses, thus reducing their costs and triggering higher voluntary compliance rates, but it primarily serves to persuade Congress to introduce legislation that would allow the states to mandate businesses to collect use tax from out-of-state customers and thus prevent double nontaxation.

10.2. THE HARMONIZATION OF INDIRECT TAXES IN THE EU

Tax harmonization in Europe has to be understood within the context of European integration, a process initiated after the Second World War.[1] The establishment of the European Coal and Steel Community (ECSC)[2] in July 1952 was the first step towards a supranational Europe. For the first time the six Member States of this organization relinquished part of their sovereignty, albeit in a limited domain, in favor of the community. This first drive towards integration soon came to a halt with the failure of the European Defense Community (EDC) in 1954. Although there was reason to fear that the effort undertaken by the ECSC was doomed to fail, the Messina Conference of June 1955 endeavored to add a new impetus to European construction. It was followed by a series of meetings of ministers or experts. A preparatory committee responsible for drafting a report on the creation of a European common market was created at the beginning of 1956. It met in Brussels under the presidency of Henri Spaak, the Belgian minister for foreign affairs at the time.[3] In April 1956, this committee submitted two drafts, which corresponded to the two options selected by the Member States:

- the creation of a general common market; and
- the creation of an atomic energy community.

The so-called "Treaties of Rome" were signed in March 1957. The first treaty established the EEC[4] and the second the European Atomic Energy Community (Euratom).[5] These two treaties entered into force on 1 January 1958. The treaty has been amended by a number of treaties, including treaties of new Member States accession. The most important amendments are as follows:

- The Treaty of Brussels, known as the "Merger Treaty," which replaced the three councils of ministers (EEC, ECSC and Euratom) on the one hand and

1. For the period after the First World War, see H. Brugman, *L'idee Europeenne 1918–1965* (Bruges, 1965); for a comprehensive description of the political situation after the Second World War, see R.R. Palmer, Joel Colton & Lloyd Kramer, *A History of the Modern World*, 10th ed. (New York: McGraw-Hill, 2007), Ch. XXII.
2. Treaty of 18 April 1951, establishing the ECSC, Tractatenblad 1951, 82 (Dutch language version), entered into force as of 23 July 1952.
3. P.H. Spaak, *Rapport des Chefs de délégation des Ministres Etrangers* (Brussels, 21 April 1956).
4. Treaty of 25 March 1957, establishing the EEC, 294–297 U.N.T.S. 17, entered into force as of 1 January 1958.
5. Treaty of 25 March 1957, establishing the Euratom.

the two commissions (EEC, Euratom) and the High Authority (ECSC) on the other hand with a single council and a single commission. This administrative merger was supplemented by the institution of a single operative budget.[6]

- The Treaty amending Certain Budgetary Provisions, which replaced the system whereby the communities were funded by contributions from Member States with that of own resources. It also put in place a single budget for the communities.[7]
- The Single European Act, which entailed the first major reform of the treaties. It extended the areas of qualified majority voting in the council, increased the role of the European Parliament (cooperation procedure) and widened community powers. It set the objective of achieving the internal market by 1993.[8]
- The Treaty on European Union, known as the "Maastricht Treaty," which brought the three communities (Euratom, ECSC, EEC) and institutionalized cooperation in the fields of foreign policy, defense, police and justice together under one umbrella, the European Union. The EEC was renamed, becoming the EC. Furthermore, this treaty created an economic and monetary union (EMU), put in place new community policies (education, culture) and increased the powers of the European Parliament (codecision procedure).[9]

10.2.1. The Objectives of the EEC Treaty

The preamble of the treaty provides clear insights into the treaty's rationale and purpose. It seeks to create an ever-closer union among the peoples of Europe and with economic and social progress of their countries by common action to eliminate the barriers that divide Europe. The essential objective is found in the strife for the constant improvements of living and working conditions. To realize this, the removal of existing obstacles is required through concerted action in order to guarantee steady expansion, balanced trade and fair competition. In addition, the differences existing between the various regions and the disadvantage of the less-favored regions need to be reduced to strengthen the unity of their economies and to ensure their harmonious development. The restriction on international trade needs to be progressively abolished by means of a common commercial policy, and the development of the prosperity of overseas countries needs to be supported and ensured. These objectives are placed within the grander goal of preserving and strengthening peace and liberty.

---

6. Treaty of Brussels, 8 April 1965, O.J. of 13 July 1967, No. 152, entered into force as of 1 July 1967.
7. Treaty amending Certain Budgetary Provisions, 22 April 1970, O.J. of 2 January 1971, No. L2, entered into force as of 1 January 1971.
8. Single European Act, 28 February 1986, O.J. of 29 June 1987, No. L169, entered into force as of 1 July 1987.
9. Treaty on European Union, 7 February 1992, O.J. of 29 July 1992, No. C191, entered into force as of 1 November 1993.

The EEC treaty[10] provided for the establishment of a common market, a customs union and common policies. Articles 2 and 3 of the treaty directly address these three issues. They state that the community's primary mission is to create a common market and specify the measures that it must undertake to achieve this objective.

10.2.2. Relationship Between the Objectives and the Tax Provisions of the Treaty

Article 2 of the EEC treaty specifies the political and economic objectives of the community as the promotion of a harmonious development of economic activities throughout the community, a continuous and balanced expansion, an increase in stability, an accelerated raising of the standard of living and closer relations between the states.

To realize these tasks, Article 2 of the original treaty offered two tools:[11]

(1) the establishment of a common market; and
(2) the progressive approximation of the economic policies of Member States.

The common market has internal and external components. Externally, its aim is to create equal treatment of foreign trade among the Member States. This would be realized by the introduction of a common customs tariff. Internally, a single economic area, including all Member States, would be created, establishing free competition among businesses regardless of their location or nationality.

The foundations for the internal component are laid down with the formulation of the four freedoms, that is, the free movement of persons, services, goods and capital.[12] The free movement of goods, the most important of the four freedoms, implies the abolishment of existing and prevention of future trade barriers. This is partly realized by founding the common market on a customs union. A customs union[13] implies the establishment of a common outer tariff, replacing the preceding tariffs of the different states and preventing the diversion of trade,[14] and the

---

10. In this section, because it offers a historical perspective, we refer to the articles in the original text of the treaty. Since its implementation, the treaty has been amended several times and the text of articles and the enumeration of the articles have been altered.
11. Currently incorporated in the twenty-one objectives of Art. 3 of the amended text of the treaty.
12. Articles 48–73 EEC (original) and Art. 14(2) EEC (consolidated version), jo. Arts 23 and 24 (free movement of goods) and Arts 39 et seq. (free movement of persons, services and capital) EEC (consolidated).
13. Articles 12–17 EEC (original) and Arts 25–31 EEC (consolidated).
14. If internal customs duties are abolished but Member States were to maintain their individual rates for trade with third countries, in reality products would be imported into the state with the lowest duties and then forwarded to the state of destination, effectively avoiding the higher rates applied by the latter state.

abolishment of internal import and export duties among the Member States. A customs union is crucial for the realization of the optimal allocation of production factors. Producers would gain access to the markets of all Member States under conditions equal to those of local producers, which would lead to increased production at least by the more efficient businesses, to concentration and specialization, and indirectly to the development of interstate trade and interdependence of their economies. The free trade principles on which the EEC is built assumes prosperity growth as a result of comparative advantages.[15] National trade policy could easily undermine the free movement of goods and a fortiori the customs union itself, but for the prevalence of the common trade policy of the EEC. The existence of a common trade policy, managed at the community level and no longer at the state level, dissociates the customs union from a free trade association.

The following two figures may help visualize the concept of a common market. Figure 18 describes the situation before the common market was realized. The six original Member States each had their own customs borders and levied duties on the importation of goods regardless of origin. In Figure 19 the common market is realized, and no duties are payable for cross-border sales between the Member States. Products arriving from third countries are subject to duties at a common tariff to ensure equal treatment of foreign trade.

Figure 18. Six Markets

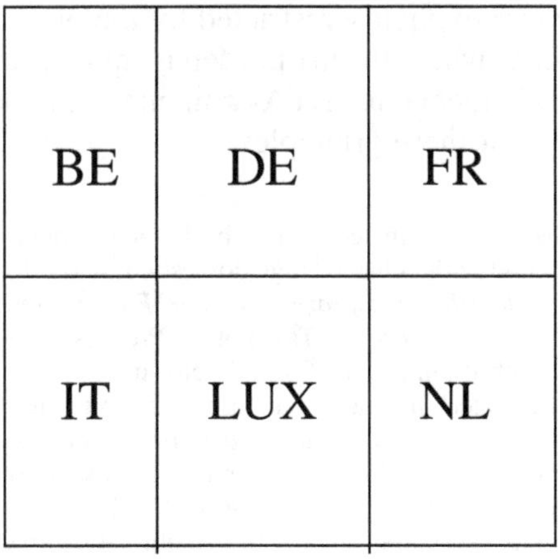

Figure 19. Common Market

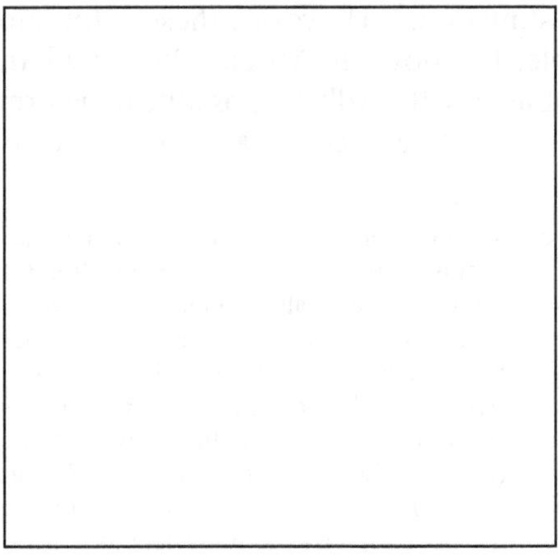

15. That is, reducing cost production from greater specialization; see G.K. Shaw, "European Economic Integration and Stabilization Policy," in *Fiscal Harmonization in Common Markets*, vol. II, ed. Carl S. Shoup (New York and London: Columbia University Press, 1967), 344.

Nevertheless, distortion of intracommunity free trade by individual Member States through discriminatory border tax adjustments (BTAs) would remain possible. It would be relatively easy to sponsor domestic production by combining a prohibitive import tax with a generous export restitution system. In this sense, the tax provisions of the treaty serve to guarantee the proper functioning of the common market, in particular the free movement of goods.

The founding states realized that differences between the states in indirect tax systems could be the route to distortion of competition. Based on past experience,[16] they feared that the abolishment of internal customs tariffs, required to constitute the customs union, would simply trigger replacement by discriminatory BTAs. The solution chosen was twofold. The European Commission was charged to investigate and determine "in what manner" harmonization of indirect taxes could be realized.[17] Until that time a transitional regime was created prohibiting discrimination at the detriment of importation[18] and to the advantage of exportation.[19] Imported goods cannot be taxed at a higher rate than similar domestically produced goods, and export restitutions of indirect tax may not exceed the tax actually levied. Implicitly, these provisions contain a choice for the destination principle. One of the problems at the time was that all of the founding Member States, with the exception of France, applied GRTs. As demonstrated in Section 5.3, exact calculation of the domestic tax burden on a certain product cannot be accommodated under a GRT system because the tax actually incurred will depend on the length of the supply chain and the level of vertical integration. As a result, it is equally impossible to determine the tax rate to be levied on importation or to be rebated on exportation. For that reason, Article 97 of the EEC Treaty allowed Member States with such a tax system to determine BTAs on the basis of estimation.[20] However, these estimations were explicitly restricted by the principles laid down in Articles 95 and 96. In reality, where the tax burden is immeasurable, it will hardly be possible to determine whether actual BTAs remain within the lines of tolerance dictated by the restrictions of these principles.

---

16. The German steel industry maintained it had been discriminated against by France through a turnover tax rate levied on importation that was higher than the average domestic rate on steel products see Walter Hahn, *Steuerpolitische Willensbildungsprozeße in der Europäischen Gemeinschaft: das Beispiel der Umsatzsteuer-Harmonisierung* (Tax Policy Process in the EU: The Example of VAT Harmonization) (Frankfurt am Main, 1988), 35 et seq.
17. Article 99 EEC (original). The phrase "in what manner" indicates that harmonization in itself is an obligation under the treaty; see Alexander J. Easson, *Tax Law and Policy in the EEC* (London: Sweet & Maxwell, 1980), 70; and Deringer Report, 26 and 34. For a contrary view, see Walter Hahn, *supra*, 51. This provision is still in place as Art. 93 EEC (consolidated) but the text has been altered to better reflect the current situation. Harmonization is still an obligation given the wording of the text, "The Council shall . . . adopt provisions for the harmonisation of . . . ," and explicitly links the purpose of harmonization to the establishment and functioning of the internal market.
18. Article 95 EEC (original) and Art. 90 EEC (consolidated). Note that the reference to a transitional period has been removed from the current text.
19. Article 96 EEC (original) and Art. 91 EEC (consolidated).
20. The provision of Art. 97 no longer exists, of course, under the current text of the treaty because all states have since introduced VATs.

10.2.3. The Need for Harmonization and the Choice for VAT

It was clear to all involved that BTAs based on estimations were in violation of the principles of neutrality and fair competition, and would be a threat to the realization of the common market. Harmonization of the general sales tax systems would be required to avoid tariff manipulation at the border in an effort to create competitive advantages for domestic traders.[21] Before making proposals in that area, the European Commission decided to seek the advice of a working group comprised of staff of the treasury departments of the Member States. It was divided into three subgroups each charged with investigating different solutions. Their conclusions, generally referred to as the ABC Report were published in 1962.[22] In addition, the so-called Fiscal and Financial Committee was established, which reported in the same year.[23] Both reports recommended to replace the current GRTs with a credit invoice method VAT (or indirect subtraction VAT) because it would guarantee economic neutrality, avoid incentives for vertical integration and enable exact calculation of BTAs.

10.2.4. Overview of the History of Sales Tax Harmonization in the EU

On the basis of these reports, the commission introduced a draft directive[24] to the European Council, suggesting harmonization in three steps. At the end of the first phase, Member States would be obliged to have abolished their existing GRTs and replaced them with a noncumulative sales tax system, leaving each state free in its choice of such a system. During the second phase, a community VAT system would be introduced, and the third phase should cumulate in the abolishment of fiscal border within the EU. The European Parliament, which at the time only had an advisory function, charged the Committee for the Internal Market with the preparation of its advice.[25] It criticized the three-step process, especially the latitude towards the Member States to temporarily introduce their own individual noncumulative sales tax system. Progress, however, was slow because of lack of support from the Member States. In fact, in those initial years the European Commission carried the whole burden of promoting tax harmonization. The Member States were not so much opposed to the idea of integration, but circumstances

---

21. Indeed, in practice the Member States displayed a continuous tendency to employ BTAs as protectionist measures; see Hahn, *Steuerpolitische Willensbildungsprozeße in der Europäischen Gemeinschaft*, at 88.
22. General Report of the Subgroups A, B and C Appointed for the Study of the Various Possibilities for the Harmonization of Turnover Taxes, EEC, Commission, Directorate General for Competition (January 1962).
23. Neumark Report, *Report of the Fiscal and Financial Committee on Tax Harmonization in the Common Market*, Report 21, Doc. SD-32 (EEC Commission, 1962).
24. Draft Directive of 31 October 1962, doc. 121/1962/-63.
25. Deringer Report.

of domestic politics determined their position. Change in the domestic political dynamics in Germany created interdependence between Bonn and Brussels that brought new life to the harmonization initiative. The German government needed European tax initiatives to break the domestic stalemate regarding the introduction of a VAT in Germany[26] and the commission needed the support of a strong ally at the council level. As a result, a majority of the council supported the principle of a community VAT making room for the commission to propose two (revised) directives in June 1964 and April 1965. It took until 1967 before the last resistance vanished.[27] Within the council a compromise was reached on the content of the Second Directive, allowing for zero rates and exemptions to accommodate the Dutch, albeit for a transitional period.

The First Directive can be characterized as a statement of intent by the states to introduce a community VAT. In addition, it functions as an explanatory memorandum to the Second Directive, where it explains political background, objectives and the economic principles of the VAT system. The Second Directive contained the modalities of the VAT system. It defined core legal terminology such as taxable person, taxable supplies, goods, services and imports;[28] determined the tax base;[29] and constituted obligations in the field of records keeping, invoicing and filing of returns.[30] The directive also constitutes the right to deduct VAT incurred on procurement to provide tax relief for taxable businesses, thus ensuring that the European VAT would, in effect, be a tax on private consumption.[31] Exports were exempt[32] and imports were taxed at the same rate as a similar domestically produced good.[33] This brought structure to the European VAT and similarity in its application by the individual Member States. Within this framework, however, Member States retained the right to determine their own standard rate as well as to subject certain goods and services to higher or lower rates.[34] In addition, Member States were allowed to determine the scope of exemptions,[35] although under the privilege of consultation, and to introduce special measures to combat fraud or for the purpose of simplification.[36] Although a broad base clearly had preference,[37] the Member States were allowed to introduce special measures for the retail sector, best suited for their

26. See Donald J. Puchala, *Fiscal Harmonization in the European Communities: National Politics and International Cooperation* (London and Dover, NH: Francis Pinter Publishers, 1984), at 44.
27. The Netherlands was the only obstacle for 2 years. For background and what changed their position, see Donald J. Puchala, *supra*, 65–85; Hahn, 160–171; R.F.W. van Brederode, *De bijzondere positie van de landbouw in de omzetbelasting* (VAT Treatment of the Agricultural Sector) (Deventer: Kluwer, 1993), 20–23.
28. See Arts 4, 5, 6 and 7 of the Second Directive.
29. Article 8 of the Second Directive.
30. Article 12 of the Second Directive.
31. Article 11 of the Second Directive.
32. Article 10(1) of the Second Directive.
33. Article 9(3) of the Second Directive.
34. Article 9 of the Second Directive.
35. Article 10(3) of the Second Directive.
36. Article 13 of the Second Directive.
37. See Art. 2(4) of the First Directive.

national circumstances.[38] Initially, the commission, supported by the conclusions in the ABC Report, proposed to include the agricultural sector in the VAT as any other business, but it had underestimated the lobbying power of this special interest group and the influence it could exercise.[39] The economic, technical and psychological objections could not be overcome, and finally a compromise was reached whereby the Member States retained the authority to design a special regime for the agricultural sector adjusted for national circumstances[40] until the commission could provide agreeable proposals for a common treatment of agricultural output.[41]

The first directives shared the main objective of realizing economic neutrality. They formed the first step of the evolutionary process towards a common European VAT system. As such, they left substantial discretion to the Member States, which proved creative and effective in optimizing their room of autonomy. Moreover, the starting positions of each Member State, technically and politically, were quite diverse as were the conditions for tax reform. It will come as no surprise, therefore, that within the EC in effect there emerged as many VAT systems as there were Member States. Explicit differences occurred in relation to the retail sector, exemptions, the deduction of input VAT,[42] agriculture and the place – of supply of cross-border services. Those differences did not lead to neutrality issues but to differences in treatment of the agricultural sector and of cross-border services. Several countries indirectly subsidized their farmers by allowing their customers a proxy input VAT credit higher than the average input VAT for the sector.[43] As a consequence of differences between Member States in tax jurisdiction rules, cross-border services were subjected to single taxation, double taxation or double nontaxation, depending on which countries were involved. The most important rationale for further harmonization was the replacement of national contributions to the EU budget with a system of own resources,[44] which would give the ECs financial autonomy.[45] Own resources are politically important beyond the issue of financial independence because they constitute a major factor in shaping the relationship between Member States, citizens and community institutions. Moreover,

38. Article 14 of the Second Directive. This was a political compromise to accommodate Italian objections; see Hahn, at 115; and Easson, at 115.
39. See Walter Hahn, *supra*, at 116.
40. Article 15(2) of the Second Directive.
41. Article 15(1) of the Second Directive.
42. Two problem areas were identified: the pro rata temporis deduction of input VAT for capital goods and the French *butoir* arrangement, which limited the deduction of input VAT in a given tax period to the amount of VAT due on sales (output VAT), effectively avoiding paying refunds; excess input VAT credit needed to be carried forward to the next tax period.
43. For Germany, the average input VAT for flat rate farmers was 3.5%, but the proxy was set at 5%; see Hahn, at 187. The Netherlands subsidized the farmers similarly over many years see van Brederode, *De Bijzondere Positie van de Landbouw in de Omzetbelasting*, 169 et seq.
44. Council Decision 70/243/EEC of 21 April 1970, O.J. 28 April 1970, No. L94/19. The principle of own resources for the communities was laid down in Art. 201 of the EEC Treaty. Direct contributions were agreed on for a transitional but undefined period.
45. The previous national contribution system allowed the Member States some scope of control over the community policies, an ability lost when the Own Resources Decision was ratified.

the choice and form of own resources are an integral part of the wider debate over the future of integration and the continuing struggle for dominance between the federal and intergovernmental visions for Europe. Those resources were customs duties, agricultural levies[46] and a percentage[47] of the uniform VAT base.[48] In 1988, the council introduced a fourth source of income, namely a percentage of gross national income (GNI)[49] of a Member State. The VAT and GNI resources qualify as EU taxes levied on the Member States.[50] The own resources revenues are remitted by the Member States on a monthly basis.[51]

The intention was to introduce the system of own resources per 1975, but delay of the implementation of the First and Second Directives in Belgium and Italy as well as the accession of new Member States to the union left the commission with no choice but to postpone the introduction of a proposal for the Sixth Directive until June 1973. However, the Member States were reluctant to commit because they had been able to maximize their respective autonomy to tailor their domestic VAT systems to domestic circumstances.[52] System changes encountered strong opposition for fear of budgetary or electoral ramifications. In addition, the need for

---

46. A logical choice given the customs union and the existence of a common agricultural policy in the EC. They are collected by the customs authorities of each Member State that will remit the proceeds minus a 25% collection fee to the communities.
47. Initially, the maximum call-in rate of VAT was limited to 1% of the base. The second Own Resources Decision 85/257/EEC of 7 May 1985, O.J. 14 May 1985, No. L128/15 raised the ceiling to 1.4% from 1 January 1986 to cover the costs of the enlargement of the community with Portugal and Spain. The 2000 Own Resources Decision 2000/597/EC of 29 September 2000, O.J. of 7 October 2000, No. L253 reduced the maximum call-in rate to the level of 0.5% of the harmonized and capped VAT base. Council Decision 2007/436/EC of 7 June 2007, O.J. of 23 June 2007, No. L163 reduces the cap to 0.3%. Lower rates apply to Austria, Germany, the Netherlands and Sweden.
48. See Art. 4(1) of Decision 70/243. The assumption was that national consumption would provide a reasonably accurate measurement of a state's ability to pay. Council Decision 88/376/EEC of 24 June 1988, O.J. 15 July 1988, No. L185/24 capped the contributions in relation to a states' gross national product (GNP). From 1988 until 1994 the base could not exceed 55% of a states' GNP. After 1995 the limit was lowered to 50% of GNP for states with a per capita GNP below 90% of the community average. This new limit has gradually been extended to all Member States. GNP has been replaced by GNI; see n. 44.
49. The GNI-based resource is obtained by applying a rate fixed each year under the budget procedure to a base representing the sum of GNIs at market prices. It is calculated by reference to the difference between expenditure and the yield of all other own resources. The GNI resource contributes the bulk of the EU budget. See Council Regulation 1287/2003 of 15 July 2003 on the harmonization of GNI at market prices (GNI Regulation) O.J. of 19 July 2003, No. L181. Council Decision 2007/436/EC of 7 June 2007, O.J. of 23 June 2007, No. L163 caps the own resources at 1.24% of the sum of all Member States' GNIs.
50. See Ben Terra, *Sales Taxation: The Case of Value Added Tax in the European Community* (Deventer and Boston Kluwer, 1988), at 72.
51. Member States credit the own resources collected to an "own resources" account opened by the commission at each national treasury or national bank. Duties, agricultural and sugar levies are credited each month as they are collected. VAT and GNI resources are made available on the first working day of the month at the rate of one-twelfth of the budgeted estimate. See Council Regulation 2028/2004 of 16 November 2004, O.J. of 27 November 2004, No. L352.
52. Hahn, 186 and 197–200.

harmonization seemed less urgent with progress to realize the EMU significantly slowing down. Pressure from the European Parliament and a decision in April 1976 by the Finance and Foreign Affairs ministers to set a deadline of 1 January 1978 for the realization of the own resources were the two key factors accelerating the harmonization process. To allow Member States sufficient time to adapt their legislation to the new directive, it was imperative to reach a compromise on its content during the year 1976. After a series of intense negotiations,[53] the states were able to reach common ground. The final version was accepted in May 1977,[54] but it took until the end of 1979 before all nine Member States had implemented the provisions of the Sixth Directive into their national VAT legislation.

The main success of the Sixth Directive was that it prevented national VAT legislation to further drift apart and, in that sense, it can be characterized as a standstill agreement.[55] In addition, the direction was set for future harmonization. However, between 1977 and 1985 no progress was made because of a lack of political commitment on the part of the states. Tax harmonization, in particular the need to abolish the tax borders between the states, regained priority as a result of rising awareness of the relative underperformance of the EU economy compared to the United States and Japan. To a large extent, Europe's economic potential remained unrealized because of a fractioned economy. The reemergence as a political objective of realizing the internal market became the engine of the harmonization process, culminating in the publication of the commission's Whitepaper on the completion of the internal market.[56] It provided a program to reach the ultimate goal of an internal market without fiscal borders as well as a timeline. The envisaged measurements are divided into three categories, namely the abolishment of physical, technical and fiscal (tax) barriers. The commission acknowledged that simply removing border controls would only lead to fraud and tax avoidance because of existing differences between the Member States in tax rates, tax structure and tax base. The core issue was how to change the existing system of BTAs, that is, taxation of imports and rebates for exports, so physical border controls would become redundant. In essence, the commission proposed to abandon the BTAs entirely, which would mean that cross-border transactions would be taxed at the appropriate rate of the country of departure. In implication, this would translate into a shift from destination to origin principle. Logistically, the recipient of the goods would be eligible to deduct the origin VAT as a credit from the domestic output VAT. Apart from rate differences, this would create a financial advantage for net exporting countries. Clearly, such a shift in tax allocation reduced the chances for the proposal to be accepted by the Member States. Abandoning the destination principle in a common market would only then be without consequences for individual states, if the community would be a single tax jurisdiction

53. *Supra*, 209 et seq.
54. Directive 77/388/EEC, O.J. of 13 June 1977, No. L145.
55. Hahn, *supra*, at 219.
56. The completion of the internal market Whitepaper by the European Commission to the European Council, Com (85)310.

for VAT purposes. One of the reasons the Member States had favored the destination principle when accepting a common system of sales taxation was to prevent supranational collection and redistribution of taxes. Anticipating these objections, the commission proposed a clearing system, under which the tax collected by the export country would be transferred to the country of consumption. In this manner, continuing application of the destination principle was secured.[57]

In the summer of 1987, the commission proposed a package of measures to accomplish the goals identified in the Whitepaper, consisting of a general statement,[58] a working document on the clearing system[59] and seven draft directives.[60] It was proposed that the Member States would accept a tariff structure of no more than two rates, which should remain within a bandwidth of 4% to 9% for the reduced rate and 14% to 20% for the standard rate. Strong opposition emerged against the tariff approximation as suggested by the commission. The English and Irish governments could not abolish the zero rate on necessities for reasons of domestic policies;[61] Denmark feared revenue loss if it were to reduce its single rate of 22% to bring it within the bandwidth.[62] Luxemburg opposed mandatory tariff approximation in an effort to protect its retail sector's competitive advantage due to Luxemburg's low standard rate. The proposed clearing system is no longer based on bilateral clearing between individual Member States but instead on central clearing monitored by the Commission. Mistrust between Member States as to the accuracy of their respective claims to the central clearing institute lay at the root of the system's rejection. The claims of the Member States would be based on information submitted by domestic businesses involved in cross-border, intracommunity trade, but inaccuracies in reporting would have no negative consequences for the drawings or contributions of the states from and to the clearinghouse.[63] It was feared by the business community that strict verifications of all claims would be required, only imposing excessive compliance costs, and for this reason it

57. In this respect the commission had not much choice because the application of the destination principle was implicitly laid down in Arts 95–97 EEC (original).
58. Com (87)320, Brussels 21 August 1987.
59. Com (87)323, Brussels 25 August 1987.
60. Com (87)321, O.J. of 18 September 1987, No. C250 (tariff approximation); Com (87)322, O.J. of 22 September 1987, No. C252 (changes to Sixth Directive); Com (87)324–328, O.J. of 18 September 1987, No. C250.
61. The Thatcher administration had made strong promises regarding the continuation of the zero rate during the previous elections; see van Brederode, *De Bijzondere Positie van de Landbouw in de Omzetbelasting*, at 41. A committee of the European Parliament also concludes that abolishment of the zero rate would be politically impossible for the UK; see Session Documents E, 1987–1988, series A doc. A2-63/87, at 7, sub 16. (De Gucht Report).
62. Estimated at about 4.5% of GDP. Whether a reduced rate would lead to revenue loss and, if so, the extent of the loss, or actually to a revenue gain is subject to debate, see our remarks on an optimum VAT rate in s. 8.2.1.3.
63. It would be irrelevant for a Member State if a business were to overclaim foreign input tax because the state would simply file a claim for the same with the clearinghouse; similarly, underpayment of tax regarding exports to other states would either lead to a reduction of its contribution to the clearinghouse or to an increase of its claim.

lobbied strongly against its introduction. Unable to overcome the objections or to find a compromise, the harmonization of VAT in the EU arrived at an impasse. Politically and legally this was a problem because with the European Act of 1987 the realization of the internal market by 1992 has become a treaty obligation.[64] It appears that the commission had underestimated the extent of which differences between the tax systems of the Member States are caused by differences in social background and political culture.[65] It would take until the end of 1989 before conceptual common ground is reached on the basis of which the commission formulated further proposals. Ultimo 1991 the council is able to agree on the content of a transitional period.[66]

The transitional system entered into force per 1993 and was supposed to terminate ultimo 1996 and be replaced by a definite system based on the origin principle. However, during the Ecofin meeting of 24 June 1991, this deadline was made more flexible, changing its character from fatal and fixed to desired and intended. Although the Member States remained committed to the date of 1997, it was also decided that the transitional system would be maintained until the time of introduction of a definite system. The transitional system is a hybrid, mixing the origin and destination principles. Most sales to final consumers are subject to the origin principle, in other words, VAT will be paid in the country of purchase and further movement across borders is ignored for tax purposes.[67] B2B sales remain subject to the destination principle. However, border verification has been abolished by the introduction of an intracommunity acquisition as a taxable event. The cross-border, intracommunity sale is relieved from tax by the application of the zero rate. On the flip side of the coin, the recipient of the good is making an intracommunity acquisition subject to VAT in the country of arrival. The verification of the transaction is shifted to the creation of a paper trail of records. The seller has to report all intracommunity sales in a separate box on the VAT return and file a quarterly listing of all sales to each individual business located in another Member State. This information is exchanged between Member States to allow cross-checking of the sales listing and the VAT return of the buyer to verify that acquisition tax is appropriately accounted for.

The business community strongly opposed a major system change shortly after the introduction of the transitional system. Businesses and tax administrations had incurred considerable start-up costs, offset by the ending of tax controls at frontiers, and they were doubtful whether the new costs of adapting to yet another system in a few years' time could be justified by likely new savings. Instead, the commission decided to carry out an extensive consultation exercise with traders, tax authorities, academic bodies and so forth on the form the "definitive" VAT

64. O.J. 1987, No. L169 amending the EEC Treaty.
65. See Sybren Cnossen, *Tax Coordination in the European Community* (Deventer: Kluwer, 1987), at 49.
66. Directive 91/680/EEC of 16 December 1991, O.J. of 31 December 1991, No. L376.
67. However, special, destination-based regimes were introduced for distance sales; cars, boats and planes; and sales to exempt bodies.

system should take. On 10 July 1996, the commission presented its proposition for the final system in the form of a work program.[68] This put forward the idea that taxation should be based on a trader's "tax domicile" so that there would be one single place of registration[69] with a redistribution mechanism based on official statistics (macroeconomic data) to ensure that VAT receipts accrue to the Member State where consumption takes place. The commission recognized that simplification measures had reached their limits and the difficulties of the transitional system were fundamental and could only be resolved on the basis of different conceptual thinking. The tax system should be designed on the idea of the EU as a single tax jurisdiction instead of as a combination of nation-states surrounded by a frontier. To fully meet the objectives of the single market and avoid the problems of the current system, a new design for VAT should provide for equal treatment of domestic supplies and intracommunity supplies, and base revenue reallocation on national final consumption data. A single VAT rate would be ideal for the purpose of avoiding distortions, but rate differences are acceptable within a certain bandwidth.

Although it presented a thorough analysis of the flaws of the transitional system, most observers were disappointed with the lack of detail. Where the White-paper proposed to introduce the origin-based definite system immediately, 10 years later a gradual milestone plan was presented to achieve that objective. This new approach of gradual transformation to the ideal VAT was as unsuccessful as the immediate transformation proposed in 1987.

In June 2000, the commission presented a strategic program for improving the operation of the VAT system within the context of the internal market,[70] geared towards four main objectives: the simplification and modernization of existing rules, more uniform application of current rules and a new system of administrative cooperation. This action program was initiated because it seemed unlikely that, given the reservations of the states, significant progress towards a common system of VAT based on the origin principle would be made in the near future. Its main objective was to give new momentum in the council towards concrete and essential improvements to the existing tax system. One of the successes was the requirement of the states to introduce a facility under which traders have the right to discharge their tax registration and returns obligations by electronic means.[71]

The 2003–2007 Fiscalis program[72] is designed to help Member States collaborate more closely in combating tax fraud through improved electronic systems for the exchange of information between national administrations, the introduction

68. "A Common System of VAT. A Programme for the Single Market," Com 328(96) final.
69. Under this rule, the location of the goods sold in terms of departure and arrival would become irrelevant. If a business registered in Italy would sell goods from France to Germany, it would charge Italian VAT. In other words, origin and destination principles would be replaced with a registration situs rule.
70. COM (2000) 348 final.
71. Directive 2002/38/EC, O.J. of 15 May 2002, No. L128.
72. Decision 2235/2002/EC of the European Parliament and the Council of December 2002, O.J. of 17 December 2002, No. L341.

of cooperation between administrations for investigations, training seminars for officials and experts of national tax administrations and exchanges of officials between national administrations. The Standing Committee on Administrative Cooperation (SCAC), jointly with the commission and the Member States, has been working hard on risk analysis, computerized audits and targeting of checks to prevent carousel fraud.

Per 2007, Directive 2006/112[73] came into effect, which is basically a recodification of the former Sixth Directive. The new directive does not offer substantive changes but restructures the former directive that had been amended several times. The rules for the transitional system are no longer presented under a separate title, but these provisions are systematically integrated on subject matter. Although the number of titles is reduced from 22 to 15, the recast directive has grown to 414 articles by cutting the former articles in smaller bites to enhance clarity and comprehensibility.

All in all, progress on the path to further harmonization since the Sixth Directive has been modest and the small steps taken regard technical detail more than grand design. However, an important step to simplification was made in 2008 with legislation[74] to change the main tax jurisdiction rule for B2B cross-border services from origin to destination based, combined with a reverse charge rule to shift the actual tax accounting to the recipient of the service (see Section 9.5.2.2).

10.2.5. Scope and Present State of the Harmonization

The introduction of VAT in the early years of the EC was a major step politically, but it was also a requisite step towards the establishment of the single market. It enabled the abolishment of customs and tariffs at the internal borders of the community, but customs control was still required for VAT, which was levied when goods arrived in the Member State of destination. The major objective of the 1985 single market program was to remove these tax adjustments at the internal borders. The commission's initial proposal was an immediate move to the origin principal: firms would invoice deliveries to other Member States in exactly the same way as domestic deliveries. However, this ran into two problems. Major shifts in revenue between Member States were unacceptable and a "clearing system" was proposed to repay VAT to the countries of consumption; and there were sharp disagreements as to the extent VAT rates would have to be aligned. A compromise was reached, embodied in the current transitional system, that, in essence, diverts the tax adjustments from the border to a business's books where it has to account for the tax otherwise due at the border.

73. Directive 2006/112 of 28 November 2006 on the common system of VAT, O.J. of 11 December 2006, No. L347.
74. Directive 2008/8/EC of 12 February 2008, O.J., 20 February 2008, L44/11-22.

Though the abolition of controls at internal borders has reduced traders' costs, many have found these savings offset by new administrative burdens. Evidence indicates that these are due more to the intrastat trade statistics requirements than to the VAT system itself. Often, cross-border movement of goods takes place within a single firm, or between companies that belong to the same group or are otherwise related. The administrative burden in keeping track of all these movements for tax and statistical purposes is considerable. If the mere cross-border transfer of goods within a single firm or transactions between related companies could be ignored for VAT purposes, approximately 80% of all movement between the Member States could be taken out of the VAT system, which would lead to a significant ease of the compliance costs.

So where does Europe currently stand in the process of harmonization? When VAT became one element of the community's so-called own resources, the Sixth Directive harmonized the tax base to ensure that the VAT would cover the same transactions in all Member States. VAT rates have been gradually converging, and only three Member States (Denmark, Finland and Sweden) currently have a standard rate outside a 15% to 21% bandwidth. Most states apply two reduced rates, others only one, and ten states apply zero rates, in most cases for isolated products such as newspapers (but in Ireland and the UK for a wide range of necessities). Differences in VAT rates would create problems if an origin-based VAT were to be introduced. Where the differences are too great, competition might be distorted. However, application of the origin principle since 1993 to purchases by most final consumers does not so far appear to have altered patterns of cross-border shopping. The main problems are the multiplicity of reduced rates and the selection and definition of the categories to which the reduced rates can apply. In addition, the European legislation allows for many options, rights and transitional arrangements, which lead to an overall system that is admittedly coherent but also extremely diverse and invested with a multitude of derogations. In effect, because of the differences in VAT, there is not a single but a segmented market with compartmentalized competition.

10.3. THE HARMONIZATION OF SALES AND USE TAXES IN THE UNITED STATES

10.3.1. Reasons for Harmonization

Tax policy and administration are, to a large extent, decentralized in the United States because each state is responsible for the financing of the public services it provides to its residents. Currently, forty-five states and the District of Columbia apply sales and use tax,[75] which contributes about 25% to 30% of their total tax

75. Alaska, Delaware, Montana, New Hampshire and Oregon do not have a state sales tax. Together, those states comprise about 3% of the US population. However, in Alaska, sales tax is levied at the local level.

revenue. Moreover, thirty-three states permit local governments (counties and towns) to levy the tax, and additional sales taxes are now levied by about 7,500 local jurisdictions, generating an average of 12% of their total revenue. The local sales and use tax is the second-largest source of tax revenue to local government. In their design and scope, the state sales taxes follow a common pattern but details, rates and coverage vary considerably.[76]

The sales tax applies only to domestic supplies, which means supplies that originate and end within the boundaries of the same state. In the case of cross-border transactions, the sales tax in the state of origin cannot apply because the goods (or services) are exported. Sales tax in the state of destination does not apply because the transaction originated in another state and is, therefore, not domestic. To fill this void, use taxes have been introduced. The use tax relates to the sales tax as the flip side of the same coin. The use tax kicks in when the sales tax fails to apply. When a good is sold to a customer in another state and is subsequently shipped to that other state, or a service is rendered to a customer located in another state, the sale will be subject to a use tax in the destination state. Because interstate commerce is the exclusive domain of the federal government, states have no authority over out-of-state suppliers. Unless the supplier has sufficient physical presence (nexus) in a state, he cannot be required to collect the use tax on sales made to customers located in another state. This leaves the states of arrival no option but to collect the use tax from the recipient of the goods or services, businesses and private consumers alike. Especially as regards sales to private consumers, compliance with the obligation to account for use tax is extremely low and, in effect, out-of-state purchases by consumers escape taxation. This lack of compliance not only results in revenue loss for the state and local government within whose jurisdiction the consumer is resident[77] but also puts local retailers, who cannot avoid charging sales tax, at a competitive (price) disadvantage. Of course, this problem has existed for decades but, from the perspectives of loss of revenue and competitive fairness, it is becoming increasingly pressing with the advancement of technologies that make remote selling and buying easier and cheaper.[78]

It is understandable that the states want to be able to require remote sellers to collect the use tax, but their efforts have been left stranded in court. In the most

---

76. For a general treatise of the sales taxes in the United States, see Robert F. van Brederode, "Introduction to the US State Sales and Use Taxes," *International VAT Monitor* 18 (4) (2007): 270–276.
77. In relation to remote sales, the US General Accounting Office estimates the revenue erosion at between USD 2.6 billion and USD 20.4 billion. The midpoint of that range, USD 11.5 billion, is about 4% of total revenue that states expect to receive from sales and use taxes. Private sector estimates range from USD 15.4 billion to USD 16.1 billion for 2003 and project a revenue loss range of USD 21.5 billion to USD 33.6 billion for 2008. See respectively: *Sales Taxes: Electronic Commerce Growth Presents Challenge; Revenue Losses Are Uncertain*, GOA Report OCE-00-165 (Washington, DC: GAO, 30 June 2000), 21; and Donald Bruce & William F. Fox, *State and Local Sales Tax Revenue Loss from E-commerce: Estimates as of July 2004* (University of Tennessee, July 2004), 5.
78. See Robert F. van Brederode, "The American Debate on Taxing Distance Sales and E-commerce," *International VAT Monitor* 18 (5) (2007): 352–361.

recent case, *Quill*,[79] the Supreme Court upheld its earlier ruling that requiring collection of use taxes by remote sellers that do not have sufficient physical presence in a state is a violation of the commerce clause of the Constitution.[80] According to the Supreme Court, such a requirement would constitute an undue burden on interstate trade, specifically because of the prohibitively high compliance cost that distance traders would encounter.[81] Because interstate commerce is the legislative domain of Congress, the latter has the power to change the physical-presence rules, thus enabling states to require use tax collection by out-of-state sellers. However, Congress has been reluctant to do so for precisely the very same reasons: the complexity of having to account for use tax in different jurisdictions and the accompanying compliance costs.

Clearly, the heart of the matter lies in the current complexity caused by the diversity of state and local sales and use taxes, and the inherent compliance costs. For example, in 2002, Walmart reported having 3,172 outlets at locations that impose a sales tax. With the differences in tax base definitions and potentially 377 different sales tax rates, it seems clear that the cost of compliance is substantial for firms.

Indeed, several bills are pending in Congress that propose guidelines for simplifying state and local sales taxes. However, the states are strongly opposed to any guidelines or criteria set at the federal level because they perceive them as an infringement of their autonomy. However, the states do realize that they cannot expect Congress to give them carte blanche authorization for collection of use taxes by out-of-state sellers, without taking measures to reduce the complexity of the tax system and the inherent compliance costs.[82] For this reason, the states have initiated the Streamlined Sales Tax Project (SSTP), which is essentially an effort to harmonize sales and use taxes on a voluntary basis. In a sense, it is a political preemptive strike to render federal guidelines obsolete in lieu of considerable streamlining of the existing legislation of the participating states and, henceforth, a significant reduction of the compliance costs.

The magnitude of the project and the institutional complexities inherent in the participation of so many parties and their special interests are described in Section 10.3.2. More specifically, the political feasibility aspects are dealt with in Section 10.3.12. The project's objective, scope and methodology are dealt with

79. *Quill Corp. v. North Dakota*, 504 US 298 (1992).
80. Article I(8), clause 3 of the US Constitution.
81. Estimates of compliance costs in a 1999 study by Ernst & Young ranged from 1% of revenue collected for large firms collecting sales tax in a single state, to 48% and 87%, respectively, for medium-sized and small firms doing business in forty-five states. See Robert J. Cline & Thomas S. Neubig, *Masters of Complexity and Bearers of Great Burden: The Sales Tax System and Compliance Costs for Multistate Retailers* (Washington, DC: Ernst & Young, 8 September 1999).
82. See Steven Maguire, "State and Local Sales and Use Taxes and Internet Commerce," CRS Report, 28 January 2005; and John L. Mikesell, "Remote Vendors and American Sales and Use Taxation: The Balance between Fixing the Problem and Fixing the Tax," *National Tax Journal* 53 (4) (2000): 1273–1285.

in Section 10.3.3. A more detailed look at the particulars of the harmonization effort is taken in Sections 10.3.5, 10.3.6, and 10.3.7.

Interestingly, the SSTP provides for financial compensation of compliance costs to sellers that collect the tax (see Section 10.3.8), an approach that should trigger the interest of businesses collecting turnover taxes in other parts of the world as well. In order to realize a high level of voluntary participation from distance sellers, the SSTP also provides for amnesty of sales and use tax due in the past (Section 10.3.9). A different, but not less important, issue is consumer privacy protection, which will be addressed in Section 10.3.10. Interestingly, the SSTP is expected to have a high degree of voluntary compliance from the business community, an assumption that will be evaluated in Section 10.3.11.

10.3.2. Legislative Aspects

The *Quill* decision implicitly requires simplification and harmonization efforts to be multilateral in nature, where it states that the complexity caused by the diversity of the sales and use taxes and the inherent compliance costs impose an undue burden on interstate commerce. It is unfeasible for the Supreme Court to overturn its earlier decisions, neither is it likely that Congress will relax the physical-presence requirements without serious progress by a large number, if not all, of the states regarding harmonization and simplification of their sales and use tax systems. It is important to realize that the current tax system is the result of the unilateral action by each of the forty-five states and the District of Columbia. Reform, although multilateral in nature and based on mutual agreement, will however, by necessity, follow that same unilateral path because there exists no institutionalized forum in which states can resolve common issues or take multilateral decisions. Involved are: the National Governors Association (NGA), the National Conference of State Legislatures (NCSL) and, to a lesser degree, the Federation of Tax Administrators (FTA) and the MTC. None of these have legislative authority. The governors and state legislators who do have that authority tend to have very distinct agendas in respect to tax policy.[83] Although the legislators and governors may all agree on the necessity of ending unfair competition for local traders and of expanding the tax base, they also want to keep their authority regarding defining the tax base and determining the general rules of sales and use taxation in their respective states.

There is a tension between tax autonomy and simplification because the two are antithetical in nature.[84] This is demonstrated by the actions of the NCSL that unanimously endorsed both the Model Act and the Streamlined Sales and Use Tax Agreement (SSUTA) (see Section 10.3.3) in January 2001 only after modifying

83. Charles E. McLure, *New Developments on State and Local Tax: E-commerce, Tax Incentives for Business and Litigation-generated Revenues*, paper for the Annual Meeting of the Association of American Law Schools (January 2001), 6.
84. *Supra*, 7.

key provisions and deleting others, especially those allowing the states to apply preferential rates to food, clothing, electricity and gas.

10.3.3. Objective and Methodology of the Streamlining Project

To overcome the compliance burden on vendors, a group of public and private entities formed the SSTP in March 2000. More than forty states joined the SSTP, along with state and local government associations, retailers and retail associations. The mission of the SSTP is to develop measures to design, test and implement a radically simplified sales and use tax system. It is envisioned that each state that has a sales and use tax adopts a Model Act that authorizes the tax authority of the state to enter into the SSUTA or "agreement"[85] with one or several other states to simplify and modernize sales and use tax administration in order to substantially reduce the burden of tax compliance for all sellers and all types of commerce. The SSUTA contains all the details of uniformity and simplification, including the standards that must be attained. In other words, the SSUTA constitutes a contractual relationship between the signatory states. The participating states are required to modify their laws to bring them into conformity with the terms of the agreement. The SSUTA is not a static agreement but basically a work in progress. Project groups work on recommendations relating to simplification, coordination and use of technology, which need to be approved by the implementing states group (see Section 10.3.5).

The first step in moving the agreement forward was to establish a group of implementing states, the Streamlined Sales Tax Implementing States (SSTIS). On 12 November 2002, the SSTIS officially approved the provisions of the agreement outlining a uniform system for the administration and collection of all sales taxes – whether collected at a physical location or remotely.

10.3.4. Participating and Associate States

Participating or full Member States are those that have been determined, by the Streamlined Sales Tax Governing Board, to have changed their sales tax administration law so that they meet all of the requirements set forth in the agreement. Sellers that register under the agreement must collect sales and use tax for all participating states, and they will be notified at the time a new state becomes a full member.

Associate Member States are those that have been determined by the governing board to be either in compliance with the agreement, albeit that the changes to their statutes and rules are not yet fully in effect, or in compliance with nearly all parts of the agreement. In either case, the necessary changes must take effect on or before 1 July 2009.

---

85. SSUTA, adopted on 12 November 2002, and was last amended on 26 February 2009.

The SSUTA came into effect on 1 October 2005, when thirteen states representing more than 20% of the population were certified as having met the requirements of the agreement. Currently, nineteen states[86] are full members and three states[87] are associate members.

10.3.5. Decision-Making Process

The governance of the SSUTA is in the hands of the governing board, which has the form of a nonprofit entity. All full and associate Member States have a seat on the board. The board is charged with:

- interpretations and amendments to SSUTA, requiring a 75% majority vote;
- certifying certified automated system (CAS)[88] and certified service providers (CSPs);[89]
- reviewing state compliance with the SSUTA;
- implementing administrative mechanisms, such as multistate audit procedures and vendor compensation; and
- handling dispute resolution.

The governing board is advised by two councils: the State and Local Advisory Council (SLAC), which mainly develops new definitions, analyzes proposed amendments and advises on requests for interpretations; and the Business Advisory Council (BAC), which includes businesses, associations and practitioners and provides input to the board, as well as to the SLAC relating to administration, interpretation and compliance with, and amendments to, the agreement.

Each participating or associate Member State may appoint up to four representatives to the governing board, but each state only has one vote. Associate Member States have all the rights and privileges of participating Member States under the agreement, except that they[90]

- are not allowed to vote on amendments to, or interpretations of, the Agreement;
- do not have access to the names of sellers or other data provided by volunteering sellers through the central registration system, unless the seller has determined that he will collect use tax on sales into the associate Member State;
- may not receive information from the governing board on companies being audited by that board, unless the state is a part of the audit;

86. Arkansas, Indiana, Iowa, Kansas, Kentucky, Michigan, Minnesota, Nebraska, Nevada, New Jersey, North Carolina, North Dakota, Oklahoma, Rhode Island, South Dakota, Vermont, Washington, West Virginia and Wyoming.
87. Ohio, Tennessee and Utah.
88. Certified automated system (see section 10.3.7.1.).
89. Certified service providers (see section 10.3.7.1).
90. Article VII(705) of the SSUTA.

- are not represented on the Compliance Review and Interpretations Committee; and
- may not vote to determine if a petitioning state is in compliance with the agreement.

10.3.6. SCOPE OF HARMONIZATION

In order to accomplish a high degree of uniformity between the sales and use tax systems of the states and, henceforth, realize simplified compliance, the SSTP is charged with developing uniform definitions and product codes, uniform sourcing (i.e., jurisdiction) rules and simpler, more uniform tax return forms. An essential element of the project is developing standards for service providers and for automated systems, as well as performance standards for multistate sellers. In essence, the SSTP is promoting software and automation technology to significantly assist in solving the complexity issue. These aspects are further dealt with later.

10.3.6.1. Registration and Administration

Under the agreement, all local sales and use taxes would be administered by the state. Sellers would only be required to register and file returns with, and remit the tax to, the state, which would redistribute the revenues to the local governments. Of course, sellers would still have to allocate the revenue to the different jurisdictions through their returns. Audits would be conducted by the state only.

10.3.6.2. State and Local Tax Base

The agreement requires the tax base for state and local jurisdictions to be identical.[91] According to the agreement, delivery charges and installation charges are to be included in the sales or purchase price, which is important to achieve neutrality between local and remote sellers.

10.3.6.3. Change of Rules and Regulations

Participating states agree to reduce the difficulties for sellers in relation to change of rules and regulations by making a reasonable effort to:

- provide sellers with advance notice of rate changes;
- ensure that rate changes come into effect on the first day of a calendar quarter;

91. However, this provision does not apply to the sales and use tax on the transfer of motor vehicles, aircraft, boats, and modular, manufactured or mobile homes. As to the latter category, the reason is that many states only tax a percentage of the value of such property in order to achieve rough parity with the tax treatment of conventional housing.

- notify sellers of legal changes in the tax base and other rules and regulations;
- not apply caps or thresholds;
- not apply multiple tax rates;
- ensure the rate for sales tax is identical to the rate for use tax;
- ensure there is only one sales and use tax rate per jurisdiction. A single rate per state is, therefore, not required; local jurisdictions would still be allowed to determine their own sales and use tax rate;
- maintain a database that describes the boundaries of all taxing jurisdictions according to the five- and nine-digit zip code;
- ensure that changes in the boundaries of local jurisdictions would apply only at the first day of a calendar quarter with a minimum of 60 days notice; and
- maintain a database of all sales and use tax rates for all jurisdictions within the state.

10.3.6.4. Uniform Jurisdiction (Sourcing) Rules

It is essential to define common rules of tax jurisdiction to prevent double taxation or nontaxation. In the EU, for VAT, these rules are referred to as the "place-of-supply rules"; in the United States, for sales and use taxes, they are called sourcing rules. Regardless of whether the product is a tangible good or a service, the following provisions have been designed to determine where sales take place, that is, which state has tax jurisdiction or, in other words, what tax rate applies and to which state the tax must be remitted.[92]

(1) Where a good or service is collected by the purchaser at a business location of the seller, the sale is sourced to that location. This rule basically refers to normal over-the-counter retail sales.
(2) Where a good or service is not collected at a business location of the seller, the sale is sourced to the location where it is received. This rule is consistent with the destination principle and would include situations where gifts, at the instigation of the buyer, are directly sent from the seller to the recipient. If there exists a difference in tax rates between the state of purchase and that of destination, the buyer could elect the most beneficial tax treatment by either buying the good at retail and sending it himself to the final recipient (taxed at the rate applicable in the state of purchase) or having the seller send it to the recipient (taxed at the rate applicable in the state of destination).
(3) In most instances, this rule will be clear. However, the *Rules and Procedures* of the project's governing board provide examples that are somewhat confusing. As an example, it gives the scenario of standard computer

92. Streamlined Sales Tax Governing Board, Inc., *Rules and Procedures*, approved on 1 October 2005, as most recently amended on 6 December 2008.

software that is electronically delivered by the seller to multiple locations of the purchaser. Because the seller can identify these multiple locations, it apparently needs to source the sales to each jurisdiction. That would be relatively simple if the seller were to invoice each recipient separately, but if the supply is invoiced to one location (e.g., a headquarters) does that mean that the seller has to attribute the total price to the individual recipients? Unfortunately, the *Rules and Procedures* do no go into such detail.

(4) Where the first two rules do not apply, the sale is sourced to the location indicated by an address for the purchaser that is available from the business records of the seller that are maintained in the ordinary course of the seller's business, unless use of this address constitutes bad faith. In other words, if the seller has no indication of where the goods or services are actually consumed, he will apply the tax rate and submit the tax to the state in which the purchaser, according to the seller's administration, has an address. Obviously, the exception for the "bad faith" situations is intended to prevent sellers from participating in schemes to evade taxes by utilizing addresses in states without sales and use tax.

(5) Where the first three rules do not apply, the sale will be sourced to the location indicated by an address for the purchaser obtained during consummation of the retail sale, including the address of a purchaser's payment instrument if no other address is available, for example, the address associated with the purchaser's credit card, provided this address does not constitute bad faith. The bad faith provision again is to prevent the use of addresses in nontaxing states, but it seems the buyer will be able to use such a ploy as long as the seller is unaware of it.

(6) Where none of the above rules apply, including the circumstance where the seller lacks sufficient information to apply the previous rules, the sale would be sourced to, in respect to tangible goods, the address from which the product was shipped or, in respect to digital goods and services, the address from which the service was provided or the product was first available for transmission by the seller.

10.3.6.5. Uniform Definitions

Under the agreement, the states and local jurisdictions are not required to tax or exempt specific items. However, in either case, items must be categorized by the product definitions provided by the agreement and, unless the agreement specifically provides otherwise, all items listed within such a category must be included, without exceptions or variations.

10.3.6.6. Uniform Tax Return Forms

Where, currently, each state has its own return forms, the agreement requires the states to develop one tax return per seller per tax period. At their discretion, the states would be allowed to require electronic filing from compliance model 1, 2 and 3 sellers (see Section 10.3.7.2).

10.3.7. Certification and Compliance Models

10.3.7.1. Certification

The SSTP provides for two types of certification. The certification is conducted by the states to determine the accuracy of reporting. The first is for CSPs,[93] which are agents certified to perform all of the seller's sales and use tax functions.[94] A CSP could play an important part in simplification because he would act as an independent specialist to whom all tasks normally performed by sellers themselves are outsourced, and the agent would be liable to the tax authorities for errors made. The software used by the CSP must be approved by the governing board and meet certification standards.[95]

The second type of certification is for software to calculate the tax due to each jurisdiction and to maintain records of each transaction. The CAS software[96] is central to the technology-based solution for sales and use tax simplification. The software must be able to link addresses to tax jurisdictions, determine whether specific goods or services are taxed or exempt, apply the correct tax rate per jurisdiction, calculate the total amount of tax due and allocate it to each jurisdiction, and prepare the required documentation.

10.3.7.2. Compliance Models

The SSTP envisions three compliance models for different types of vendors. In model 1, sellers would employ a CSP to perform all their sales and use tax functions. It is likely that small businesses would employ this model. CSPs are intended to enable a business to outsource most of its sales tax administration responsibilities. The software system of a CSP will identify which goods and services are taxable, will apply the appropriate tax rate, will interface with the seller's accounting system, and will file the tax return and remit the tax to the appropriate tax authorities. Each participating and associate Member State will have certified the accuracy of the software and will provide liability relief to the sellers for errors that may result in the incorrect calculation of the tax amount (by shifting the liability to

93. Currently, four CSPs have a contract with the governing board: Avalara, Exactor, Speedtax and Taxware.
94. The agent only represents the seller in his capacity as a vendor and is not responsible for the seller's obligation to remit use tax on its own purchases.
95. Calculation accuracy standards and Technology standards (e.g., ISO 17799, SAS70).
96. The software needs approval from the governing board and must meet certification standards, for example, calculation accuracy standards and technology standards (e.g., ISO 17799, SAS70). Currently, only two providers, Speedtax and Taxware, have achieved the distinction of being a CAS.

the CSP). In addition, the services rendered by CSPs will be paid for by the participating states by compensating the CSPs (see Section 10.3.8).

In model 2, sellers would retain their responsibility in respect to sales and use taxes and use CAS software to perform these functions. This model seems appropriate for medium-sized companies. The CAS software will identify which goods and services are taxable, will apply the appropriate tax rate, and can interface with the seller's accounting system. Although the business that uses CAS software remains responsible for filing the tax return and paying the tax, each participating Member State will have certified the accuracy of the software and will provide liability relief for errors that may result from the incorrect calculation of the tax amount. Sellers that use CAS software will be able to file their returns electronically. The costs of the CAS software are borne by the businesses employing them.

Finally, model 3 sellers use their own systems to make their tax calculations on the basis of performance standards determined by the individual participating states with which the seller has entered into a performance agreement. To be eligible for this regime, it is required for a seller, or an affiliated group of sellers using the same system, to have sales in at least five participating states and total revenue of at least USD 500 million.

10.3.8. Financial Compensation for Businesses

The participating states will provide monetary compensation for the implementation of new technology and voluntary registration, that is, registration in a state where registration is not required because the seller lacks sufficient nexus. In addition, CSPs receive a percentage of the revenue generated as compensation for the general costs of collecting the use tax. In a report prepared by PricewaterhouseCoopers[97] on the basis of a survey among 13,000 retailers, ten categories of compliance cost are identified:

- training of personnel on sales tax;
- documenting exempt sales;
- customer services relating to sales tax issues;
- sales tax related software and license fees;
- programming and servicing cash registers;
- preparing tax returns and related costs;
- dealing with sales tax audits[98] and appeals;

97. PricewaterhouseCoopers, *Retail Sales Tax Compliance Costs: A National Estimate* (7 April 2006).
98. Audits can be conducted by the individual states, the MTC, and by local governments. In at least six states (Alabama, Alaska, Arizona, Colorado, Mississippi and Louisiana), the local governments have active and aggressive audit practices. There is enough demand by local governments for audit services, which are contracted to private audit firms, who claim to serve hundreds of local governments. If only one out of ten of Walmart's local operations and half the state operations were audited each year, Walmart would face more than 1.25 audits per day.

- unrecovered sales tax caused by bad debts;
- debit/credit card fees on sales tax collections; and
- other compliance costs.

The top cost categories for small retailers are as follows: (1) preparing tax returns, (2) documenting exempt sales and (3) training of personnel. Medium-sized retailers concur with the first two categories but rank debit/credit card fees as third. For large retailers, the ranking is: (1) debit/credit card fees, (2) unrecovered tax due to bad debts and (3) training of personnel.

The standard contract between the governing board and CSPs provides for compensation according to a formula that awards compensation rates based on the amount of taxes due by the seller to all participating and associate Member States combined. The compensation is as follows:

- 8% for the first USD 250,000 in taxes due;
- 7% for taxes due between USD 250,000 and USD 1 million;
- 6% for taxes due between USD 1 million and USD 2.5 million;
- 5% for taxes due between USD 2.5 million and USD 5 million;
- 4% for taxes due between USD 5 million and USD 10 million;
- 3% for taxes due between USD 10 million and USD 25 million; and
- 2% for taxes due for more than USD 25 million.

When the amount of taxes due by the seller reaches the next bracket, the compensation must be adjusted as soon as is practicable to avoid overcompensation, but no later than the next tax remittance to the participating and associate Member States after the new level has been reached. For example, if taxes are remitted monthly and, from the beginning of the year until the end of 1 month, the total amount of taxes due by a seller to all participating and associate Member States combined rises from USD 225,000 to USD 300,000 at the end of the following month, in addition to 8% of USD 225,000 (USD 18,000, which the CSP received in the preceding months), the CSP receives 8% of USD 25,000 (USD 2,000) and 7% of USD 50,000 (USD 3,500) for the current month, and the remainder (USD 75,000 – USD 5,500 = USD 69,500) must be remitted for that month. Sales and use taxes on sales by that seller sourced to participating or associate Member States in which the seller is not registered voluntarily are to be disregarded for the purposes of the compensation scheme.

When remitting the taxes due for a reporting period in which the compensation percentage has been adjusted, the CSP is expected to make the best effort to allocate the change to the individual participating and associate Member States. Unless the CSP uses a method that consistently applies the rate change more

---

Few audit processes are more difficult for a firm or corporate tax department to deal with than use tax audits. Use tax audits require the storage and retrieval of information on thousands of transactions that are carried out in thousands of tax jurisdictions. Large and small firms that engage in multistate B2B transactions are asked to verify that they have either collected from their customers the use tax due, or that the customers have paid the use tax to the appropriate tax authorities.

precisely, he must attribute the change proportionately to the participating and associate Member States, regardless of which individual sales were made before or after the compensation was adjusted during the period. In the preceding example, unless he uses a more accurate allocation method, the CSP would charge all participating and associate Member States 8% on one-third, and 7% on two-thirds, of the taxes owed to each of them for that month.

The rates of compensation are reset annually for services performed on behalf of each seller. Regardless of the total amount of taxes due by the seller to the participating and associate Member States for the preceding year, the rate at the beginning of the following year will return to 8% on the first USD 250,000 of taxes due from each seller and that rate is to be adjusted according to the procedure set forth previously. For the purposes of resetting the compensation rate to 8% annually, the 1-year period for each seller begins on the first day of the month in which sales and use taxes are remitted for that seller to any participating or associate Member State, and a new year begins on each anniversary thereafter.

For the purposes of determining when a rate adjustment level is reached, affiliated sellers must be treated as a single seller, if they would qualify as "related persons" for income tax purposes.[99]

It is important to realize, that the compensation is only awarded in respect to sales made to states in which the seller registers for use tax collection voluntarily. If registration in a particular state is mandatory, for example, because the seller has sufficient physical presence (nexus) there, or if a seller forfeits status as a "volunteer" tax collector in a state for whatever reason, no compensation will be paid under the terms of the CSP contract in respect to taxes due to that particular state.[100]

Individual Member States and associate Member States are allowed to provide supplementary compensation to CSPs, in accordance with their own laws, but none has done so.

There is no requirement under the SSTP for compensation of model 2 and 3 sellers who basically administer their own use tax collection. Currently, however, twenty-five states allow firms to keep a portion of the sales tax they collect. In most states, these vendor discounts range from 0.5% of the taxes collected to 3% in some states. Many states that offer discounts for sales tax compliance do not extend them to use tax collections.

10.3.9. Amnesty

Under the SSUTA, on becoming a participating member, each state must provide a 1-year amnesty period for tax, interest and penalties to vendors who register as use tax collectors in respect to sales made prior to the date of registration, unless they

99. Under ss 267(b) or 707(b) of the Internal Revenue Code.
100. In that event, the seller and CSP have to agree on the terms of compensation for the services rendered by the CSP in collecting taxes for the seller in that state.

are subject to an audit or have received notice of an audit at the time of registration. The registration must take place within 12 months of the effective date of the state's participation in the agreement. The amnesty even applies if the vendor has physical presence (nexus) in the state. The amnesty only applies to the tax due on sales made, not to tax due from the vendor in his capacity as purchaser. To obtain amnesty, vendors must register in all participating states of the agreement through the Central Registration System, including registration in states that join the agreement later. The SSUTA came into effect on 1 October 2005, but additional states continue to join as full or associate members. The original amnesty period is past, unless the seller uses CSP or CAS software, which reduces the overall amnesty benefit and complicates the decision as to whether registration will result in a net benefit. The most significant drawback to registration is the requirement to file sales and use tax returns in all the participating states for a minimum of 3 years, including states in which the registrant would not otherwise have a legal requirement to file. Any seller who received an amnesty from any state will lose that amnesty if he cancels registration within 36 months of the date of registration.

10.3.10. Consumer Privacy Protection

Another and fundamental issue is the effect of the sales and use tax harmonization or streamlining on consumer privacy. Apart from any records that distance sellers may keep and use in accordance with the privacy policy that they have adopted, electronic commerce permits an Internet purchaser to maintain a level of anonymity. With few exceptions, the government cannot obtain vendor records without following appropriate search warrant procedures designed to protect the purchaser's fundamental right to privacy. The audit procedures proposed under the SSTP, and the access to personal data that they seem to allow, leaves consumers vulnerable to misuse of sensitive information and potentially violates the consumers' constitutional rights of privacy and due process. According to some, consumer privacy protection is an issue that has not been appropriately addressed in the current agreement.[101] The SSUTA acknowledges the importance of privacy protection, especially in relation to consumers dealing with model 1 sellers, and requires CSPs to only use systems that ensure anonymity as a condition for certification by the governing board. The collection, use and retention of personally identifiable information are only allowed where required to ensure the validity of exemptions from taxation. States are required to inform individuals of the information retained and provide them access to the information with the right to correct inaccuracies. When the information is no longer needed for the purpose for which it has been collected, it must be deleted.[102]

101. Renee Giachino & Jeffrey Mazzella, *Simplification Is Not the Easy Answer* (Alexandria, VA: Center for Individual Freedom, July 2001). <www.cfif.org>
102. Article III(321) of the SSUTA.

10.3.11. The Voluntary Compliance Assumption

The most interesting supposition made by the supporters of the SSTP is the assumption that remote B2C vendors will volunteer to collect the use tax when the compliance process is made simple, transparent and straightforward. More than 1,000 businesses have taken advantage of the simplifications offered by the agreement by volunteering to comply and collect use taxes from their remote sales but, given the tens of thousands of remote sellers in the United States, this is hardly sufficient proof of the validity of the proposition. It appears that its validity depends on the existence of both economic and sociological advantages for the remote sellers. Individuals and firms certainly contribute to society on a voluntary basis without receiving monetary compensation, for example, through offering services or support to religious or youth organizations. In addition, voluntary compliance with legal requirements that benefit society, such as environmental protection legislation, is also quite common. In both instances, the compensation for the benefactor lies in the recognition by society of the individual's altruistic behavior or the corporate entity's social responsibility thus displayed. Convention as to what constitutes appropriate behavior plays an important role. Generally, it makes good public relations for a firm to be perceived as a good corporate citizen, in other words to abide by the accepted conventions. Firms are very sensitive to their public image because it has a strong influence on the success and, ultimately, the profitability of their business.[103] The widespread practice of tax-avoidance schemes and the epidemic growth of utilization of offshore tax shelters by corporations to reduce or at least postpone taxation have not met serious financial or social repercussions. It seems that tax avoidance and noncompliance with the tax regime are not identified as pressing problems by society at large; otherwise, firms would be more reluctant in employing tax-avoidance schemes. Use tax collection is at present not part of the relationship between remote vendors and state and local governments. Quite the contrary, noncompliance seems to be the accepted convention. Remote vendors have battled in both political and legal arenas over nexus and prevailed in two landmark cases before the Supreme Court (see Section 10.3.1). It seems unlikely that remote vendors are willing to voluntarily concede the nexus protection for which they have so long fought. Even in situations where they have nexus in a given state, efforts are made to avoid use tax collection, for example, by establishing an affiliate firm without physical presence (nexus) in the state through which they channel mail-order and Internet sales. Under those circumstances, the parent company argues that it is under no obligation to collect use taxes because it is not participating in these sales, and the affiliate entity claims the same, but for the reason of absence of nexus.[104]

---

103. Robert Gibbons, "Incentives in Organizations," *Journal of Economic Perspectives* 12 (4) (1998): 115–132.

104. This is common practice employed by both remote and traditional vendors, such as Borders, Barnes and Noble, Gateway, Saks Fifth Avenue and Nordstrom's. See, Robert F. van Brederode, "The American Debate on Taxing Distance Sales and E-commerce," 352–361.

If current behavior regarding tax compliance is an indication for the likelihood of voluntary compliance in the context of use tax collection, there seems no reason for optimism. The states do have optimistic expectations of collective behavior regarding voluntary use tax collection. However, if a sufficient number of firms comply with use tax collection, political pressure to mandate compliance will probably diminish. As a consequence, noncomplying vendors will engage group pressure at strongly reduced levels as well. The compliance by many opens the door for abuse through noncompliance by a few. This possibility in itself poses a variant of the prisoner's dilemma to each individual firm, contemplating joining the collective effort, which consequently, raises concerns regarding the likelihood of voluntary compliance.[105]

From another angle, voluntary compliance will also, and to a large extent, depend on a cost-benefit analysis undertaken by individual firms. As indicated in Section 10.3.8, the compliance costs are considerable, especially in respect to payments made by credit or debit cards, which will be the case with most remote sales. Where these costs are easy to identify, direct benefits are far more difficult to attribute. The harmonization itself and simplified audit procedures are clearly beneficial to businesses. From a financial perspective, the compensation scheme will play an important role in the analysis as well. In addition, businesses have to assess the impact that taxation will have on their sales volume and profit margin.[106] The actual situation will be different for each firm, and the decision to participate in voluntary use tax collection will depend on a variety of factors, including the existing level of tax expertise, the type of products sold, and the nature and size of the business, for example, an exclusively virtual store seller as compared to a traditional retailer with an affiliate firm for remote sales. A traditional retailer, for example, may benefit from voluntary use tax collection through reduced audit and compliance costs, and the compensation offered for the tax collection. However, price increases resulting from the tax collection on distance sales may lead to loss of market share or sales volume. Basically, each firm would compare the financial outcome of the current situation (model 1) with the anticipated outcome under the voluntary compliance model (model 2). The assumption is that voluntary use tax compliance is likely when the profits under model 2 are equal to or greater than those under model 1. To take a closer look at this, we take the following factors into account: current sales volume with no tax (*S*), sales volume loss due to the use tax[107] (*SL*), profit rate (*p*), compensation received as a percentage or margin of the tax collected (*M*), cost of compliance as a percentage of the tax collected (*C*) and tax rate (*t*).

---

105. Mancur Olson, *Logic of Collective Action* (Cambridge, MA: Harvard University Press, 1971).
106. It is estimated that the effective application of sales and use tax to Internet sales would reduce the number of online shoppers by 24%. See Austan Goolsbee, "In a World without Borders: The Impact of Taxes on Internet Commerce," *Quarterly Journal of Economics* 115 (2) (2000): 561–576.
107. Assuming price-elastic demand, that is, the percentage decrease of demand is larger than the percentage increase of the price.

In equation: Model 1 $\leq$ Model 2, or $pS \leq (M - C)t(S - SL) + p(S - SL)$

The left side of the equation represents the current profit level, whereas the two terms on the right side represent the profits from collecting the tax and the profits from the new sales level, respectively.

In a recent study,[108] a simulation decision-making model was developed to assess the likelihood of voluntary compliance, based on financial criteria as identified previously. Although the model does not provide exact predictions of the proportion of firms that would find use tax collection beneficial, it did demonstrate that for a large minority of firms (about 42%), voluntary tax collection would be profitable under the right conditions, most of which are under the control of public policy. Strong incentives are required to induce firms to voluntary use tax collection, especially significantly lower compliance costs and increased compensation levels for the collection of use taxes.

10.3.12. Political Feasibility

Interstate political cooperation does not have a strong performance record and poses many complexities. There have been some successes in the past, notably the MTC, which provides an excellent example of an alliance between states that has facilitated uniformity between the states in terms of audit coverage and administrative performance. However, this is, in essence, an effort to enforce compliance and does not require the states to accommodate any request from the business community for legislative change or harmonization. Moreover, within the Member States of the MTC there is disagreement over strategy and tactics.[109] Another example of interstate tax cooperation is the multistate charter on collecting the motor fuel tax from the interstate trucking industry. Indeed, states have shown that they are willing to cooperate when they share a mutual interest, for example, in legal cases before the Supreme Court. Since the mid-1980s, the states have filed a series of so-called amicus curiae briefs with the Court. The briefs are written to reflect the combined position of the participating states. This practice proves that states can cooperate; however, those briefs are limited to issues that are narrow and technical. The briefs are absent when issues involve policies and politics that may differ between states.[110]

Unfortunately, on the flip side of the coin, states and local governments often openly compete for new and old businesses by offering a variety of sales tax

108. Gary C. Cornia, David L. Sjoquist & Lawrence C. Walters, "Sales and Use Tax Simplification and Voluntary Compliance," *Public Budgeting & Finance* 24 (1) (2004): 1–31.
109. David Brunori, "The Politics of State Taxation: Now More Than Ever MTC Is Needed," Tax Analysts Reference: 1999 STT 152-28 (3 August 1999).
110. Edward B. Laverty & Kenneth T. Palmer, "State and Local Governmental Interest Groups before the Supreme Court: Implications for Intergovernmental Policy," *Public Administration Quarterly* 24 (4) (2001): 522–537.

incentives.[111] The question is whether the states are willing and able to move beyond this stage of competition and forgo some of these policy options by agreeing to more uniformity. Although all states share a budgetary interest in the success of the SSTP, there is no reason to assume that they agree on the steps needed to simplify the sales and use taxes. In addition, internal state politics play a vital role as well. During the initial planning stages of the SSTP, the NCSL adopted a proposal that was different from the SSTP document that had been drafted by the NGA, the FTA, and the MTC. Moreover, political party affiliation may have an impact at the state level as well. Most Republicans seem opposed to taxing Internet or remote sales, whereas most Democrats support it. Nevertheless, and this signifies how complex and unpredictable local politics can be, the strongest supporter of the streamlining project is the Republican governor of Utah.

What is politically significant is that three politically and economically important states, California, Massachusetts and New York, are currently not participating in the project. This not only poses a challenge to but also may, in the end, compromise the success of the SSTP.

10.3.13. Conclusions

The Streamlining Project is an important development in creating a level economic playing field for all sellers, regardless of their location (within or outside a state's borders) and regardless of product format (physical or digitized). From a different perspective, it will prove to be essential as well to the success of the states in securing congressional support for requiring remote vendors to collect use tax on their out-of-state sales. Nevertheless, it seems that the prevention of revenue loss is crucial for the states, more so than mitigating economic distortions. The states seem to be satisfied with the SSTP realizing a level of simplification just sufficient to obtain congressional support for their tax collection efforts. The positions taken by Congress and the Supreme Court concerning nexus have created a momentum for tax reform. It is regrettable that the states do not exploit this opportunity to fundamentally change their sales and use tax laws by broadening the tax base and eliminating clear flaws in the current legislation. Nevertheless, the SSTP may prove successful, provided sufficient incentives are created to induce the business community to cooperate.

111. Wallace E. Oates & Robert M. Schwab, "Economic Competition among Jurisdictions: Efficiency Enhancing or Distortion Inducing?," *Journal of Public Economics* 35 (3) (1998): 333–354; and Daphene A. Kenyon & John Kincaid, *Competition among States and Local Governments: Efficiency and Equity in American Federalism* (Washington, DC: The Urban Institute, 1991).

Chapter 11

Revenue Allocation within Federal and Common Markets

11.1. INTRODUCTION

Adopting separate VAT systems in subordinate jurisdictions belonging to a single economic entity is fraught with difficulties. Differences in tax bases, rates and legal definitions as well as potential jurisdiction disputes over cross-border transactions may create excessive compliance costs for businesses, trigger mistakes and confusion, and lead to double or double nontaxation. Tax coordination serves the purposes of supporting free trade, creating economies of scale, ensuring fair competition, preventing economic distortions, and realizing the optimal allocation of production factors and prosperity growth through the creation of comparative advantages (see the motives for creating the European common market, discussed in Section 10.2).

Discussions about tax reform occur in the United States on a regular basis, both in academic circles and at the political level. Over the years, many proposals have been made for the introduction of a federal consumption tax, in the form of a VAT, an RST, subtraction VATs or hybrid tax forms (see Section 7.3). None of the proposals offers a solution for coordinating a federal consumption tax with the states' sales and use taxes.

We start by presenting a short overview of the economic similarities of VAT and RST. In addition, the most important imperfections of the RSTs as currently applied at the subnational level in the United States are described (Section 11.2).

No decision has been made yet to introduce a federal consumption tax in the United States, neither is there consensus as to the preferred system of such a tax, but questions would arise concerning the cooperation of federal and subnational governments and how revenue should be allocated among the states, especially in relation to cross-border sales.

Revenue allocation among states and between the federal and subnational levels of governments is not an issue limited to the United States. Canada has a national VAT and subnational sales taxes, and both India and Brazil have consumption taxes at the federal and state levels. Last, but not least, the EU has a harmonized system of VAT, the revenue of which is shared among the Member States and the supranational level. Revenue allocation includes the problem of finding an appropriate methodology to deal with the taxation of cross-border transactions on the basis of the destination principle. For the purpose of providing context, we take a closer look at the theoretical models for cooperation between federal and states consumption taxes in Section 11.3. In Section 11.4, we discuss several proposals, submitted over the years, for the allocation of VAT revenue, particularly as regards interstate sales. All these proposals have in common that they revolve around their respective solution for handling tax rate variation among the states. Most proposals, such as the EU clearinghouse (Section 11.4.1), viable integrated VAT (VIVAT) (Section 11.4.2) and compensating VAT (C-VAT) (Section 11.4.3) are limited to interstate relationships, The dual VAT system (Section 11.4.4) and digital VAT (D-VAT) (Section 11.4.5) offer solutions for the coordination of federal and state consumption taxes.

The focus of this chapter is on the United States because introducing a federal consumption tax while RSTs are currently levied at the state level offers an excellent opportunity to fine-tune the tax system in respect to the taxation of private consumption. The discussion, however, is equally relevant to other federal and common markets. The premises of the final section of this chapter are that the states' and the federal governments will find common ground and create a uniform consumption tax system, which is briefly described in Section 11.4.6.1. This model has the advantage that it offers an integrated consumption tax system at both the national and subnational levels. Because a single tax rate would be introduced, complexities caused by rate variation among states and cross-border sales issues are avoided. We will demonstrate how a single national tax rate could be calculated (Section 11.4.6.2) and, most importantly, how revenue could be accurately allocated to the federal government and among the individual states on the basis of macroeconomic data (Section 11.4.6.3).

11.2. RST VERSUS VAT

RSTs and VATs offer two economically equivalent alternatives for collecting a broad, indirect transaction-based tax on consumptive expenditure. The taxes differ only in how they are administered. In its most common variant, the credit invoice method, the VAT is levied at each stage of the manufacturing and distribution chain, regardless of whether the sale is made to a private consumer or to another business. The seller has to remit the tax thus collected to the revenue service. The tax due by sellers is generally referred to as output VAT. To ensure that the VAT is a tax on final consumption, and not a business tax, business purchasers have the right to deduct the tax they have incurred on their purchases (input VAT) from the tax due on their sales (output VAT). For example, if a business buys components for USD 800 and sells the final product for USD 1,000, its value added, therefore, being USD 200, it will pay VAT (let us say at 20%) to the component seller for an amount of USD 160 and will charge USD 200 in VAT to its purchaser. However, it will remit USD 40 (200 – 160) to the revenue service, which constitutes exactly 20% of its added value. Through the credit mechanism, businesses are effectively relieved from the tax and only final consumption by private households remains taxed.

RSTs in the United States do not have a deduction mechanism (tax credit) to relieve businesses from input taxes. To ensure that sales tax is, indeed, a consumption tax, the sales tax systems as applied in the United States seek to exempt business-to-business sales through suspension certificates. Most commonly, US sales tax systems apply exemptions for B2B sales when goods are bought for resale[1] or for materials and component parts to be physically incorporated into other goods destined to be sold (known as the "physical ingredient" rule). For example, leather sold to a shoe manufacturer is exempt under the latter rule. However, a wide range of business assets remain that are subject to the tax, even though they are used to produce final products that are themselves subject to the sales tax.[2] Research shows that final consumers contribute approximately 60% of the states' sales tax revenues, and the remaining 40% comes from businesses.[3] The business share of all general sales taxes measured for 2003 varied from 28% in Idaho to 67% in Louisiana and exceeded 50% in eight states, with a national average of 42.8%. In 2006, the national average was 44%.[4]

With some minor exceptions, although their share in the total consumption has risen considerably over the years, services remain outside the scope of sales tax. This is especially distortive where services can be substituted for goods, for example, the sale of books and music in digitalized form instead of on a physical carrier or in physical format. In addition, to reduce the assumed regressivity of the sales tax, many goods, such as food and other groceries, medical, educational and

1. The definition of "resale" may vary from state to state. Some states apply the resale exemption under the restriction that the goods must be resold in the same physical form as they were purchased, which narrows the scope of the exemption considerably. See Perry D. Quick & Michael J. McKee, "Sales Tax on Services: Revenue or Reform?," *National Tax Journal* 41 (1988): 398.
2. See Robert F. van Brederode, "Introduction to the US State Sales and Use Taxes", *International VAT Monitor* 18 (4) (2007): 270–276. For a more extensive treatise, see Tax Foundation, *State and Local Sales Taxes*, Research Publication no. 23 (New York: Tax Foundation, 1970); and John F. Due & John L. Mikesell, *Sales Taxation: State and Local Structure and Administration,* 2nd ed. (Washington, DC: The Urban Institute, 1994).
3. Raymond J. Ring, "Consumer's Share and Producer's Share of the General Sales Tax", *National Tax Journal* 52 (1) (1999): 79–90.
4. Robert Cline, Tom Neubig & Andrew Phillips, *Total State and Local Business Taxes: Fifty-State Estimates for Fiscal Year 2006* (study prepared by Ernst & Young LLP in conjunction with the Council on State Taxation, February 2007).

other goods and services, are exempt, that is, not taxed.[5] Because of exemptions for most services and a large number of goods, only about 37% of the total consumption in the United States is actually subject to sales tax.[6] In conclusion, the design of the sales taxes in the United States fails with respect to scope because it covers only a portion of total consumption.

A separate problem is mail-order and Internet sales. Cross-border purchases are subject to use tax in the state of destination, but voluntary compliance, especially by private consumers, is extremely low. States cannot require firms engaged in these types of sales to collect use taxes from their customers unless they have sufficient nexus, that is physical presence in the state.[7] In relation to remote sales, the US General Accounting Office (GAO) estimates the revenue erosion at between USD 2.6 billion and USD 20.4 billion. The midpoint of that range, USD 11.5 billion, is about 4% of total revenue that states expect to receive from sales and use taxes.[8] Estimates by private researchers of the loss range from USD 15.4 billion to USD 16.1 billion for 2003, and they project a revenue loss ranging from USD 21.5 billion to USD 33.6 billion for 2008.[9] Equally important are the detrimental economic consequences of nontaxation, at least by prevailing practice, of distance sales. Nontaxation of distance sales violates the principle of neutrality that should exist between different methods of production and distribution of goods, and should apply to consumer preferences as well. Clearly, traditional retailers are placed at a competitive disadvantage when distance sales of similar goods remain untaxed. Although, from a legal perspective, distance sales are taxed through the imposition of use tax, in practice, because of the significant lack of compliance, no taxation effectively takes place.

---

5. The rules on exemptions vary widely. Food for off-premises consumption is generally exempt, whereas restaurant meals are not. About half the states exempt prescription drugs, sometimes also nonprescription drugs and orthopedic appliances. Clothing is exempt in a few states and subject to a reduced rate in others. A large number of states exempt products subject to excise taxes, such as gasoline. Utilities supplies, such as gas, electricity, telephone and water; local transportation; repair services; laundry and dry cleaning; hairstyling, barber shop and beauty parlor services; and general admissions (e.g., to zoos, museums or theaters) may all share in exempt treatment in a considerable number of states. Professional services, such as financial, accounting, legal and medical services, are generally exempt. In addition to these objective exemptions, also subjective exemptions apply: purchases made by entities of the federal, state and local government and by philanthropic, religious and educational organizations are also generally exempt.
6. Donald Bruce & William F. Fox, "E-commerce in the Context of Declining State Sales Tax Bases", *National Tax Journal* 53. (4) (February 2000): 1373–1388; Robert Cline, John Mikesell, Tom Neubig & Andrew Phillips, *Sales Taxation on Business Inputs*, Council on State Taxation (25 January 2005): 1.
7. *National Bellas Hess v. Dept. of Revenue for the State of Illinois*, 386 US 753 (1967), and *Quill Corporation v. North Dakota*, 504 US 298 (1992).
8. General Accounting Office, "Sales Taxes: Electronic Commerce Growth Presents Challenge, Revenue Losses Are Uncertain", GAO Report OCE-00-165 (Washington, DC: GAO, 30 June 2000), 21.
9. Donald Bruce & William F. Fox, State and Local Sales Tax Revenue Loss from E-commerce: Estimates as of July 2004 (University of Tennessee, July 2004), 5.

In principle, the two apparently dissimilar taxes differ only (but importantly) in the mechanism they use to relieve business purchases from tax, allowing the tax to apply to consumption. In practice, the sales taxes as currently applied in the United States are imperfect because of insufficient relief for business inputs and the narrow tax base. However, these flaws are not inherent to sales taxes but the result of poor design only. It is feasible to have a broad-based sales tax that provides relief to all business inputs. What is needed is a truly broad definition of business inputs. Certainly, that would lead to problems in the realm of definition, mixed use of products (both private and business), and change of use (from business to private and vice versa), but that is true for VAT as well. There is no reason to assume that an RST cannot be designed in a truly tax neutral manner similar to a VAT.

11.3. COOPERATION MODELS

If a federal consumption tax were introduced, regardless of whether it were a sales tax or a VAT, the core question would relate to tax coordination between the state sales taxes and the federal consumption tax. Several formats are, conceptually at least, feasible. The most important variations are the following. The federal consumption tax could be an independent tax levied in addition to state sales taxes; the federal tax could be levied as a surcharge on state sales taxes; or, the states could adopt the federal tax and levy their taxes as a surcharge on the federal tax. Last, but not least, the federal and state governments could join forces in designing a single combined consumption tax.

11.3.1. Separate Federal and Subnational Taxes

A separate national RST (NRST), levied independently from the state sales taxes and with its own tax base, rate, definitions, exemptions, and so forth, would complicate the work of state tax collection and increase the problems that businesses face in complying with multiple tax bases. Currently, forty-five states and the District of Columbia levy a form of sales tax. Moreover, thirty-three states permit local governments (counties and towns) to levy the tax, and additional sales taxes are now levied by about 7,500 local jurisdictions. Adding an additional governmental level of consumption taxation would increase the already excessive compliance costs for businesses.

Alternatively, the federal consumption tax could copy the tax base of the state sales taxes. This would strongly reduce the extra compliance cost generated by a federal tax. Basically, businesses would file a copy of their state sales tax return and remit the federal tax rate. In effect, the federal government would levy and administer forty-six different sales taxes, and in addition be required to levy its own design sales tax in the five states that currently do not have a sales tax. This does not seem to be a practical way to introduce a national consumption tax. A US federal tax piggybacked on the existing state taxes would be completely inappropriate for a national tax because of the considerable state-by-state differences in the tax. Attempting to levy a national tax as a supplement to state sales taxes would be ill advised because there is simply insufficient uniformity in what states tax and exclude to allow a linked federal tax to be fair and efficient. That seems to remain true even when the harmonization of state sales taxes under the streamlining project would be reasonably successful. As a result, certain sales of goods (and services) would be subject to federal consumption tax in one state but not in another, depending on the tax base formula of the individual states. This would violate the principle of equality.

Moreover, an NRST generally following the pattern of the state taxes would not be a general and uniform tax on consumption. State RSTs are partial consumption taxes and partial business purchase taxes. They exempt many household purchases of goods, are narrowly selective in their coverage of household service purchases, and apply to a wide array of business inputs, including the purchase of capital assets. This hybrid tax would not generate the performance enhancers on savings, investment and economic development that a uniform and general consumption tax would.

11.3.2. Federal Surcharge

The least change would occur when a federal tax would be levied as a surcharge on existing state taxes.[10] The US federal government could follow that path, matching the federal tax to each individual state tax and arranging for the states to collect on its behalf, which would reduce compliance costs for businesses and would simplify tax collection and enforcement. The federal consumption tax would still have the format of 46 different sales taxes and a separate design would still be required to cover sales in the states that do not have a sales tax. All the other objections and concerns mentioned under Section 11.3.1 would remain unsolved.

11.3.3. State Surcharge

Another possibility would be for the states and localities to adapt their sales taxes to the federal tax and levy a surcharge on the federal tax base. That would have the advantage of a common tax base for the nation as a whole, reducing compliance

10. In the EU, the VAT is levied as a national tax, but the Member States must remit a certain percentage of the tax base to the supranational level (the EU) on the basis of Decision 70/243 of 21 April 1970, OJ 1970, no. L 94, 19 et seq., which replaced contributions by the Member States as funding for the EU with direct income (own resources); see Section 10.2.4. However, the VAT charge is not a tax collected by the states from taxpayers on behalf of the EU, but rather a tax on the states themselves.

costs for firms significantly. In addition, it would improve the efficiency of the domestic market relative to the EU common market. In the past, the United States had an advantage over Europe because of large domestic market. There existed no single European market, but national domestic markets only, protected by national tariffs. This fragmentation hindered economic efficiency, but with the birth of the European Union, Europe's economic growth has been phenomenal. Taxation can play an important role in economic dominance. In the mid-seventeenth century, England was gaining the economic upper hand over rival France because England modernized its tax collecting system while France maintained an essentially feudal system inadequate to finance a modern state.[11] The higher degree of uniformity of its consumption tax system (VAT) provides the EU with an economic advantage. If the states and federal government would agree to use a common tax base for the purpose of consumption taxes, the United States would at once close that gap.

State and local surcharges, however, would still require firms to file sales tax returns in all states and local jurisdictions where they do business. The current problems with determining state tax jurisdiction over mail-order and Internet sales, in essence determined by the nexus standard of *Quill*, would remain, and it is feasible, if not likely, that these sales would become subject to the federal consumption tax only thus depriving the states of an important additional source of revenue (see Section 11.3.2) and maintaining the current detrimental effects on competitive neutrality. These problems would be resolved under a combined state and federal consumption tax system, basically imposing a single VAT or RST and developing a system to adequately distribute the revenues between the national and subnational levels of government.

Assuming that the federal consumption tax would have a broad base, including services, the states would benefit from this broader base as well, and the inequalities explained under Section 11.3.1 would disappear or at least be significantly reduced. We describe such a system in detail in Section 11.4.6.

11.4. AGGREGATE LEVEL OF REVENUE SHARING

11.4.1. EU Clearing House System

In the early 1990s, the European Commission proposed the definite VAT system under which intracommunity sales would be treated in the same way as domestic sales. International sales, for example, transactions with third countries, would remain subject to zero rating, but all other sales would be taxed at rates applicable

11. Mikael Priks, *Optimal Rent Extraction in Pre-industrial England and France: Default Risk and Monitoring Costs*, CESifo Working Paper Series no. 1464 (May 2005); Michael S. Kimmel, *Absolutism and Its Discontents: State and Society in Seventeenth-Century France and England* (New Brunswick, NJ, 1988).

Figure 20. Distribution Flow for Clearinghouse VAT

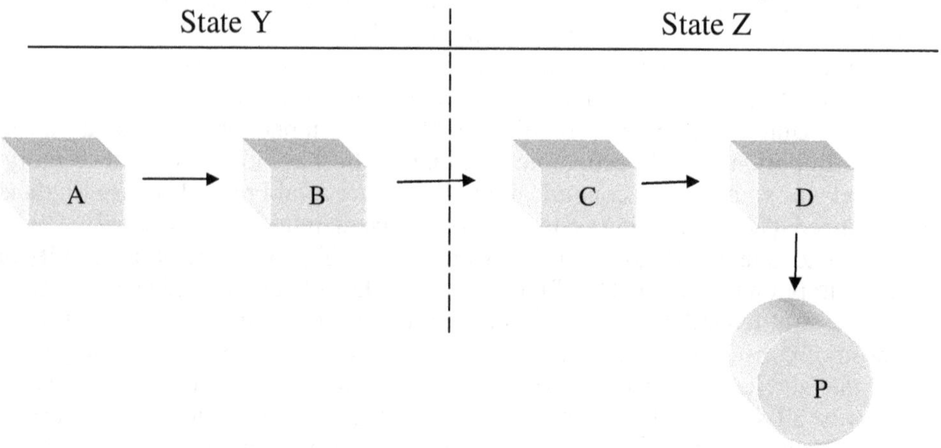

in the country of origin. A cross-border sale by a Portuguese seller to a Spanish customer, for instance, would be subject to Portuguese tax. Taxing cross-border sales within a common market has the benefit of retaining the collection chain and would reduce the possibilities for fraud. However, to retain the character of the VAT as a consumption tax, a taxable buyer should be eligible for a tax credit. Under the definite system, the buyer would deduct the tax paid on the foreign procurement as a credit from the output VAT due in his resident state. In our example the Spanish buyer would deduct Portuguese VAT from the output VAT due in Spain. In other words, Spain would refund tax to a resident business that has been collected by another state. Such a system would be to the advantage of net-exporting countries. This is prevented under the proposed definite system by creating a clearinghouse to reallocate revenues among the Member States to arrive, in essence, at accruing exactly the same revenue to Member States as currently is under the transitional arrangement of zero rating intracommunity transactions. Although this system has been identified as an origin tax, it is essentially hybrid in character because the revenue, via clearing, would accrue to the destination state.

Company A sells to company B located in the same state Y for USD 100 plus USD 19 in VAT. B makes a cross-border sale at USD 200 to C in state Z within the federation/common market. This sale is subject to the VAT in state Y, and B will add USD 38 to its price. B can deduct the VAT paid on the purchase from A and remits USD 19 to the taxing authorities. Subsequently, C sells for USD 300 to company D, which is also a resident of state Z. The VAT rate in state Z is 16%. C has to charge USD 48 in domestic VAT and remits (USD 48 – USD 38) = USD 10 to state Z revenue. Finally, D sells to private consumer P for USD 400 and has to charge USD 64 in VAT. D has to remit (USD 64 – USD 48) = USD 16 to the state revenue. As a result, the states receive together exactly 16% over the final consumer price, as demonstrated in Table 47.

Table 47. Tax Distribution under a Clearinghouse VAT

Seller	Sales Price	VAT	Total	Input Credit	To Treasury
A	100	19	119	—	19
B	200	38	238	19	19
C	300	48	348	38	10
D	400	64	464	48	16

Total tax receipts: Country Y: USD 38
Country Z: USD 26
USD 64

However, under the destination principle the total tax should have accrued to country Z. This is realized through a payment of USD 38 by country Y to the clearinghouse, which in turn pays the same amount to country Z.

Each cross-border transaction leads either to a payment obligation for a state or to a refund claim. Clearing between countries, of course, will take place not per transaction, but periodically. Figure 21 presents a simplified model of the clearinghouse with only four countries. To demonstrate the workings of the clearinghouse, all sales and purchases have the same value of USD 100; only the tax rate is different.

Figure 21. VAT Clearinghouse

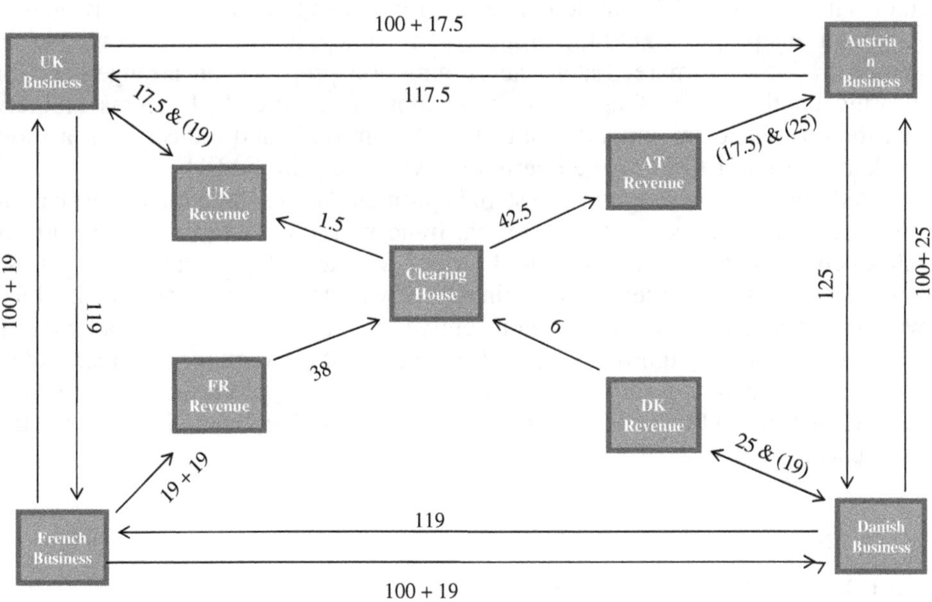

A UK business buys product from a French company and pays USD 100 plus USD 19 in French VAT. The French company also sells product for the same amount to a Danish customer. The French company has to remit the tax for a total of USD 38 to the French revenue. The customers deduct the French VAT paid from their output VAT due in respectively the UK and Denmark. The UK business also makes sales to an Austrian company for USD 100 plus USD 17.5 in tax, which it remits to the UK revenue. The Austrian company also sourced product from the Danish business for USD 100 plus USD 25 in Danish VAT. The Austrian company receives a refund from the Danish revenue for all the foreign tax paid at USD 42.5. The Danish business has to remit USD 25 to the Danish revenue but receives a credit for the VAT paid to the French business.

The position of the respective revenues relative to the clearinghouse is as follows. The French revenue received a total of USD 38 in tax in relation to cross-border sales to other Member States and needs to remit this to the clearinghouse. The Danish revenue collected USD 25 on a cross-border sale and credited USD 19 for French VAT paid by a resident business. As a result, the Danish revenue has to pay USD 6 to the clearinghouse. The UK revenue received USD 17.5 on a cross-border sale and credited USD 19 in French VAT, and will, therefore, receive a refund of USD 1.5 from the clearinghouse. The Austrian revenue only refunded foreign VAT and will be compensated for USD 42.5 in foreign VAT it refunded to the Austrian business.

In reality, clearing involves quite an administrative constraint due to the shear volume of transactions. Within the EU, several billion cross-border transactions take place annually between the 27 Member States. The original proposal was for each Member State to claim repayment of the total input tax, paid to domestic traders in relation to their intracommunity procurement on the basis of invoices.[12] Although this proposal held the promise of accuracy, it was also perceived as an administrative nightmare. Later, the commission proposed an arrangement for clearing on the basis of aggregate consumption statistics.[13] It seems unlikely that there is sufficient support, political and from trade and industry, for a short implementation of the so-called definite VAT system in the EU.

Although the clearinghouse system is promoted as a safeguard against carousel fraud, it is an illusion to believe that fraud will altogether disappear with its introduction. Other forms of fraud will surface. The advantage of the clearinghouse system is that cross-border sales within the EU will no longer be zero rated, which would, indeed, remove an important incentive for carousel or missing trader fraud. However, as long as significant rate differences exist between the Member States, it remains lucrative to remit false purchase invoices to suggest procurement in high tax jurisdictions, while in fact the product was bought locally, and cash in the tax difference.

12. COM (87)322/2 of 21 August 1987.
13. Commission 1996.

11.4.2. Viable Integrated VAT

The VIVAT model has been developed for cross-border trade within the EU[14] but can be applied by any federal system where the states levy consumption taxes.[15] The obvious purpose is to alleviate the problems currently encountered by traders and tax authorities when dealing with cross-border sales, while at the same time preserving a certain level of fiscal autonomy for the states or at the subnational level through the application of the destination principle.

Under the VIVAT proposal, international sales will be relieved from tax through zero rating, but intracommunity sales would be taxed at a uniform rate. That same uniform rate would also apply to domestic transactions between taxable persons, but each state would retain full autonomy to determine the tax rates for domestic sales to consumers. In essence, this system combines a uniform VAT with a subnational RST. Under the current VAT system in the EU, sellers must administratively distinguish between domestic supplies, intracommunity supplies and export supplies. Under VIVAT, a seller must distinguish between export supplies, transactions with registered customers and sales to private consumers. The VIVAT retains the audit and collection trail, generally perceived as a beneficial element of VAT, and relies on a clearing system to allocate the tax to the destination country.

The rate for the B2B sales, the intermediate rate, could be set at whatever level desired by the states, but higher rates provide more protection for revenues at the early stages of the supply chain. A rate higher than the retail rate applicable to sales to consumers is possible, but this would lead to refunds for retailers in the case where the difference between the intermediate rate and the retail rate is more than the average profit margin of the retailer. In the example in Figure 22, assume an intermediate rate of 10% and a retail rate for sales to consumers of 15%.

The application can best be explained by demonstrating the supply chain covering consecutive transactions in two different jurisdictions.

Company A sells for USD 100 to company B located in the same state Y, and company A will collect 10% tax from B by increasing the price with the VAT. Company B sells for USD 200 to C located in another state and applies the same VAT rate of 10% because C is a taxable person. Company B deducts the tax paid to A as a credit from the tax due on the sale and remits the difference (USD 20 – USD 10) = USD 10 to the tax authorities. Company C sells to company D for USD 300 and charges USD 30 in tax. C remits (USD 30 – USD 20) = USD 10 to the tax authorities. Finally, D sells to a private consumer P for USD 400 and increases the price with 15% tax. D remits (USD 60 – USD 30) = USD 30 to the tax authorities.

---

14. Michael Keen & S. Smith, "Viva VIVAT!" *International Tax and Public Finance* 7 (6) (2000): 741–751; and Michael Keen, *VIVAT, C-VAT and All That: New Forms of Value-Added Tax for Federal Systems*, IMF Working Paper (WP/00/83) (Washington, DC: IMF, April 2000), also published in the *Canadian Tax Journal* 48 (2) (2000): 409–424.
15. According to Richard M. Bird & Pierre-Pascal Gendron, *The VAT in Developing and Transitional Countries* (Cambridge, 2007), 125, n. 28, the VIVAT system is not very applicable in developing countries.

Figure 22. Distribution Flow for VIVAT

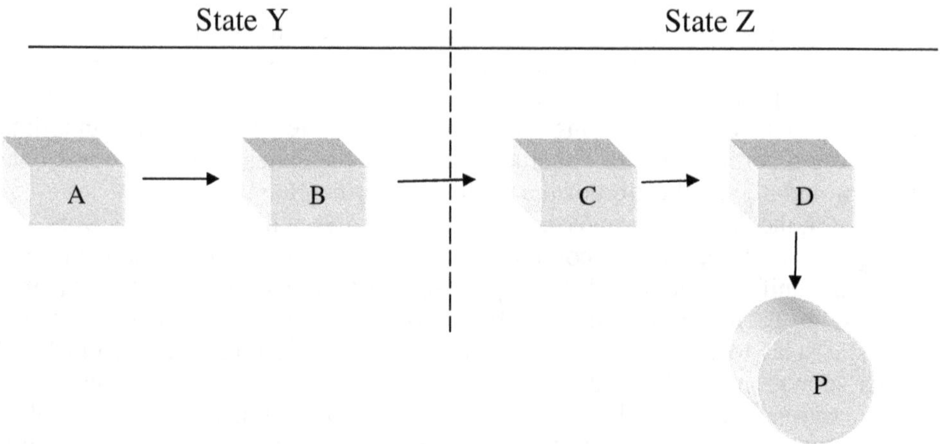

The result of all tax actually remitted in the course of the chain is the collection of USD 60, which is exactly 15%, the statutory retail rate of the final sales price (see Table 48).

Table 48. Tax Distribution under a VIVAT

Seller	Sales Price	Tax	Total	Input Credit	To Treasury
A	100	10	110	—	10
B	200	20	220	10	10
C	300	30	330	20	10
D	400	60	460	30	30
Total					60

Clearing will be required between the states within a federation or common market to ensure the realization of the destination principle. In our example, state Y needs to pay the tax it collected on the sales from A to B and from B to C for a total of USD 20 to state Z which, in addition to the tax directly collected by state Z on the sales between C and D and from D to the consumer, would give state Z the required revenue of USD 60.

VIVAT offers the advantage of preserving the VAT chain in cross-border sales within federal or common markets. In addition, it provides compliance symmetry regarding B2B sales, where it removes the distinction between domestic and intrastate sales, at the same time it creates an asymmetry by treating B2C sales differently from B2B sales.

The VIVAT shares strong similarities with the C-VAT, discussed in the next section.

11.4.3. Compensating VAT

The C-VAT tax is focused on assuring the actual taxation of interstate sales.[16] Assume that in a federal state there exists a federal or central consumption tax and subnational (state) consumption taxes. At the state or subnational level, independent rates can be imposed, but interstate transactions, that is, cross-border sales within the federation, will be subjected to a compensating tax, the C-VAT. In short, individual states would zero rate both international and interstate sales, but the latter would be subject to federal consumption tax and the C-VAT. Domestic sales are subject to federal tax and state consumption tax. International sales would be zero rated altogether and interstate sales would be subject to federal VAT and C-VAT. Registered buyers in the state of arrival would be eligible to a credit for C-VAT paid against the federal consumption tax. The subsequent domestic sale would be subject to the tax in the state of arrival. If we assume that the domestic tax rate is 10% in all states, the federal VAT is 15% and the C-VAT is 10%, the chain of transactions shown in Figure 23 will demonstrate that the total tax revenue received both at the state and federal levels is exactly equal to the tax rate applied to the final sales price.

Company A sells to company B located in the same state Y for USD 100 plus USD 10 in state tax and USD 15 in federal tax. B makes an interstate sale at USD 200 to C in state Z within the federation. This sale is zero rated from state Y's

Figure 23. Distribution Flow for C-VAT

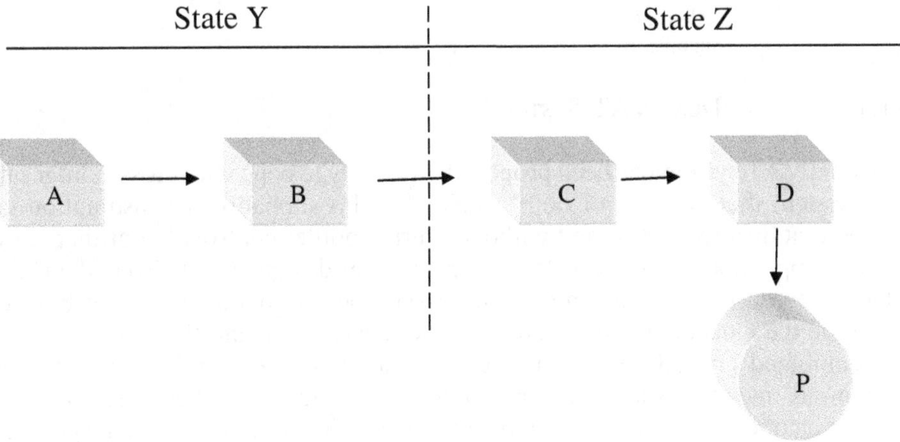

16. Charles E. McLure, "Implementing Subnational VATs on Internal Trade: The Compensating VAT (C-VAT)", *International Tax and Public Finance* 7 (6) (2000): 723–740; and R. Varsano, "Subnational Taxation and Treatment of Interstate Trade in Brazil: Problems and Proposed Solution", in *Decentralization and Accountability of the Public Sector,* eds. S.J. Burki & G. Perry, Annual World Bank Conference on Development in Latin America and the Caribbean (Washington, DC: World Bank, 2000).

perspective but will be subject to federal tax at USD 30 and C-VAT at USD 20. B can deduct from the federal and C-VAT taxes due on the later sale the amount of federal tax paid to A. As a result, B receives a refund from the state revenue for USD 10 and pays (USD 50 – USD 15) = USD 35 to the federal government. Subsequently, C sells to company D, which is also a resident of state Z. C has to charge USD 30 in domestic state sales tax and remit USD 30 to state Z's revenue. C also receives a refund of USD 5 from the federal government because his input tax is higher than the output VAT. D subsequently sells to private consumer P for USD 400 and has to charge USD 40 in state tax and USD 60 in federal tax. D has to remit (USD 40 – USD 30) = USD 10 to the state revenue and (USD 60 – USD 45) = USD 15 to the federal revenue. As a result, the states receive exactly 10% and the federal government receives exactly 15% over the final consumer price, as demonstrated in Table 49.

Table 49. Tax Distribution under a C-VAT

Seller	Sales Price	State VAT	Federal VAT	C-VAT	Total Tax: State	Total Tax: Federal/C-VAT
A	100	10	15	—	10	15
B	200	—	30	20	(10)	50 – 15 = 35
C	300	30	45	—	30	45 – 50 = (5)
D	400	40	60	—	40 – 30 = 10	60 – 45 = 15

Total tax receipts: State Y: 0
Federal: 60
State Z: 40

11.4.4. Dual VAT System

The dual VAT system has been proposed especially to cope with cross-border sales in a system that consists of both a federal and a subnational consumption tax, imposed at different rates, and without internal border controls.[17] For that reason it could apply not only in Canada, for which it was designed, but also in the United States when a federal consumption tax would be introduced, or in the EU. It is based on the Quebec model where both the federal GST and the provincial VAT are combined and administered at the subnational level. Under the dual VAT system all interstate sales are zero rated. Imports from another state within the federation or common market will be taxed when the importer resells the goods. In

17. Richard M. Bird & Pierre-Pascal Gendron, "Dual VATs and Cross-border Trade: Two Problems, One Solution?" *International Tax and Public Finance* 5 (1998): 429–442; and Richard M. Bird & Pierre-Pascal Gendron, "C-VAT, VIVAT, and Dual VAT: Vertical 'Sharing' and Interstate Trade," *International Trade and Public Finance* 7 (2000): 753–761. See also, Richard M. Bird & Pierre-Pascal Gendron, *The VAT in Developing and Transitional Countries* (Cambridge, 2007), 152 et seq., where the authors compare the dual VAT with the C-VAT.

Figure 24. Distribution Flow for Dual VAT System

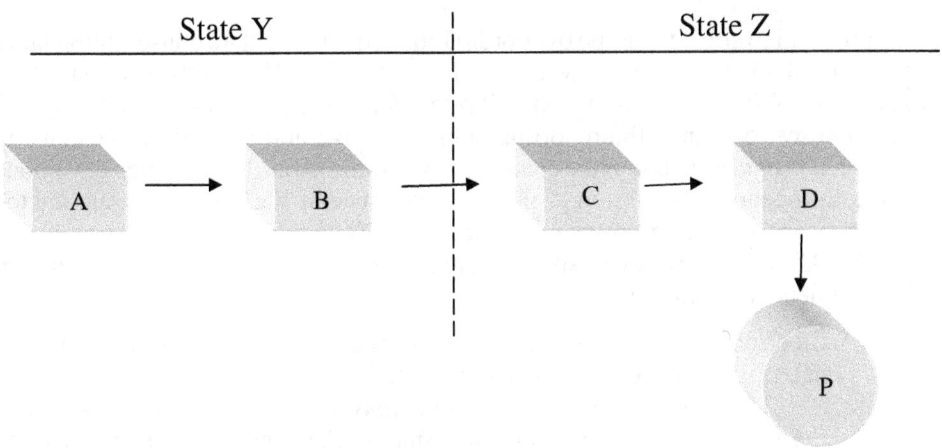

Figure 24, we demonstrate how the dual VAT system works on the basis of the same transaction flow used to describe the C-VAT.

Company A sells goods for USD 100 to company B located in the same state Y. The dual tax VAT rate in state Y is 25%, consisting of a 10% state component and a 15% federal component. Therefore, A has to charge USD 125 to B, which the latter can deduct as an input tax credit. B exports the goods for USD 200 to C in state Z, which is a zero rated sale. As a result, B will actually receive a refund of the tax paid to A because the tax due on the outputs is zero. As a registered business, C does not have to account for any VAT regarding his purchase from B nor is he eligible for any input tax credit because the purchase was zero rated. The subsequent sale to D for USD 300 is subject to the dual VAT rate in his state Z, which is 27%, consisting of a federal component of 15% and a state component of 12%. C will be charging USD 300 + USD 81 VAT = USD 381. In turn, D will be able to recuperate the tax paid to C as an input credit because he is making a domestic sale to consumer P for USD 400 + USD 108 = USD 508 (see Table 50).

Table 50. Tax Distribution under a Dual VAT System

Seller	Sales Price	Tax	Total	To Treasury
A	100	25	125	25
B	200	0	200	(25)
C	300	81	381	81
D	400	108	508	108 − 81 = 27

Total tax receipts: State Y: 0
Federal: 60
State Z: 48

11.4.5. Digital VAT

One proposal to solve the issue of coordination federal and state consumption taxes is by introducing a federal-level digital (D) VAT.[18] The D-VAT is based on existing VAT systems, making explicit reference to the ABA Model or Vatopia,[19] and proposes to change the reporting, administrative and payment provisions. In essence, it proposes to adopt the electronic tax administration principles developed by the European Commission,[20] in combination with the third-party automated collection and reporting provisions of the SSUTA.

D-VAT identifies seven specific areas where modifications from standard VAT models are required.

(1) Electronic notices, returns, periodic and recapitulative statements, tax determinations and payments mandated.

The D-VAT would require all taxpayers to file electronically,[21] with the exception of special rules for small traders and for invoices issued to final consumers (see item 7).

(2) Third-party invoicing, tax calculation, return-filing authorized.

This is a two-part modification, combining elements from the EU VAT and the SSUTA. From the first, D-VAT borrows the provision that allows third-party invoicing.[22] From the latter, it adopts the provisions dealing with CSPs and CASs as discussed in Section 10.3.7.

According to Ainsworth, these concepts are more effective within the D-VAT than under the SSUTA because of the "self-policing" character of a credit invoice VAT. Buyers and sellers have an incentive to assure correct determinations in a VAT, whereas under the SSUTA the accuracy of the digital record depends on state oversight of the CSP or the CAS.

(3) Use of uniform product and service identifier codes.

The D-VAT would require the digital identification of each good or service sold on the basis of existing product codes used for trade reporting purposes. These product codes need to be mentioned on the periodical VAT return and other statements and would be available to the taxing authorities.

---

18. Richard T. Ainsworth, *The Digital VAT (D-VAT)*, Boston University, School of Law, Working Paper Series, Law and Economics, no. 06-22. Also published in *Virginia Tax Review* 25 (2006): 875–927.
19. Vatopia is a VAT model developed by Alan Schenk and included as Appendix B in Alan Schenk & Oliver Oldman, *Value Added Tax: A Comparative Approach* (New York, Cambridge University Press, 2007).
20. Council Directive 2001/115/EC of 20 December 2001, O.J. L.15 (2002), 24 et seq., with a view to simplifying, modernizing and harmonizing the conditions laid down for invoicing regarding the VAT.
21. This provision would essentially adopt the reporting requirement under Art. 250(2) of Directive 2006/112 except that electronic filing would not be elective.
22. Article 220 of Directive 2006/112.

(4) For the United States, state RST piggybacking encouraged.

The D-VAT would encourage states to piggyback on the federal database. However, the states would be able to retain their fiscal autonomy and there is no need for them to copy the federal tax system or tax base, although they could. Copying only the federal database would certainly contribute to minimizing or avoiding the controversy in the United States revolving around fiscal federalism.

As a multistage consumption tax, the D-VAT will record goods and services transactions along the whole supply chain, not only on transactions between retailers and final consumers. For that reason, the federal database will be more accurate and comprehensive than the information that can be subtracted from the retail state sales tax base. In turn, this would benefit the states in their verification efforts.

(5) State access to the federal database at a national level.

The federal database would contain information regarding the names and addresses of customers, bill-to and ship-to locations, which would enable states to identify sales made to consumers within their state, regardless of where the seller is located. This has the additional benefit that states can enforce use tax compliance in cases where the seller cannot be obliged to collect tax as the result of the *Quill* decision. Congressional action would no longer be needed to close this loophole in tax collection (see Sections 9.6.1.3 and 9.6.1.6).

(6) Digital relief from the regressivity of taxing consumption.

The assumed regressivity of a VAT (see Section 4.4.2) leads to calls for providing relief to low-income households. Generally, a VAT cannot easily accommodate that, and measurements designed to provide such relief have proven to be inaccurate. Most commentators believe that it is better to keep the VAT "pure" and provide relief through tax expenditures elsewhere.[23] The D-VAT enables accurate targeting of households in need of assistance and support to neutralize the regressive effects of VAT. It can target both eligible persons and eligible transactions. When states piggyback the federal database, this can be accomplished at both levels of government. The idea is to remove the tax from selective transactions (such as clothing, certain foods and medical or educational services, identified via the product codes) through the use of a procurement card issued to eligible low-income household members, which would allow them to make zero rated[24] purchases of these items. It would constitute a simple, straightforward and flexible system of providing relief,

23. The ABA Model VAT, for that very reason, does not provide any relief from the assumed regressive effect and suggests that such relief should be accommodated outside the VAT regime.
24. To allow the seller to fully recover input VAT regardless of whether a sale is made to a low-income person or a regular customer.

accommodating tax policy needs insofar, of course, as one truly believes a VAT to be regressive.

(7) Small business and final consumer exemptions added.

The D-VAT provides for an exemption of small traders from the mandatory electronic filing requirements but not from taxing their sales. This is to prevent an unreasonable burden associated with digital compliance. For those businesses, traditional paper compliance would remain the norm.

A second exemption regards sales directly to final consumers. Although retailers would be required to keep digital records, they would be allowed to present their customers with paper receipts (such as supermarket or department stores' sales slips). This makes sense because final consumers do not have to file reports or consumption tax returns with the tax authorities.

11.4.6. Combined Federal and Subnational Sales Tax

The combined federal and subnational sales tax variant tries to unite the best of two worlds. It is an attempt to create a straightforward system of consumption tax with low administrative and compliance costs, comprehensibly levied at the national and subnational level at an integral, single rate, while maintaining sufficient tax autonomy for the subnational level. In essence, it is a variation of the system currently applied in Germany, where the VAT revenue is shared between the federal and subnational governments, in the sense that the states (Länder) receive some of the revenue on a formula basis. In this section, we apply the variant to the US situation, but it could serve as a model for other federal and common markets as well. A truly national consumption tax would be designed at a single rate, which would include the weighted average of the state and local sales taxes. A single tax for federal, state and local purposes would significantly reduce the administrative and compliance efforts and costs. Businesses would file a single return to cover all their sales made in the United States in a given tax period. Economic neutrality could be realized by broadening the tax base, that is, including services and eliminating or reducing preferential treatment. Taxing mail-order and Internet sales would also become feasible because the tax rate nationwide is the same, and tax allocation among the states would occur after collection. Nexus issues would disappear as will be explained in Sections 11.4.6.1 and 11.4.6.3. The economic distortions and inequalities as described in Section 11.3.1 would disappear. A combined federal and state tax would improve the overall efficiency of the domestic market. Economies of scale would arise in relation to public finance when design and management would be elevated to the federal level, and revenue distribution, on the basis of a preagreed-on formula, would flow from federal to state government and from state to local government. The economic benefits may be obvious, but politically this option is controversial. Clearly, states would be hesitant to participate, fearing loss of tax autonomy. However, the most important decisions regarding whether to introduce a state consumption tax and the level of taxation (the tax rate) would remain the prerogative of the states. The tax base and the overall design would be determined at the national level. In this section we assume that the states will accept a combined consumption tax despite the loss of autonomy because of the obvious economic advantages and the potential revenue increase such a national tax would offer.

11.4.6.1. Brief Description of the Combined Tax System

For the purpose of this discussion, it is irrelevant which type of consumption tax is selected (VAT, RST or other). Nor is it necessary to elaborate on each and every technical detail because the focus is on tax allocation methodology and tax rate calculation. A brief overview, however, is required to provide a certain minimal level of context.

The national tax would have a broad base, thus eliminating the economic distortions of the current state sales taxes. The national consumption tax would provide for a mechanism through which businesses would receive full relief for the tax paid on their inputs. Of course, full relief is not entirely without problems and potential risks of fraud. However, a best-practice approach should be able to fine-tune arrangements for problem areas, such as mixed use (e.g., both private and business use) and change of use (e.g., from business to private or vice versa). In addition, special arrangements are required for financial services, real property, secondhand goods sales, returned goods and trade-ins. Based on the experience under the US sales taxes of the states, as well as the experience with avoidance and evasion schemes in use under consumption taxes in other countries, it is relatively straightforward to identify risk industries and to profile taxpayer groups that are more likely inclined to take a liberal view regarding their obligations to comply. The tax could be administered by the states or, alternatively, by the federal government. From a tax collection perspective that does not make a principle difference. Tax collection by the states offers the benefit of tax administration by agencies that are experienced with a consumption tax. The states that currently do not have a sales tax could either introduce one or decline to do so, in which case the tax administration and collection in these states would fall on the federal government or the tax agency of another state as a subcontractor of the former.

In addition, mail-order and Internet sales would simply be taxed at the single rate. All mail-order and Internet sales to US residents would be taxable. In cases where the tax is administered by the states, mail-order and Internet sales need to be reported to the state in which the seller is resident. Were the tax to be administered at the federal level, these sales need to be reported to the federal agency charged with its administration. Special rules need to be determined for sales by foreign-based companies. It would be feasible, for example, that foreign-based mail-order and Internet sellers do not need to register but will be given the opportunity to do so. Goods from outside the United States would be included in the customs declaration and taxed at the time and point of entry. Most of these goods would be handled by third-party carriers such as UPS and FedEx, who would be obliged to pay the tax on importation and would in turn charge the tax to the customer on delivery, unless the tax had been charged by the foreign seller to the US resident, and the foreign seller is registered for consumption tax in the United States. Services will be included in the tax base. Jurisdiction rules need to be developed to ensure that services supplied to US residents by foreign service suppliers are deemed taxable in the United States. Coordination with trade partners will be required in this respect to prevent double taxation and double nontaxation. In case the customer is a registered taxable person for consumption tax purposes, it would be possible to reverse the tax liability to the customer. For sales to private consumers, mail-order and Internet sellers would be required to register if and when their sales to the United States exceed a certain *de minimis* threshold. Similar rules already exist in the EU for VAT purposes and seem to work satisfactorily. The current problem with mail-order and Internet sales is that they escape taxation where nexus is absent. When a consumption tax is levied at the national level, nexus with a particular state becomes irrelevant. What remains is the necessity to properly allocate the revenue of these sales among the states. Tax allocation is dealt with in Section 11.4.6.3.

States would still determine the tax rate for their state, even under a single rate national tax, and be allowed to change the rate effective January 1 of the next year.

11.4.6.2. Calculation of the Single National Tax Rate

The national tax rate (**t***n*) will compose of a federal rate (**t***f*) and a weighted average states rate (**wat***s*). The federal rate will depend on the revenue that the federal government needs to generate. It is feasible that the federal tax will serve the purpose of generating additional revenue or replacing existing taxes, for instance personal and corporate income taxes, payroll taxes or other taxes. The fair tax proposals, introduced in Congress every year since 1999, are a good example of initiatives to replace income-type taxes with a consumption-type tax.[25] Clearly, if a national sales tax serves to replace existing taxes (on a budget-neutral basis), as envisioned under the Fair Tax Act, the federal rate will likely be more than 35% on an exclusive basis,[26] and a combined federal/state rate could be more than 40%, a rate sufficiently high to raise concerns of tax evasion and fraud. It is also possible, that the federal tax will serve as both an additional tax and as a replacement for other taxes. This is not the place to have a detailed discussion on the benefits and

25. It was introduced for the last time in 2007 to the 110th Cong. HR 25/S 1025 (the Fair Tax Act of 2007) was introduced by, respectively, Representative John Linder (R-GA) with 68 cosponsors in the House on 1 April 2007 and by Senator Saxby Chambliss (R-GA) with 4 cosponsors in the Senate on 29 March 2007.

26. Supporters of the fair tax proposals quote a 23% tax-inclusive tax rate, which is 30% on a tax-exclusive basis. Taking into account a reasonable assumption of base erosion of 20%, calculations in academic research for the appropriate tax rate range between 35% and 40%. See Robert F. van Brederode, "Towards a Federal Consumption Tax," *International VAT Monitor* 19 (2) (2008): 114–120.

setbacks of either choice. In this section, it is assumed that the federal tax will be levied as an additional tax at a rate of 10%.

Calculation of the states tax rate, that is, a single rate for all states combined, is relatively complicated. Thirty-three states allow local jurisdictions to levy sales taxes in addition to the state tax. The local tax level needs to be included in an overall state tax rate. When revenue (*R*) is determined by applying the statutory tax rate (***t***) to total taxable consumption (*C*), that is $tC = R$, the combined local and state tax rate for a given state can be calculated by dividing total combined sales tax revenue in a state by total taxable consumptive expenditure:

$$t = \frac{R}{C}$$

If we assume that the new national tax will not be distorted by any exemptions, which is not unreasonable given the existing broad-base proposals for a national consumption tax, the calculations are demonstrated for all states in Table 51.

Under a combined national sales tax, the state tax base would more or less double from about 40%[27] currently to about 80% (corrected for a 20% base erosion), and in effect reduce the average tax rate to about half the current one. However, business procurement would be fully relieved from the tax, which would reduce sales and use tax revenue for all states combined with USD 124.7 billion,[28] and would result in an upward effect on the tax rate. This effect would vary among states, depending on the volume of business procurement relative to total (private and business) expenditure. The integration of local tax rates with the state tax rate will also have an upward effect, which will depend on the monetary volume of local tax revenue relative to state sales tax revenue. The new tax rates (**t***s*) found in Table 51 are, in most cases, significantly lower than the current statutory state sales tax rates, but in some states (e.g., Hawaii, South Dakota and Wyoming) the new rate is higher than the statutory rate.

Unless government consumptive expenditure would be exempt, which is not the case under the fair tax proposals, the states and local governments need to raise additional income to finance the federal tax (**t***f*) incurred by them on their inputs, which would lead to an increase of the average tax rate. Assuming a federal exclusive tax rate (**t***f*) of 10%, state and local governments would pay about USD 135 billion to the federal government. By comparison, the total nationwide revenue generated by state sales and use taxes for the year 2005 was USD 245 billion. Although some may argue that it is systematically correct for subnational governments to pay consumption tax levied by the national government, one could make the argument that it makes no economic sense for one sector of tax

27. Because most services remain outside the scope of the current sales tax and many goods are exempt in an effort to reduce regressivity, in the end about 38% of the total consumption in the United States is actually subject to sales tax. See Bruce & Fox, "E-commerce in the Context of Declining State Sales Tax Bases"; Cline et al., 1.
28. Cline, Neubig & Phillips.

Table 51. State Tax Rates on Revenue-Neutral Basis

State	Current Tax Rate		Total Sales/Use Tax Revenue (USD billions)*	Total Private Consumption** (USD billions)	Combined State Tax Rate (**t***s*)
	State	Local			
Alabama	4	1–5	3.53	66.0	5.35
Alaska	—	1–7	0.16	16.5	0.97
Arizona	5.6	0–3	7.02	93.5	7.51
Arkansas	6	0.5–4.75	3.33	38.5	8.65
California	6.25	1–2.5	37.57	720.0	5.22
Colorado	2.9	1–5	4.39	93.5	4.69
Connecticut	6	—	3.27	88.0	3.72
Delaware	—	—	—	27.5	—
District of Columbia	5.75	—	0.84	38.5	2.18
Florida	6	0.5–2.5	20.08	297.0	6.76
Georgia	4	1–3	7.66	159.5	4.80
Hawaii	4	—	2.14	22.0	9.72
Idaho	6	0–5	1.13	22.0	5.14
Illinois	6.25	0–4	8.36	247.5	3.38
Indiana	6	—	5.00	104.5	4.78
Iowa	5	0–2	2.16	55.0	3.93
Kansas	5.3	0–3	2.52	49.5	5.09
Kentucky	6	—	2.60	60.5	4.30
Louisiana	4	2–7	5.68	82.5	6.88
Maine	5	—	0.93	22.0	4.23
Maryland	5	—	2.87	110.0	2.61
Massachusetts	5	—	3.89	143.0	2.72
Michigan	6	—	8.07	165.0	4.89
Minnesota	6.5	0–1	4.27	104.5	4.08
Mississippi	7	—	2.59	33.0	7.85
Missouri	4.225	0.5–4.75	4.86	93.5	5.20
Montana	—	—	—	11.0	—
Nebraska	5.5	0.5–1.5	1.77	33.0	5.36
Nevada	6.5	0–1.25	3.06	49.5	6.18
New Hampshire	—	—	—	22.0	—
New Jersey	7	—	6.55	192.5	3.40
New Mexico	5	0.125–2.8125	2.15	33.0	6.52
New York	4	3–4.625	21.10	429.0	4.92
North Carolina	4.25	13	6.24	154.0	4.05
North Dakota	5	1–2.5	0.48	11.0	4.36

Table 51. (contd)

State	Current Tax Rate		Total Sales/Use Tax Revenue (USD billions)*	Total Private Consumption** (USD billions)	Combined State Tax Rate (**t***s*)
	State	Local			
Ohio	5.5	0.5–2	9.65	198.0	4.87
Oklahoma	4.5	1–7	2.93	55.0	5.33
Oregon	—	—	—	60.5	—
Pennsylvania	6	0–1	8.26	214.5	3.85
Rhode Island	7	—	0.84	22.0	3.82
South Carolina	5	0–2	3.03	57.5	5.27
South Dakota	4	1–2	0.83	11.0	7.55
Tennessee	7	1.5–2.75	7.57	94.0	8.05
Texas	6.25	0.5–2	20.25	440.0	4.60
Utah	4.75	1.25–3.35	2.18	38.5	5.66
Vermont	6	—	0.31	11.0	2.82
Virginia	4	1	4.04	154.0	2.62
Washington	6.5	0.5–2.4	10.64	121.0	8.79
West Virginia	6	—	1.09	22.0	4.95
Wisconsin	5	0–0.6	4.3	99.0	4.34
Wyoming	4	0–2	0.68	11.0	6.18

Source: US Census Bureau 2005.
* For state and localities combined, in rounded numbers.
** Private household consumption is not compiled in the United States on a per state basis. Private consumption has been based on US Department of Labor and US Bureau of Labor Statistics numbers for the year 2005, Report 998, February 2007, which estimates spending of an average of USD 46,409 per consumer unit, given a total of 117,356 million units. Allocation to individual states has been made on the basis of gross state product (GSP) ratios. As a result, the estimates found are rather rough indications and not fairly precise calculations. This is acceptable, however, because our purpose is merely to demonstrate the methodology of calculating the **t***s* and wa**t***s*, and of allocating the total consumption tax revenue over the states.

consumers to pay to another sector of tax consumers.[29] It only leads to needless pumping around of moneys.[30] Because the subnational governments would increase their state tax rates (**t***s*) to finance the payment of the federal tax (**t***f*), it

29. Following the distinction made by the Austrian school of economic thought between taxpayers and tax consumers.
30. Under VAT in Europe, government consumption is taxed. Interestingly in this context, several Member States have created a special equalization fund to reimburse subnational governments for VAT paid on their inputs.

seems simpler and more direct to exempt the consumptive expenditures of subnational governments and increase the federal tax rate to generate the same amount of revenue for the federal government. Instead of paying tax over state and local government consumption first to the state through a higher rated state tax (**t***s*), the consumers in a given state would pay the same directly to the federal government through a higher federal tax rate (**t***f*) applied to their own consumptive expenditures. Although this is true on a national level, or within a single state, within a federation exemption of subnational governments', consumptive inputs may lead to distortions. The payment that the state must make for the federal tax (**t***f*) is a function of the relative size of each state and local government. Exempting the subnational governments' consumptive inputs would benefit states with large governments relative to states with smaller-sized governments. Preferential treatment would be given to states that choose to consume via government expenditure over states that prefer to consume via private consumption. By redirecting consumption from the private sector to the government sector, large-government states could edge out or increase a comparative price advantage over smaller-government states. This cannot be compensated through an increased federal tax rate (**t***f*) because the additional tax would be paid by all consumers nationally and not only by consumers in the state with a large-government sector. The disparity is particularly striking if the state with a relatively large government also has a relatively small population.

Assuming that no exemption for government consumptive inputs will be provided, the necessary state and local tax rate (**t***s*) for a given state must equal the amount required to replace existing state and local sales tax revenues (*sR*) plus the amount required to finance the national consumption tax imposed by the federal government on state and local government consumption (*gC*) and investment (*gI*) divided by the state tax base (*sC*). In equation:

$$\frac{sR + (\mathbf{t}f[gC + gI])}{sC}$$

The state tax rate necessary to generate the same revenue for the state and local jurisdictions as well as compensation for the federal tax paid on government consumptive spending by a given federal tax rate of 10% is estimated in Table 52 for all the states.

The total amount of revenue needed to pay the federal tax (**t***f*) is more than half the amount of current total sales and use tax revenue. Roughly USD 380 billion will be needed.

After calculating the applicable rate (**t***s*) for each state, an average state tax rate (**wat***s*) must be determined, which should give equal bearing to the relative economic performance of each state. The choice would be to determine the relative weight of a state's tax rate to the basket of tax rates either on the basis of total consumptive expenditure of the state relative to total national consumptive expenditure, or on the basis of a state's gross product relative to the gross product of other states. The former would imply a choice for the destination principle and the latter a preference for the origin principle. In this discussion, the choice is made for gross state product (GSP) because it appears to be a more accurate yardstick for economic performance than the consumption level of a state.

Table 52. State Tax Rate Required When Government Consumption Is Taxed

State	Total Sales Tax Revenue (*sR*) (USD billions)*	**t***f* (*gC* + *gI*) (USD billions)**	Total Private Consumption (*sC*) (USD billions)	Required Tax Rate (**t***s*)
Alabama	3.53	1.98	66.0	8.35
Alaska	0.16	0.60	16.5	4.61
Arizona	7.02	2.30	93.5	9.97
Arkansas	3.33	1.07	38.5	11.43
California	37.57	19.02	720.0	7.86
Colorado	4.39	1.88	93.5	6.71
Connecticut	3.27	1.58	88.0	5.51
Delaware	—	0.39	27.5	1.42
District of Columbia	0.84	0.63	38.5	3.82
Florida	20.08	8.02	297.0	9.46
Georgia	7.66	3.50	159.5	7.00
Hawaii	2.14	0.63	22.0	12.59
Idaho	1.13	0.51	22.0	7.45
Illinois	8.36	5.13	247.5	5.45
Indiana	5.00	2.63	104.5	7.30
Iowa	2.16	1.29	55.0	6.27
Kansas	2.52	0.99	49.5	7.09
Kentucky	2.60	1.48	60.5	6.74
Louisiana	5.68	1.79	82.5	9.05
Maine	0.93	0.67	22.0	7.27
Maryland	2.87	2.18	110.0	4.59
Massachusetts	3.89	3.43	143.0	5.12
Michigan	8.07	4.48	165.0	7.61
Minnesota	4.27	2.54	104.5	6.52
Mississippi	2.59	1.22	33.0	11.55
Missouri	4.86	2.07	93.5	7.41
Montana	—	0.37	11.0	3.36
Nebraska	1.77	0.84	33.0	7.91
Nevada	3.06	1.06	49.5	8.32
New Hampshire	—	0.51	22.0	2.32
New Jersey	6.55	4.06	192.5	5.51
New Mexico	2.15	0.92	33.0	9.30
New York	21.10	12.68	429.0	7.87
North Carolina	6.24	3.39	154.0	6.25
North Dakota	0.48	0.27	11.0	6.82
Ohio	9.65	4.95	198.0	7.37
Oklahoma	2.93	1.30	55.0	7.69
Oregon	—	1.53	60.5	2.53
Pennsylvania	8.26	5.91	214.5	6.61

Table 52. (contd)

State	Total Sales Tax Revenue (*sR*) (USD billions)*	t*f* (*gC* + *gI*) (USD billions)**	Total Private Consumption (*sC*) (USD billions)	Required Tax Rate (t*s*)
Rhode Island	0.84	0.49	22.0	6.05
South Carolina	3.03	1.91	57.5	8.59
South Dakota	0.83	0.31	11.0	10.36
Tennessee	7.57	2.83	94.0	11.06
Texas	20.25	8.42	440.0	6.52
Utah	2.18	1.02	38.5	8.31
Vermont	0.31	0.32	11.0	5.73
Virginia	4.04	2.72	154.0	4.39
Washington	10.64	3.18	121.0	11.42
West Virginia	1.09	0.76	22.0	8.41
Wisconsin	4.3	2.46	99.0	6.83
Wyoming	0.68	0.34	11.0	9.27
	244.87	135.37	5,560	

* Sales and use tax for states and localities combined, not including tax on motor fuel, alcohol, tobacco and public utilities.

** The US Census Bureau does not compile totals per state for public consumption and investment. Government consumption and investment has been estimated by taking the total direct expenditure of state and localities, and deducting categories of expenditure that are not consumptive in nature, such as wages, salaries, insurance trust contributions, interest, subsidies and assistance. The most recent numbers available are for the year 2005.

Because the relative weight of each state tax rate fluctuates with the change of a state's GSP relative to the GSP of other states, the national tax rate needs to be periodically recalculated. To avoid possibly wide variation, it seems wise to apply the average GSP for a state over a number of years and adjust the group of years annually by dropping the oldest year and adding a more recent one. This is demonstrated in Table 53.

Table 53. Continuing Average GSP (5 Years)

2005	2006	2007	2008	2009					
	2006	2007	2008	2009	2010				
		2007	2008	2009	2010	2011			
			2008	2009	2010	2011	2012		
				2009	2010	2011	2012	2013	
					2010	2011	2012	2013	2014

Assuming that the combined federal and state consumption tax will be effective as of the year 2011, the average GSP of each state would be calculated on the basis of statistical material available for the most recent year prior to 2011, which would probably be the year 2009, and the four preceding years. The first group of years would, therefore, span from 2005 to 2009. For the next year, 2012, the average GSP for each state would be determined on the bases of information collected in relation to the year group 2006 to 2010, and so on.

The calculation of the weighted average state tax rate is demonstrated in Table 54. Because statistical data for the year groups noted previously are not yet available, the GSPs for the year 2005 is used to stay consistent with the reference year of other available data. The GSP is expressed as a percentage of the GDP of the United States (US = 100). The tax rates per state are taken from Table 52.

Table 54. Weighted Average State Tax Rate

State	Average GSP*	Tax Rate (**t***s*)	Weighted Rate (**wat***s*)
Alabama	1.2	8.35	0.1002
Alaska	0.3	4.61	0.0138
Arizona	1.7	9.97	0.1694
Arkansas	0.7	11.43	0.0800
California	13.1	7.86	1.0296
Colorado	1.7	6.71	0.1140
Connecticut	1.6	5.51	0.0881
Delaware	0.5	1.42	0.0071
District of Columbia	0.7	3.82	0.0267
Florida	5.4	9.46	0.5108
Georgia	2.9	7.00	0.2030
Hawaii	0.4	12.59	0.0503
Idaho	0.4	7.45	0.0298
Illinois	4.5	5.45	0.2452
Indiana	1.9	7.30	0.1387
Iowa	1.0	6.27	0.0627
Kansas	0.9	7.09	0.0638
Kentucky	1.1	6.74	0.0741
Louisiana	1.5	9.05	0.1357
Maine	0.4	7.27	0.0291
Maryland	2.0	4.59	0.0918
Massachusetts	2.6	5.12	0.1331
Michigan	3.0	7.61	0.2283

Table 54. (contd)

State	Average GSP*	Tax Rate (t*s*)	Weighted Rate (wat*s*)
Minnesota	1.9	6.52	0.1239
Mississippi	0.6	11.55	0.0693
Missouri	1.7	7.41	0.1259
Montana	0.2	3.36	0.0067
Nebraska	0.6	7.91	0.0474
Nevada	0.9	8.32	0.0749
New Hampshire	0.4	2.32	0.0093
New Jersey	3.5	5.51	0.1928
New Mexico	0.6	9.30	0.0558
New York	7.8	7.87	0.6138
North Carolina	2.8	6.25	0.1750
North Dakota	0.2	6.82	0.0136
Ohio	3.6	7.37	0.2653
Oklahoma	1.0	7.69	0.0769
Oregon	1.1	2.53	0.0278
Pennsylvania	3.9	6.61	0.2578
Rhode Island	0.4	6.05	0.0242
South Carolina	1.1	8.59	0.0945
South Dakota	0.2	10.36	0.0207
Tennessee	1.8	11.06	0.1990
Texas	8.0	6.52	0.5216
Utah	0.7	8.31	0.0581
Vermont	0.2	5.73	0.0114
Virginia	2.8	4.39	0.1229
Washington	2.2	11.42	0.2512
West Virginia	0.4	8.41	0.0336
Wisconsin	1.8	6.83	0.1229
Wyoming	0.2	9.27	0.1185
Weighted Average	Rate (wat*s*) =		**7.3404**

Source: US Bureau of Economic Analysis.

The national tax rate (**t***n*) is the sum of the federal tax rate (**t***f*) and the weighted average state tax rate (wat*s*). In equation: **t***n* = **t***f* + wat*s*

Assuming a federal tax of 10%, the combined federal and states tax rate would be 10 + 7.34 = 17.5% (rounded up for simplicity reasons).

The tax rate would not be static. Apart from fluctuations in relative economic performance, which would be reflected in the average GSP per state, states would be allowed to change their state tax rate, effective 1 January of the following year. This would allow states to retain some, but important, fiscal and budgetary autonomy.

11.4.6.3. Macroeconomic Method of Revenue Allocation

It is essential to find a method to allocate to each state its share of total revenue that is appropriate relative to the share of other states. Each state wants its fair share and the challenge is to find a method that ensures the fairness of revenue allocation. Between nation-states, as well as within common or federal markets, the standard solution is to determine tax jurisdiction and hitherto allocate tax revenue for consumption tax purposes on the basis of either the origin principle or the destination principle, the latter requiring a mechanism of border tax adjustments.

When macroeconomic data are used, border adjustments are avoided and firms would no longer be required to register in every state in which they do business. Registration would be limited to either that with the federal agency charged with the consumption tax administration or, in cases when the states retain that authority, with the state where a firm has its principle US office.

Regardless of whether the tax is administered and collected at the state level or at the federal level, the allocation of revenue should be in the hands of an independent clearinghouse. Revenue is initially allocated to the states or withheld by the states from tax collected on the basis of data from the previous year, except for the first year where allocation will initially be based on estimates made by the clearinghouse. Annually, the clearinghouse will make precise calculations, and surplus states will remit revenue to the clearinghouse, which in turn will pay out to deficit states. Clearing for the federal government is not necessary, of course, because the federal share will always be determined on the basis of the weight of the federal tax rate (**t***f*) relative to the national rate (**t***n*) times the amount of revenue collected (*R*):

$$\frac{\mathbf{t}f}{\mathbf{t}n} \times R.$$

All states and localities combined would receive

$$\frac{\mathrm{wats}}{\mathbf{t}n} \times R.$$

Assuming total national annual consumption of USD 5.56 trillion,[31] the revenue at 17.5% would be USD 973 billion. Allocation between the federal government and the states as demonstrated in Table 55.

Table 55. Revenue Allocation between the Federal Government and the States

Total consumption tax collected	973 billion
To federal government 100/175	556 billion
To states 75/175	417 billion

31. The calculations are based on an assumption of no base erosion. If tax base erosion were 20%, the combined tax rate (**t***n*) would have to increase to 21.87% to generate the same tax revenue.

The difference between the revenue needed by the states on a budget-neutral basis at USD 380 billion and the amount generated in our calculations, USD 417 billion, is caused by the cumulative rounding up of all numbers.

The relative economic performance of a state may vary over time. The economy in one state may grow, but in another state it may decrease. For that reason, the annual revenue allocation among the states should be adjusted relative to the change in economic performances of the states. This can be accomplished by applying the same weighted state tax rate (wat*s*) as a tool to determine revenue allocation among the states. Tax allocation is determined by dividing the state wat*s* (swat*s*) for a given state by the wat*s* for all states combined (twat*s*) and multiplying the result with the revenue generated for all states combined (*tR*):

$$\frac{\text{swat}s}{\text{twat}s} \times tR. = sR.$$

This is demonstrated in Table 56 for all states on the basis of the combined revenue of USD 417 billion. In turn the states need to allocate part of the revenue to the localities.

Table 56. Revenue Allocation among States

State	GSP-based State Tax Rate (wat*s*)	wat*s*-Based Revenue Allocation (USD billions)
Alabama	0.1002	5.69
Alaska	0.0138	0.78
Arizona	0.1694	9.62
Arkansas	0.0800	4.54
California	1.0296	58.49
Colorado	0.1140	6.47
Connecticut	0.0881	5.00
Delaware	0.0071	0.40
District of Columbia	0.0267	1.51
Florida	0.5108	29.01
Georgia	0.2030	11.53
Hawaii	0.0503	2.85
Idaho	0.0298	1.69
Illinois	0.2452	13.92
Indiana	0.1387	7.88
Iowa	0.0627	3.56
Kansas	0.0638	3.62
Kentucky	0.0741	4.20
Louisiana	0.1357	7.70
Maine	0.0291	1.65
Maryland	0.0918	5.21
Massachusetts	0.1331	7.56

Table 56. (*contd*)

State	GSP-based State Tax Rate (wat*s*)	wat*s*-Based Revenue Allocation (USD billions)
Michigan	0.2283	12.96
Minnesota	0.1239	7.03
Mississippi	0.0693	3.93
Missouri	0.1259	7.15
Montana	0.0067	0.38
Nebraska	0.0474	2.69
Nevada	0.0749	4.25
New Hampshire	0.0093	0.52
New Jersey	0.1928	10.95
New Mexico	0.0558	3.16
New York	0.6138	34.87
North Carolina	0.1750	9.94
North Dakota	0.0136	0.77
Ohio	0.2653	15.07
Oklahoma	0.0769	4.36
Oregon	0.0278	1.58
Pennsylvania	0.2578	14.64
Rhode Island	0.0242	1.37
South Carolina	0.0945	5.37
South Dakota	0.0207	1.17
Tennessee	0.1990	11.30
Texas	0.5216	29.63
Utah	0.0581	3.30
Vermont	0.0114	0.64
Virginia	0.1229	6.98
Washington	0.2512	14.27
West Virginia	0.0336	1.90
Wisconsin	0.1229	6.98
Wyoming	0.1185	6.73
		416.77

11.4.6.4. Final Remarks and Conclusions

The discussion on tax reform and tax coordination between the federal and state level is still parochial in nature. The United States could generate an important advantage if the parties involved at both levels would allow for a globally comparative approach when determining the appropriate level and methodology of taxation. It is counterproductive for each state and local jurisdiction to adhere to the historic American tradition of fiscal decentralization, when markets have evolved from local to national, and are in the process of becoming global platforms.

Since the mid-nineteenth century, the United States has created a large single market, outsizing the competition. This has made the United States the economic leader of the world, effectively, since the First World War, and it has been recognized as such since the end of the Second World War. It is essential to maintain a tax system that supports the competitive edge, not one that erodes it. The EU is slowly creating a common market under fiscal conditions increasingly superior to the ones in the United States. Globalization inherently leads to increased international competition between nation-states, federations of states, and common economic markets. Integrated emerging markets, such as China and India, with a consumer base, when developed, several times that of the United States, may gain the competitive edge if the United States does not respond adequately to the global economic challenge. What was true for France in the past compared to England will prove equally true for the United States in relation to the EU and challenging emerging markets unless the United States provides for an innovative fiscal policy. This would require open-minded cooperation between the national and subnational levels of government towards a common economic goal. An essential step forward would be the creation of a comprehensive system of consumption tax for the Unites States as a whole that would maximize market efficiency by eliminating existing distortions. Out-of-the-box thinking would be a requirement towards success. It is important for policymakers at both the federal and state levels to realize that it is imperative to avoid the past fiscal policy mistakes of France and, instead, ensure we will create a fiscal environment that provides a competitive advantage. The existing sales tax system with multiple levels of taxation is archaic. A single consumption tax, generating revenue for both the federal and subnational governments, could be an engine to economic advancement, provided it is properly designed to avoid border tax adjustments, avoid jurisdiction competition and reduce compliance costs. This section serves to illustrate that such a tax system would be rather straightforward. A national, broad-based consumption tax could generate more revenue for federal, state and local governments at reduced compliance and administrative costs. At a single rate, revenue allocation on the basis of macroeconomic data seems feasible and efficient. Such a tax, especially when applied to partially replace current income taxes, would generate a boost in economic performance and improve the US investment climate.

11.5 CONCLUSIONS

Tax coordination serves a number of purposes, including promoting free trade, ensuring fair competition, preventing economic distortions and realizing enhanced prosperity. Revenue allocation among states and between the federal and subnational levels of governments is an important element of tax coordination. Revenue allocation includes the problem of finding an appropriate methodology to deal with the taxation of cross-border transactions on the basis of the destination principle.

All proposals in scholarly literature revolve around handling tax rate variation among the states, but none of them has been implemented.

The discussion in the United States for a national consumption tax is becoming more serious because it is undeniable that the federal government will need additional revenue to finance the expected rise in the cost of health care and to ensure that foreign investors will keep buying American debt with which the economic stimulus plan and bail-out plans for the financial institutions is essentially financed. This would open a unique opportunity for tax reform through the creation of an integrated consumption tax system for both the national and the subnational level with a single rate. Previously we demonstrated how a single national tax rate could be calculated and how revenue could be accurately allocated to the federal government and among the individual states on the basis of macroeconomic data. Although this is an alternative that should be of particular interest to policymakers, it is far from certain that such a system would be accepted and implemented because of the complex political dynamics, specifically the precarious balance between federal power and state autonomy. On the basis of the experience in Canada, we may expect the states to continue their current retail taxes if a federal VAT were to be introduced.

Partly, tax coordination solutions are driven by the urge to avoid fraud. Zero rating cross-border transactions within a common market essentially removes the tax burden at the weakest point in the supply chain, that is, when these transactions leave the control of one jurisdiction and enter the control of another. Where the zero rate is perceived as the main factor triggering fraud, replacing it with a positive rate, an approach adopted under the clearinghouse, VIVAT and C-VAT proposals, prima facie seems to be a logical choice. However, it is naïve to believe that this would provide a definite solution for the problem of fraud. Indeed, temporarily fraud would decline, but in reality these measures would only divert fraud schemes. They would disappear on one front, simply to emerge somewhere else. Zero rates are inherent to the destination principle and, although their application could be avoided for cross-border transactions within common or federal markets, they remain essential in relation to sales to third countries, unless a feasible global clearing methodology could be applied.

It appears more realistic and practical to adhere to proven methods of protecting the revenue interest, such as restricting the input VAT deduction to the level of output VAT (the French *butoir* rule) in essence ensuring that no money would actually be refunded, in combination with a carry forward of excess input VAT. This would provide the revenue with more precious time to investigate the legitimacy of claims. In addition, it should be considered to introduce the status of reliable trader within the context of VAT, similar in concept to Authorized Economic Operator (AEO) for customs purposes in the EU[32] and Customs-Trade

32. Companies that are able to ensure and verify that their business transactions are transparent and safe will be able to obtain the new AEO certificates. The certification will allow businesses to identify safe and reliable partners for local, as well as international, business transactions. In addition, its holder will benefit from simplified procedures, priority customs clearance and relief from the requirement to provide customs guarantees.

Partnership against Terrorism (C-TPAT) in the United States,[33] to create a mutually beneficial cooperation between the business community and revenue agencies to combat fraud. See also the remarks in Section 9.7.3.5.

33. Customs-Trade Partnership against Terrorism is a voluntary government business initiative to build cooperative relationships that strengthen and improve the overall international supply chain and US border security. It is based on the recognition that the highest level of cargo security can only be realized through close cooperation with the ultimate owners of the international supply chain, such as importers, carriers, consolidators, licensed customs brokers and manufacturers.

Chapter 12
Tax Policy Lessons

The first question policy makers face is whether sales or consumption taxes deserve serious consideration when designing or reforming a tax system. Especially in the United States, this question arises in the context of fully or partially replacing the current income taxes. Most economists contend that consumption taxes offer advantages in terms of simplicity, efficiency and fairness. The general opinion is that income is difficult to measure accurately, with capital gains and depreciations as notable problem areas. These problems do not arise under a consumption tax because capital expenditures are expensed and capital gains irrelevant. Consumption taxes are considered to be efficient mainly because they do not tax savings and thus eliminate the intertemporal consumption distortion. In addition, this stimulates investment and will lead to economic growth. However, distortions remain under a consumption tax between purchased and nonpurchased goods and services, most notably leisure, which is not subject to tax.

Consumption taxes are inadequate as a tool to achieve distributional goals. Although progression can be realized, at least theoretically, within a consumption tax through rate variation and exemptions, it leads to adverse complexities, while hardly realizing the objectives for which they have been created because it is virtually impossible to identify goods and services that are exclusively used by either the rich or the poor. This may provide an argument for creating a tax system that consists of a combination of an income tax and a general sales tax.

The fairness of a consumption tax is a source of concern and of lively debate. A broad-based consumption tax is perceived as fair because individual consumption is an adequate indicator of someone's living standard. Therefore, consumption appears to provide a fair tax base. However, many opponents of a consumption tax point to its regressive character, especially compared to income taxes. A tax is considered regressive when low-income groups pay more relative to their income. As we have seen in Section 4.4.2.5, this argument can be made because savings remain untaxed under a consumption tax and the savings rate rises relative with income. Not all agree. It seems that the regressivity depends on how it is calculated. Measured over a limited time period, such as annual income, consumption taxes are, indeed, regressive. However, measured on the basis of a consumer's lifetime income, the tax is close to proportional. Taking a time capsule has the disadvantage of assuming that income is stagnant and income progression or income variation absent. Moreover, most consumers make decisions based on their reasonable expectations of long-term income development. For these reasons we have supported the life cycle analysis of regressivity; however, it should be noted that not all economists agree on this issue. Although it is true that countermeasures could be taken within the design of a consumption tax to mitigate or reduce the perceived regressivity, or even to make the tax progressive, the general consensus is that the tools to do this, rate variation and exemptions, are too blunt for the job and lead to economic distortions, while adding significantly to the complexity of the tax. Generally, taxes are inadequate vehicles to achieve vertical equity. It makes far more sense to address poverty directly through measures taken on the expenditure side of the budget.[1] A revenue-neutral shift from income to consumption taxation would in itself result in high-income taxpayers receiving a tax cut. This may create political difficulties in countries that seek to partially replace income tax with a consumption tax, but not, or to a lesser extent, in countries that intend to introduce a consumption tax in addition to an existing income tax, which remains unchanged.

Another aspect of fairness is found in the neutrality of a well-designed broad-based consumption tax. In essence, this is a nondiscrimination argument. A consumption tax, in its ideal form, covers all goods and services and is levied on all businesses regardless of their legal organization (corporate and noncorporate) and their extent of economic integration. As a consequence, exemptions, as found in the European VAT model, insofar as they erode the tax base, also reduce the neutrality of a consumption tax. Although there may exist a political or practical rationale for exemptions under, for example, a VAT, they violate the very essence of the tax and have, therefore, been characterized as cancerous by Maurice Lauré in his evaluation of the French VAT.[2] The need and rationale for exemptions are discussed later in this section.

If policy makers conclude that a sales tax is needed, the next question is which particular type of sales tax best serves the needs. Although highly criticized, GRTs offer the advantage of simplicity, and they are efficient as long as they are levied at low rates. However, the distortions that turnover tax create, such as the incentive for vertical integration and tax cascading, has provided the case in the past for the introduction of less distortionary, but still highly revenue-productive, sales taxes.

The choice between a RST and a VAT is not an easy one because they are close cousins. Even if it is true that a VAT is superior, it is not a knockout victory. It also depends on approach and perspective. Rothbard prefers the RST over income

1. Liam Ebrill et al., *The Modern VAT* (Washington, DC: IMF, 2001), at 112.
2. Maurice Lauré, *Au Secours de la T.V.A.* (Rescue the VAT) (Paris: Presses Universitaires de France, 1957).

tax and VAT on more philosophical grounds because "the sales tax surely has the great advantage, for most of us, of eliminating the despotic power of the government over the life of every individual, as in the income tax, or over each business firm, as in the VAT, and it would not skew individual preferences as would specific excise taxes."[3] His argument is partly based on economics, but it is mostly argued from the perspective of privacy and business information protection.

From a technical perspective, the difference between a RST and a VAT is primarily administrative in nature, and all advantages attributed to VAT derive from that difference.[4] VAT is collected at each stage of the production and distribution chain. Each business collects the tax as an add-on to the price, regardless of whether the buyer is a business or a private consumer (output VAT). However, a business holds a credit for the tax paid on its procurement (input VAT), which is exercised against the tax liability arising from sales. As a result, a business only remits the difference between output and input VAT to the taxing authority. In comparison, RST is only collected by retailers, the final stage of the distribution chain. It seems risky and problematic to concentrate all taxability at the retail stage, generally seen as the weakest link in the distribution chain from a compliance perspective. Under the fractioned collection system of a VAT, only a portion of the tax is at risk in any transaction, which reduces the incentive to be dishonest. Most of the tax will be received before a product or service reaches the final stage from large-scale manufacturers and wholesalers who are less prone to cheat. Proponents of the RST contend that collecting tax along the whole production and distribution chain simply creates more opportunities for fraud. Collection at a single stage offers the advantage that it allows the taxing authority to concentrate its audit efforts at this single stage as well. In addition, the retail sector is dominated in terms of sales volume by large firms that are much less likely to cheat. Under this reasoning the problem would be concentrated with small retailers.

Another difference is that the credit invoice method VAT depends on invoices issued by the seller. The invoice is essential for the buyer (if a business) because without it the latter cannot exercise his right to deduct the input VAT. For this reason, it is generally believed that a purchaser will insist on the issuing of an invoice and, although this does not guarantee the actual remittance of the tax by the seller, this does create a paper trail supporting tax audits and enabling cross-checks of input VAT credit claims against payments made by sellers. Some refer to this as the self-enforcing or self-policing effect of the credit invoice VAT, although its actual value may be less as proponents of the tax advocate. However, the emergence of complex carousel schemes in the EU proves that no sales tax system is immune to fraud, and invoices can, of course, be falsified.

---

3. Murray N. Rothbard, "The Consumption Tax: A Critique," *Review of Austrian Economics* 7 (2) (1994): 75–90.
4. Many studies have been conducted over the years comparing VAT to and evaluating it against a RST; see, for example, George R. Zodrow, "The Sales Tax, the VAT, and Taxes in Between – or, Is the Only Good NRST a VAT in Drag?," *National Tax Journal* 52 (3) (1999): 429–442.

VAT is also perceived to be less susceptible than a RST to evasion in the form of false input VAT claims regarding business purchases of goods or services that are actually used for private purposes of the business owner. This argument is probably more psychological in nature where it contends that it is harder to make these false statements regarding the use of a product directly to the tax authorities, as under a VAT, instead of directly to the sellers as under a RST.

An advantage of VAT is its ability to enable tax relief on business inputs. If it is well designed, that is with no or only the bare minimum of exemptions, a VAT removes the tax burden from businesses through the input VAT deduction mechanism. RSTs do not offer such a technique and depend on an inaccurate system of exemption certificates. The holder of such a certificate is allowed to purchase goods without the seller charging sales tax. In the United States, states have been restrictive in determining which goods are eligible for exempt purchases for fear of tax evasion by routing private consumption of goods via business purchases. Moreover, some explicit policy choices have been made to tax capital goods as well as certain intermediate goods. As a result, about 40% of business inputs are taxed, which violates the legal character of a consumption tax and reduces efficiency gains offered by a (partial) shift from income tax to consumption tax. In an effort to raise revenue, legislative proposals have been introduced in several states to further restrict the exemptions.

The credit invoice VAT also makes border tax adjustments easy to incorporate. By applying a zero rate on exported goods (and services) with full right to deduct input VAT, exports leave the country tax free. Because the tax burden is equal to the tax rate times the sales price or value of a good, taxing at importation creates a level playing field between imported goods and domestically produced goods. This is not feasible under a RST to the extent that business inputs are taxed and pyramiding occurs. Exports will not be fully relieved, where tax is hidden in the price, and imports will be undertaxed relative to domestic goods.

As exemptions under a VAT offer less of an incentive because of the input VAT credit restrictions associated with it, there appears to be less political pressure to obtain exempt status under VAT than under a RST.

The VAT as applied in the EU meets the requirements of a general tax on private consumption because it is characterized by a broad tax base, including most goods and services, and has an efficient system of input tax credit to enable the shifting forward of the tax. The system is not perfect. Exemptions under VAT, whatever the rationale or perceived justification for their existence, violate the legal character of the VAT insofar as it results in the taxation of business procurement. Where the nondeductible input VAT is shifted forward to the consumer, tax cascading will occur which will lead to overcollection of tax relative to the value of the consumption, and economic distortions may arise. Although the EU model since its adoption has been able to create a large following, its imperfections have encouraged other jurisdictions to modify the model and to incorporate many improvements to strengthen the overall system. The New Zealand VAT was the trendsetter in this respect and has, in turn, become a model itself for other countries to more or less copy. By reducing the number of exemptions, the so-called modern

VAT has an improved C-efficiency of more than 96% compared to approximately 50% for the traditional VAT as applied in the EU.

Because the sales tax in the United States only covers less than 40% of all consumptive expenditure, its characterization as a general tax is questionable. Moreover, in addition to taxing private consumption, it appears to tax a large proportion of business procurement as well.

As to the treatment of sales and resales of personal tangible property, whether B2B, B2C or C2C, during its economic life cycle, as secondhand goods or as trade-ins, VAT offers satisfactory solutions to prevent overcollection of tax where sales tax often fails.

However, these conclusions do not disqualify sales tax per se, nor do they imply the superiority of VAT because the flaws in the design of the sales tax as applied in the United States are certainly not beyond repair. Special rules to prevent overtaxation in cases of intermediary life cycle sales could be considered, and the EU VAT treatment could be used as guidance. Preventing taxation of business procurement seems urgent as well, but it may be less straightforward within sales tax. Clearly, where the sales tax is intended to be a tax on private consumption, business expenditure must be relieved from the tax. The current system of exemptions is incomplete and arbitrary. Unfortunately, the budget restraints caused by the economic depression early in the twenty-first century has lead states to move in the direction of abolishing exemptions altogether, or at least of reducing their number, basically undermining the legal character of the tax or changing it fully into a business tax.

Overall, the VAT seems to slightly have the upper hand, in particular because it has a wider scope (including most services), provides an adequate way of relieving business inputs from tax through the input VAT credit system, creates a paper trail that allows authorities to effectively examine claims and liabilities, and reduces revenue loss by ensuring that illegal operators are at least input taxed.

The VAT offers no advantage over RST in regard to taxing difficult-to-tax sectors such as farmers, financial institutions, real estate, small enterprises, and the public and charity sectors.

These difficult-to-tax sectors offer themselves challenges and lessons. What can be learned from the treatment of the agricultural sector in the EU is that, although the choice for a special regime for economic or developmental reasons is easy to understand and accept, policy makers need to realize how difficult it has proven, even in developed countries as those in the EU, to eliminate special treatment at some time in the future when conditions have changed. Therefore, special regimes should have an expiration date and should be accompanied by a strategic plan containing strict criteria, which cannot be overruled, to determine whether a regime should be continued or dissolved. In principle, the agricultural sector should be treated the same as any other business sector. However, the sector is important because of the essential nature of what it produces and, as a result, it has significant political clout. There is no reason for special treatment of the agricultural sector per se, but in many countries this sector is dominated by a large quantity of small farmers, many of whom, particularly in developing countries, lack sufficient schooling to fulfill the administrative requirements of a VAT. Instead of a separate regime, it seems better to treat farm businesses as any other small business. Small traders are, in most countries, excluded from the VAT as long as their annual turnover does not exceed a certain threshold. This enhances the efficiency of the tax because it eliminates from the tax base taxpayers whose administration and compliance costs are greater than the revenue they generate.

Identifying the tax base for financial services is particularly difficult because the charge for financial services is often a spread that may be only a few basis points. Moreover, only part of this charge is for the service of financial intermediation, and it is impossible to unbundle it from the other fees. Where the VAT is designed to be levied on explicit fees, it is, as a consequence, inadequate to tax margin fees. Under the EU model, these services are exempt and, therefore, effectively input taxed. When delivered directly to consumers, these services are, in effect, subject to a reduced rate (see Section 8.2.4.3.2), which has the unintended effect of encouraging consumers to take out loans rather than acquire fully taxed commodities. The treatment of the financial sector has been the subject of numerous studies, and a solution could be found in taxing explicit fees and applying the cash flow method on the remainder services.

The actual situation in the EU demonstrates how complicated a special regime for the public sector can be. Their activities may be exempt, out of scope, non-taxable or taxable under the VAT, depending on many, and rather vaguely defined, criteria. As a result, public bodies, their suppliers, their customers and, indeed, their competitors encounter legal uncertainty, incur increased compliance costs and face economic distortions. From an economic perspective, full taxation of the public sector has strong preference because it offers administrative simplicity, accountability and transparency. New Zealand is the only country that has fully accomplished the optimum structure.

The problems posed by immoveable property are very similar to those of other capital goods. Generally, during its life cycle, real estate changes hands several times and it may be used for different purposes. An extra dimension is added by the appreciation over time of real estate, which sets it apart from most other durables. Taxing each real estate transaction, regardless of whether it takes place between taxable persons or private persons, is theoretically most correct and would solve the problems encountered under the current treatment in most jurisdictions, combining exemptions with mandatory and optional taxation. Taxing private individuals for the sale of real estate seems feasible, provided that the legal mediators of the sale will be charged with withholding the tax. Subjecting long-term residential leases to the VAT would require also taxing the rental value of owner-occupied property, at least from the perspective of neutrality, but this would be politically controversial.

General sales taxes are capable of generating large amounts of revenue, but rate variation, as a result of political pressures to correct social inequities, erodes the tax base and the neutrality of the tax. Moreover, rate variation complicates the tax and leads to enhanced administration and compliance costs and increases the opportunities for evasion through misclassification.

Multiple rates have been the norm under VAT for many years, but the number of countries applying a single rate has risen from 25% to almost 55%. Rate variation is defended on equity arguments, but social policy can much better be accomplished through direct expenditures for the benefit of lower-income groups. Moreover, it appears that the advantages of a single rate, such as compliance simplification, enhanced enforcement and reduced tax evasion, outweigh the benefits generated by multirates.

Tax coordination between jurisdictions within a common or federal market is a necessity if the objective is to prevent double taxation or double nontaxation. In the EU there are specific tax jurisdiction rules to address this issue. In the United States the problem hinges on the concept of nexus. Harmonization of scope and definitions is desirable to prevent excessive compliance costs for businesses. It is reasonable for policy makers to keep these costs in mind, where businesses are used as, generally unpaid, tax collectors, and the success of raising revenue ultimately depends on their efforts and cooperation. Harmonization and cooperation becomes more urgent when general sales taxes are levied at both the national and subnational levels. Several models for cooperation have been developed to prevent double (non-) taxation, combat fraud with cross-border transactions and keep compliance costs in check. A fully integrated national and subnational general sales tax would be preferred because it offers the largest extent of synergy benefits; this is hard to accomplish, however, because of the political need to maintain the precarious balance between federal/supranational power and subnational autonomy.

In the United States, most propositions have been made for the introduction of a federal sales tax with coerced cooperation from the states. However, it seems better to take an integrated approach, which ensures proper administrative alignment between a federal sales or consumption tax and the existing state RSTs. Sales tax coordination in the United States is problematic where more than 7,500 jurisdictions are involved with nonharmonized bases and nonuniform rates, and where the taxes are implemented through a diverse set of destination and origin-based sourcing rules.[5] The SSUTA is a relatively recent initiative to harmonize the subnational sales taxes in the United States and can account for some clear achievements, but several important states are still not participating.

Regardless of whether the choice would be made for a combined RST or a VAT, a single tax is feasible with revenue allocation based on macroeconomic data and leaving a reasonable measurement of autonomy to the states. Where the world has seen significant technological change since VAT was introduced in Europe, such a combined tax could feasibly be levied applying the latest computer technology, thus creating a D-VAT, but it is doubtful, regardless the obvious benefits it may offer, that political consensus can be reached to make such an innovative step into unknown territory.

5. Richard T. Ainsworth, *The Digital VAT (D-VAT)*, Boston University, School of Law, Working Paper Series, Law and Economics, no. 06-22. Also published in *Virginia Tax Review* 25 (2006): 875–927.

Bibliography

Aaron, Henry J. "The Political Economy of a Value-added Tax in the United States: a Consumption Tax Symposium." *Tax Notes* (1988): 1111 et seq.

Aaron, Henry J. (ed.). *The Value-added Tax: Lessons from Europe.* Washington, DC: The Brookings Institute, 1981.

ABC Report. General Report of the Subgroups A, B, and C Appointed for the Study of the Various Possibilities for the Harmonization of Turnover Taxes. EEC, Commission, Directorate General for Competition. Brussels, January 1962.

Adams, Thomas S. "Fundamental Problems of Federal Income Taxation." *Quarterly Journal of Economics* 35 (1921): 527–556.

Agha, Ali & Jonathan Haughton. "Designing VAT Systems: Some Efficiency Considerations." *Review of Economics and Statistics* 78 (2) (1996): 303–308.

Ahmad, Ehtisham & Stephen Ludlow. *The Distributional Consequences of a Tax Reform on a VAT for Pakistan.* Working Papers, no. 238. Washington, DC: World Bank, August 1989.

Ainsworth, Richard T. *The Digital VAT (D-VAT).* Boston University, School of Law, Working Paper Series, Law and Economics, no. 06-22. Also published in *Virginia Tax Review* 25 (2006): 875–927.

Ainsworth, Richard T. *UK Car-Flipping: The VAT Fraud Market-Place and Certified Solutions.* Boston University School of Law, Working Papers Series, Law and Economics no. 07-19, 2007. <www.bu.edu/law/faculty/scholarship/workingpapers/2007.html>.

Aizenman, Joshua & Yothin Jinjarak. "The Collection Efficiency of the Value Added Tax: Theory and International Evidence. Paper 605 presented at the Department of Economics, University of California, Santa Cruz, 1 August 2005. <http://repositories.cdlib.org/ucscecon/605>.

Amand, Christian, Gottfried Schellmann & Rob Vermeulen, ''Immovable Property and VAT: Lessons from Past Experience.'' *International VAT Monitor* 16 (5) (2005): 325–334.

Andel, Norbert. ''Problems of Government Expenditure Harmonization in a Common Market.'' In *Fiscal Harmonization in Common Markets*, vol. I, edited by Carl S. Shoup. New York and London, 1967, 311–353.

Andrews, William D. ''A Consumption or Cash Flow Personal Income Tax.'' *Harvard Law Review* 87 (1974): 1113–1167.

Annacondia, Fabiola & Walter van der Corput. ''Overview of General Turnover Taxes and Tax Rates.'' *International VAT Monitor* 19 (2) (2008): 2–11.

Atkins, Chris. *A Twentieth Century Tax in the Twenty-First Century: Understanding State Corporate Tax Systems.* Background Paper, no. 49. Washington, DC: Tax Foundation, September 2005.

Atkins, Chris. *Establishing Physical Presence: Borders Online Case Reveals Court Disharmony in Applying Physical Presence Rules to State Sales Taxes*. Fiscal Fact no. 67. Washington, DC: Tax Foundation, 26 September 2006.

Auerbach, Alan J., Laurence J. Kotlikoff, Kent Smetters & Jan Walliser. *Fundamental Tax Reform and Macroeconomic Performance.* In Joint Committee on Taxation Tax Modeling Project and 1997 Tax Symposium Papers. Washington, DC: US Government Printing Office, 1997.

Auerbach, Alan & Roger Gordon. *Taxation of Financial Services under a VAT*. University of California at Berkeley: Mimeo, 2001.

Auerbach, Alan J. & Kevin A. Hassett (eds.). *Toward Fundamental Tax Reform.* Washington, DC: American Enterprise Institute for Public Policy Research, 2005.

Aujean, Michel, Peter Jenkins & Satya Poddar. ''A New Approach to Public Sector Bodies.'' *International VAT Monitor* 10 (4) (1999): 144–149.

Aujean, Michel. ''Application of VAT to Public Bodies: The EU VAT System, Current Issues and Proposals.'' In *VAT in Africa*, edited by Richard Krever. Pretoria University Law Press, 2008, 71–79.

Azcárate, Tomas Garcia. *El impuesto sobre el valor añadido y la agricultura española: unos primeros resultados* (The Value Added Tax on the Spanish Agricultural Sector: First Findings). Hacienda Pública Española, no. 99, Madrid, 1986.

Bacchetta, Philippe & Eric Van Wincoop. ''A Scapegoat Model of Exchange-Rate Fluctuations.'' *American Economic Review*, May 2004, 114–118.

Barrand, Peter. ''The Taxation of Nonprofit Bodies and Government Entities under the New Zealand GST.'' *International VAT Monitor* 10 (1) (1991): 1–19.

Baum, Donald N. ''Economic Effects of Eliminating the Sales Tax Exemption for Food: An Applied General Equilibrium Analysis.'' *Journal of Economics* 24 (1) (1998): 125–148.

Beyer, Vicki & Koji Ishimura. ''The Progress of the Japanese National Consumption Tax.'' *Revenue Law Journal* 3 (2) (1993): 115–124.

Beyer, Vicky. ''Japan's Consumption Tax: Settled in to Stay.'' *Revenue Law Journal* 10 (1) (2000): 98–106.

Bickley, James M. *Flat Tax Proposals and Fundamental Tax Reform: An Overview.* Congressional Research Service Brief for Congress (30 September 2004).

Bickley, James M. *Value-Added Tax: A New U.S. Revenue Source?* CRS Report, 22 August 2006, 11–12.

Bird, Richard M. & Pierre-Pascal Gendron. ''Dual VATs and Cross-border Trade: Two Problems, One Solution?'' *International Tax and Public Finance* 5 (1998): 429–442.

Bird, Richard M. & Pierre-Pascal Gendron. ''CVAT, VIVAT, and Dual VAT: Vertical 'Sharing' and Interstate Trade.'' *International Trade and Public Finance* 7 (2000): 753–761.

Bird, Richard M. ''A New Look at Local Business Taxes.'' *Tax Notes International* 30 (2003): 695.

Bird, Richard M. & Pierre-Pascal Gendron. *The VAT in Developing and Transitional Countries*. Cambridge, 2007.

Board of Governors of the federal Reserve Board, *Report of the Board of Governors of the Federal Reserve Board on State and Local Taxation of Banks* (1972).

Bradford, David. *Blueprints for Basic Tax Reform.* 2nd edn. Washington, DC: US Department of the Treasury, 1984.

Bradford, David. *Untangling the Income Tax.* Harvard University Press, 1986.

Bradford, David. *Blueprints for International Tax Reform.* American Enterprise Institute, 2001.

Bradford, David. *The X Tax in the World Economy.* 3, 5 CSPS Working Paper no. 93. August 2003. </www.princeton.edu/~ceps/workingpapers/93bradford.pdf>.

Bradford, David. ''A System for the Twenty-First Century.'' In *Toward Fundamental Tax Reform*, edited by Alan J. Auerbach & Kevin A. Hassett. Washington, DC: American Enterprise Institute for Public Policy Research, 2005.

Brederode, R.F.W. van. ''De rechten van de mens in het belastingrecht'' (Human Rights in Tax Law). *Weekblad voor Fiscaal Recht* 5779 (1987): 749–759.

Brederode, Robert F.W. van. ''Justice and Judgement, Methods of Judicial Interpretation in Value Added Taxation.'' *International VAT Monitor* 10 (1990): 13–20.

Brederode, R.F.W. van. *De bijzondere positie van de landbouw in de omzetbelasting* (VAT Treatment of the Agricultural Sector). Deventer: Kluwer, 1993.

Brederode, Robert F. van. ''VAT's Regressivity: Empirical Truth or Political Correctness.'' *International VAT Monitor* 18 (2) (2007): 86–92.

Brederode, Robert F. van. "Introduction to the US State Sales and Use Taxes." *International VAT Monitor* 18 (4) (2007): 270–276.

Brederode, Robert F. van. "The American Debate on Taxing Distance Sales and E-commerce." *International VAT Monitor* 18 (5) (2007): 352–361.

Brederode, Robert F. van. "Towards a Federal Sales Tax." *International VAT Monitor* 19 (2) (2008): 114–120.

Brederode, Robert F. van. "The Re-emergence of Gross Receipt Taxes in the US." *International VAT Monitor* 19 (3) (2008): 182–191.

Brederode, Robert F. van. "The Metamorphosis of Corporate Income Tax into a Value Added Tax." *International VAT Monitor* 19 (4) (2008): 266–275.

Brederode, Robert F. van. "Revenue Distribution under Federal/State Consumption Tax." *Tax Notes* 121 (8) (2008): 953–963.

Brederode, Robert F. van. "A Normative Evaluation of Consumption Tax Design: The Treatment of the Sales of Goods under VAT in the EU and Sales Tax in the US." *The Tax Lawyer: The State and Local Tax Edition* (forthcoming).

Brederode, Robert F. van. "The Morality of Coerced Tax Collection." *The Journal of Accounting, Ethics & Public Policy* (forthcoming) (2009).

Brown, Harry Gunnison. "The Incidence of a General Sales Tax." In *Readings in the Economics of Taxation*, edited by Richard A. Musgrave & Carl S. Shoup. Homewood, IL, 1959, 330–339.

Brown, Lorrie Jo. "Sales Tax Compliance Costs for E-tailers Revisited: A Critique of the Ernst & Young Study." *State Tax Notes* 18 (4) (2000): 315–317.

Bruce, Donald & William F. Fox. "E-commerce in the Context of Declining State Sales Tax Bases." National Tax Journal 53 (4) (2000): 1373–1388.

Bruce, Donald & William F. Fox. State and Local Sales Tax Revenue Loss from E-commerce: Estimates as of July 2004. University of Tennessee, July 2004.

Brugman, H. *L'idée Européenne 1918–1965*. Bruges, 1965.

Brunori, David. "The Politics of State Taxation: Now More Than Ever MTC Is Needed." Tax Analysts Reference: 1999 STT 152-28 (3 August 1999).

Carlson, George N. & Melanie K. Patrick. "Addressing the Regressivity of a Value-added Tax." *National Tax Journal* 42 (3) (1989): 339–351.

Carroll, Robert J. *The 2001 and 2003 Tax Relief: The Benefit of Lower Tax Rates*. Fiscal Fact, no. 141. Washington, DC: Tax Foundation, 23 August 2008.

Caspersen, Erik & Gilbert Metcalf. "Is a Value Added Tax Regressive? Annual versus Lifetime Incidence Measures." *National Tax Journal* 47 (4) (1994): 731–746.

Chamberlain, Andrew & Patrick Fleenor. *Tax Pyramiding: The Economic Consequences of Gross Receipt Taxes.* Special Report, no.147. Washington, DC: Tax Foundation, December 2006.

Chia, Ngee-Choon & John Whalley. "The Tax Treatment of Financial Intermediation." *Journal of Money, Credit, and Banking* 31 (4) (1999): 704–719.

Cline, Robert J. & Thomas S. Neubig. Masters of Complexity and Bearers of Great Burden: The Sales Tax System and Compliance Costs for Multistate Retailers. Washington, DC: Ernst & Young, 8 September 1999.

Cline, Robert, John Mikesell, Tom Neubig & Andrew Phillips. *Sales Taxation on Business Inputs*. Council on State Taxation, 25 January 2005.

Cline, Robert, Tom Neubig & Andrew Phillips. *Total State and Local Business Taxes: Fifty-State Estimates for Fiscal Year 2006*. Study prepared by Ernst & Young LLP in conjunction with the Council on State Taxation, February 2007.

Cnossen, Sybren. "The Netherlands." In *The Value-added Tax: Lessons from Europe*, edited by Henry J. Aaron. Washington, DC: The Brookings Institute, 1981.

Cnossen, Sybren. *Tax Coordination in the European Community*. Deventer: Kluwer, 1987.

Cnossen, Sybren. "Administrative and Compliance Costs of the VAT: A Review of the Evidence." *Tax Notes* 63 (1994): 1609–1626.

Cnossen, Sybren. "VAT Treatment of Immovable Property." In *Tax Law Design and Drafting*, vol. 1, edited by Victor Thuronyi. Washington DC: IMF, 1996, 231–245.

Cnossen, Sybren. "Global Trends and Issues in Value Added Taxation." *International Tax and Public Finance* 5 (1998): 399–428.

Cnossen, Sybren. "VAT Treatment of Financial Services." In *International Studies in Taxation: Law and Economics*. Series on International Taxation no. 21, edited by Gustaf Lindencrona, Sven-Olof Lodin & Bertil Wiman. The Hague: Kluwer Law International, 1999.

Congressional Budget Office (CBO). *Cost Estimate of Senate Bill (S) 150, the Internet Nondiscrimination Act, 9 September 2003*. Contained in 108th Cong., 1st Session Report 108-155. Washington, DC: CBO, 29 September 2003.

Congressional Budget Office (CBO). *Economic Issues in Taxing Internet and Mail-order Sales*. Washington, DC: CBO, October 2003.

Conrad, Robert F. *Value Added Taxation and Real Estate*. Discussion Paper, DRD-224. World Bank, Washington, DC, February 1987.

Conrad, Robert & Anca Grozav. "Real Property and VAT." In *VAT in Africa*, edited by Richard Krever. Pretoria University Law Press, 2008, 81–112.

Cornia, Gary C., David L. Sjoquist, & Lawrence C. Walters. "Sales and Use Tax Simplification and Voluntary Compliance." *Public Budgeting & Finance* 24 (1) (2004): 1–31.

Council on State Taxation. *Total State and Local Business Taxes: A Fifty-State Study of the Taxes Paid by Business in FY 2003*. Study prepared by Ernst & Young LLP for the Council on State Taxation, January 2004.

Daly, Michael. "The WTO and Direct Taxation." *The World Economy* 29 (5) (2006): 527–557.

Denie, Arthur H.R.M. *De Overheid in de Omzetbelasting* (VAT Treatment of the Public Sector). Deventer: Kluwer, 1987.

Deringer Report. Report on behalf of the Commission for the Internal Market. European Parliament Session Docs. 1963-4, no. 56, 20 August 1963.

Dijk, Harpert van & Guido Lubbers. "The VAT Compensation Fun(d)?" *International VAT Monitor* 11 (1) (2000): 6–9.

Due, John F. *Sales Taxation*. London, 1957.

Due, John F. *Government Finance*, 1977.

Due, John F. & John L. Mikesell. *Sales Taxation: State and Local Structure and Administration*. 2nd edn. Washington, DC: The Urban Institute, 1994.

Duverne, D. "Coordinate Audits of Income Tax and VAT." Presented at the Conference on Administrative Aspects of a Value-added Tax, Washington, DC, October 1990.

Easson, Alexander J. *Tax Law and Policy in the EEC*. London: Sweet & Maxwell, 1980.

Ebrill, Liam, Michael Keen, Jean-Paul Bodin & Victoria Summers. *The Modern VAT*. Washington, DC: IMF, 2001.

Edmiston, Kelly D. & Richard M. Bird. *Taxing Consumption in Jamaica: The GCT and the SCT*. ITP Paper 0414, International Tax Program, Rotman School of Management, University of Toronto, December 2004, <www.rotman.utoronto.ca/iib/ITP0414.pdf>.

Eisenstein, Martin I. "The Constitutional Limits on Sales Taxation of Cyberspace." *State Tax Notes* (24 February 1997): 601–605.

Entin, Stephen J. *Tax Incidence, Tax Burden, and Tax Shifting: Who Really Pays the Tax?* The Heritage Foundation, Center for Data Analysis, Report 04–12, 5 November 2004. <www.heritage.org/research/taxes/cda04-12.cfm>.

Ervin, R. Todd. "State Taxation of Financial Institutions: Will Physical Presence or Economic Presence Win the Day?" *Virginia Tax Review* 19 (2000): 515 et seq.

Farmer, Paul & Richard Lyal. *EC Tax Law*. Oxford: Clarendon Press, 1994.

Federal Reserve Bank of Chicago. Letter no. 154, June 2000.

Feria, Rita de la. *The EU VAT Treatment of Public Sector Bodies: Slowly Moving in the Wrong Direction*. Oxford University Centre for Business Taxation, Working Paper 08/08 (2008).

Foster, J.D. *International Aspects of Tax Reform*. Washington, DC: Tax Foundation, April 2000.

Fox, William F. & Matthew N. Murray, "The Sales Tax and Electronic Commerce: So What's New." *National Tax Journal* (19) 50 (3) (1997): 573–592.

Fox, William F. & Matthew N. Murray. "A National Retail Sales Tax: Consequences for the States." Paper presented at the Symposium on Federal Tax Reform and the States. Washington, DC: National Press Club, 13 May 2005.

Francis, James. "The Florida Sales Tax on Services: What Really Went Wrong?" In *The Unfinished Agenda for State Tax Reform*, edited by Steven D. Gold. Denver: National Conference of State Legislatures, 1988.

Fullerton, Donald & Diane L. Rogers. "Lifetime versus Annual Perspectives on Tax Incidence." *National Tax Journal* 44 (1991): 277–287.

Fullerton, Donald & Diane L. Rogers. *Who Bears the Income Tax Burden?* Washington, DC: The Brookings Institute, 1993.

Gale, William G. "The Required Tax Rate in a National Sales Tax." *National Tax Journal* 52 (3) (1999): 443–458.

Garber, Harry D. & David G. Raboy. "Value-added Taxation of Financial Services." In *VAT, Orthodoxy and New Thinking*, edited by Murray L. Weidenbaum, David G. Raboy & Ernest S. Christian, Jr. Boston: Kluwer Academic Publishers, 1989, 163–184.

Gendron, Pierre-Pascal. "Value-Added Tax Treatment of Public Bodies and Non-profit Organizations." *Bulletin for International Fiscal Documentation* 59 (11) (2005): 514–526.

Gendron, Pierre-Pascal. *Value-added Tax Treatment of Financial Services: A Developing Country Perspective*. ITP Paper 0606, International Tax Program, Rotman School of Management, University of Toronto, August 2006. <www.rotman.utoronto.ca/iib/ITP0606.pdf>.

General Accounting Office. *Sales Taxes: Electronic Commerce Growth Presents Challenge, Revenue Losses Are Uncertain*. GAO Report OCE-00-165. Washington, DC: General Accounting Office, 30 June 2000.

Giachino, Renee & Jeffrey Mazzella. *Simplification Is Not the Easy Answer*. Alexandria, VA: Center for Individual Freedom, July 2001. <www.cfif.org>.

Gibbons, Robert. "Incentives in Organizations." *Journal of Economic Perspectives* 12 (4) (1998): 115–132.

Gillis, Malcolm. *The VAT and Financial Services*. Development Research Department, Discussion Paper, report no. DRD-220. Washington, DC: World Bank, February 1987.

Goldberg, Daniel S. *E Tax: The Flat Tax as an Electronic Credit VAT*. Legal Studies Research Paper, no. 2005-59. University of Maryland School of Law.

Goolsbee, Austan. "In a World without Borders: The Impact of Taxes on Internet Commerce." *Quarterly Journal of Economics* 115 (2) (2000): 561–576.

Gordon, Roger, Laura Kalambokidis, Jeffrey Rohaly, & Joel Slemrod. "Toward a Consumption Tax and Beyond." *American Economic Review* 94 (2) (2004): 161–65.

Gossen, Hermann Heinrich. *Die Entwicklung der Gesetze des menschlichen Verkehrs und der daraus fließenden Regeln für menschliches Handeln* (The Development of the Laws of Human Intercourse and the Consequent Rules of Human Action), 1854.

Gottfried, Peter & Wolfgang Wiegard. "Exemption versus Zero Rating: A Hidden Problem of VAT." *Journal of Public Economics* 46 (1991): 307–328.

Grabower, Rolf, Detlef Herting & Gottfried Schwarz. *Die Umsatzsteuer, ihre Geschichte und gegenwärtige Gestaltung im In und Ausland* (Turnover Taxes: Their History and Present Design Here and Abroad). Köln, 1962.

Granville, Jane G. *Corporate Tax Reform and International Competitiveness*. Congressional Research Service Report no. 86-42E. Washington, DC, 25 February 1986, 1–2.

Grierson, Scot R. "State Taxation of the Information Superhighway: A Proposal for Taxation of Information Services." *Loyola of Los Angeles Entertainment Law Journal* 16 (3) (1996): 603–655.

Grossekettler, Heinz. "Die Umsatzsteuer aus ökonomischer Sicht" (Turnover Taxes from an Economic Perspective). In *Freiheit, Gleichheit, Effizienz: Ökonomische und verfassungsrechtliche Grundlagen der Steuergesetzgebung* (Freedom, Equality and Efficiency: Economic and Constitutional Principles of Tax Legislation), edited by Kirchhof, Paul und Manfred J.M. Neumann. Frankfurter Institut – Stiftung Marktwirtschaft und Politik, 2001, 70–84.

Grubert, Harry & James Mackie. "Must Financial Services Be Taxed under a Consumption Tax?" *National Tax Journal* 53 (1) (2000): 23–40.

Hahn, Walter. *Steuerpolitische Willensbildungsprozeße in der Europäischen Gemeinschaft: das Beispiel der Umsatzsteuer-Harmonisierung* (Tax Policy Process in the EU: The Example of VAT Harmonization). Frankfurt am Main, 1988.

Haig, Robert M. "The Concept of Income – Economic and Legal Aspects." In *Readings in* the *Economics of Taxation,* edited by Richard A. Musgrave & Carl S. Shoup. 1959, 54 et seq.

Hall, Arthur. *The High Cost of Tax Compliance for U.S. Business*. Special Report. Washington, DC: Tax Foundation, November 1993.

Hall, Arthur P. *The Compliance Costs and Regulatory Burden Imposed by the Federal Tax Laws*. Special Brief. Washington, DC: Tax Foundation, January 1995.

Hall, Robert E. & Alvin Rabushka. *The Flat Tax*. Stanford, CA: Hoover Institution Press, 1995.

Hanhart, J.C. *De BTW in schema's en tabellen* (VAT in Figures and Tables). Alphen aan den Rijn/Brussel: Samson, 1968.

Harrison, Graham & Russell Krelove. *VAT Refunds: A Review of Country Experience*. IMF Working Paper WP/05/218. Washington, DC: IMF, November 2005.

Hawkins, Richard R. "Popular Substitution Effects: Excess Burden Estimates for General Sales Taxes." *National Tax Journal* 55 (4) (2002): 755–769.

Hellerstein, Walter. "Federal Constitutional Limitations on Congressional Power to Legislate Regarding State Taxation of Electronic Commerce." *National Tax Journal* 53 (4) (2000): 1307–1325.

Hemmings, Richard & John A. Kay "The United Kingdom." In the *Value-added Tax: Lessons from Europe*, edited by Henry J. Aaron. Washington, DC: The Brookings Institute, 1981.

Henderson, David. "Limitations of the Laffer Curve as a Justification for Tax Cuts." *Cato Journal* 1 (1) (1981): 45–52.

"HM Revenue and Customs: Measuring Indirect Tax Losses." *The Economist* (2005).

Hoekman, Bernard. "The WTO: Functions and Basic Principles." In *Development, Trade, and the WTO: A Handbook*, edited by Bernard M. Hoekman, Aaditya Mattoo & Philip English. Washington, DC: World Bank Publications, 2002.

Hoffman, Lorey Arthur, Satya Poddar & John Whalley. "Taxation of banking Services Under a Consumption Type, Destination Base VAT." *National Tax Journal* 40 (1987): 547–554.

Honohan, Patrick (ed.). *Taxation of Financial Intermediation: Theory and Practice for Emerging Economies.* World Bank/Oxford University press, 2007.

Hufbauer, Gary Clyde & Carol Gabyzon. *Fundamental Tax Reform and Border Tax Adjustments*, Policy Analysis in International Economics 43. Washington, DC: Institute for International Economics, 1996.

Hufbauer, Gary Clyde. *The Foreign Sales Corporation Drama: Reaching the Last Act?* Institute for International Economics, Policy Brief no. PB02-10. Washington, DC, 2002.

Huizinga, Harry, "A European VAT on Financial Services?" *Economic Policy* (2002) 17 (35): 497–534.

IBFD, *Survey on the Recovery of Input VAT in the Financial Sector*, Amsterdam, December 2006.

Iorwerth, Aled Ab & John Whalley. "Efficiency Considerations and the Exemption of Food from Sales and Value Added Taxes." *Canadian Journal of Economics* 35 (1) (2002): 166–182.

Ireland, Tax Strategy Group (2001). Vat Issues (01/08) [Online]. *Department of Finance*. <www.finance.gov.ie/publications/tsg01/0108.doc>.

Irish Commission on Taxation. Third Report of the Irish Commission on Taxation: Indirect Taxation 71. Dublin, June 1984.

Ishi, Hiromitsu. *The Japanese Tax System*. 2nd edn. Clarendon Press, 1993.

Jack, William. "The Treatment of Financial Services under a Broad – based Consumption Tax." *National Tax Journal* 53 (4) (2000): 841–851.

Jackson, John H. *The World Trade Organization: Structure of the Treaty and the Institution, Sovereignty, the WTO and Changing Fundamentals of International Law*. Cambridge University Press, 2006.

Jorgenson, Dale W. "The Economic Impact of Fundamental Tax Reform." Testimony before the House Ways and Means Committee, 6 June 1995.

Jorgenson, Dale W. "The Economic Impact of Fundamental Taxing Consumption." Testimony before the House Ways and Means Committee, 27 March 1996. [per Ch. 6, fn. 62]

Joulfaian, David & James Mackie. "Sales Taxes, Investment, and the Tax Reform Act of 1986." *National Tax Journal* 45 (1992): 89–105.

Kaldor, Nicholas. *An Expenditure Tax*. London: George Allen & Unwin, 1955.

Kapteyn, Paul J.G., A.M. McDonnell, Kamiel J.M. Mortelmans & Christiaan W.A. Timmermans. *The Law of the European Union and the European Communities*, 4th edn. Kluwer Law International, 2008.

Kaylor, Herbert. "The Experience of Several Cities in Implementing a Commuter Tax." *State Tax Today* (2004): 133.

Keen, Michael. *VIVAT, C-VAT and All That: New Forms of Value-added Tax for Federal Systems*. IMF Working Paper (WP/00/83). Washington, DC: IMF, April 2000; also published in the *Canadian Tax Journal* 48 (2) (2000): 409–424.

Keen, Michael & S. Smith. "Viva VIVAT!" *International Tax and Public Finance* 7 (6) (2000): 741–751.

Keen, Michael & Jack Mintz. "The Optimal Threshold for a Value-added Tax." *Journal of Public Economics* 88 (3, 4) (2004): 559–576.

Keen, Michael & Stephen Smith. *VAT Fraud and Evasion: What Do We Know, and What Can Be Done?* IMF Working Paper [WP/07/31], Washington, DC: IMF, February 2007.

Keen, Michael. *VAT Attacks!* IMF Working Paper [WP/07/142]. Washington, DC: IMF, June 2007.

Kenyon, Daphene A. & John Kincaid. *Competition among States and Local Governments: Efficiency and Equity in American Federalism*. Washington, DC: The Urban Institute, 1991.

Kessler, Martha. *FTA Opposes Nexus Change Bill, Favors Expansion of Sales Tax Collection Duty*. Bureau of National Affairs, Daily Tax Report, no. 113, 12 June 2000.

Keynes, John Maynard. *The General Theory of Employment, Interest and Money*, London, 1936.

Kimmel, Michael S. *Absolutism and Its Discontents: State and Society in Seventeenth-century France and England*. New Brunswick, NJ, 1988.

Koenig, Evan F. "Achieving 'Program Neutrality' under a National Retail Sales Tax." *National Tax Journal* 52 (4) (1999): 683–698.

Kotlikoff, Laurence J. *The Economic Impact of Replacing Federal Income Taxes with a Sales Tax*. Policy Analysis no. 193. Washington, DC: Cato Institute, 15 April 1993.

Krever, Richard (ed.). *VAT in Africa*. Pretoria University Law Press, 2008.

Laffer, Arthur B. *The Laffer Curve: Past, Present, and Future*. The Heritage Foundation, Backgrounder 1765, www.heritage.org/Research/Taxes/bg1765.cfm, 1 June 2004.

Lauré, Maurice. *La taxe sur la valeur ajoutée* (The Value Added Tax). Paris, 1952.

Lauré, Maurice. *Au Secours de la T.V.A.* (Rescue the VAT). Paris : Presses Universitaires de France, 1957.

Laverty, Edward B. & Kenneth T. Palmer. "State and Local Governmental Interest Groups before the Supreme Court: Implications for Intergovernmental Policy." *Public Administration Quarterly* 24 (4) (2001): 522–537.

Maguire, Steven. *State and Local Sales and Use Taxes and Internet Commerce*. CRS Report, 28 January 2005.

Marshall, Alfred. *Principles of Economics*, 8th edn. (1890). Philadelphia, 1920 (reprinted 1982).

Matthews, Kent & Jean Lloyd-Williams. "Have VAT Rates Reached Their Limit? An Empirical Note." *Applied Economics Letters* 7 (2) (2000): 111–115.

Matthews, Kent. "VAT Evasion and VAT Avoidance: Is There a European Laffer Curve for VAT?" *International Review of Applied Economics* 17 (1) (2003): 105–114.

McIntyre, Michael J. & Richard D. Pomp. "A Policy Analysis of Michigan's Mislabeled Gross Receipt Tax." *Wayne Law Review* 53 (2007): 1275–1319. Available at <www.law.wayne.edu/mcintyre/text/mcintyre_articles/MGRT-McIntyre_Pomp.pdf>.

McLaren, John (ed.). *Institutional Elements of Tax Design and Reform*. Technical Paper no. 539, Washington, DC: World Bank, 2003. <www.bu.edu/law/faculty/scholarship/workingpapers/2007.html>.

McLure, Charles E. "Electronic Commerce, State Sales Taxation, and Intergovernmental Relations." *National Tax Journal* 50 (4) (1997): 731–749.

McLure, Charles E. "Achieving a Level Playing Field for Electronic Commerce." *State Tax Notes* 14 (1998): 1767–1783.

McLure, Charles E. "Implementing Subnational VATs on Internal Trade: The Compensating VAT (C-VAT)." *International Tax and Public Finance* 7 (6) (2000): 723–740.

McLure, Charles E. *New Developments on State and Local Tax: E-commerce, Tax Incentives for Business and Litigation-generated Revenues*. Paper for the Annual Meeting of the Association of American Law Schools. January 2001.

McMahon, Peter. *Consumption Taxation and Financial Services*. Vol. LXXXVIIIb. International Fiscal Association. 2003 Sydney Congress, Australian Branch Report.

McNie, William M. "The Origin Principle and Transport Costs." In *Fiscal Harmonization in Common Markets*, vol. I, edited by Carl S. Shoup. New York and London: Columbia University Press, 1967, 265–311.

Meade, James. *The Structure and Reform of Direct Taxation*. London: Allen & Unwin, 1978.

Menchik, Paul & Martin David. "The Incidence of a Lifetime Consumption Tax." *National Tax Journal* 35 (1982): 189–203.

Messere, Ken. *Tax Policy in OECD Countries*. Amsterdam, 1993.

Mikesell, John L. "Remote Vendors and American Sales and Use Taxation: The Balance between Fixing the Problem and Fixing the Tax." *National Tax Journal* 53 (4) (2000): 1273–1285.

Mikesell, John L. *Gross Receipt Taxes in State Government Finances: A Review of Their History and Performance*. Background Paper, no. 53. Washington, DC: Tax Foundation, January 2007.

Mill, John Stuart. *Principles of Political Economy*. 1848.

Modigliani, Franco. "The Role of Intergenerational Transfer and Life Cycle Saving in the Accumulation of Wealth." *Journal of Economic Perspectives* 2 (2) (1998): 15–23.

Montesquieu, Charles de. *De l'Esprit des Lois* (The Spirit of Laws), 1748.

Moor, A.E. de. *De belasting over de toegevoegde waarde en haar betekenis voor de ondernemer* (Value Added Tax and Its Meaning for Traders). Alphen aan den Rijn/Brussel: Samson, 1967.

Moore, Stephen & John Silvia. *The ABCs of the Capital Gains Tax*. Policy Analysis no. 242. Washington, DC Cato Institute, 4 October 1995.

Morris, William H. "Proposed Business Activities Tax Signals Renewed Interest in U.S. VAT." *The Journal of International Taxation* (October 1994): 466–470.

Moszer, Max. "A Comment on the Laffer Model." *Cato Journal* 1 (1) (1981): 23–44.

Musgrave, Richard A. & Carl S. Shoup (eds.). *Readings in the Economics of Taxation*. Homewood, IL, 1959.

Musgrave, Richard A. & Peggy B. *Public Finance in Theory and Practice*, 5th edn. 1989.

Musgrave, Peggy B. "Consumption Tax Proposals in the International Setting." In *Tax Conversations: A Guide to the Key Issues in the Tax Reform Debate*, edited by Richard Krever. Boston: Kluwer Law International, 1997, 447–470.

Nam, Chang Woon, Andrea Gebauer, & Rüdiger Parsche. *Is the Completion of the EU Single Market Hindered by VAT Evasion*? CESifo Working Paper, no. 974, 2003.

National Commission on Economic Growth and Tax Reform. *Unleashing America's Potential.* Washington, DC, January 1996.

National Retail Federation. *The Level-Playing Field and Beyond: Position Paper on the Framework for a Fair, Workable, and Simplified Sales and Use Tax System.* Washington, DC, March 2001.

Nederstigt, W.F. *Economische Beoordeling van Omzetbelastingen.* (Economic Evaluation of Turnover Taxes). Deventer: Kluwer, 1964.

Neubig, Thomas S. & Harold L. Adrion. "Value Added Taxes and Other Consumption Taxes: Issues for Insurance Companies." *Tax Notes* (22 November 1993): 1001–1011.

Neumark Report. *Report of the Fiscal and Financial Committee on Tax Harmonization in the Common Market.* Report 21, Document SD-322. EEC Commission, 1962.

Notenboom Report. Budget Committee of the European Parliament, Doc. 360/73, 14 February 1974.

Oates, Wallace E. & Robert M. Schwab, "Economic Competition among Jurisdictions: Efficiency Enhancing or Distortion Inducing?" *Journal of Public Economics* 35 (3) (1998): 333–354.

OECD. Consumption Tax Trends: VAT/GST and Excise Rates, Trends and Administration Issues, 2006 Edition. <www.sourceoecd.org/taxation/9264014179>.

Oldman, Oliver & Alan Schenk. "The Business Activities Tax: Have Senators Danforth and Boren Created a Better Value Added Tax?" *Tax Notes International* (2 January 1995): 55–74.

Olson, Mancur. *Logic of Collective Action.* Cambridge, MA, Harvard University Press, 1971.

Orzechoski, William P. *Border Tax Adjustments and Fundamental Tax Reform.* Background Paper no. 39. Washington, DC: Tax Foundation, November 2001.

Palmer, R.R., Joel Colton & Lloyd Kramer. *A History of the Modern World.* 10th edn. New York: McGraw-Hill, 2007.

Payne, James L. *Costly Returns: The Burdens of the U.S. Tax System.* San Francisco, Institute for Contemporary Studies Press, 1993.

Ploeger, L.F. (ed.). *Fiscale Encyclopedie "De Vakstudie," Deel XIX, Wet op de Omzetbelasting 1954*, (loose-leaf), Deventer: Kluwer, suppl. 62, April 1968.

Poddar, Satya & Morley English, "Taxation of Financial Services under a Value Added Tax: Applying the Cash Flow Approach." *National Tax Journal* 50 (1) (1997): 89–111.

Pomp, Richard D. & Oliver Oldman. "A Normative Inquiry into the Base of a Retail Sales Tax: Casual Sales, Used Goods, and Trade–ins." *National Tax Journal* 43 (4) (1990): 427–437.

Poterba, James M. "Lifetime Incidence and the Distributional Burden of Excise Taxes." *American Economic Review* 79 (2) (1989): 325–330.

Poterba, James M. "Is the Gasoline Tax Regressive?" *Tax Policy and the Economy* 5 (1991): 145–164.

PricewaterhouseCoopers. Retail Sales Tax Compliance Costs: A National Estimate. 7 April 2006.

PricewaterhouseCoopers. "Study to Increase the Understanding of the Economic Effects of the VAT Exemption for Financial and Insurance Services." Final report to the European Commission, 2 November 2006.

Priks, Mikael. Optimal Rent Extraction in Pre-industrial England and France: Default Risk and Monitoring Costs. CESifo Working Paper Series no. 1464. May 2005.

Puchala, Donald J. "European Fiscal Harmonization: Politics during the Dutch Interlude." In *Contemporary Perspectives on European Integration*, edited by Leon Hurwitz. Westport, CT, 1980, 209–224.

Puchala, Donald J. *Fiscal Harmonization in the European Communities: National Politics and International Cooperation*. London and Dover, NH: Francis Pinter Publishers, 1984.

Quick, Perry D. & Michael J. McKee. "Sales Tax on Services: Revenue or Reform?" *National Tax Journal* 41 (1988): 398.

Quigley, Paul. "The New European VAT Directive." *International VAT Monitor* 18 (2) (2007): 158–164.

Raboy, David G. "International Implications of Value-added Taxes." In *The Value Added Tax: Orthodoxy and New Thinking*, edited by Murray L. Weidenbaum, David G. Raboy & Ernest S. Christian, Jr. Boston: Kluwer Academic Publishers, 1989, 131–163.

Raboy, David G. & Cliff Massa III. "Who Bears the Burden of Consumption Taxes?" In *The Value Added Tax: Orthodoxy and New Thinking*, edited by Murray L. Weidenbaum, David G. Raboy & Ernest S. Christian, Jr. Boston: Kluwer Academic Publishers, 1989, 39–69.

Reugebrink, J. *Omzetbelasting* (Turnover Tax). Amsterdam: Fiscale Studieserie no. 6, FED, 1962.

Ring, Raymond J. "Consumer's Share and Producer's Share of the General Sales Tax." *National Tax Journal* 52 (1) (1999): 79–90.

Rothbard, Murray N. *Power and Market: Government and the Economy*, 2nd edn. Kansas City, 1977.

Rothbard, Murray N. "The Consumption Tax: A Critique." *Review of Austrian Economics* 7 (2) (1994): 75–90.

Rousseau, Jean Jacques. *Discours sur l'Economie Politique* (Treatise on Political Economics), 1755.

Rousslang, Donald J. "Should Financial Services Be Taxed under a Consumption Tax? Probably." *National Tax Journal* 55 (2) (2002): 281–291.

Schenk, Alan & Oliver Oldman. "Analysis of Tax Treatment of Financial Services under a Consumption-Style VAT: A Report of the American Bar Association, Section of Taxation, Committee on Value Added Tax." *Tax Lawyer* 181 44 (1991).

Schenk, Alan. "Recent Activity in the United States Involving Value Added Tax." *VAT Monitor* (August/September 1992): 2 et seq.

Schenk, Alan. "VAT Debate Stimulated by Tax Reform Hearings in the United States." *VAT Monitor* (4) (July/August 1995): 204–210.

Schenk, Alan. "Japanese Consumption Tax after Six Years: A Unique VAT Matures." *Tax Notes International* 11 (21) (1995): 1379–1393.

Schenk, Alan & Howell H. Zee. "Treating Financial Services under a Value Added Tax: Conceptual Issues and Country Practices." In *Taxing the Financial Sector: Concepts, Issues, and Country Practices*, edited by Howell H. Zee. Washington, DC: International Monetary Fund, 2004, 60–74.

Schenk, Alan & Oliver Oldman. *Value Added Tax: A Comparative Approach*. New York: Cambridge University Press, 2007.

Schmölders, G. *Die Umsatzsteuern* (Turnover Taxes). Amsterdam, 1966.

Schneider, Friedrich. The Size of the Shadow Economies of 145 Countries All over the World: First Results over the Period 1999 to 2003. Discussion Paper, no. 1431. Institute for the Study of Labor (IZA), 2004.

Schneider, Friedrich. "Shadow Economies around the World: What Do We Really Know?" *European Journal of Political Economy* 21 (3) (2005): 598–642.

Seligman, Edwin R.A. *Progressive Taxation in Theory and Practice*. 1908.

Senate Committee on Banking, Housing and Urban Affairs, 94th Congress, *Report of the Advisory Commission on Intergovernmental Relations on State and Local "Doing Business" Taxes on Out-of-State Financial Depositories* 23 (1975).

Shaviro, Daniel. "An Economic and Political Look at Federalism in Taxation." 90 *Michigan Law Review* 90 895, 902 (1992): 895 et seq.

Shaw, G.K. "European Economic Integration and Stabilization Policy." In *Fiscal Harmonization in Common Markets*, vol. II, edited by Carl S. Shoup. New York and London: Columbia University Press, 1967, 344–440.

Sheppard, Lee A. "Business Taxpayers Resist State Tax Nexus in Courts and Congress." *Tax Notes* 87 (6, 8) (2000): 740–747.

Shoup, Carl S. (ed.). *Fiscal Harmonization in Common Markets*, vols I and II. New York and London: Columbia University Press, 1967.

Siemens, Carl Friedrich von. *Veredelte Umsatzsteuer* (Improved Turnover Tax). 2nd edn. Siemensstadt, 1920.

Silvani, Carlos & S. Wakefield. "The Relationship between Tax Rates and Tax Yield." Paper presented at the thirty-sixth General Assembly of the Inter-American Centre of Tax Administrators (CIAT). Québec, May 2002.

Simons, Henry C. *Personal Income Taxation: The Definition of Income as a Problem of Fiscal Policy*. Reprint. University of Chicago Press, 1965, (1938).

Slemrod, Joel. ''Which Is the Simplest Tax System of Them All?'' In *Economic Effects of Fundamental Tax Reform*, edited by Henry J. Aaron & William G. Gale. Washington, DC: The Brookings Institution, 1996.

Smith, Adam. *Inquiry into the Nature and Causes of the Wealth of Nations*. New York: The Modern Library, 1937 (1776).

Smith, Dan Throop & Bertrand Fox. *An Analysis of Value Added Taxation in the Context of the Tax Restructuring Act of 1980*. Washington, DC: The Financial Executives Research Foundation, 1981.

Snyder, Francis G. *Law of the Common Agricultural Policy*. London, 1985.

Spaak, P. Henri. Rapport des Chefs de délégation des Ministres étrangers. Brussels, 21 April 1956.

Strauss, Robert P. ''Federal Consumption Taxes: Implications for the State and Local Sector.'' *Tax Notes* (22 February 1999): 1173–1190.

Sullivan, Clara K. ''Indirect Taxation and Goals of the European Economic Community.'' In *Fiscal Harmonization in Common Markets*, vol. II, edited by Carl S. Shoup. New York and London: Columbia University Press, 1967, 1–103.

Sullivan, Clara K. ''Potential Rates of Value-Added Tax in the European Economic Community.'' In *Fiscal Harmonization in Common Markets*, vol. II, edited by Carl S. Shoup. New York and London: Columbia University Press, 1967, 173–207.

Swinkels, Joep J.P. ''Scope of the Self-supply Rule under EU VAT.'' *International VAT Monitor* 19 (3) (2008): 175–181.

Swinkels, Joep J.P. ''Some Aspects of Input Tax Deduction under the Pro Rata of the EU VAT System.'' *International VAT Monitor* 19 (5) (2008): 343–350.

Tait, Alan A. *Value Added Tax: International Practice and Problems*. Washington, DC: IMF, 1988.

Tax Foundation. *State and Local Sales Taxes*. Research Publication no. 23. New York: Tax Foundation, 1970.

''A Tax Net Full of Holes.'' *The Economist*, 13 May 2006.

Terkper, Seth A. ''VAT in Ghana: Why It Failed.'' *Tax Notes International* 12 (1996): 1801–1816.

Terra, Ben. *Sales Taxation: The Case of Value Added Tax in the European Community*. Series on International Taxation, no. 8. Deventer-Boston: Kluwer, 1988.

Terra, Ben. *The Place of Supply in European VAT*. London-The Hague-Boston: Kluwer Law International, 1998.

Thiel, Servaas van. ''EEC: Public Authorities as Taxable Persons for VAT.'' *International VAT Monitor* 9 (2) (1990): 28–34.

Toder, Eric J. "Consumption Tax Proposals in the United States." In *Tax Conversations: A Guide to the Key Issues in the Tax Reform Debate*, edited by Richard Krever. Boston: Kluwer Law International, 1997, 159–186.

Tuk, C.P. *Inleiding tot de Omzetbelasing* (Introduction to the Turnover Tax). Gorinchem: J. Noorduijn en Zoon, 1956.

Turnier, William J. "VAT: Minimizing Administration and Compliance Costs, a Consumption tax Symposium." *Tax Notes* (7 March 1988): 1257 et seq.

US Department of Commerce. *A Nation Online: How Americans Are Expanding Their Use of the Internet*. Washington, DC, February 2002.

US Department of Labor. *The Underground Economy in the United States*. Washington, DC: US Department of Labor, 1992.

US Department of the Treasury. *Tax Reform for Fairness, Simplicity, and Growth, Vol. 3, The Value Added Tax*. Washington, DC: US Department of the Treasury, November 1984.

US Department of the Treasury. *Integration of the Individual and Corporate Tax Systems – Tax Business Income Once*. Washington, DC: GPO, 1992.

US Joint Committee on Taxation. *Impact on State and Local Governments and Tax-Exempt Organizations of Replacing the Federal Income Tax*. Washington, DC: U.S. Government Printing Office, 1996.

Varsano, R. "Subnational Taxation and Treatment of Interstate Trade in Brazil: Problems and Proposed Solution." In *Decentralization and Accountability of the Public Sector*, edited by S.J. Burki & G. Perry. Annual World Bank Conference on Development in Latin America and the Caribbean. Washington, DC: World Bank, 2000.

Vermand Report. Series Competition-Harmonization of Legislation, no. 24. Brussels, 1973.

Wagner, Adolph D. *Finanzwißenschaft* (Public Finance), vol. 2. Leipzig/Neurenberg, 1880.

Wagner, Johann. *Direkte Steuern und Welthandelsrecht – Das Verbot ertragsteuerlicher Exportsubventionen im Recht der WTO* (Direct Taxation and International Trade Law: The Prohibition of Export Subsidies under WTO Law). Nomos, Baden-Baden, 2006.

Wanniski, Jude. "Taxes, Revenues, and the 'Laffer Curve'." *The Public Interest*. winter 1978.

Warren, Alvin C. "The Proposal for an Unlimited Savings Allowance." *Tax Notes* vol. 68, no. 28 (August 1995): 1103 et seq.

Washington State Tax Structure Study Commission. *Tax Alternatives for Washington State: A Report to the Legislature*. Vols 1 & 2. November 2002, 110–112.

Webley, Paul, Caroline Adams & Henk Elffers. *Value Added Tax Compliance.* Paper presented at the conference Behavioral Public Finance: Towards a New Agenda. University of Michigan Business School. Ann Arbor, 23 April 2004–24 April 2004.

Weidenbaum, Murray L, David G. Raboy & Ernest S. Christian, Jr. (eds.). *The Value Added Tax, Orthodoxy and New Thinking*. Boston: Kluwer Academic Publishers, 1989.

Woodward, Colin. ‘‘The New UK Approach to Carousel Fraud.’’ *International VAT Monitor* 17 (4) (2006): 240–241.

Yang, Xaoqiang. ‘‘VAT Treatment of Government Procurement: A Comparative Analysis.’’ *International VAT Monitor* 16 (5) (2005): 342–348.

Youngman, Joan M. ‘‘Tax on Land and Buildings.’’ In *Tax Law Design and Drafting*, vol. 1, edited by Victor Thuronyi. Washington DC: IMF, 1996, 264–291.

Zee, Howell H. ‘‘A New Approach to Taxing Financial Intermediation Services under a Value Added Tax.’’ *National Tax Journal* 58 (1) (2005): 77–92.

Zimmerman, Dennis. *Economic Issues in Taxing Internet and Mail-order Sales*. Congressional Budget Office (CBO) paper. Washington, DC: CBO, October 2003.

Zodrow, George R. ‘‘The Sales Tax, the VAT, and Taxes in Between – or, Is the Only Good NRST a ‘VAT in Drag’?’’ *National Tax Journal* 52 (3) (1999): 429–442.

Zodrow, George R. ‘‘Evaluating the Case for a Temporary Moratorium on the Taxation of Electronic Commerce.’’ *State Tax Notes* 19 (2000): 1515–1521.

Zodrow, George R. ‘‘Network Externalities and Indirect Tax Preferences for Electronic Commerce.’’ *International Tax and Public Finance* 10 (1) (2003): 79–97.

Zodrow, George R. ‘‘Optimal Commodity Taxation of Traditional and Electronic Commerce.’’ *National Tax Journal* 59 (1) (2006): 7–31.

Index

SERIES ON INTERNATIONAL TAXATION

1. Alberto Xavier, *The Taxation of Foreign Investment in Brazil*, 1980 (ISBN 90-200-0582-0)
2. Hugh J. Ault and Albert J. Rädler, *The German Corporation Tax Law with 1980 Amendments*, 1981 (ISBN 90-200-0642-8)
3. Paul R. McDaniel and Hugh J. Ault, *Introduction to United States International Taxation*, 1981 (ISBN 90-6544-004-6)
4. Albert J. Rädler, *German Transfer Pricing/Prix de Transfer en Allemagne*, 1984 (ISBN 90-6544-143-3)
5. Paul R. McDaniel and Stanley S. Surrey, *International Aspects of Tax Expenditures: A Comparative Study*, 1985 (ISBN 90-654-4163-8)
6. Kees van Raad, *Nondiscrimination in International Tax Law*, 1986 (ISBN 90-6544-266-9)
7. Sijbren Cnossen (ed.), *Tax Coordination in the European Community*, 1987 (ISBN 90-6544-272-3)
8. Ben Terra, *Sales Taxation. The Case of Value Added Tax in the European Community*, 1989 (ISBN 90-6544-381-9)
9. Rutsel S.J. Martha, *The Jurisdiction to Tax in International Law: Theory and Practice of Legislative Fiscal Jurisdiction*, 1989 (ISBN 90-654-4416-5)
10. Paul R. McDaniel and Hugh J. Ault, *Introduction to United States International Taxation* (3rd revised edition), 1989 (ISBN 90-6544-423-8)
11. Manuel Pires, *International Juridicial Double Taxation of Income*, 1989 (ISBN 90-6544-426-2)
12. A.H.M. Daniels, *Issues in International Partnership Taxation*, 1991 (ISBN 90-654-4577-3)
13. Arvid A. Skaar, *Permanent Establishment: Erosion of a Tax Treaty Principle*, 1992 (ISBN 90-6544-594-3)
14. Cyrille David and Geerten Michielse (eds), *Tax Treatment of Financial Instruments*, 1996 (ISBN 90-654-4666-4)
15. Herbert H. Alpert and Kees van Raad (eds), *Essays on International Taxation*, 1993 (ISBN 90-654-4781-4)
16. Wolfgang Gassner, Michael Lang and Eduard Lechner (eds), *Tax Treaties and EC Law*, 1997 (ISBN 90-411-0680-4)
17. Glória Teixeira, *Taxing Corporate Profits in the EU*, 1997 (ISBN 90-411-0703-7)
18. Michael Lang *et al.* (eds), *Multilateral Tax Treaties*, 1998 (ISBN 90-411-0704-5)
19. Stef van Weeghel, *The Improper Use of Tax Treaties*, 1998 (ISBN 90-411-0737-1)
20. Klaus Vogel (ed.), *Interpretation of Tax Law and Treaties and Transfer Pricing in Japan and Germany*, 1998 (ISBN 90-411-9655-2)
21. Bertil Wiman (ed.), *International Studies in Taxation: Law and Economics; Liber Amicorum Leif Mutén*, 1999 (ISBN 90-411-9692-7)

22. Alfonso J. Martín Jiménez, *Towards Corporate Tax Harmonization in the European Community*, 1999 (ISBN 90-411-9690-0)
23. Ramon J. Jeffery, *The Impact of State Sovereignty on Global Trade and International Taxation*, 1999 (ISBN 90-411-9703-6)
24. A.J. Easson, *Taxation of Foreign Direct Investment*, 1999 (ISBN 90-411-9741-9)
25. Marjaana Helminen, *The Dividend Concept in International Tax Law: Dividend Payments Between Corporate Entities*, 1999 (ISBN 90-411-9765-6)
26. Paul Kirchhof, Moris Lehner, Kees van Raad, Arndt Raupach and Michael-Rodi (eds), *International and Comparative Taxation: Essays in Honour of Klaus Vogel*, 2002 (ISBN 90-411-9841-5)
27. Krister Andersson, Peter Melz and Christer Silfverberg (eds), *Liber Amicorum Sven-Olof Lodin*, 2001 (ISBN 90-411-9850-4)
28. Juan Martín Jovanovich, *Customs Valuation and Transfer Pricing: Is It Possible to Harmonize Customs and Tax Rules?*, 2002 (ISBN 90-411-9888-1)
29. Stefano Simontacchi, *Taxation of Capital Gains under the OECD Model Convention: With Special Regard to Immovable Property*, 2007 (ISBN 978-90-411-2549-1)
30. Michael Lang, Josef Schuch, and Claus Staringer (eds), *Tax Treaty Law and EC Law*, 2007 (ISBN 978-90-411-2629-0)
31. Duncan Bentley, *Taxpayers' Rights: Theory Origin and Implementation*, 2007 (ISBN 978-90-411-2650-4)
32. Sergio André Rocha, *Interpretation of Double Taxation Conventions: General Theory and Brazilian Perspective*, 2008 (ISBN 978-90-411-2822-5)
33. Robert F. van Brederode, *Systems of General Sales Taxation: Theory, Policy and Practice*, 2009 (ISBN 978-90-411-2832-4)

www.ingramcontent.com/pod-product-compliance
Lightning Source LLC
LaVergne TN
LVHW020645300926
849161LV00004B/821